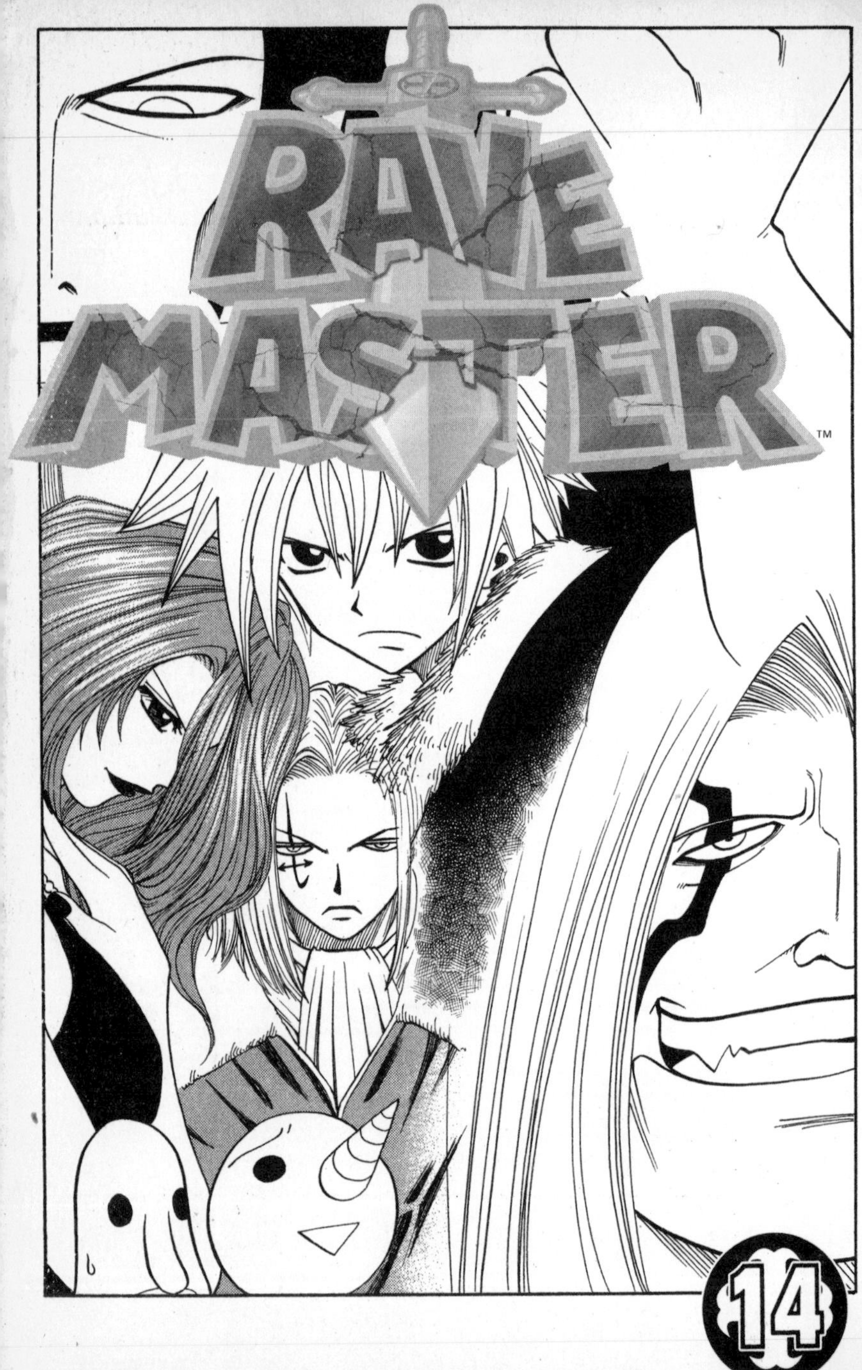
RAVE MASTER™
14

Rave Master Vol. 14
Created by Hiro Mashima

Translation - Jeremiah Bourque
English Adaptation - Jake Forbes
Copy Editor - Peter Ahlstrom
Retouch and Lettering - Anthony Daulo
Production Artist - Jose Macasocol, Jr.
Cover Design - Al-Insan Lashley

Editor - Tim Beedle
Digital Imaging Manager - Chris Buford
Pre-Press Manager - Antonio DePietro
Production Managers - Jennifer Miller and Mutsumi Miyazaki
Art Director - Matt Alford
Managing Editor - Jill Freshney
VP of Production - Ron Klamert
Editor-in-Chief - Mike Kiley
President and C.O.O. - John Parker
Publisher and C.E.O. - Stuart Levy

A 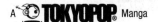 Manga

TOKYOPOP Inc.
5900 Wilshire Blvd. Suite 2000
Los Angeles, CA 90036

E-mail: info@TOKYOPOP.com
Come visit us online at www.TOKYOPOP.com

ISBN: 1-59532-019-9

First TOKYOPOP printing: April 2005
10 9 8 7 6 5 4 3 2 1
Printed in the USA

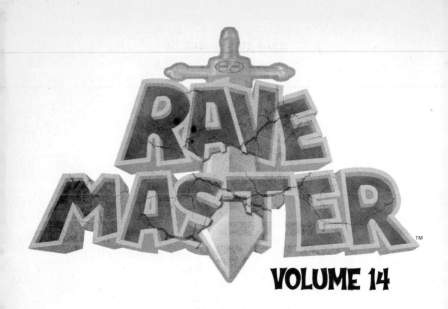

VOLUME 14

Story and Art by

HIRO MASHIMA

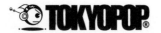

HAMBURG // LONDON // LOS ANGELES // TOKYO

THE STORY SO FAR...

While Demon Card and the Oracion Six gather their forces in preparation for their search for **Sinclaire,** the five true Dark Brings, Haru and his friends travel South to find the fourth **Rave Stone.** There they befriend **Celia,** a mermaid, who tells them of an ongoing genocide of their people being committed by the **Onigami,** a race of water-dwelling warriors. The Onigami leader has allied himself with **Pumpkin Doryu,** the commander of the **Ghost Attack Squad,** and together the two villains have created one of the most destructive weapons in existence—a weapon that is powered by the magic found within all merpeople. Upon discovering this, Haru's group vows to put a stop to it, only to be attacked moments later by the Onigami navy.

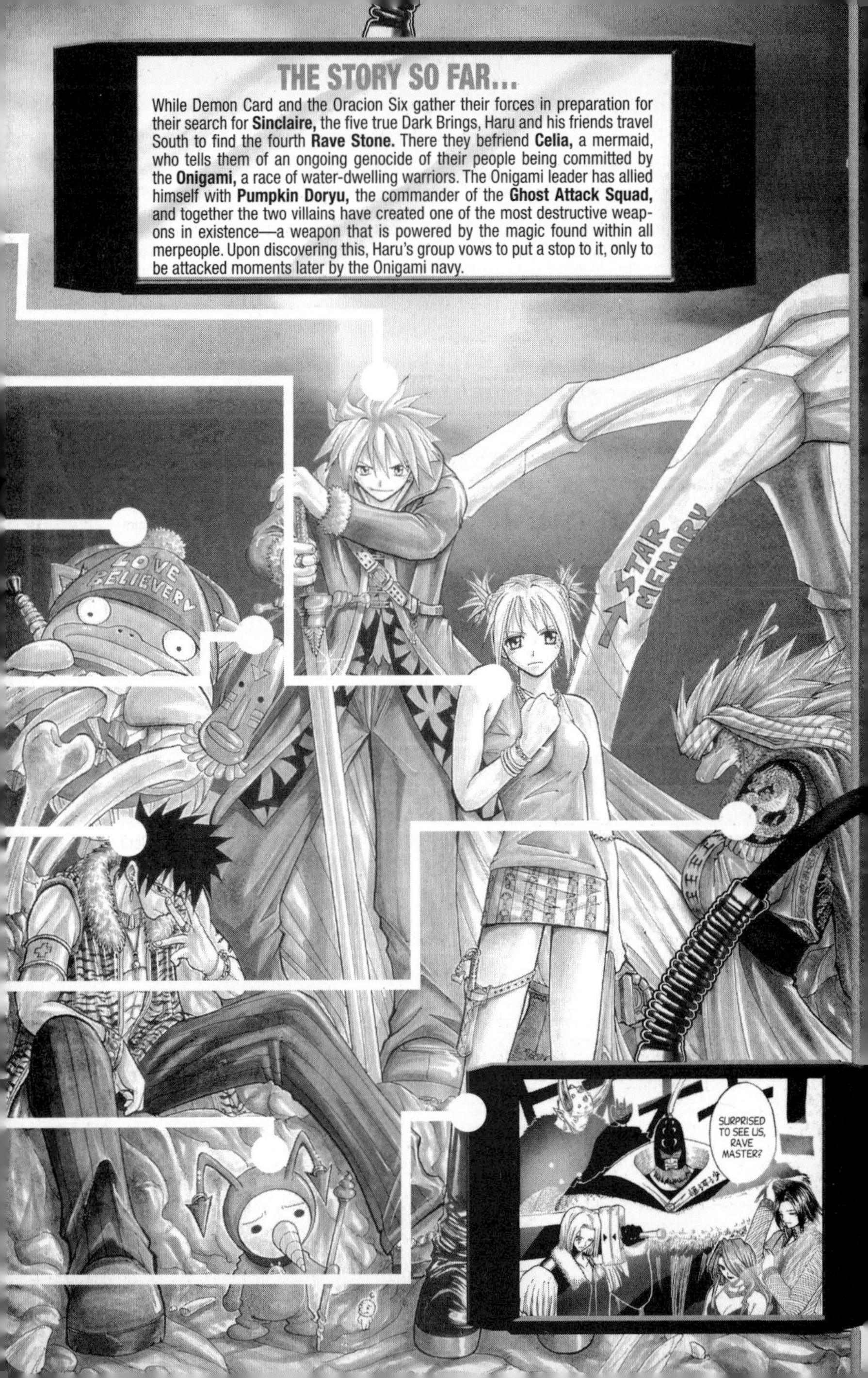
LOVE BELIEVER
STAR MEMORY
SURPRISED TO SEE US, RAVE MASTER?

THE RAVE MASTER CREW

HARU GLORY

A small-town boy turned savior of the world. As the **Rave Master** (the only one capable of using the holy weapon RAVE), Haru set forth to find the missing Rave Stones and defeat Demon Card. He fights with the **Ten Powers Sword,** a weapon that takes on different forms at his command. With Demon Card seemingly out of the way, Haru now seeks the remaining two Rave Stones in order to open the way to Star Memory.

ELIE

The girl without memories. Elie joined Haru on his quest when he promised to help her find out about her past. She's cute, spunky and loves gambling and shopping in equal measures. Locked inside of her is the power of **Etherion.**

RUBY

A "penguin-type" sentenoid, Ruby loves rare and unusual items. After Haru saved him from Pumpkin Doryu's gang, Ruby agreed to sponsor Haru's team in their search for the ultimate rare treasures: the Rave Stones!

GRIFFON KATO (GRIFF)

Griff is a loyal friend, even if he is a bit of a coward. His rubbery body can stretch and change shape as needed. Griff's two greatest pleasures in life are mapmaking and peeping on Elie.

MUSICA

A **"Silverclaimer"** (an alchemist who can shape silver at will) and a former street punk who made good. He joined Haru for the adventure, but now that Demon Card is defeated, does he have any reason to stick around?

LET

A member of the Dragon Race, he was formerly a member of the Demon Card's Five Palace Guardians. He was so impressed by Haru's fighting skills and pureness of heart that he made a truce with the Rave Master. After passing his Dragon Trial, he gained a human body, but his blood is still Dragon Race.

PLUE

The **Rave Bearer,** Plue is the faithful companion to the Rave Master. In addition to being Haru's guide, Plue also has powers of his own. When he's not getting Haru into or out of trouble, Plue can be found enjoying a sucker, his favorite treat.

THE ORACION SIX

Demon Card's six generals. Haru defeated Shuda after finding the Rave of Wisdom. The other five generals were presumed dead after King destroyed Demon Card Headquarters.

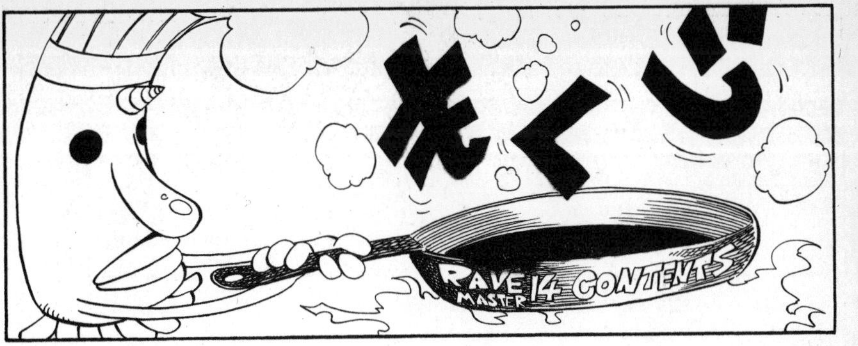
もくじ
RAVE MASTER 14 CONTENTS

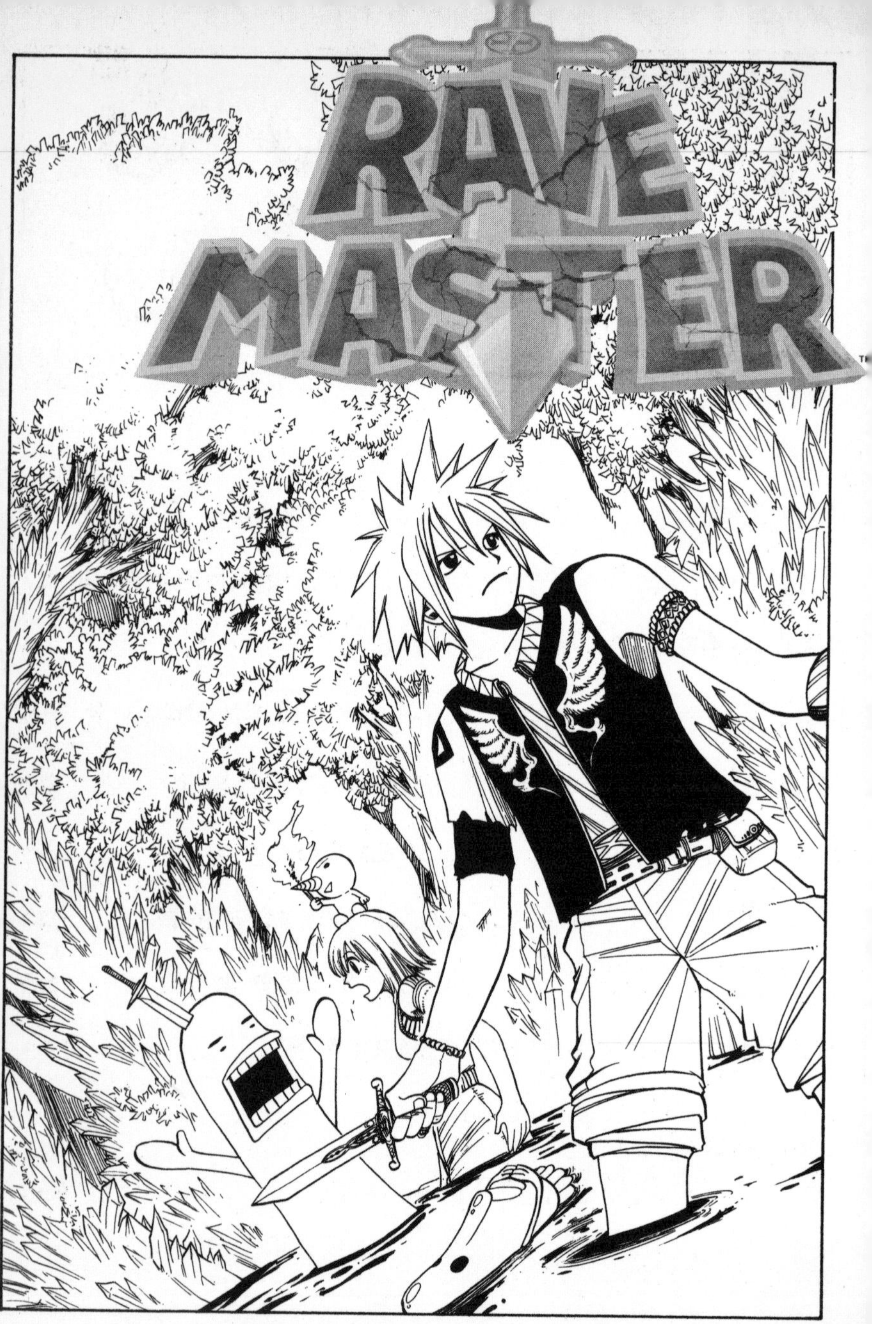
RAVE MASTER

RAVE:106 ✚ INFILTRATING SYAORAN!

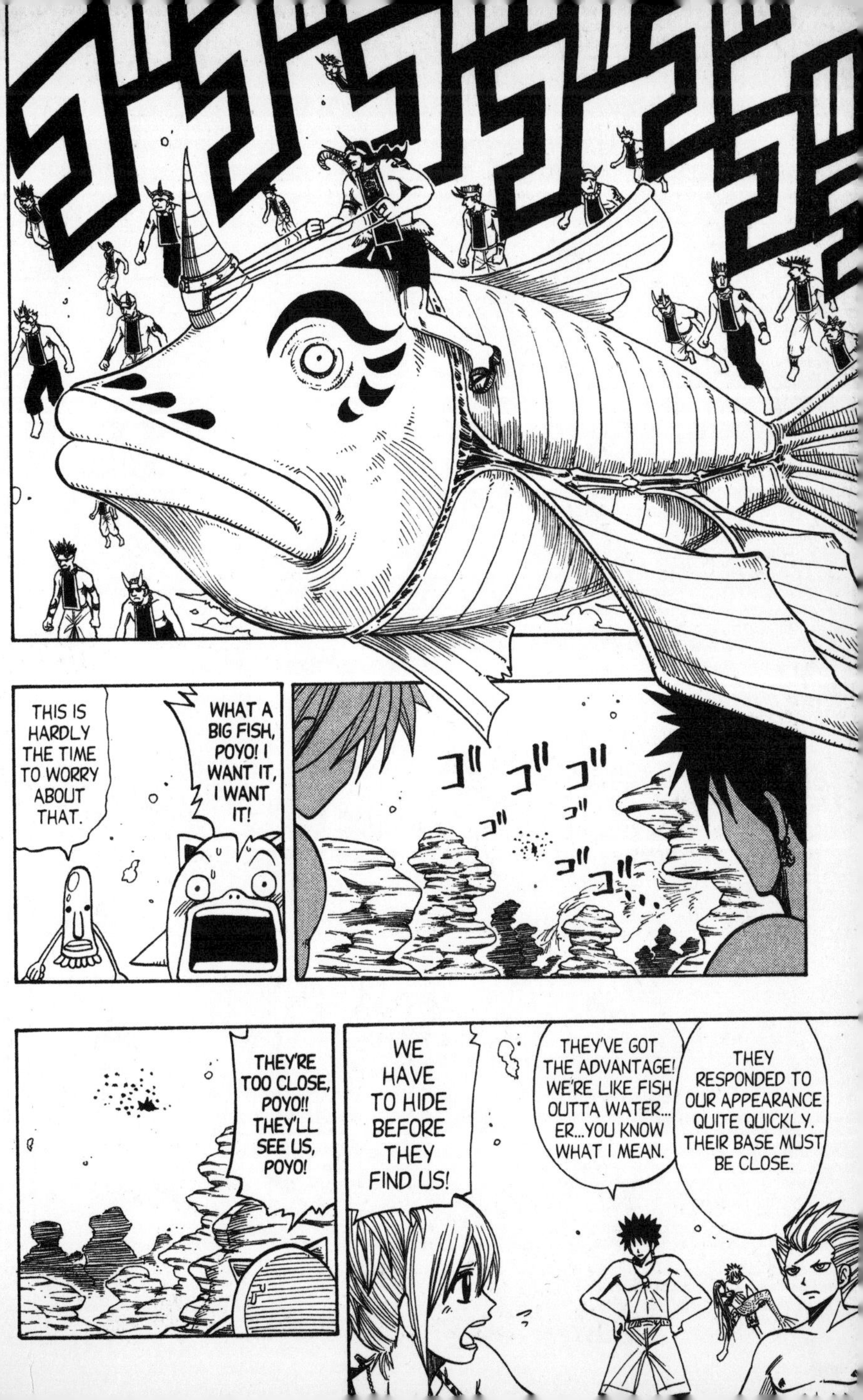
WHAT A BIG FISH, POYO! I WANT IT, I WANT IT!
THIS IS HARDLY THE TIME TO WORRY ABOUT THAT.
THEY RESPONDED TO OUR APPEARANCE QUITE QUICKLY. THEIR BASE MUST BE CLOSE.
THEY'VE GOT THE ADVANTAGE! WE'RE LIKE FISH OUTTA WATER... ER...YOU KNOW WHAT I MEAN.
WE HAVE TO HIDE BEFORE THEY FIND US!
THEY'RE TOO CLOSE, POYO!! THEY'LL SEE US, POYO!

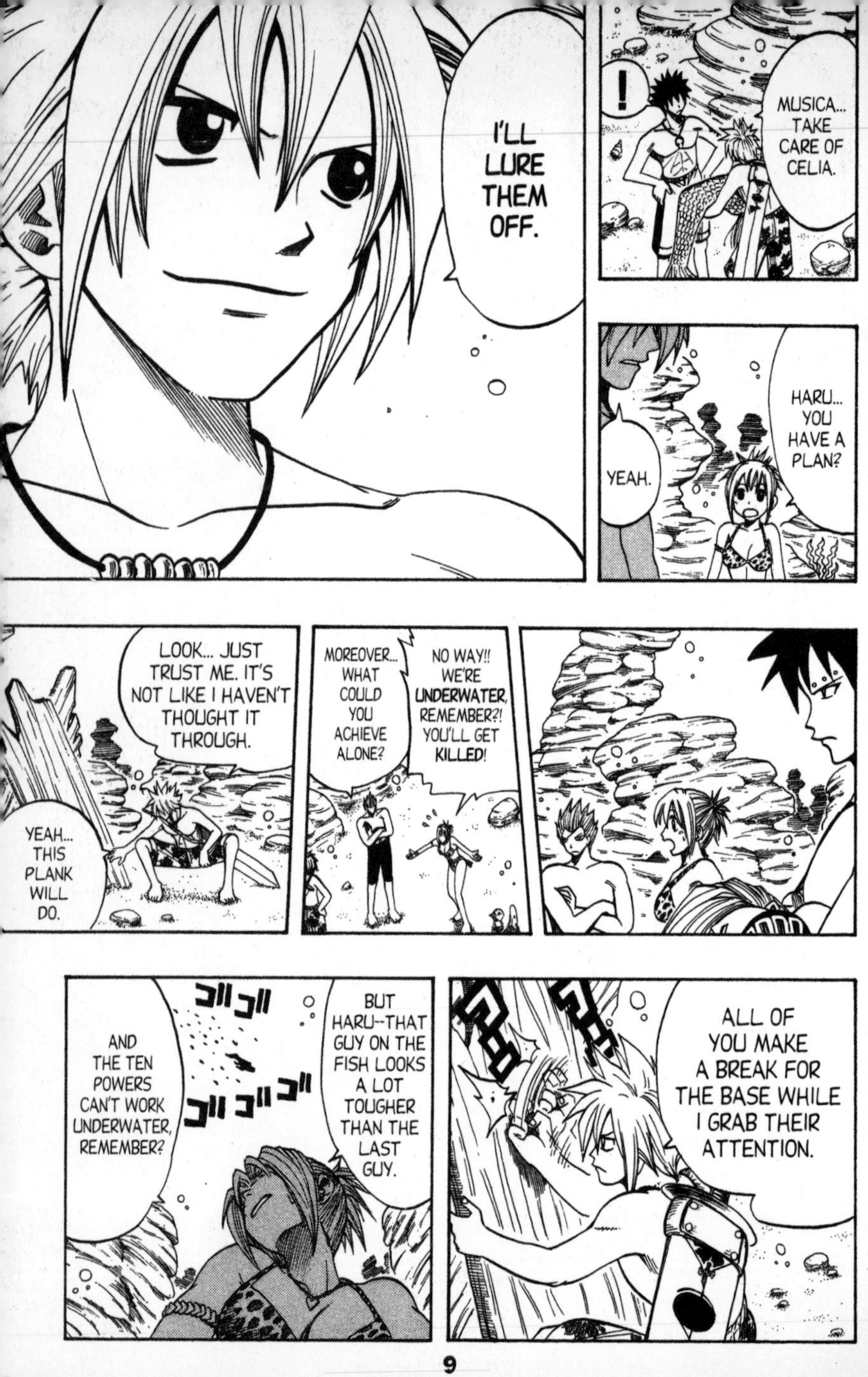
!
MUSICA... TAKE CARE OF CELIA.
HARU... YOU HAVE A PLAN?
YEAH.
I'LL LURE THEM OFF.
NO WAY!! WE'RE UNDERWATER, REMEMBER?! YOU'LL GET KILLED!
MOREOVER... WHAT COULD YOU ACHIEVE ALONE?
LOOK... JUST TRUST ME. IT'S NOT LIKE I HAVEN'T THOUGHT IT THROUGH.
YEAH... THIS PLANK WILL DO.
ALL OF YOU MAKE A BREAK FOR THE BASE WHILE I GRAB THEIR ATTENTION.
BUT HARU--THAT GUY ON THE FISH LOOKS A LOT TOUGHER THAN THE LAST GUY.
ゴゴ
ゴゴゴ
AND THE TEN POWERS CAN'T WORK UNDERWATER, REMEMBER?

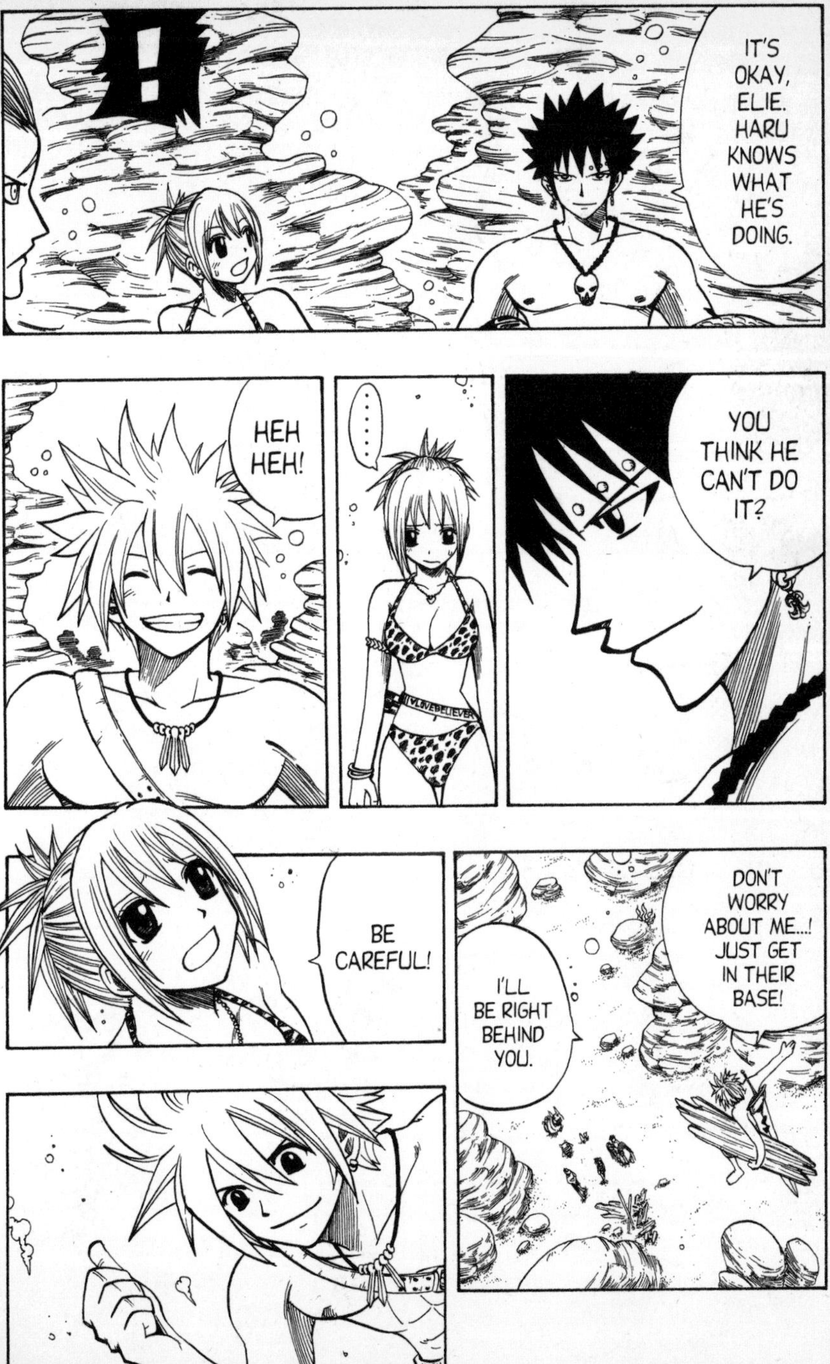
IT'S OKAY, ELIE. HARU KNOWS WHAT HE'S DOING.
!!
YOU THINK HE CAN'T DO IT?
......
HEH HEH!
DON'T WORRY ABOUT ME...! JUST GET IN THEIR BASE!
I'LL BE RIGHT BEHIND YOU.
BE CAREFUL!

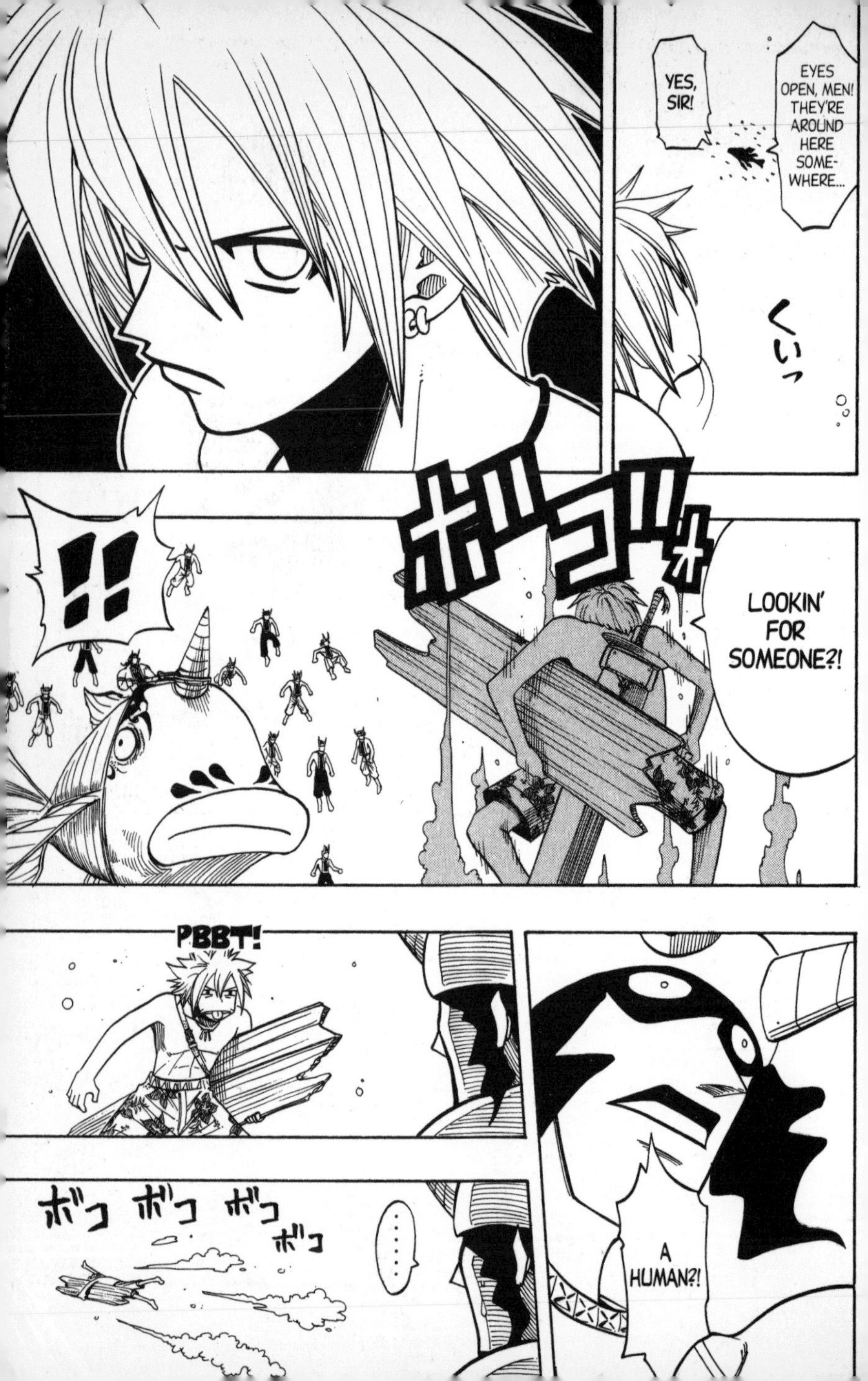
EYES OPEN, MEN! THEY'RE AROUND HERE SOME-WHERE...
YES, SIR!
くいっ
LOOKIN' FOR SOMEONE?!
!!
A HUMAN?!
PBBT!
ボコ ボコ ボコ ボコ
......

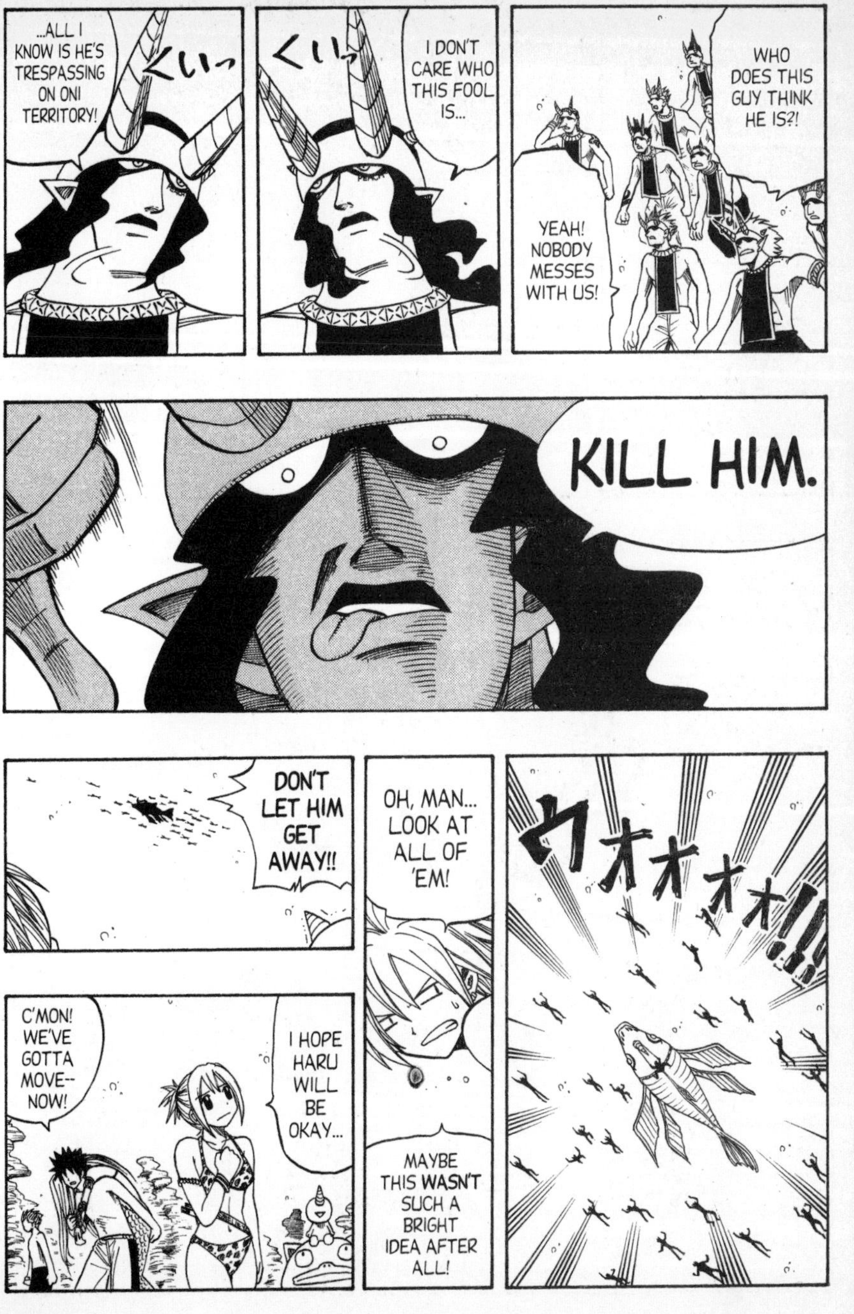
WHO DOES THIS GUY THINK HE IS?!
YEAH! NOBODY MESSES WITH US!
くいっ
I DON'T CARE WHO THIS FOOL IS...
くいっ
...ALL I KNOW IS HE'S TRESPASSING ON ONI TERRITORY!
KILL HIM.
ウオオオオ!!!
OH, MAN... LOOK AT ALL OF 'EM!
MAYBE THIS WASN'T SUCH A BRIGHT IDEA AFTER ALL!
DON'T LET HIM GET AWAY!!
I HOPE HARU WILL BE OKAY...
C'MON! WE'VE GOTTA MOVE-- NOW!

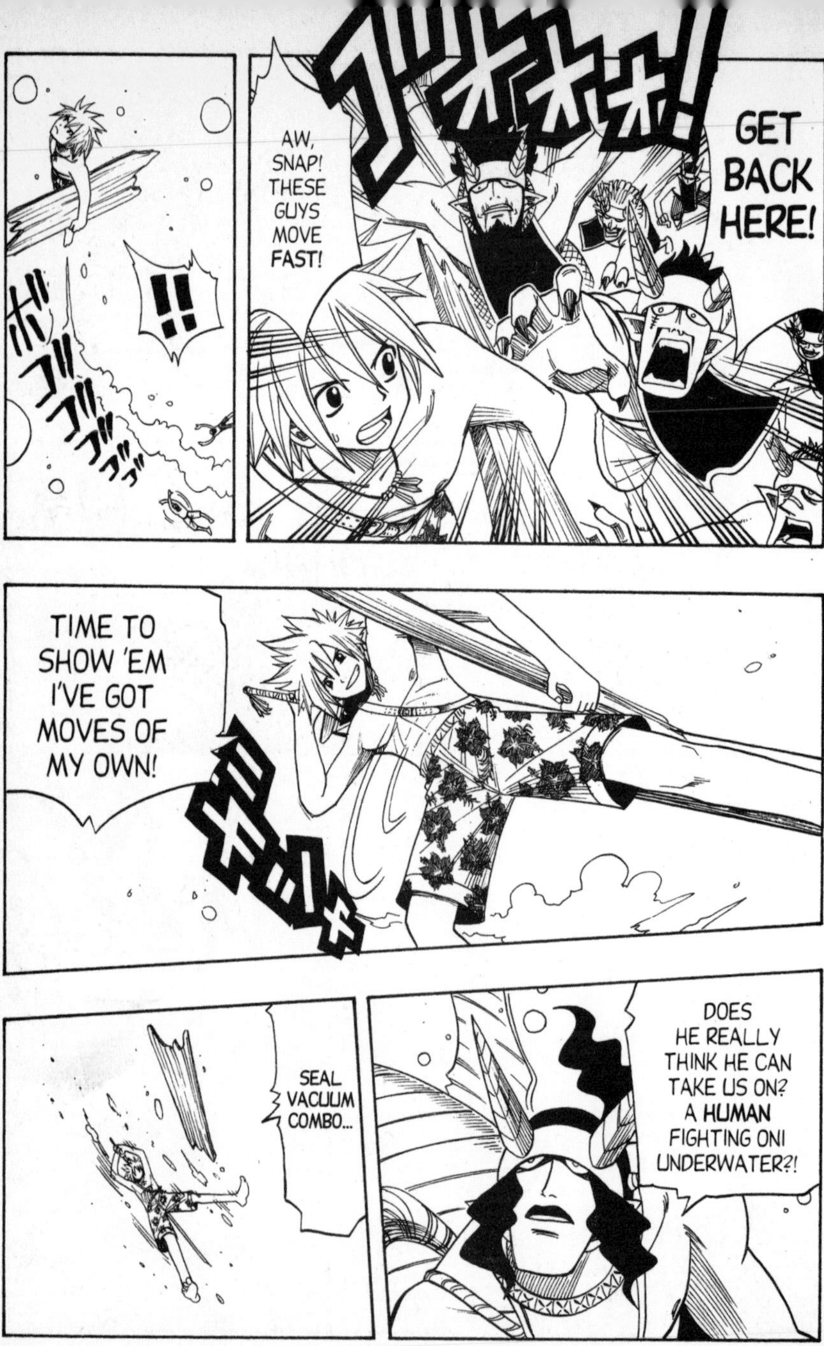
GET BACK HERE!
AW, SNAP! THESE GUYS MOVE FAST!
!!
TIME TO SHOW 'EM I'VE GOT MOVES OF MY OWN!
DOES HE REALLY THINK HE CAN TAKE US ON? A **HUMAN** FIGHTING ONI UNDERWATER?!
SEAL VACUUM COMBO...

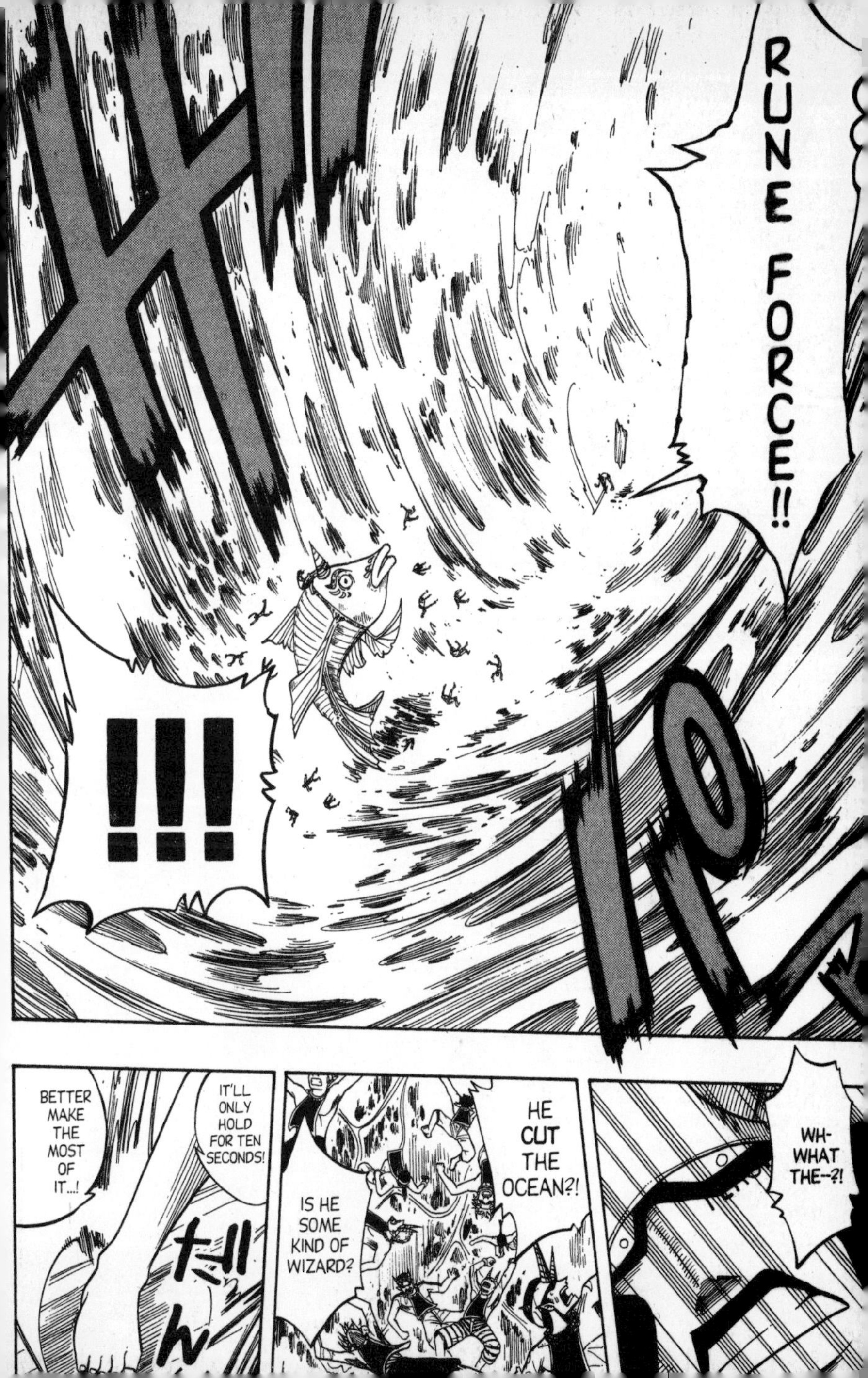
RUNE FORCE!!
!!!
WH-WHAT THE--?!
HE CUT THE OCEAN?!
IS HE SOME KIND OF WIZARD?
IT'LL ONLY HOLD FOR TEN SECONDS!
BETTER MAKE THE MOST OF IT...!

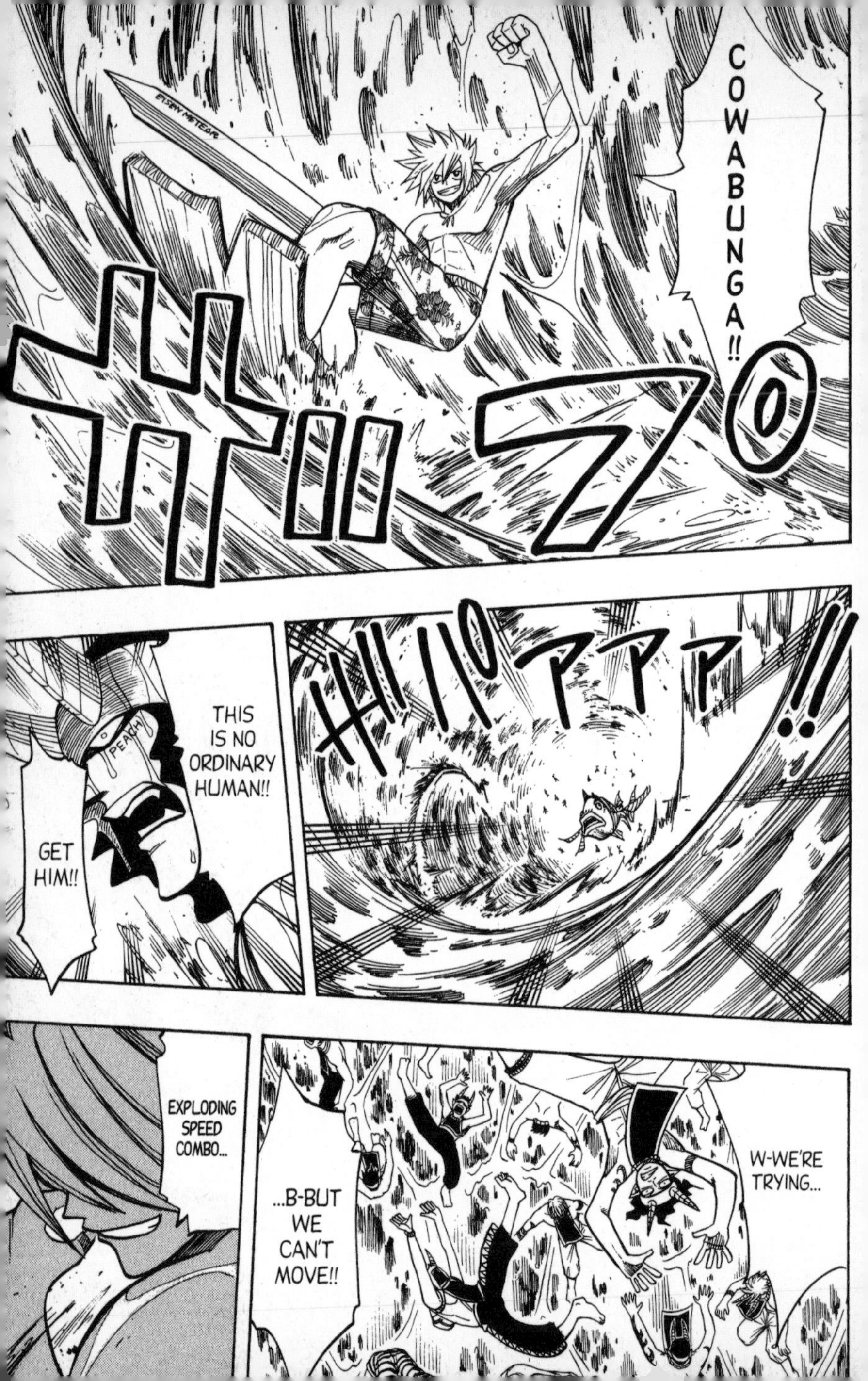
EISEN METEOR
COWABUNGA!!
THIS IS NO ORDINARY HUMAN!!
PEACH
GET HIM!!
W-WE'RE TRYING...
...B-BUT WE CAN'T MOVE!!
EXPLODING SPEED COMBO...

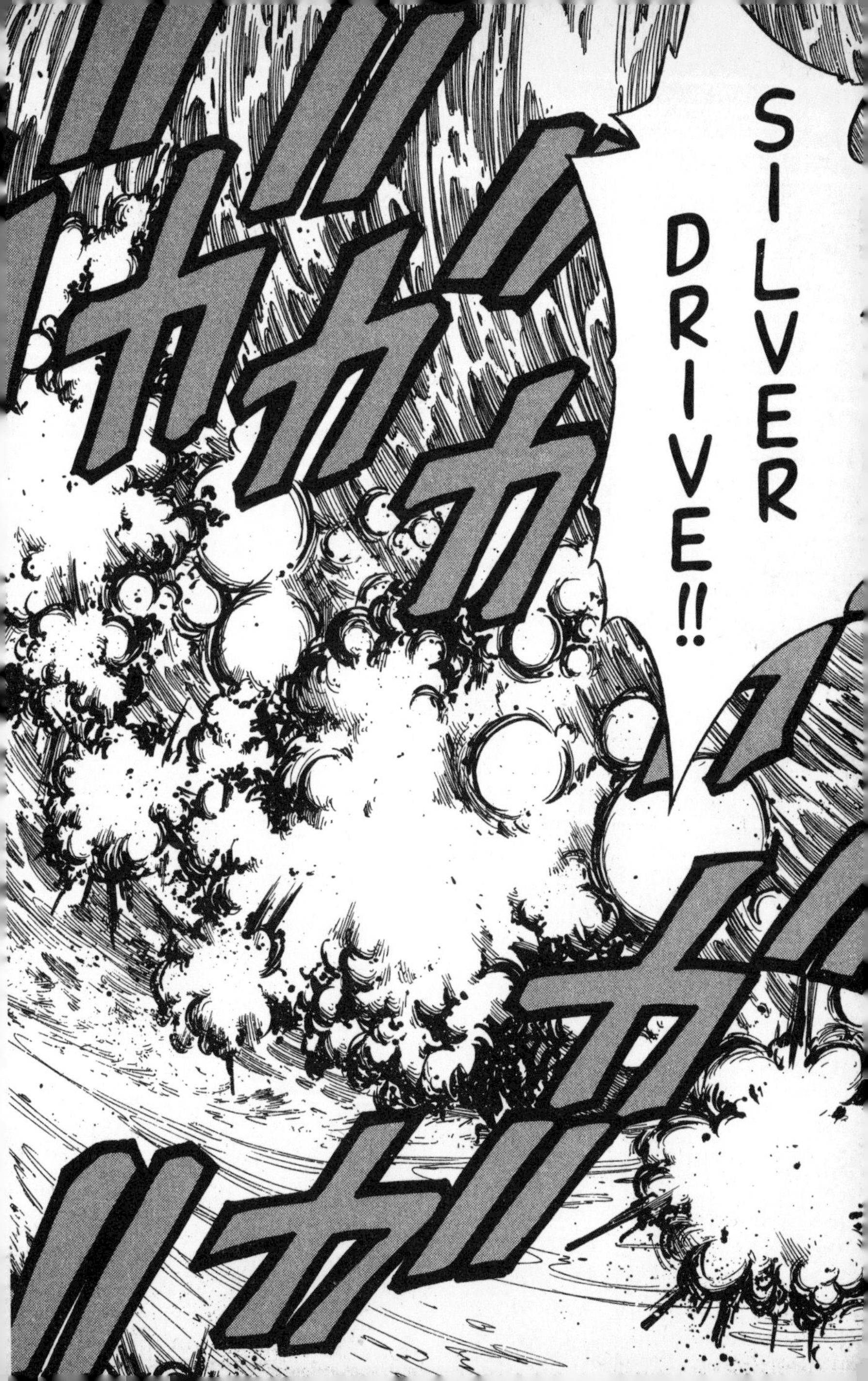
SILVER DRIVE!!

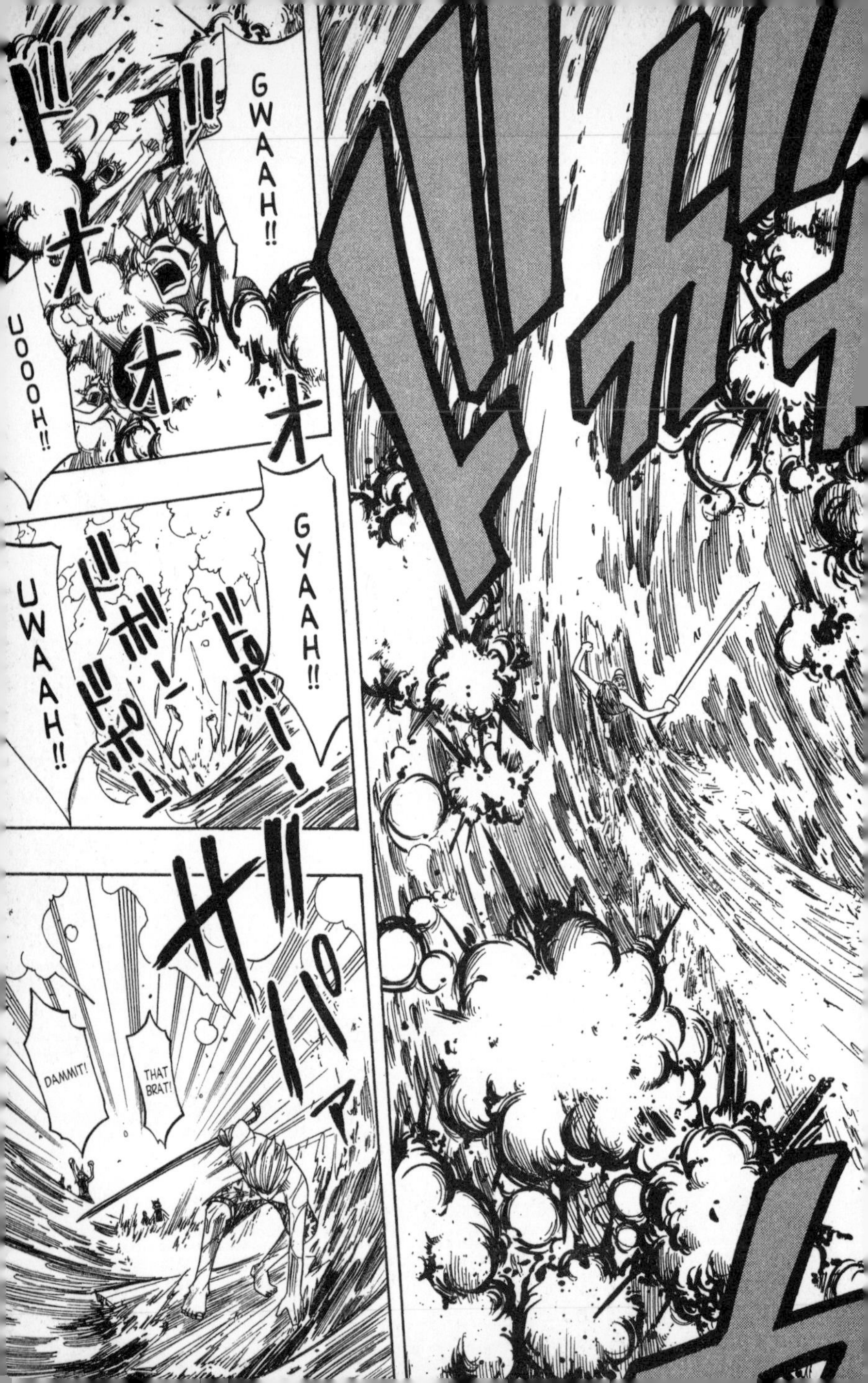
GWAAH!!
UOOOOH!!
GYAAH!!
UWAAH!!
THAT BRAT!
DAMMIT!

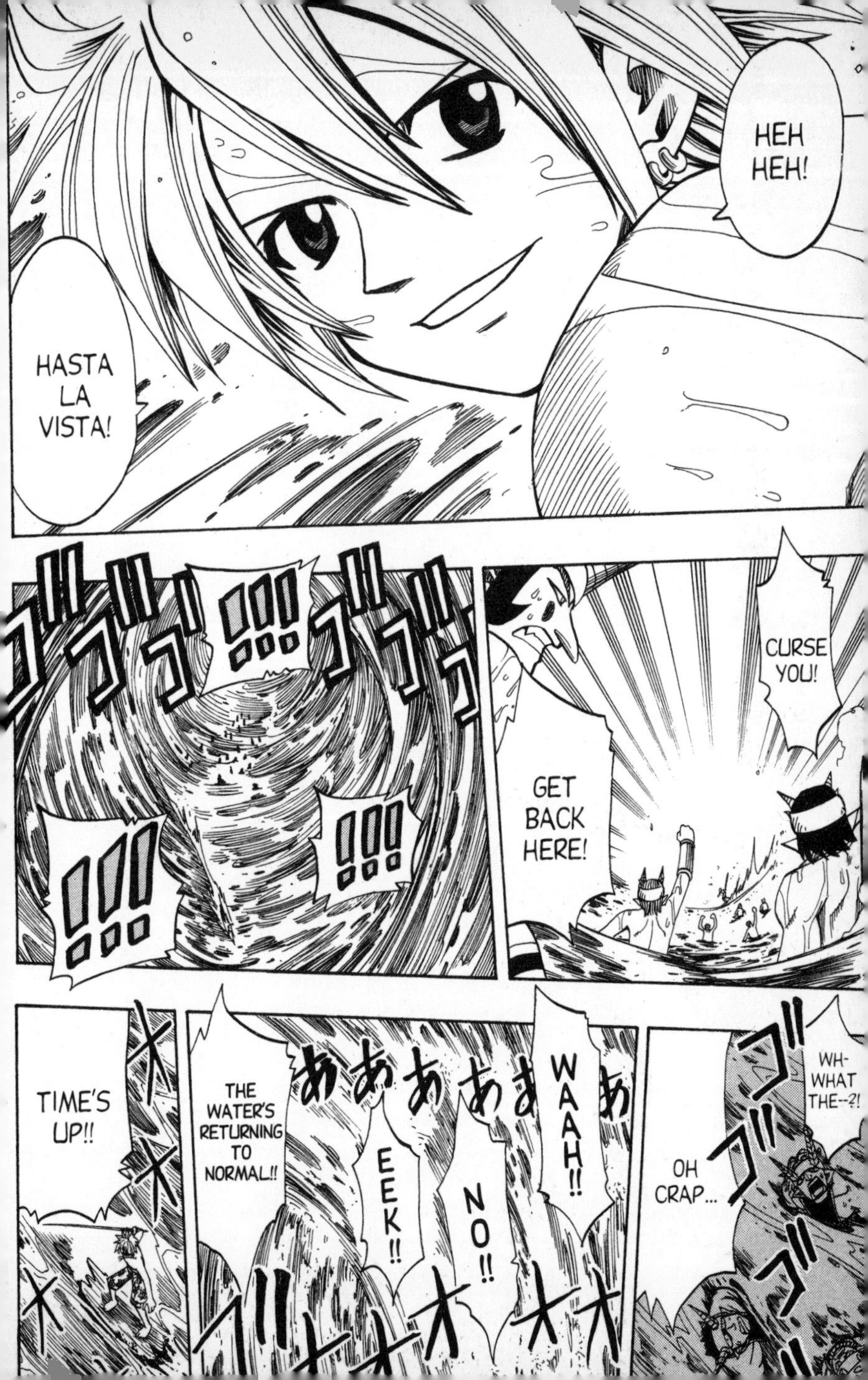
HEH HEH!
HASTA LA VISTA!
CURSE YOU!
GET BACK HERE!
!!!
!!!
WH-WHAT THE--?!
OH CRAP...
WAAH!!
NO!!
EEK!!
THE WATER'S RETURNING TO NORMAL!!
TIME'S UP!!

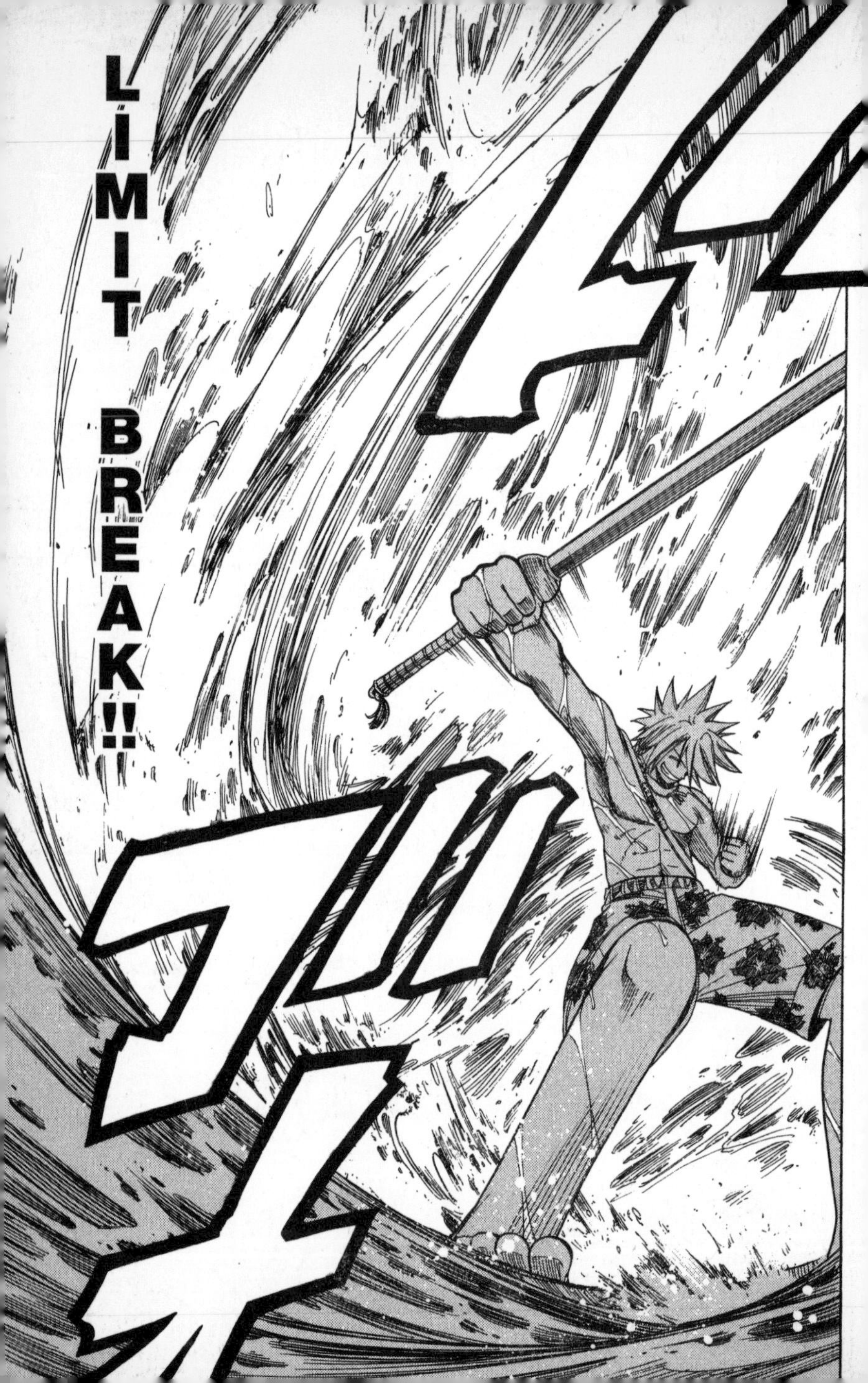
LIMIT BREAK!!

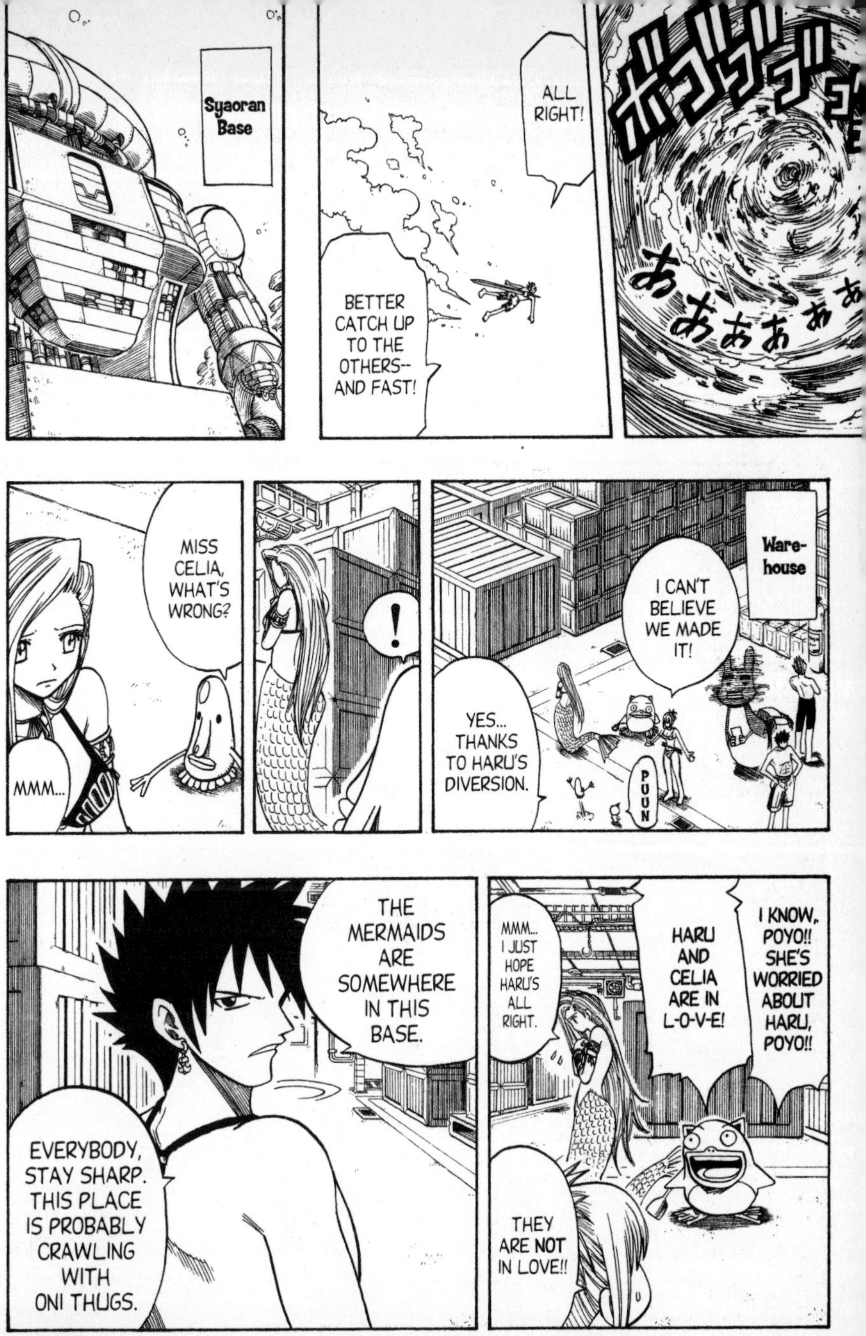
ああああああ
ALL RIGHT!
BETTER CATCH UP TO THE OTHERS-- AND FAST!
Syaoran Base
Ware-house
I CAN'T BELIEVE WE MADE IT!
YES... THANKS TO HARU'S DIVERSION.
PUUN
!
MISS CELIA, WHAT'S WRONG?
MMM...
I KNOW, POYO!! SHE'S WORRIED ABOUT HARU, POYO!!
HARU AND CELIA ARE IN L-O-V-E!
MMM... I JUST HOPE HARU'S ALL RIGHT.
THEY ARE NOT IN LOVE!!
THE MERMAIDS ARE SOMEWHERE IN THIS BASE.
EVERYBODY, STAY SHARP. THIS PLACE IS PROBABLY CRAWLING WITH ONI THUGS.

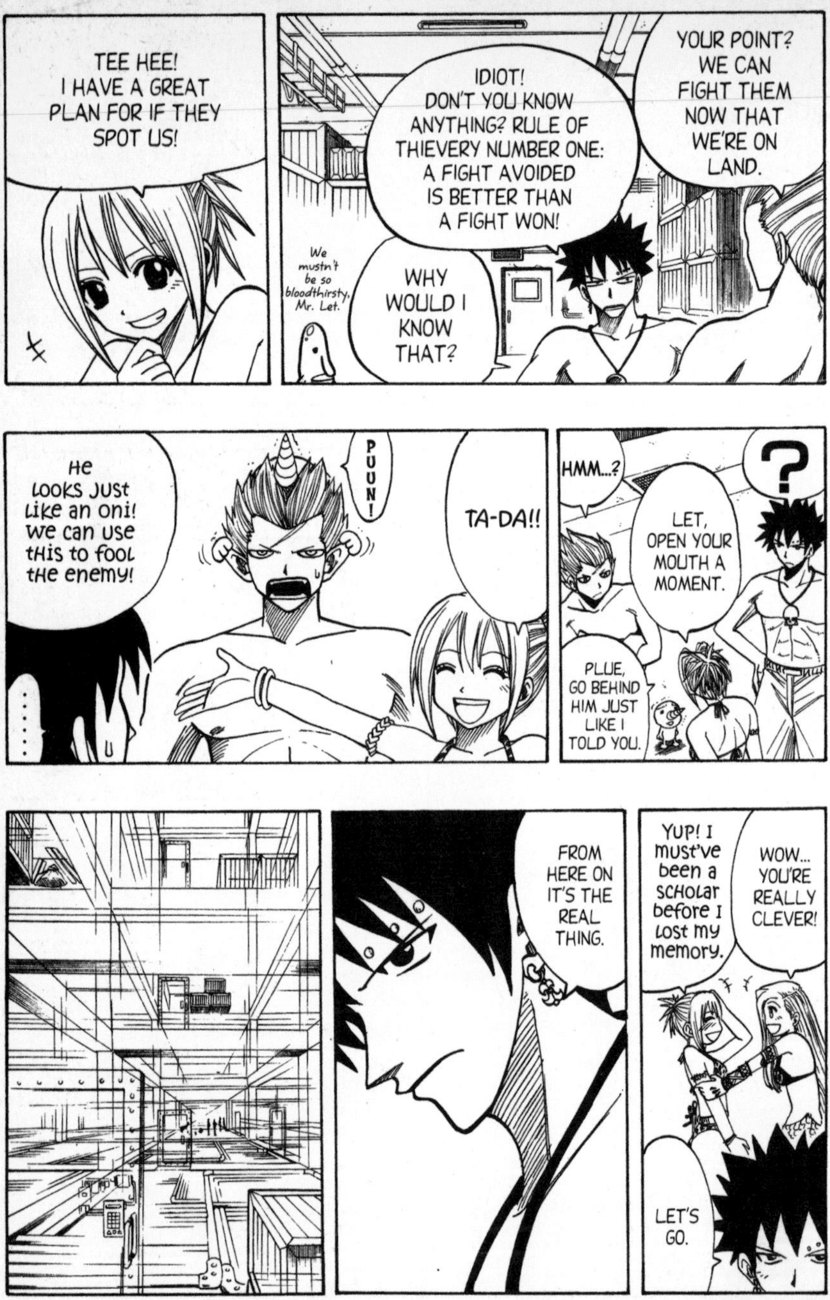
YOUR POINT? WE CAN FIGHT THEM NOW THAT WE'RE ON LAND.
IDIOT! DON'T YOU KNOW ANYTHING? RULE OF THIEVERY NUMBER ONE: A FIGHT AVOIDED IS BETTER THAN A FIGHT WON!
WHY WOULD I KNOW THAT?
We mustn't be so bloodthirsty, Mr. Let.
TEE HEE! I HAVE A GREAT PLAN FOR IF THEY SPOT US!
?
HMM...?
LET, OPEN YOUR MOUTH A MOMENT.
PLUE, GO BEHIND HIM JUST LIKE I TOLD YOU.
TA-DA!!
PUUN!
He looks just like an oni! We can use this to fool the enemy!
......
WOW... YOU'RE REALLY CLEVER!
YUP! I must've been a scholar before I lost my memory.
LET'S GO.
FROM HERE ON IT'S THE REAL THING.

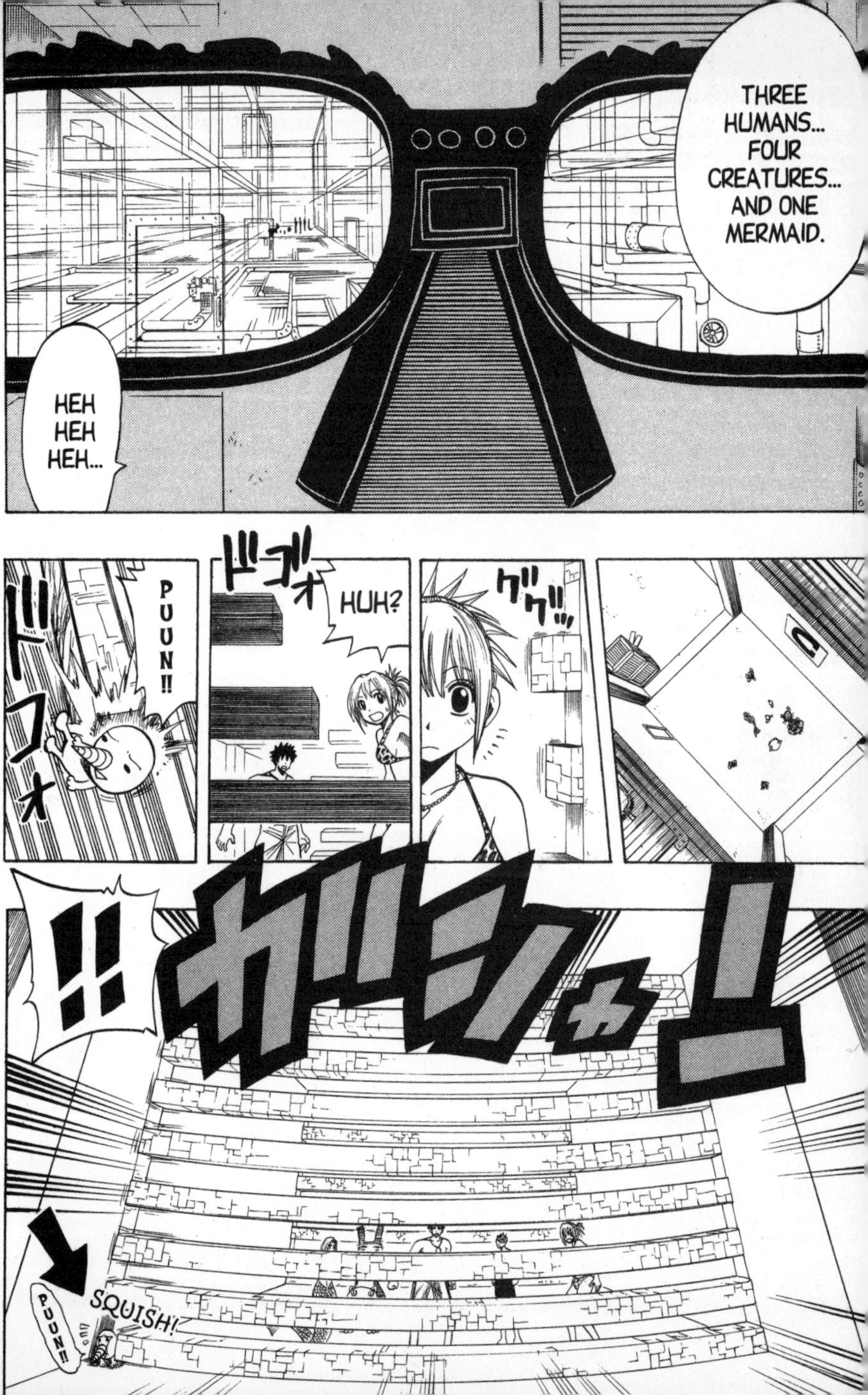
THREE HUMANS... FOUR CREATURES... AND ONE MERMAID.
HEH HEH HEH...
ドゴォ
HUH?
PUUN!!
!!
SQUISH!
PUUN!!

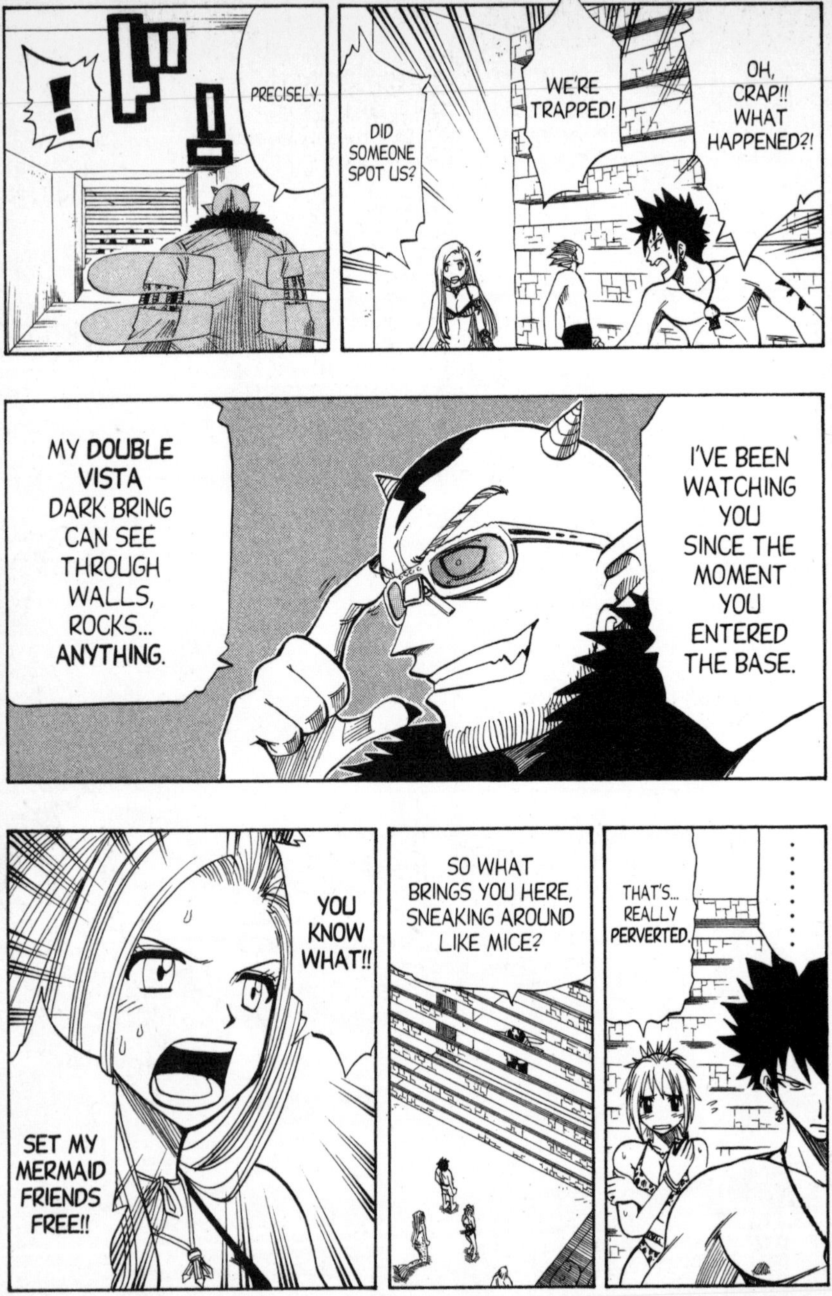
OH, CRAP!! WHAT HAPPENED?!
WE'RE TRAPPED!
DID SOMEONE SPOT US?
PRECISELY.
!
I'VE BEEN WATCHING YOU SINCE THE MOMENT YOU ENTERED THE BASE.
MY DOUBLE VISTA DARK BRING CAN SEE THROUGH WALLS, ROCKS... ANYTHING.
......
THAT'S... REALLY PERVERTED.
SO WHAT BRINGS YOU HERE, SNEAKING AROUND LIKE MICE?
YOU KNOW WHAT!!
SET MY MERMAID FRIENDS FREE!!

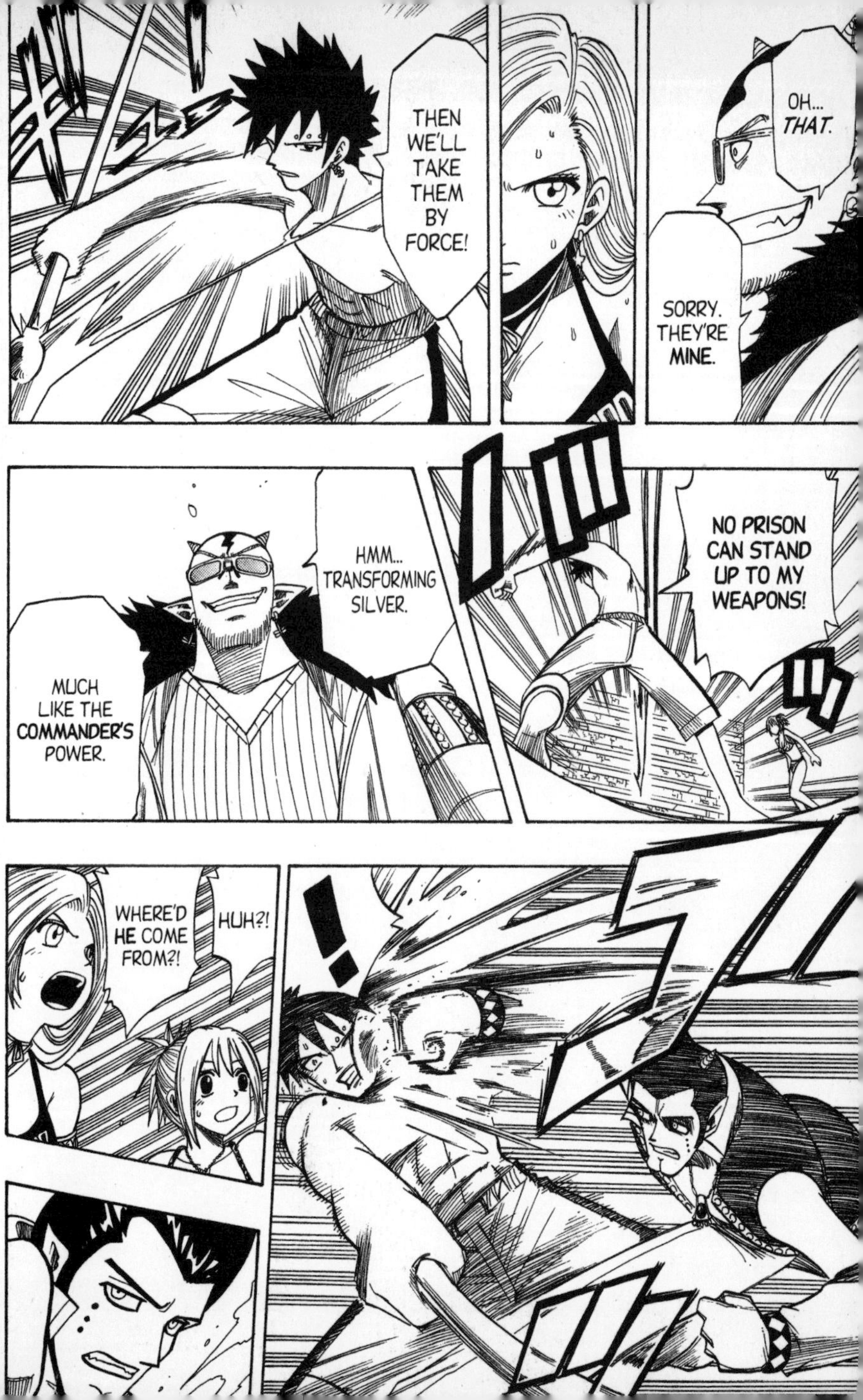
OH... THAT.
SORRY. THEY'RE MINE.
THEN WE'LL TAKE THEM BY FORCE!
NO PRISON CAN STAND UP TO MY WEAPONS!
HMM... TRANSFORMING SILVER.
MUCH LIKE THE COMMANDER'S POWER.
HUH?!
WHERE'D HE COME FROM?!

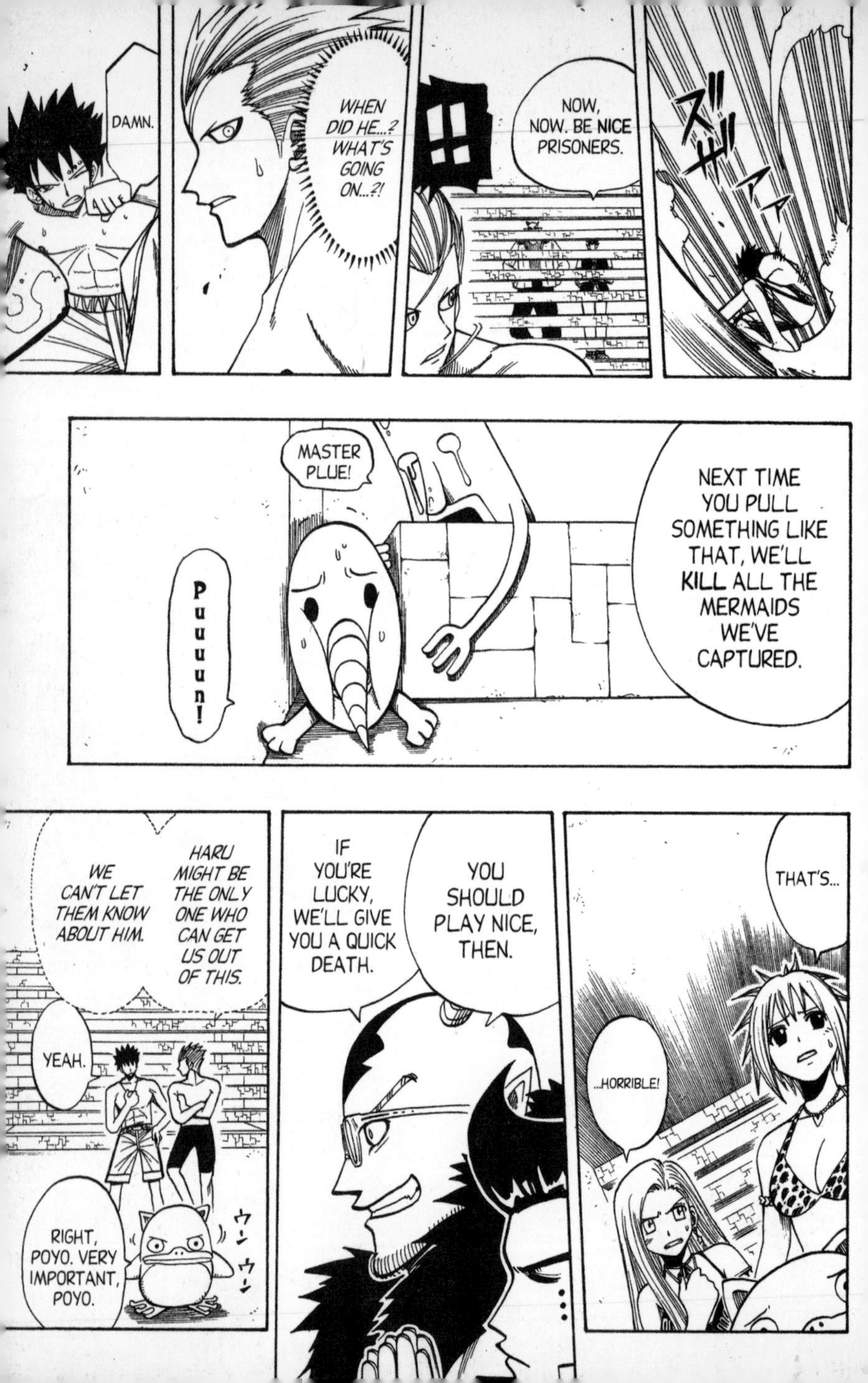
ズザァァ
NOW, NOW. BE NICE PRISONERS.
WHEN DID HE...? WHAT'S GOING ON...?!
DAMN.
NEXT TIME YOU PULL SOMETHING LIKE THAT, WE'LL KILL ALL THE MERMAIDS WE'VE CAPTURED.
MASTER PLUE!
Puuuun!
THAT'S...
...HORRIBLE!
YOU SHOULD PLAY NICE, THEN.
IF YOU'RE LUCKY, WE'LL GIVE YOU A QUICK DEATH.
HARU MIGHT BE THE ONLY ONE WHO CAN GET US OUT OF THIS.
WE CAN'T LET THEM KNOW ABOUT HIM.
YEAH.
RIGHT, POYO. VERY IMPORTANT, POYO.

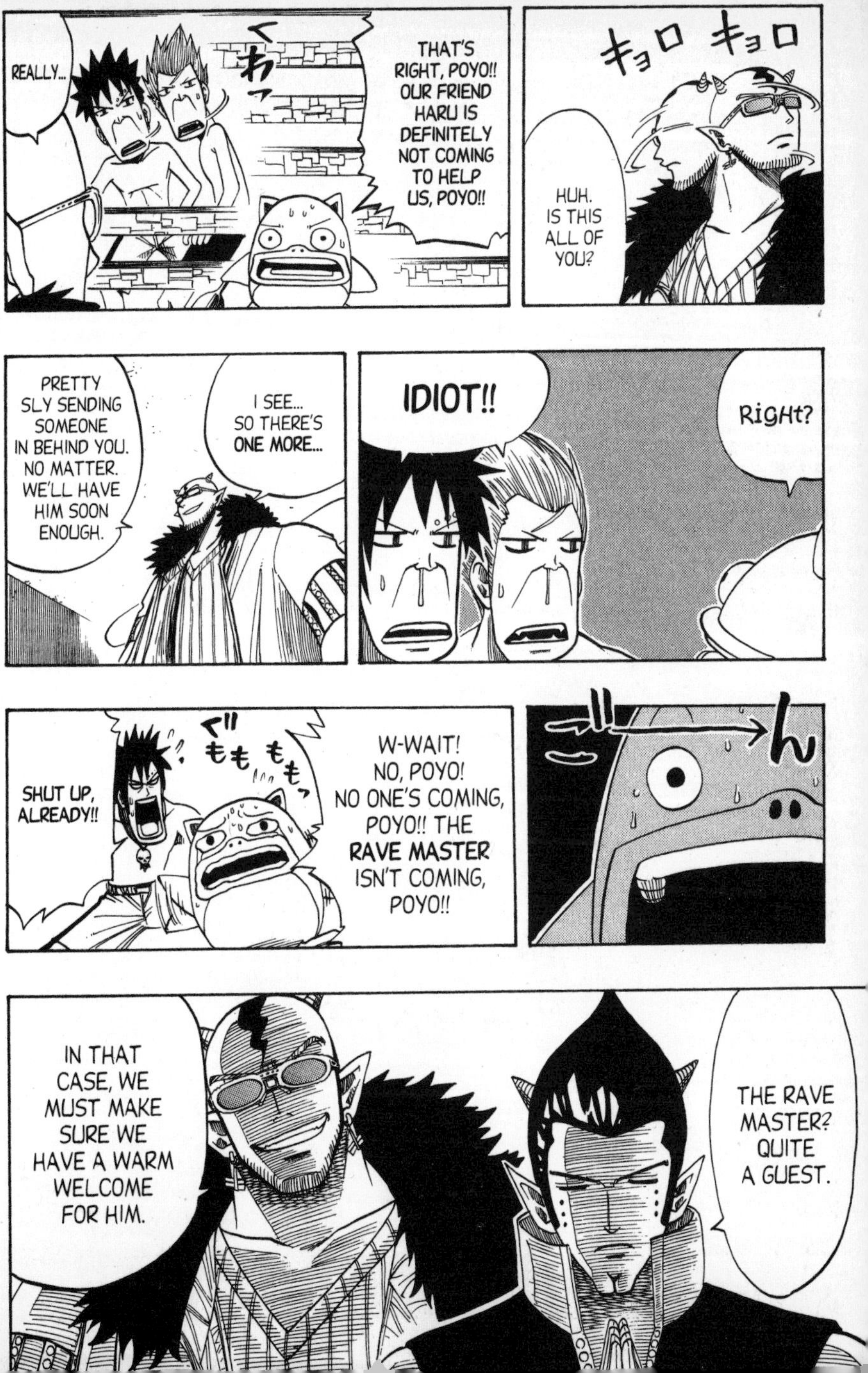
キョロ キョロ
HUH. IS THIS ALL OF YOU?
THAT'S RIGHT, POYO!! OUR FRIEND HARU IS DEFINITELY NOT COMING TO HELP US, POYO!!
くわっ
REALLY...
Right?
IDIOT!!
I SEE... SO THERE'S ONE MORE...
PRETTY SLY SENDING SOMEONE IN BEHIND YOU. NO MATTER. WE'LL HAVE HIM SOON ENOUGH.
W-WAIT! NO, POYO! NO ONE'S COMING, POYO!! THE RAVE MASTER ISN'T COMING, POYO!!
SHUT UP, ALREADY!!
THE RAVE MASTER? QUITE A GUEST.
IN THAT CASE, WE MUST MAKE SURE WE HAVE A WARM WELCOME FOR HIM.

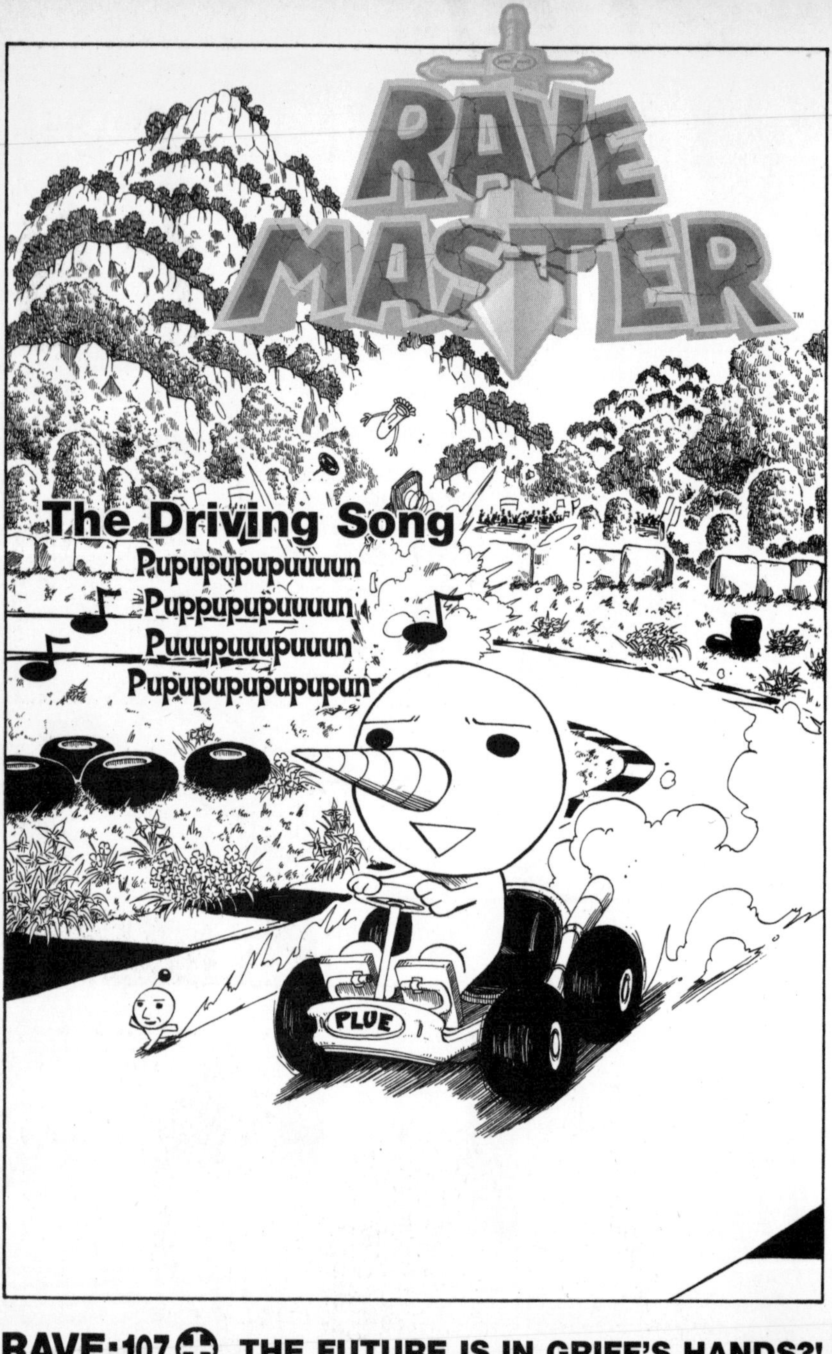
RAVE MASTER™
The Driving Song
Pupupupupuuuun
Puppupupuuuun
Puuupuuupuuun
Pupupupupupupun
PLUE

RAVE:107 THE FUTURE IS IN GRIFF'S HANDS?!

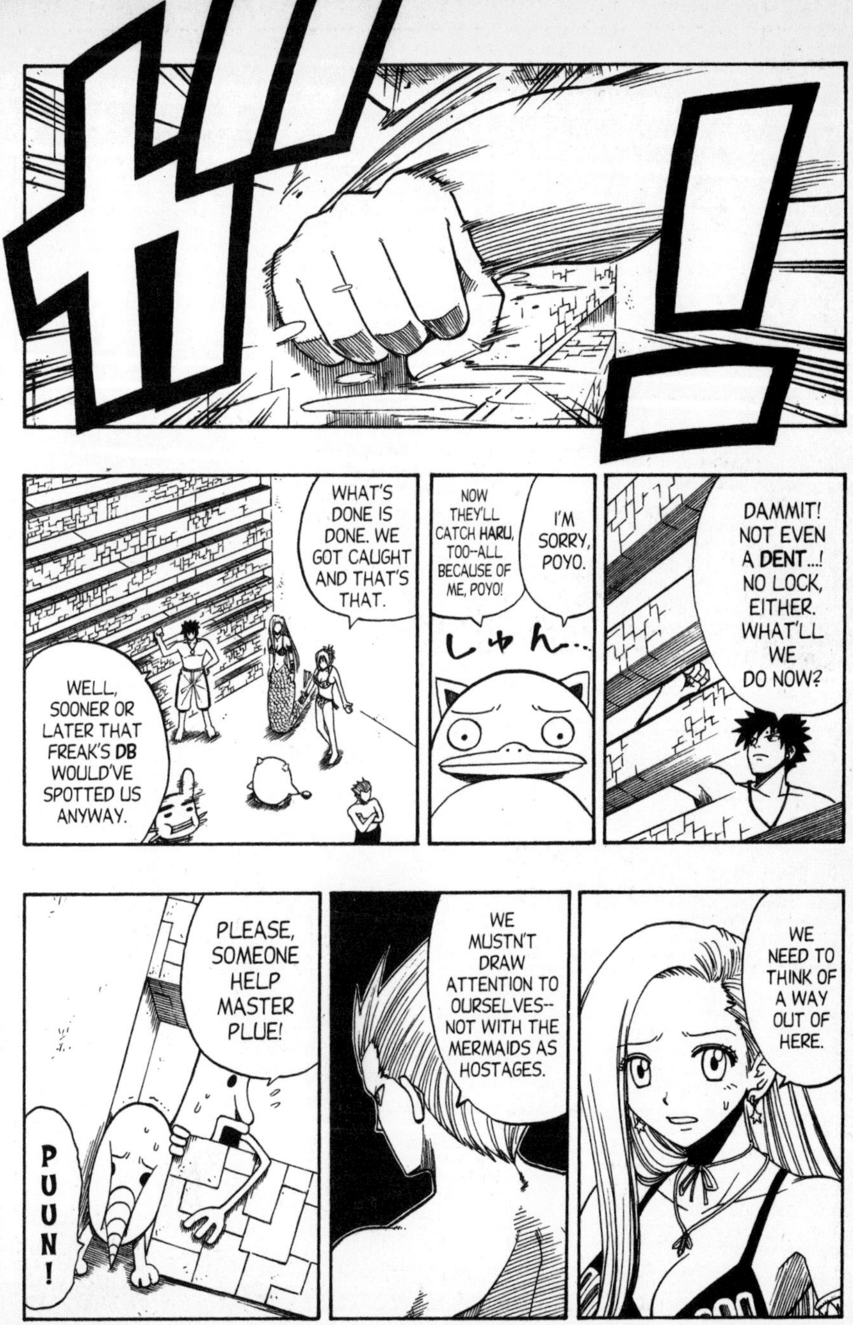
DAMMIT! NOT EVEN A DENT...! NO LOCK, EITHER. WHAT'LL WE DO NOW?
I'M SORRY, POYO.
NOW THEY'LL CATCH HARU, TOO--ALL BECAUSE OF ME, POYO!
しゅん...
WHAT'S DONE IS DONE. WE GOT CAUGHT AND THAT'S THAT.
WELL, SOONER OR LATER THAT FREAK'S DB WOULD'VE SPOTTED US ANYWAY.
WE NEED TO THINK OF A WAY OUT OF HERE.
WE MUSTN'T DRAW ATTENTION TO OURSELVES--NOT WITH THE MERMAIDS AS HOSTAGES.
PLEASE, SOMEONE HELP MASTER PLUE!
PUUN!

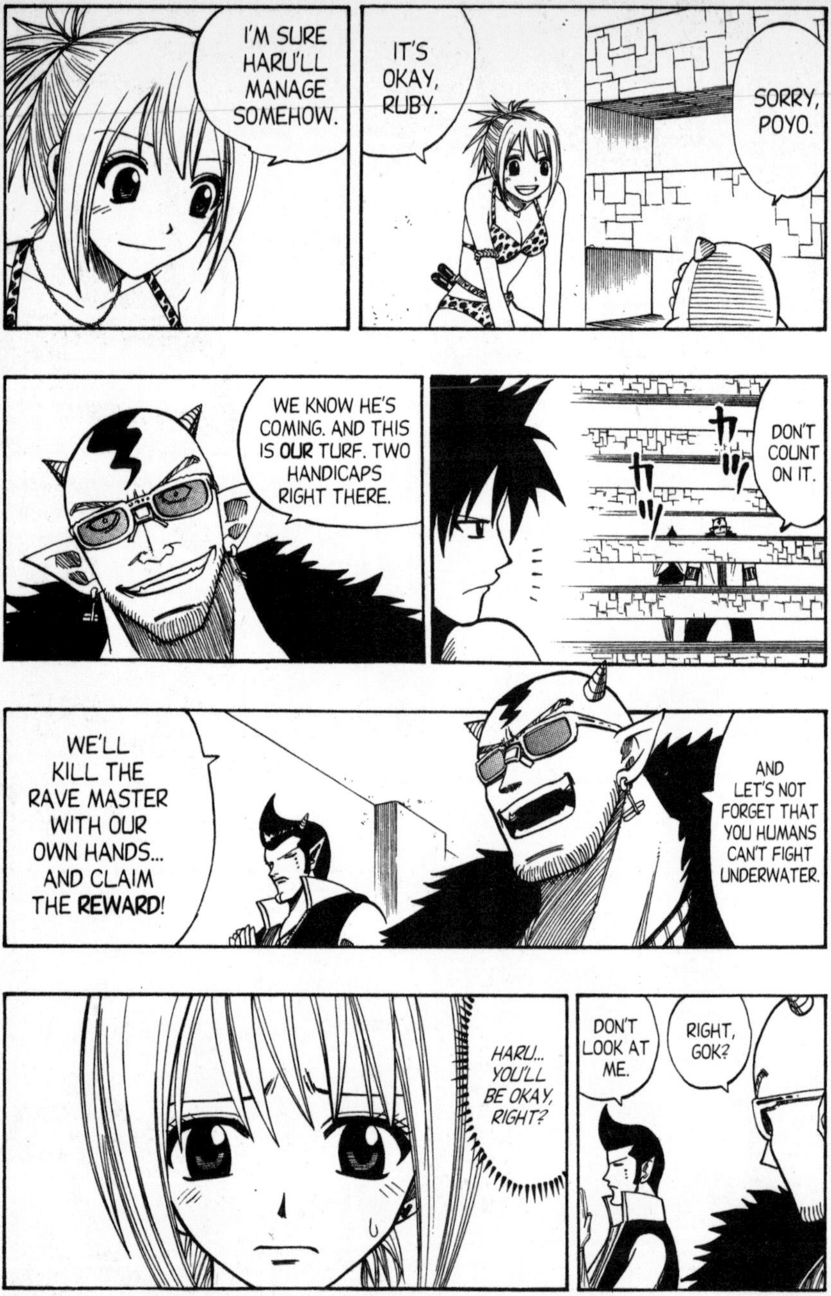
SORRY, POYO.
IT'S OKAY, RUBY.
I'M SURE HARU'LL MANAGE SOMEHOW.
DON'T COUNT ON IT.
カッ
カッ
WE KNOW HE'S COMING. AND THIS IS OUR TURF. TWO HANDICAPS RIGHT THERE.
AND LET'S NOT FORGET THAT YOU HUMANS CAN'T FIGHT UNDERWATER.
WE'LL KILL THE RAVE MASTER WITH OUR OWN HANDS... AND CLAIM THE REWARD!
RIGHT, GOK?
DON'T LOOK AT ME.
HARU... YOU'LL BE OKAY, RIGHT?

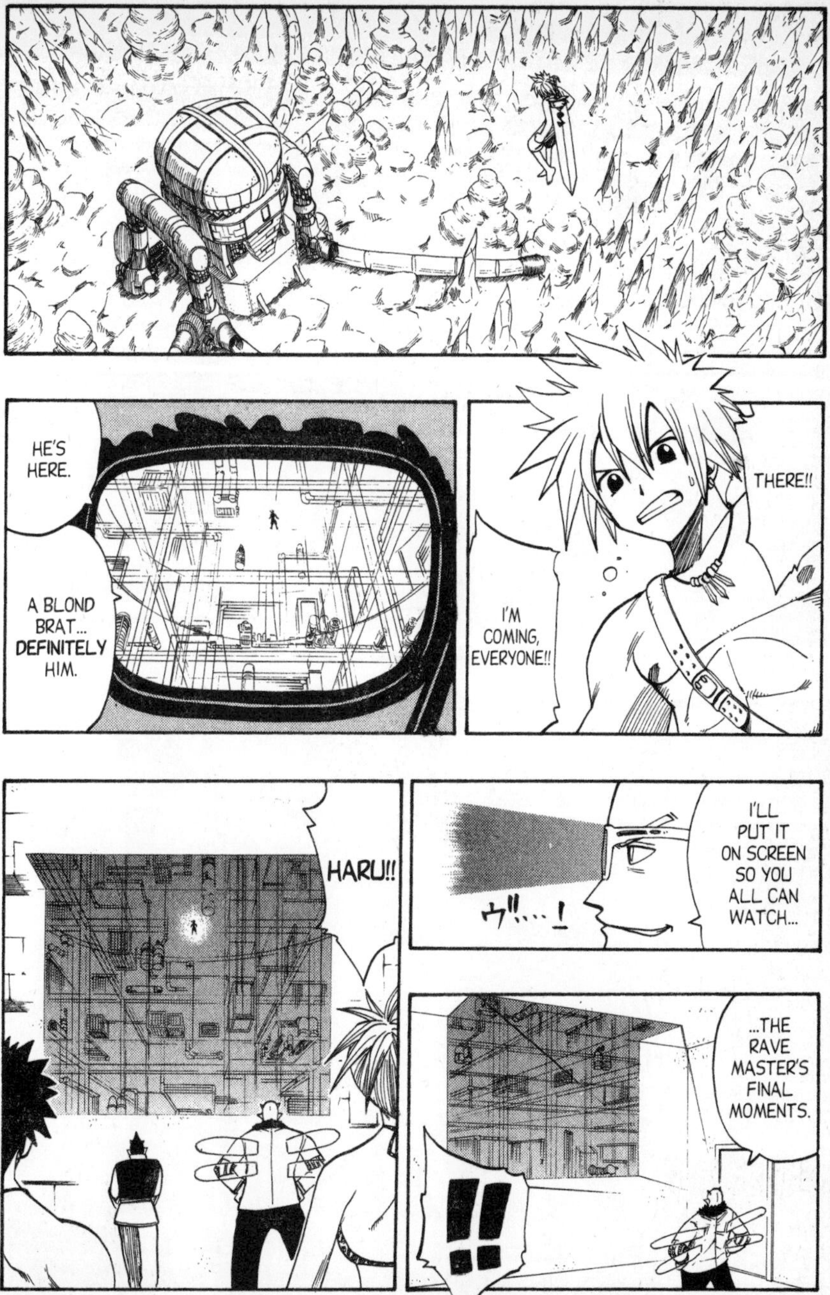
THERE!!
I'M COMING, EVERYONE!!
HE'S HERE.
A BLOND BRAT... DEFINITELY HIM.
I'LL PUT IT ON SCREEN SO YOU ALL CAN WATCH...
ウ‼…!
...THE RAVE MASTER'S FINAL MOMENTS.
!!
HARU!!

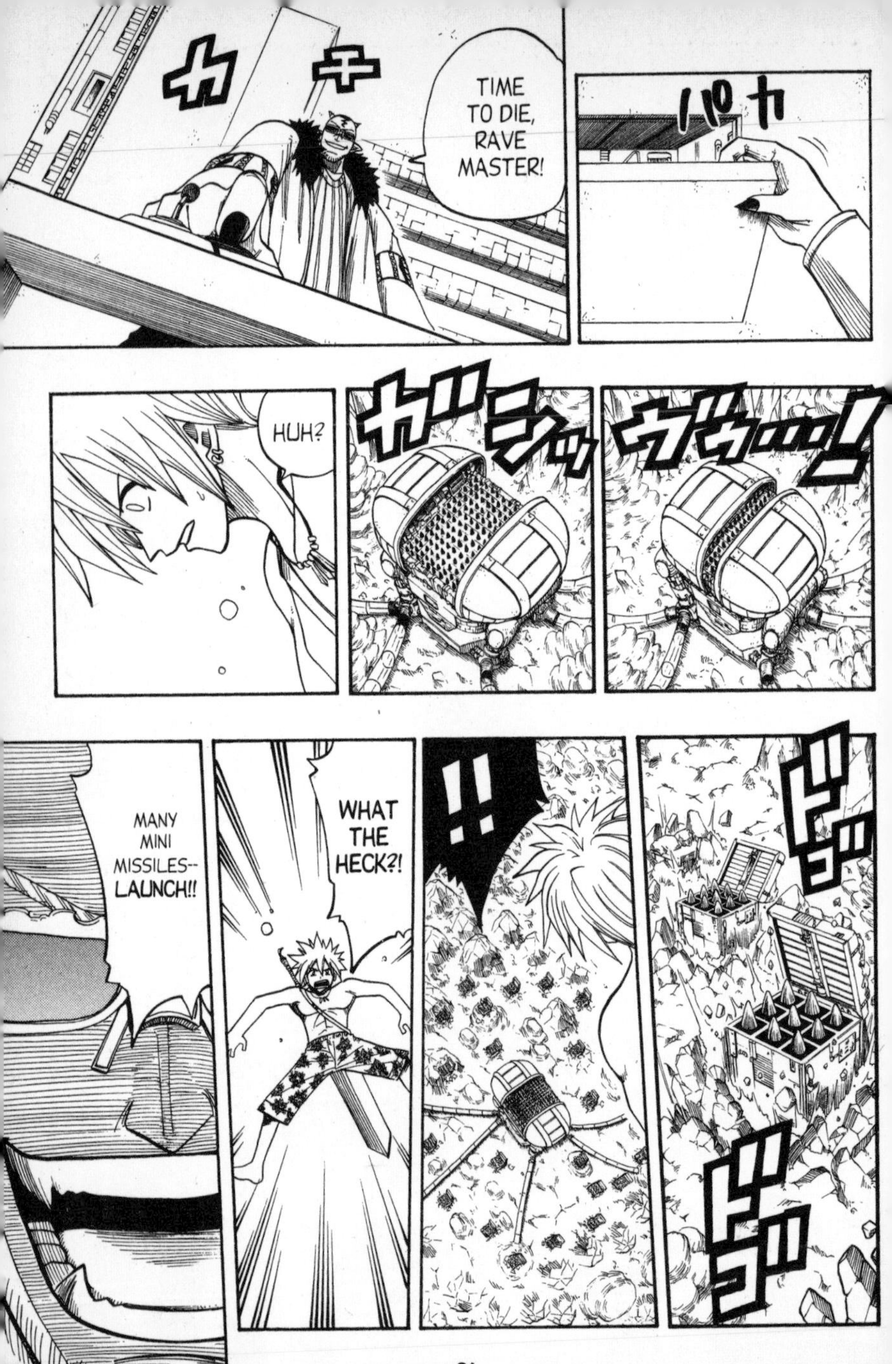
パカ
カチ
TIME TO DIE, RAVE MASTER!
HUH?
!!
WHAT THE HECK?!
MANY MINI MISSILES-- LAUNCH!!

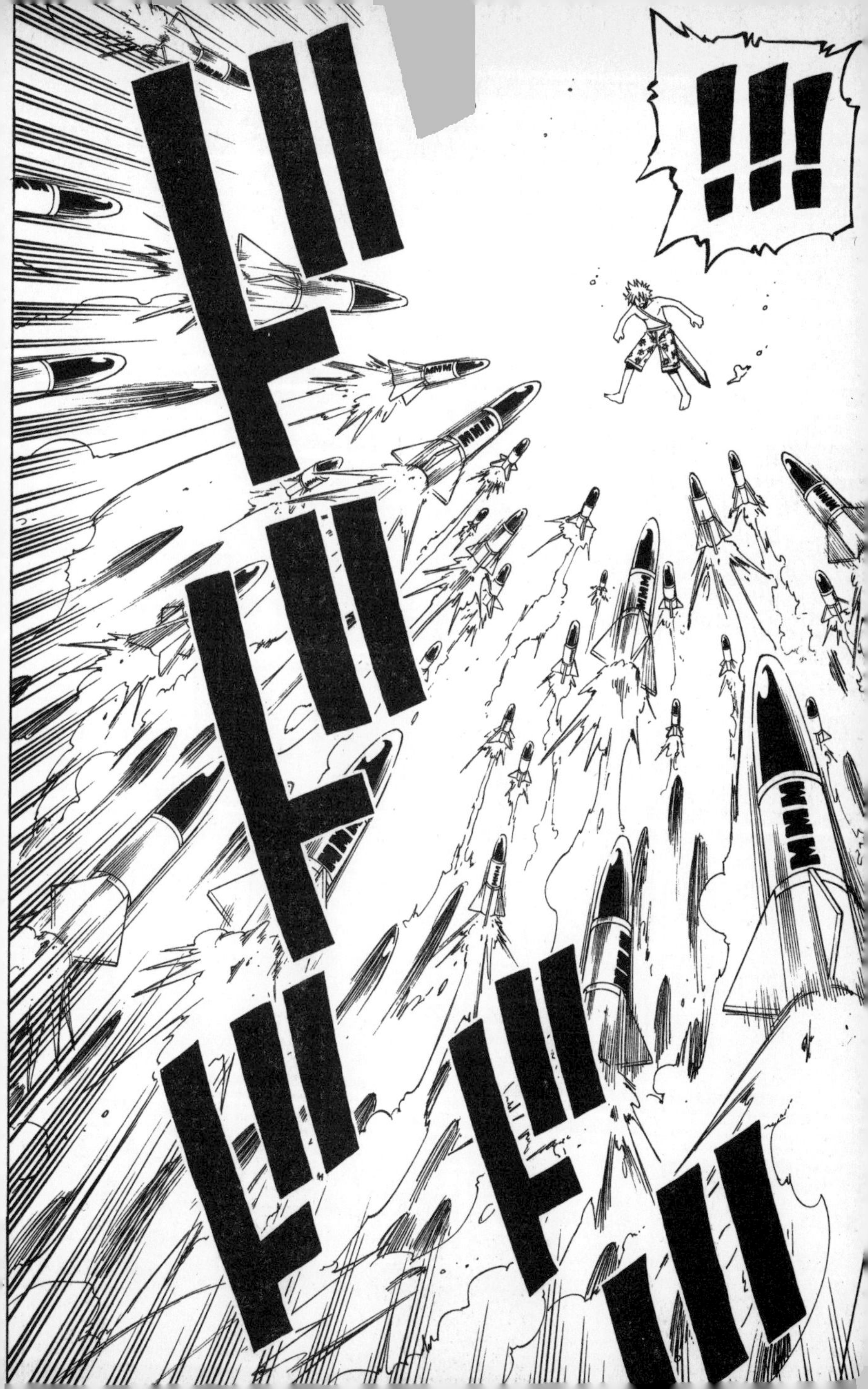
!!!
ド!!
ド!!
ド!!
ド!!
ド!!
MMM

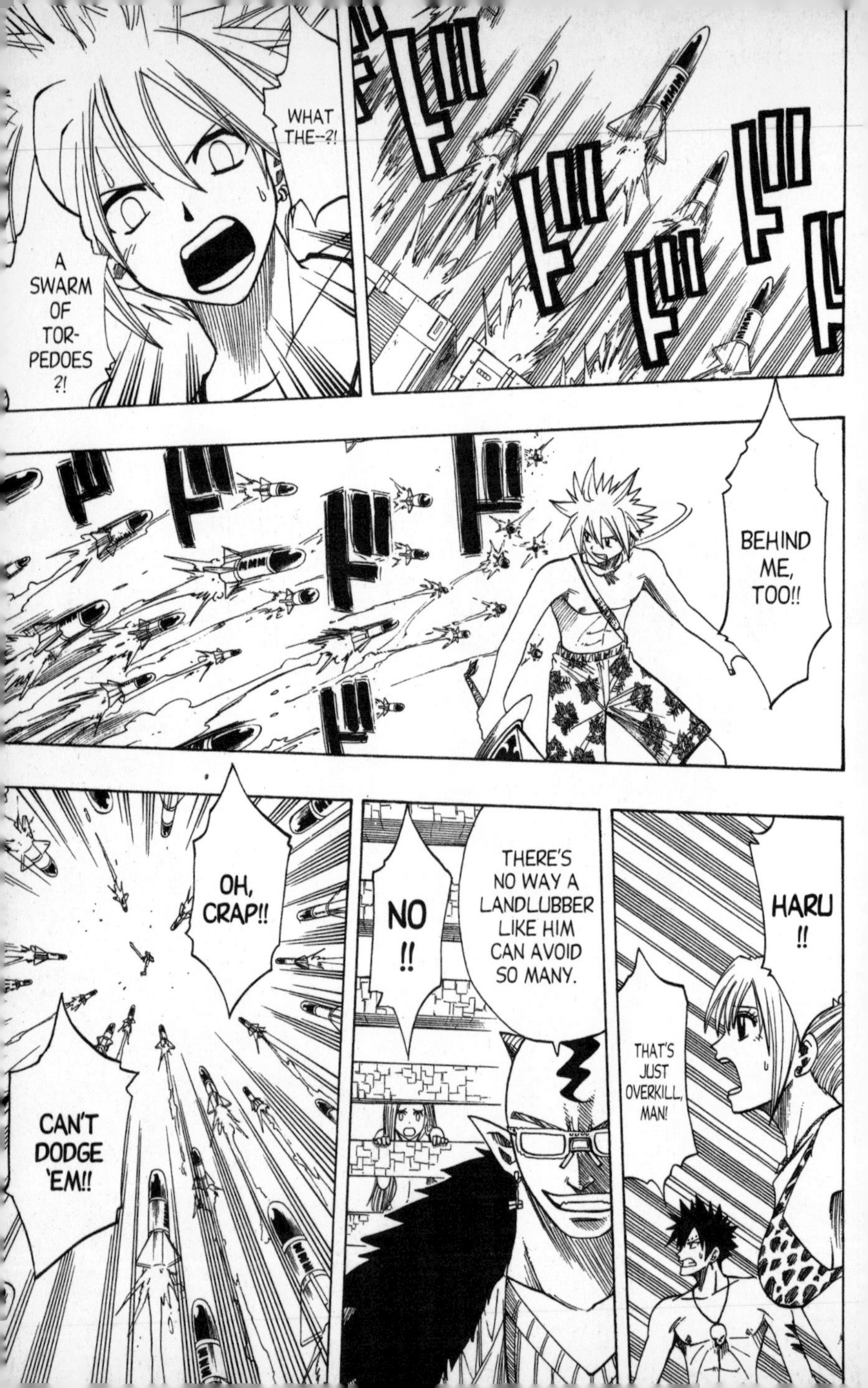
WHAT THE--?!
A SWARM OF TORPEDOES?!
BEHIND ME, TOO!!
HARU!!
THAT'S JUST OVERKILL, MAN!
THERE'S NO WAY A LANDLUBBER LIKE HIM CAN AVOID SO MANY.
NO!!
OH, CRAP!!
CAN'T DODGE 'EM!!

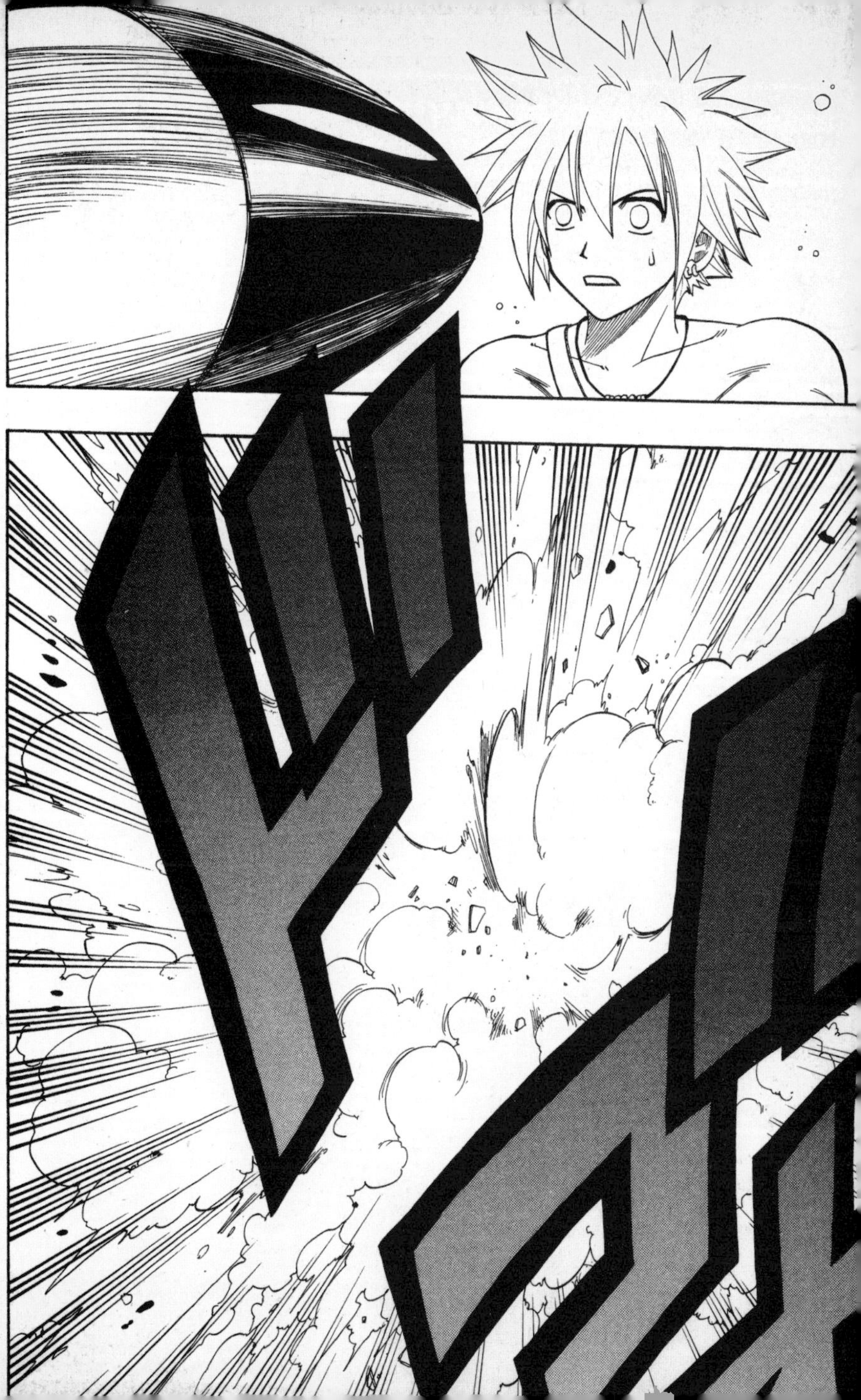

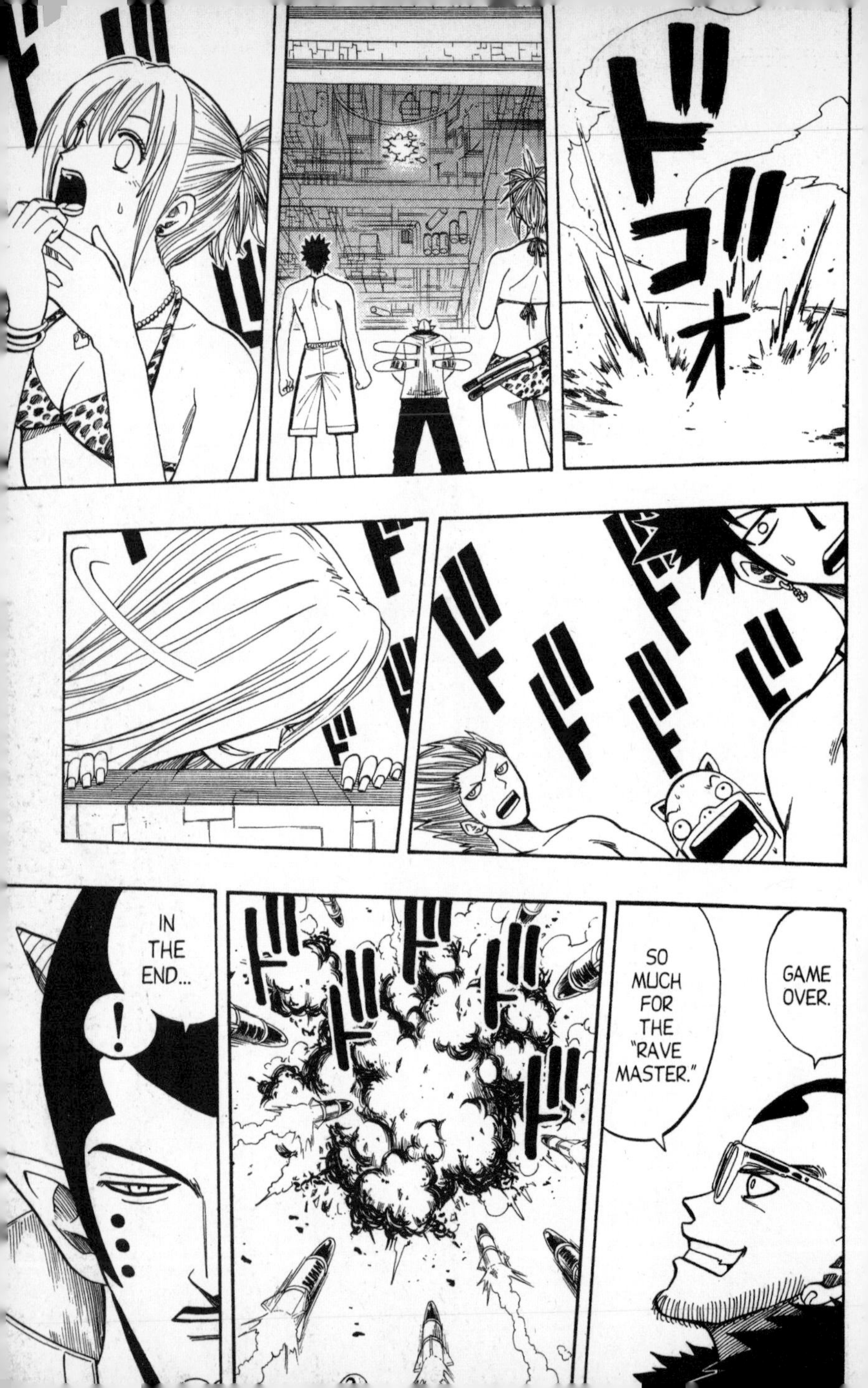
GAME OVER.
SO MUCH FOR THE "RAVE MASTER."
IN THE END...
!

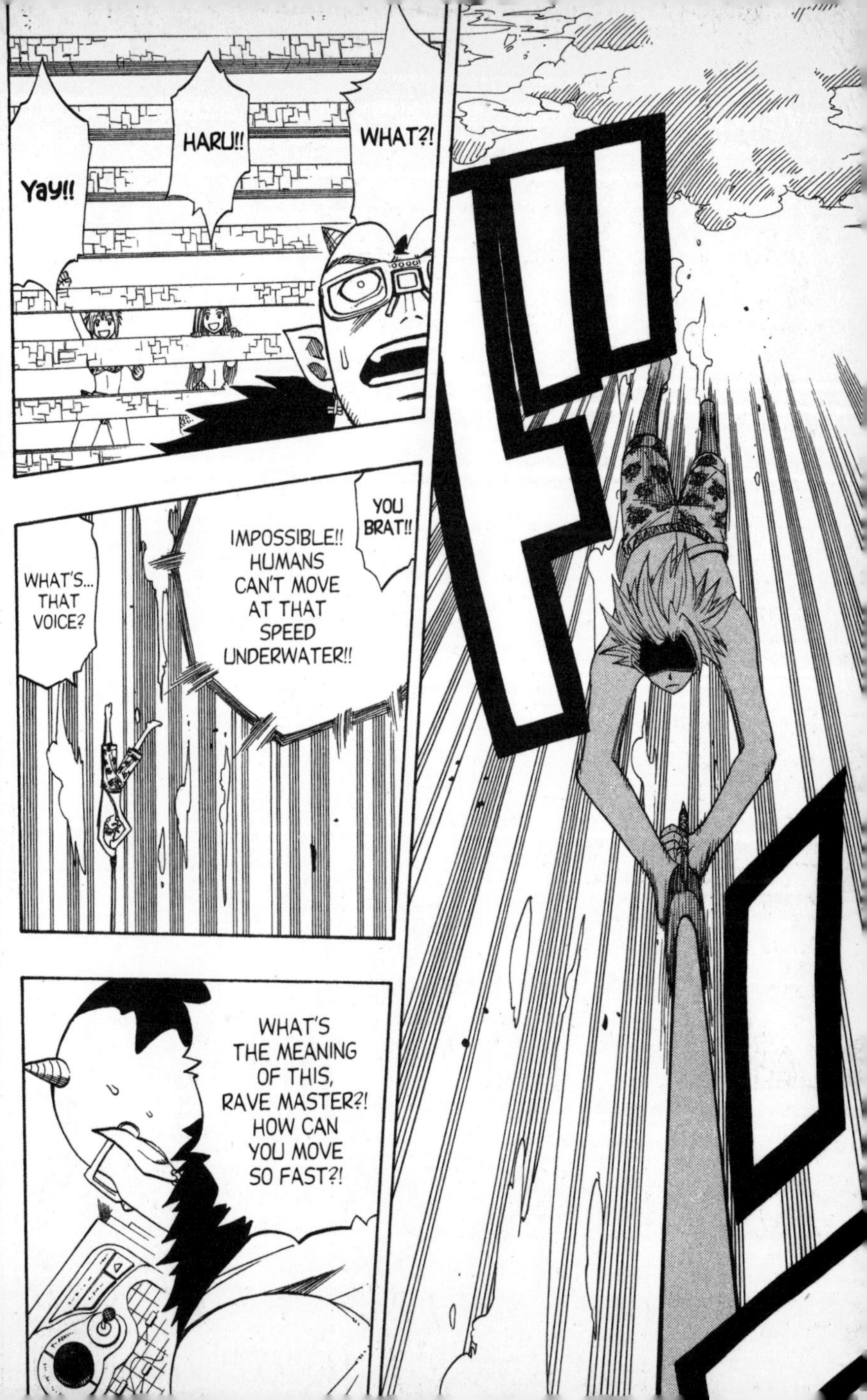
WHAT?!
HARU!!
Yay!!
YOU BRAT!!
IMPOSSIBLE!! HUMANS CAN'T MOVE AT THAT SPEED UNDERWATER!!
WHAT'S... THAT VOICE?
WHAT'S THE MEANING OF THIS, RAVE MASTER?! HOW CAN YOU MOVE SO FAST?!

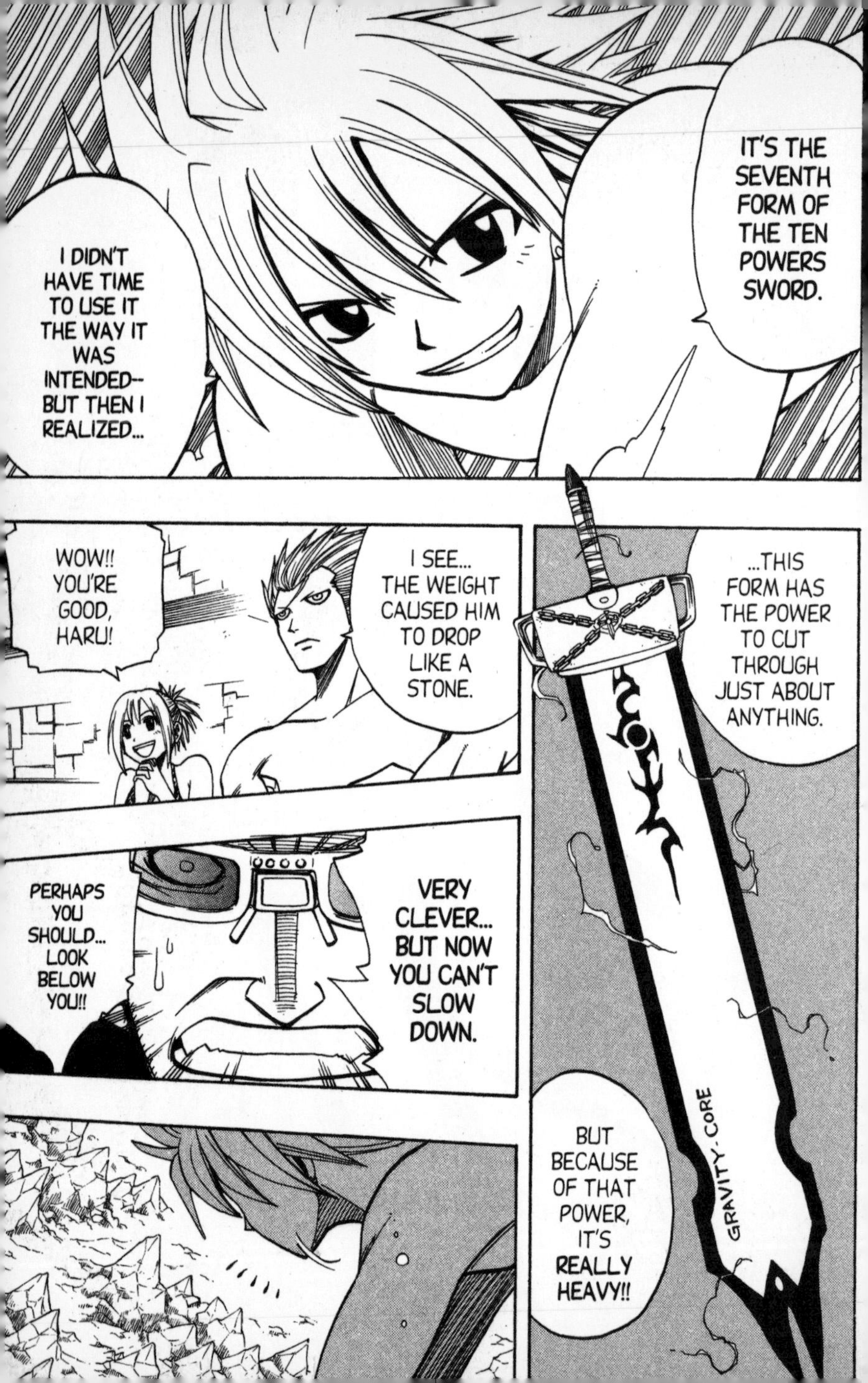
IT'S THE SEVENTH FORM OF THE TEN POWERS SWORD.
I DIDN'T HAVE TIME TO USE IT THE WAY IT WAS INTENDED-- BUT THEN I REALIZED...
...THIS FORM HAS THE POWER TO CUT THROUGH JUST ABOUT ANYTHING.
BUT BECAUSE OF THAT POWER, IT'S REALLY HEAVY!!
GRAVITY-CORE
I SEE... THE WEIGHT CAUSED HIM TO DROP LIKE A STONE.
WOW!! YOU'RE GOOD, HARU!
VERY CLEVER... BUT NOW YOU CAN'T SLOW DOWN.
PERHAPS YOU SHOULD... LOOK BELOW YOU!!
......

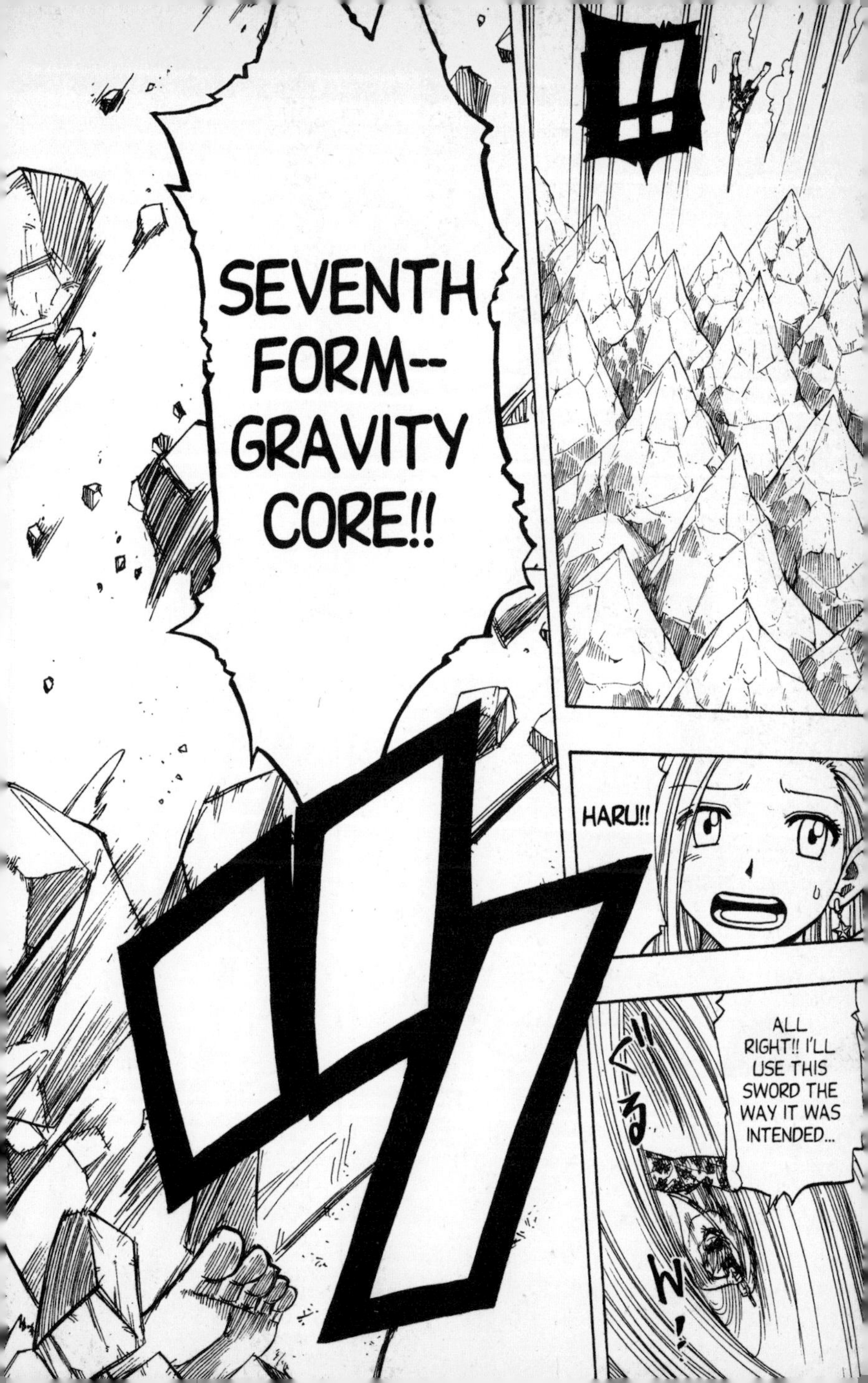
!!
HARU!!
ALL RIGHT!! I'LL USE THIS SWORD THE WAY IT WAS INTENDED...
ぐるん!
SEVENTH FORM-- GRAVITY CORE!!

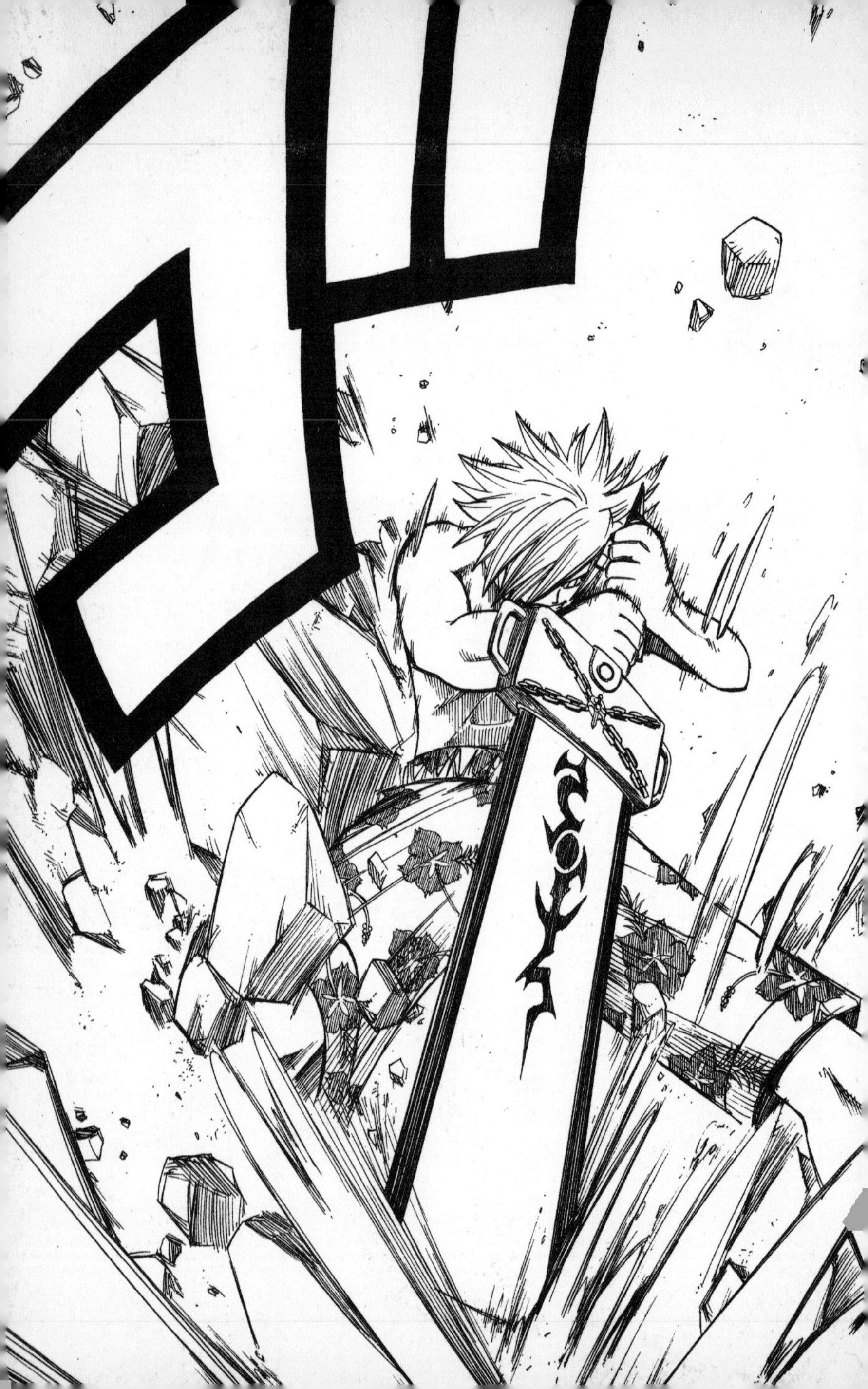

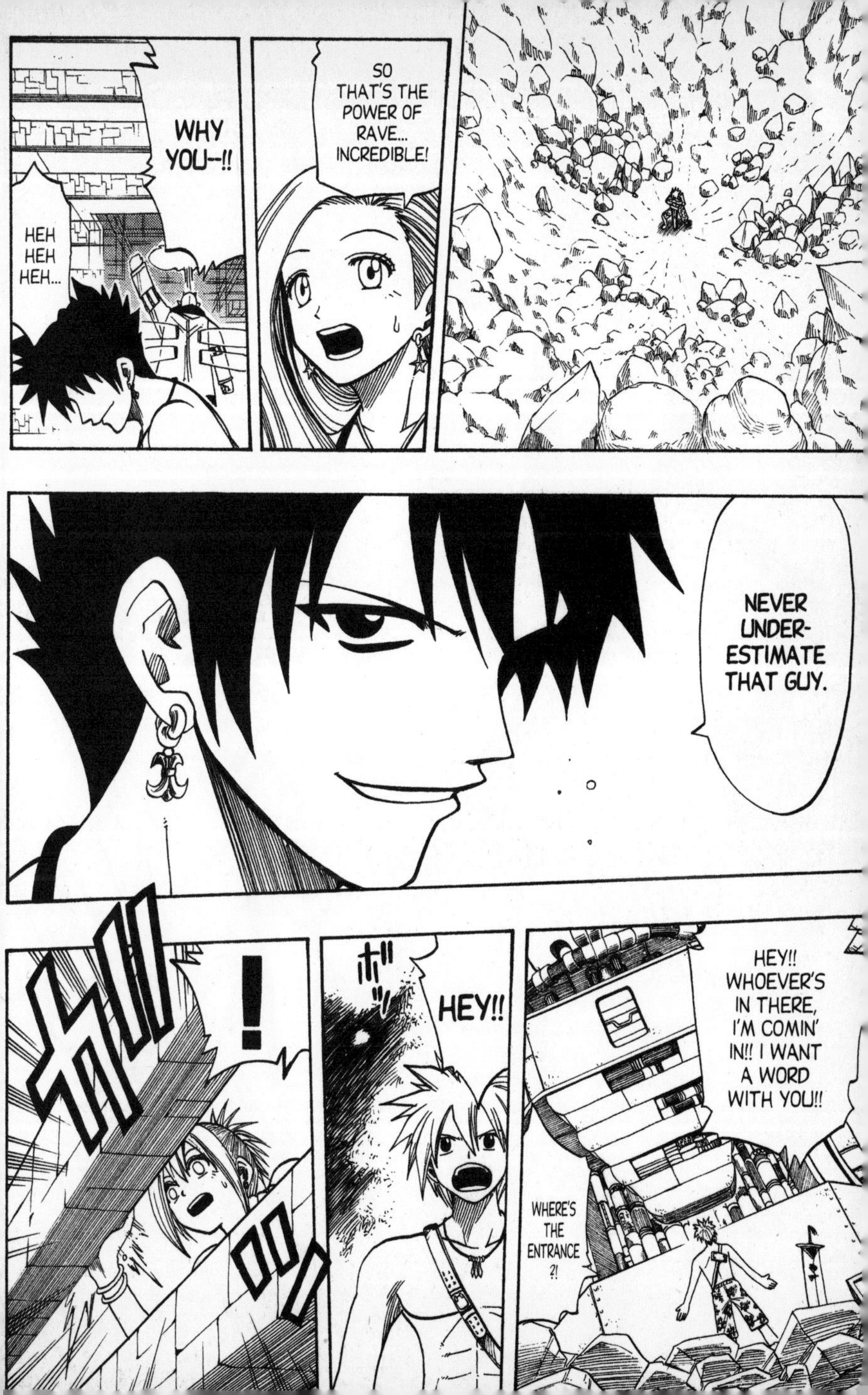
SO THAT'S THE POWER OF RAVE... INCREDIBLE!
WHY YOU--!!
HEH HEH HEH...
NEVER UNDER-ESTIMATE THAT GUY.
HEY!! WHOEVER'S IN THERE, I'M COMIN' IN!! I WANT A WORD WITH YOU!!
WHERE'S THE ENTRANCE ?!
HEY!!
!

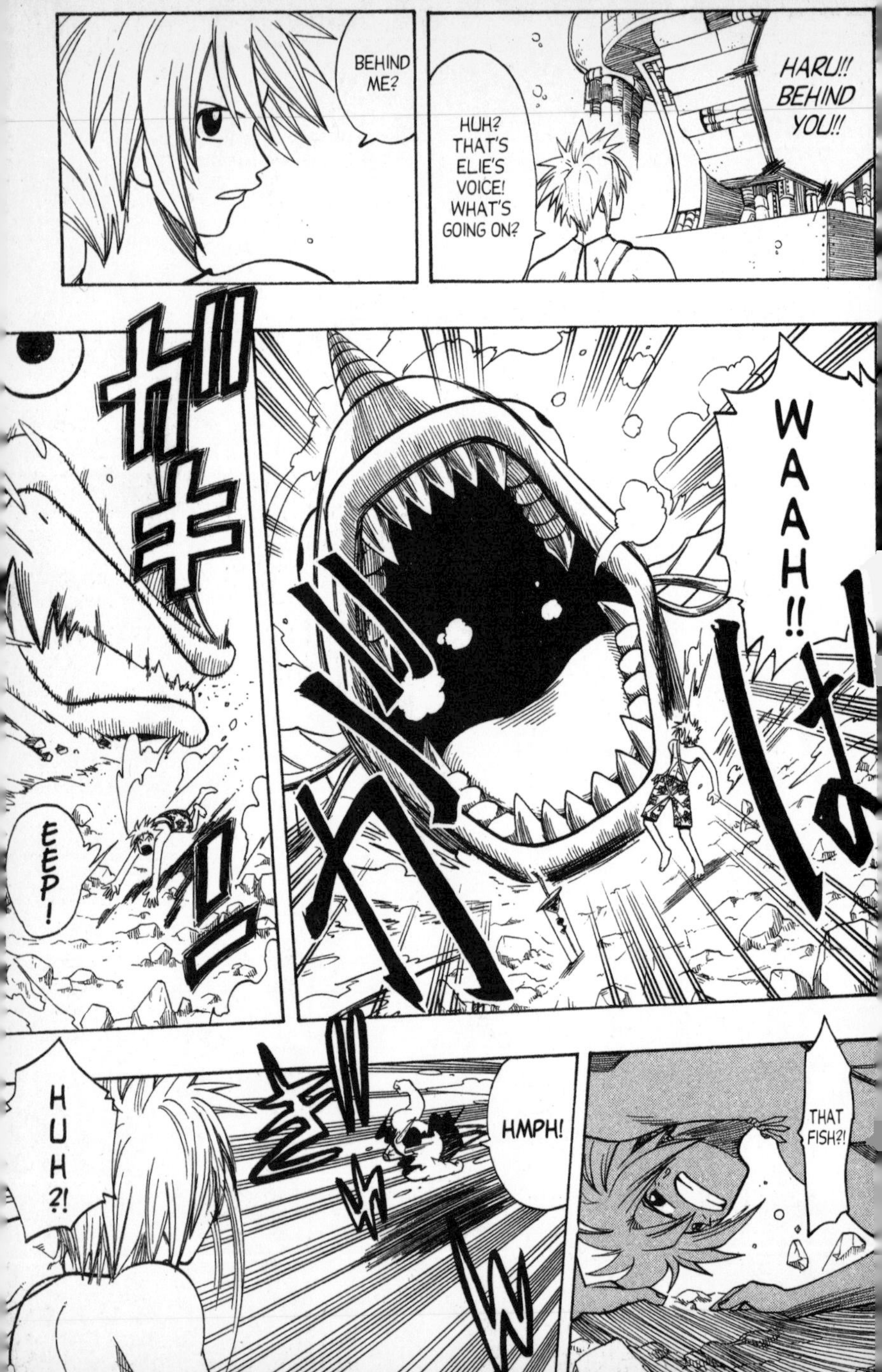
HARU!! BEHIND YOU!!
HUH? THAT'S ELIE'S VOICE! WHAT'S GOING ON?
BEHIND ME?
WAAAH!!
EEEP!
THAT FISH?!
HMPH!
HUH?!

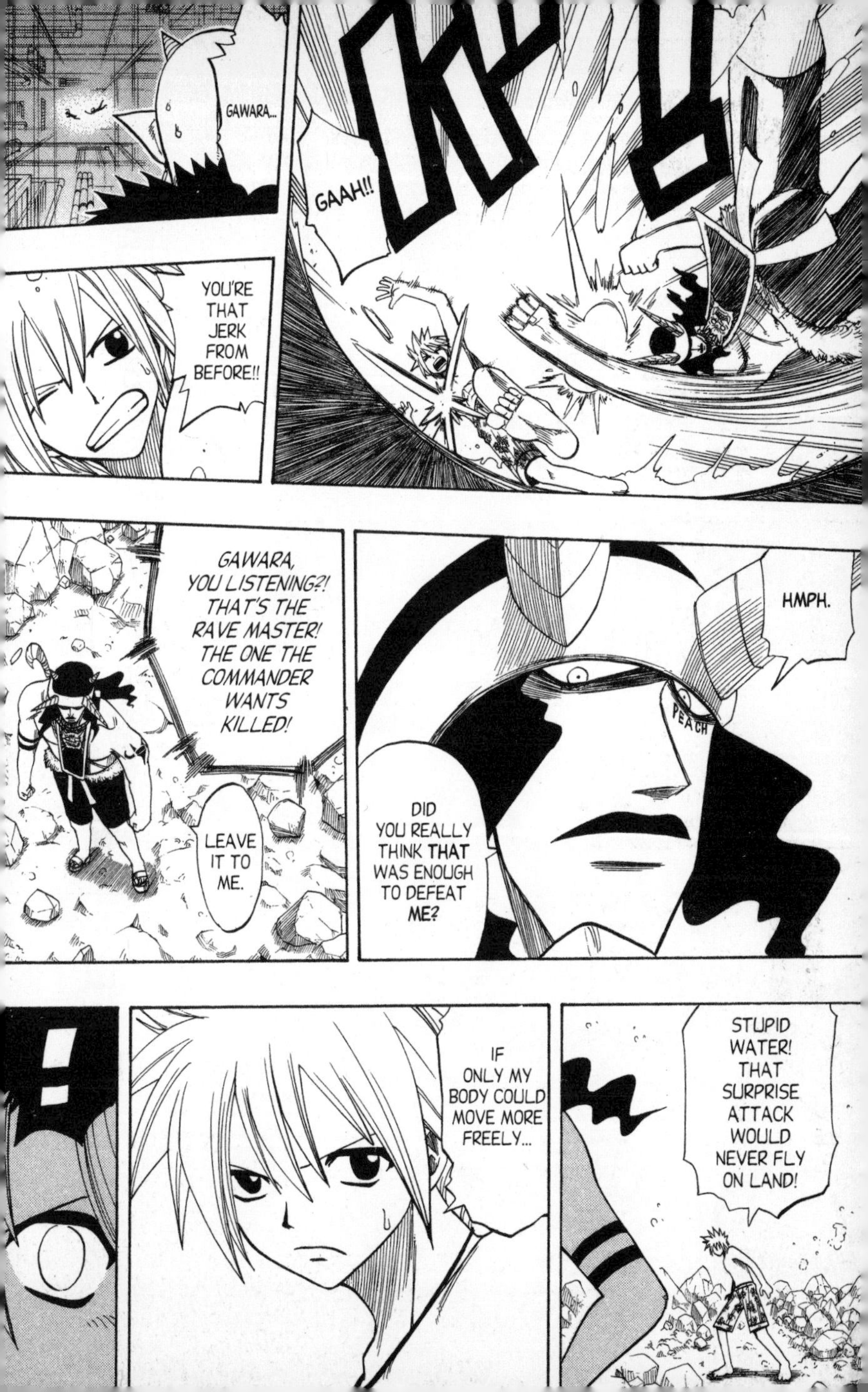
GAAH!!
GAWARA...
YOU'RE THAT JERK FROM BEFORE!!
HMPH.
PEACH
DID YOU REALLY THINK THAT WAS ENOUGH TO DEFEAT ME?
GAWARA, YOU LISTENING?! THAT'S THE RAVE MASTER! THE ONE THE COMMANDER WANTS KILLED!
LEAVE IT TO ME.
STUPID WATER! THAT SURPRISE ATTACK WOULD NEVER FLY ON LAND!
IF ONLY MY BODY COULD MOVE MORE FREELY...
!

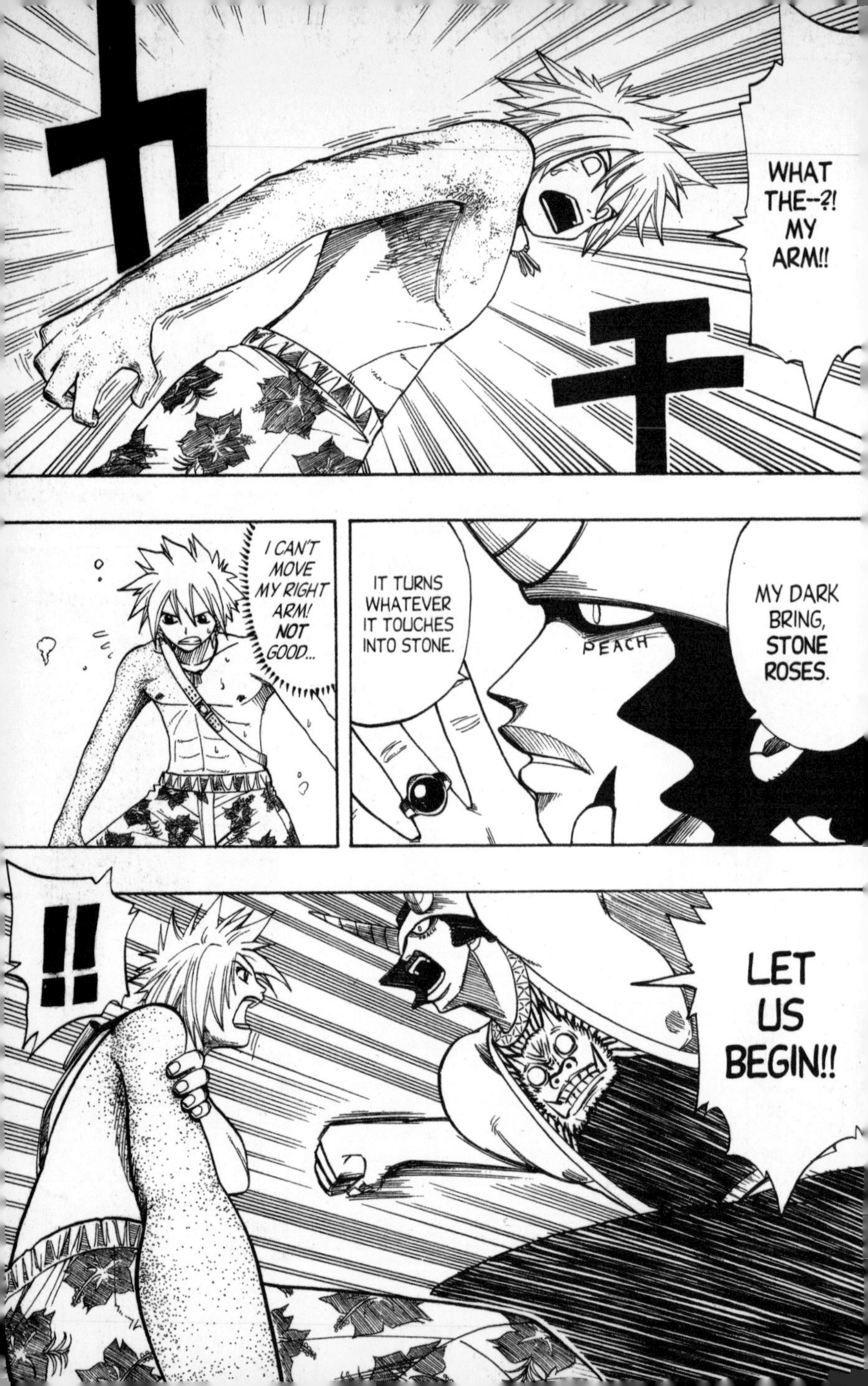
WHAT THE--?! MY ARM!!
カチ
MY DARK BRING, STONE ROSES.
PEACH
IT TURNS WHATEVER IT TOUCHES INTO STONE.
I CAN'T MOVE MY RIGHT ARM! NOT GOOD...
LET US BEGIN!!
!!

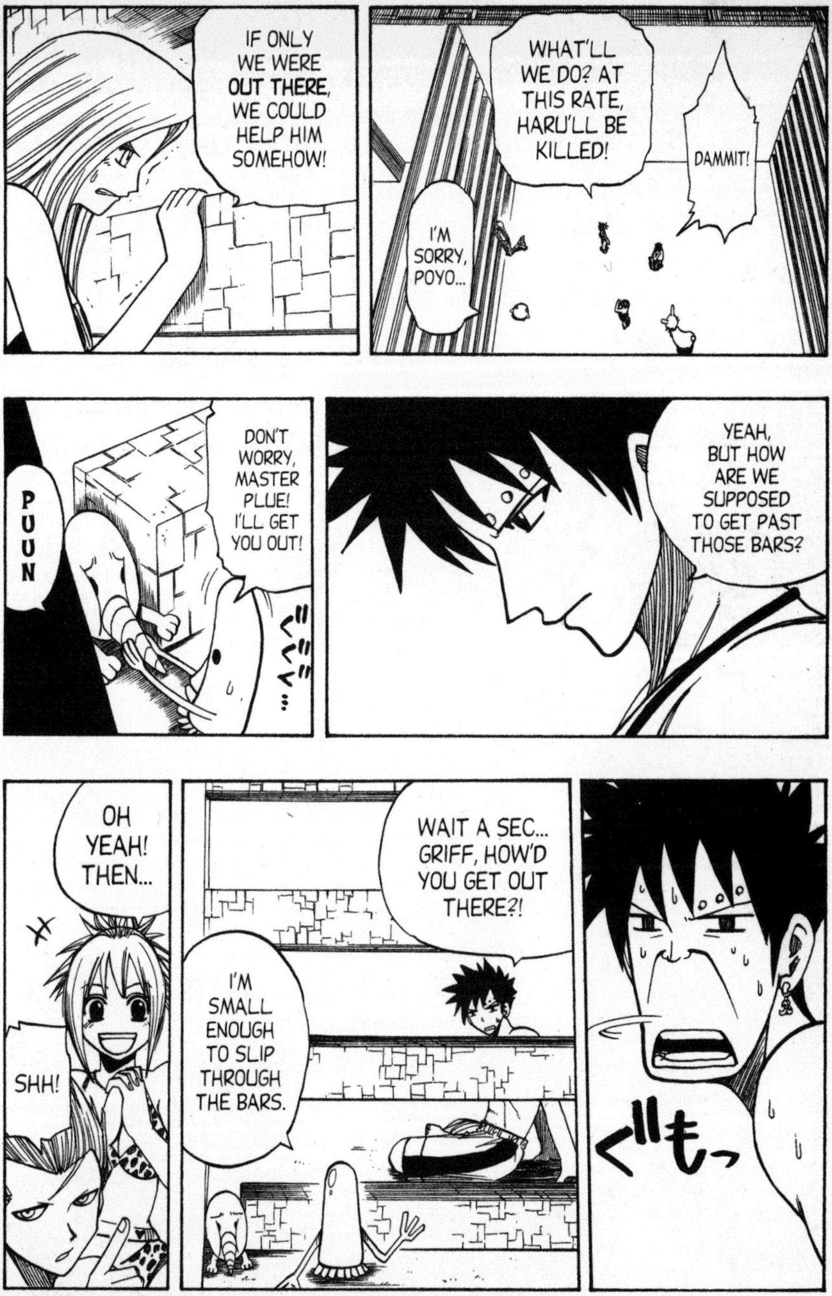
WHAT'LL WE DO? AT THIS RATE, HARU'LL BE KILLED!
DAMMIT!
I'M SORRY, POYO...
IF ONLY WE WERE **OUT THERE**, WE COULD HELP HIM SOMEHOW!
YEAH, BUT HOW ARE WE SUPPOSED TO GET PAST THOSE BARS?
DON'T WORRY, MASTER PLUE! I'LL GET YOU OUT!
ぐいぐい…
PUUN
ぐもっ
WAIT A SEC... GRIFF, HOW'D YOU GET OUT THERE?!
I'M SMALL ENOUGH TO SLIP THROUGH THE BARS.
OH YEAH! THEN...
SHH!

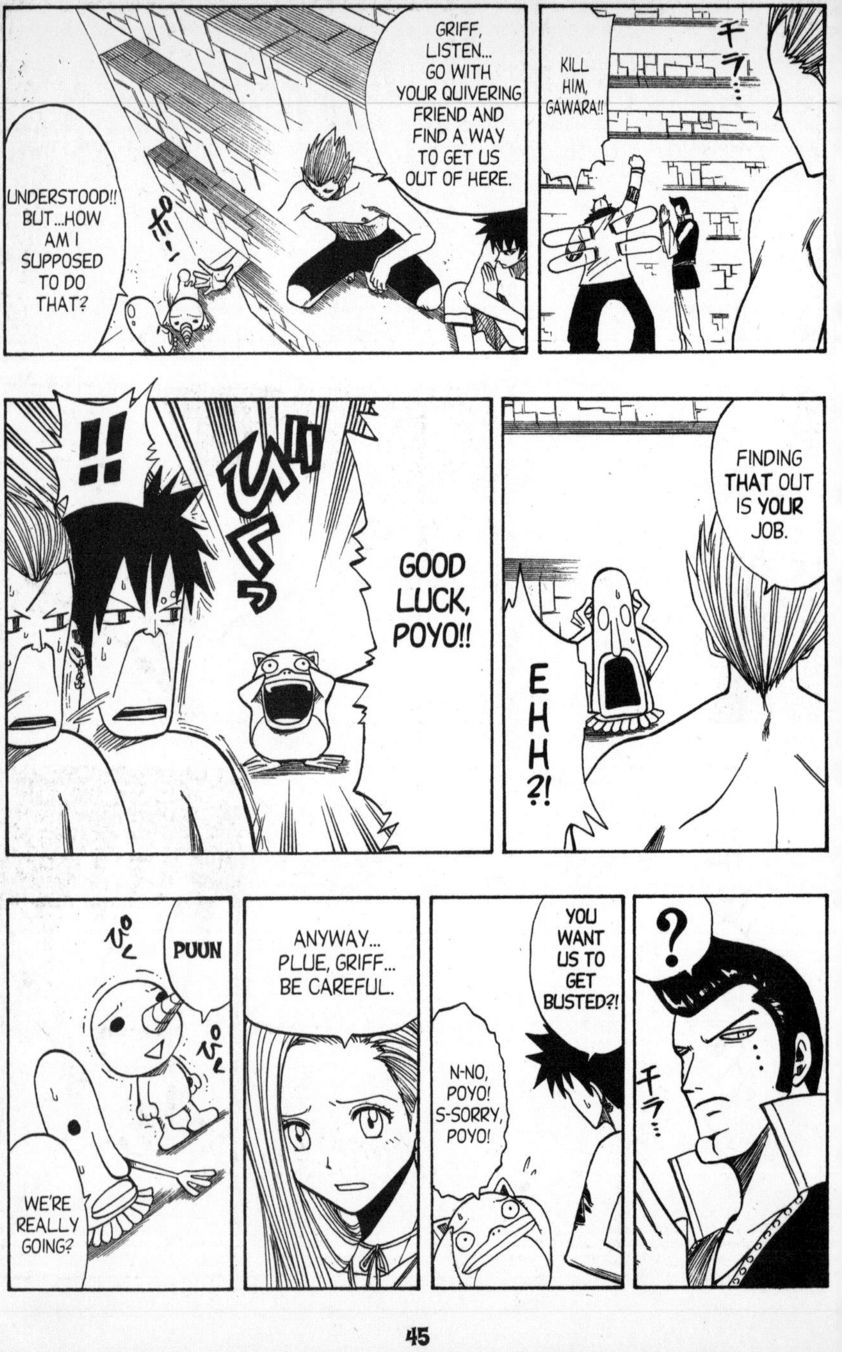
チラ…
KILL HIM, GAWARA!!
GRIFF, LISTEN... GO WITH YOUR QUIVERING FRIEND AND FIND A WAY TO GET US OUT OF HERE.
UNDERSTOOD!! BUT...HOW AM I SUPPOSED TO DO THAT?
FINDING THAT OUT IS YOUR JOB.
EHH?!
!!
GOOD LUCK, POYO!!
?
チラ…
YOU WANT US TO GET BUSTED?!
N-NO, POYO! S-SORRY, POYO!
ANYWAY... PLUE, GRIFF... BE CAREFUL.
PUUN
WE'RE REALLY GOING?

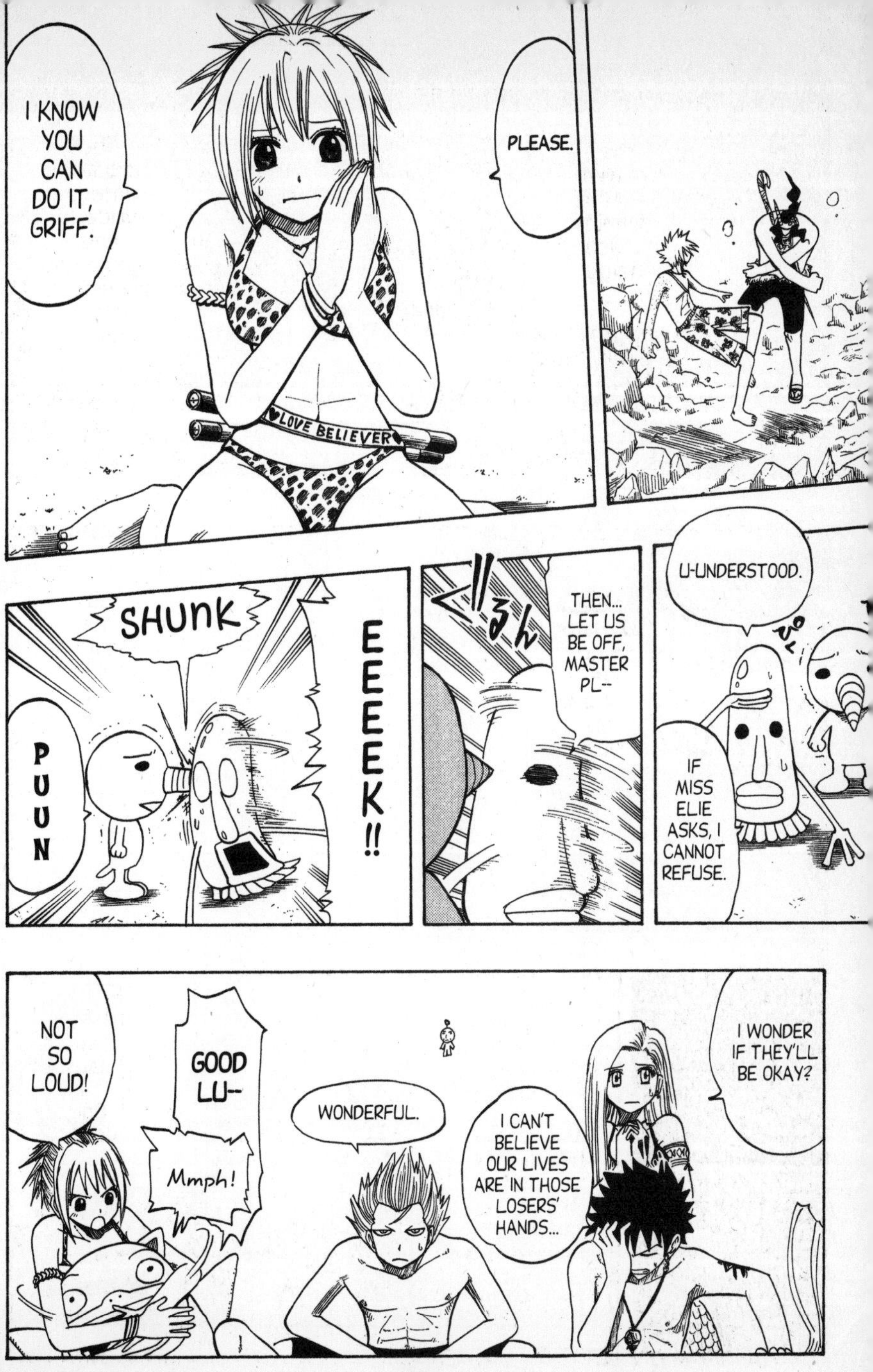
PLEASE.
I KNOW YOU CAN DO IT, GRIFF.
U-UNDERSTOOD.
IF MISS ELIE ASKS, I CANNOT REFUSE.
THEN... LET US BE OFF, MASTER PL--
EEEEEK!!
SHUNK
PUUN
I WONDER IF THEY'LL BE OKAY?
I CAN'T BELIEVE OUR LIVES ARE IN THOSE LOSERS' HANDS...
WONDERFUL.
GOOD LU--
Mmph!
NOT SO LOUD!

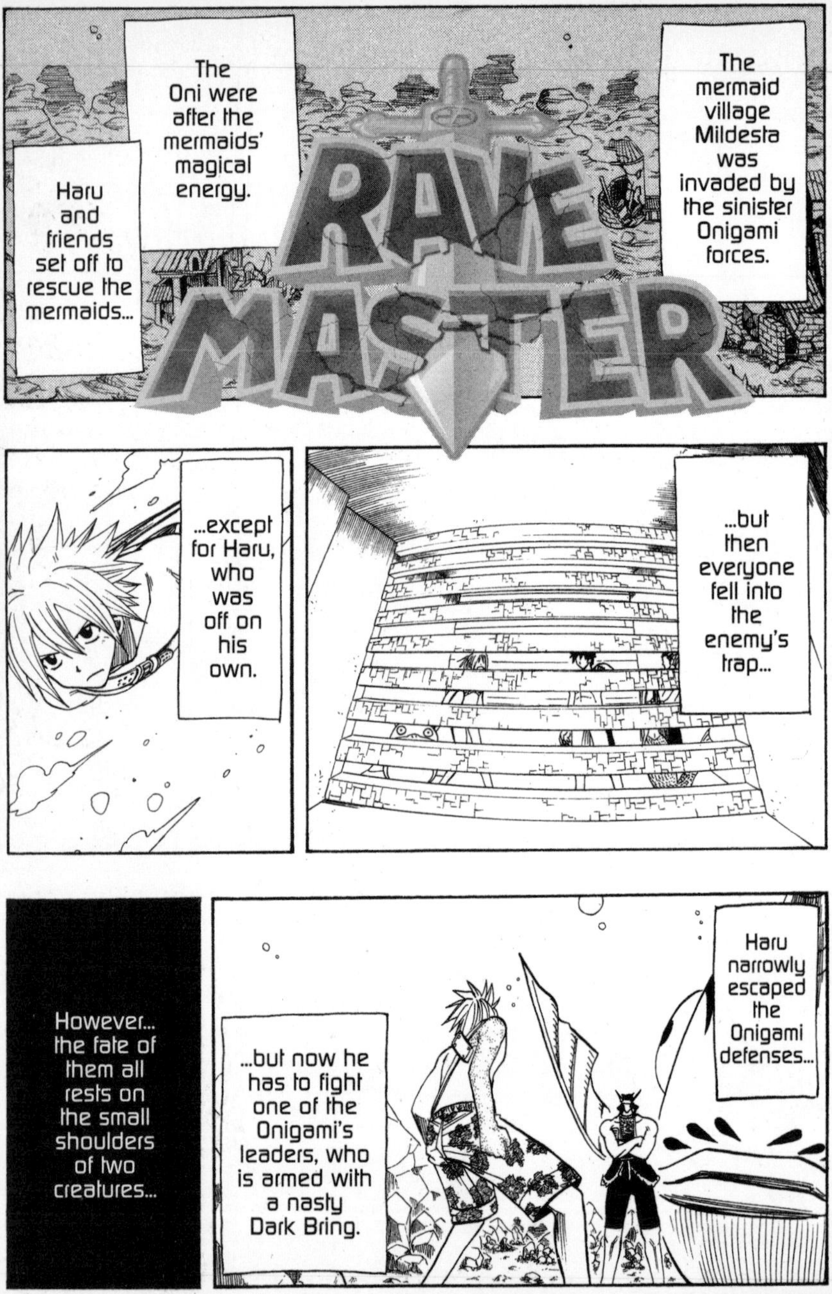
RAVE MASTER
The mermaid village Mildesta was invaded by the sinister Onigami forces.
The Oni were after the mermaids' magical energy.
Haru and friends set off to rescue the mermaids...
...but then everyone fell into the enemy's trap...
...except for Haru, who was off on his own.
Haru narrowly escaped the Onigami defenses...
...but now he has to fight one of the Onigami's leaders, who is armed with a nasty Dark Bring.
However... the fate of them all rests on the small shoulders of two creatures...

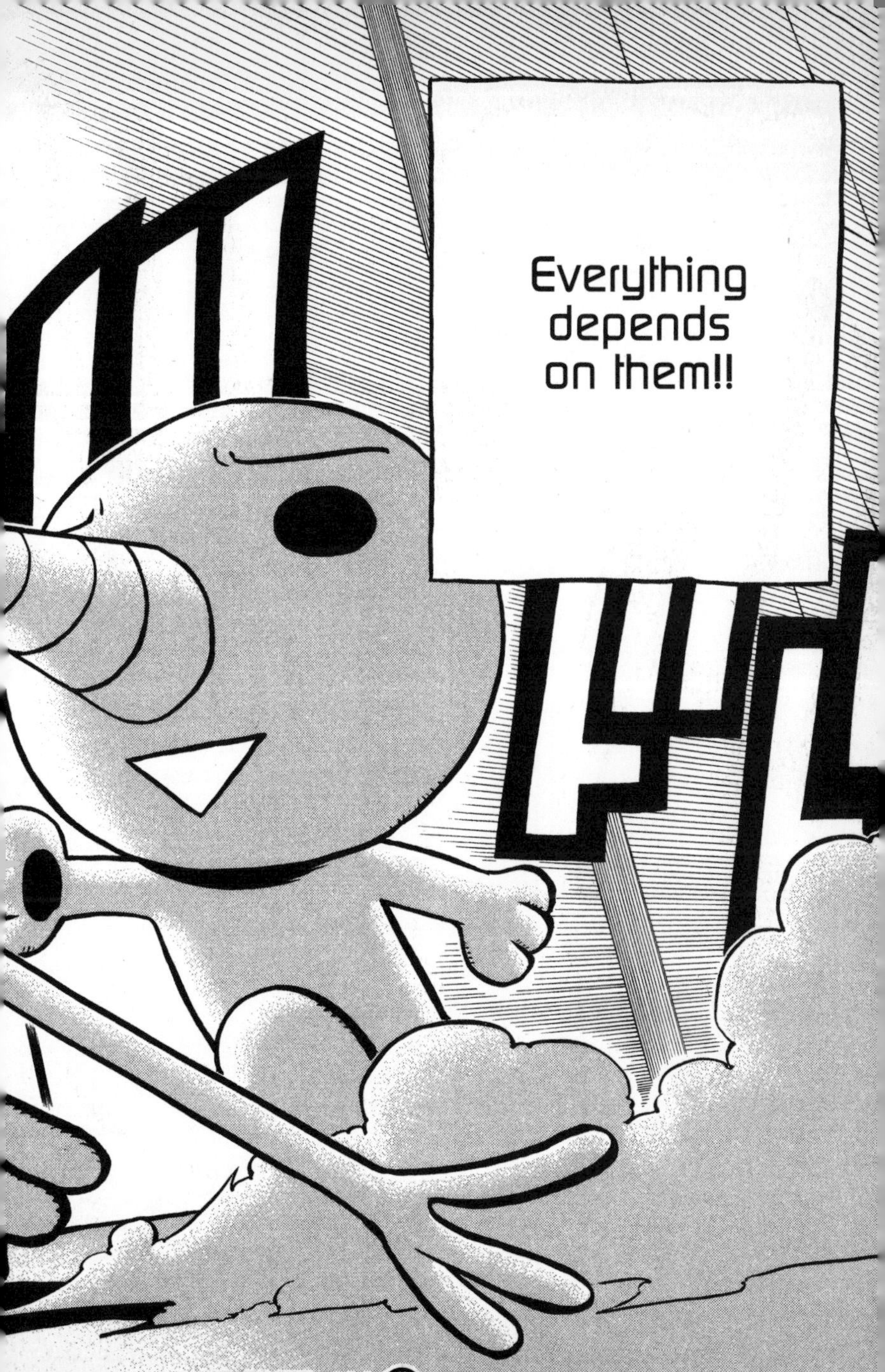
Everything depends on them!!

RAVE:108 MAD DASH?!

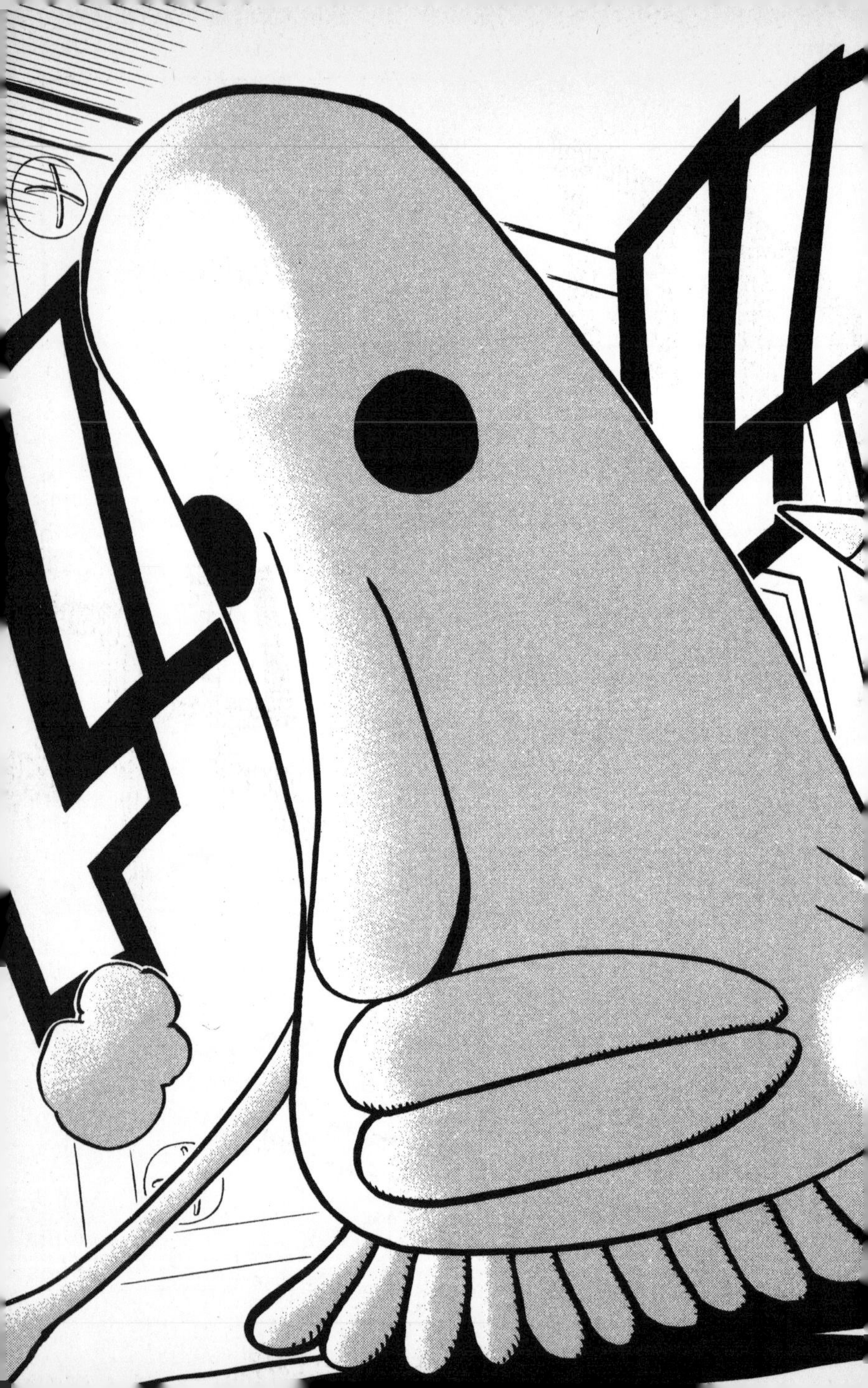

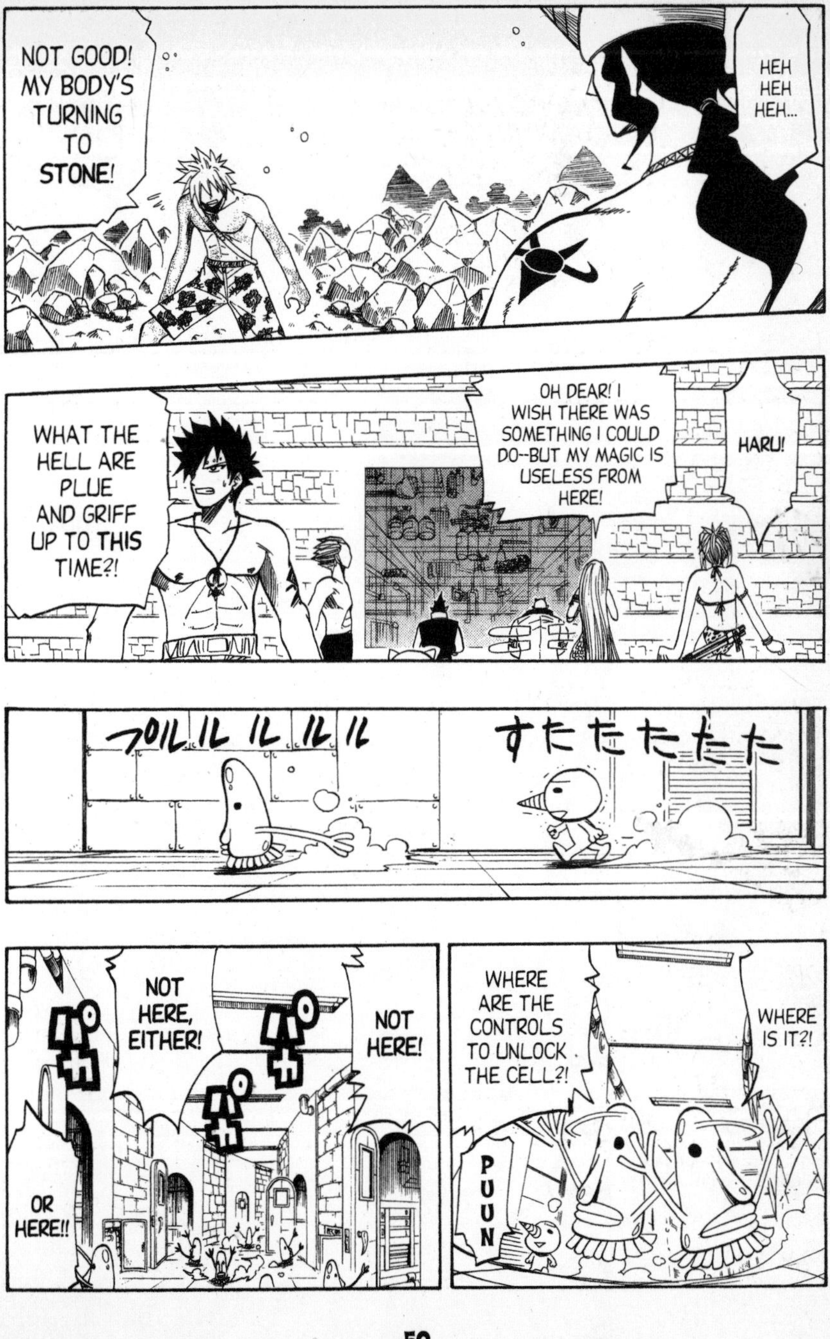
HEH HEH HEH...
NOT GOOD! MY BODY'S TURNING TO STONE!
HARU!
OH DEAR! I WISH THERE WAS SOMETHING I COULD DO--BUT MY MAGIC IS USELESS FROM HERE!
WHAT THE HELL ARE PLUE AND GRIFF UP TO THIS TIME?!
すたたたたた
フィルルルル
WHERE IS IT?!
WHERE ARE THE CONTROLS TO UNLOCK THE CELL?!
PUUN
NOT HERE!
パカ
NOT HERE, EITHER!
パカ
パカ
OR HERE!!

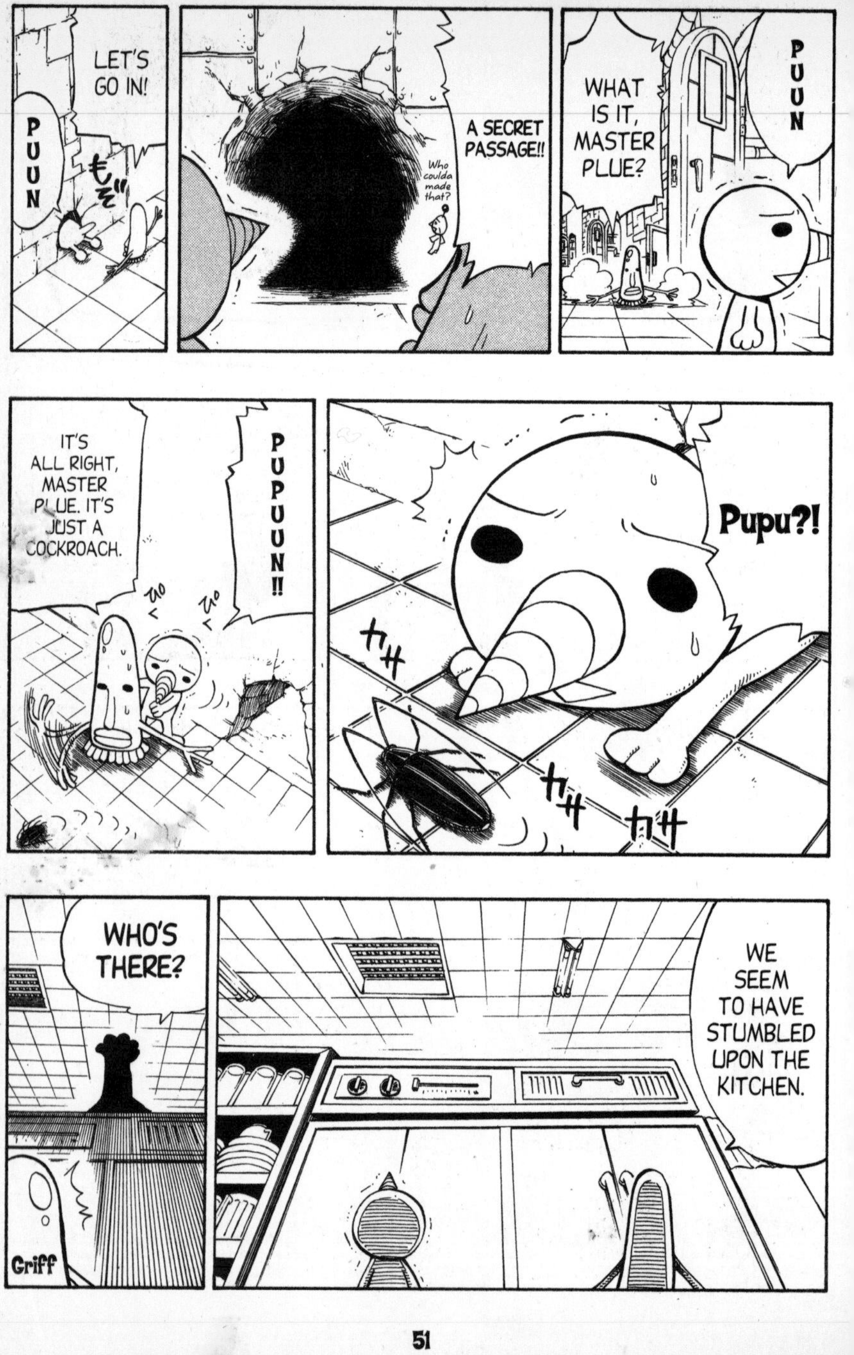
PUUN
WHAT IS IT, MASTER PLUE?
A SECRET PASSAGE!!
Who coulda made that?
LET'S GO IN!
PUUN
Pupu?!
カサ
カサ
カサ
PUPUUUN!!
IT'S ALL RIGHT, MASTER PLUE. IT'S JUST A COCKROACH.
WE SEEM TO HAVE STUMBLED UPON THE KITCHEN.
WHO'S THERE?
Griff

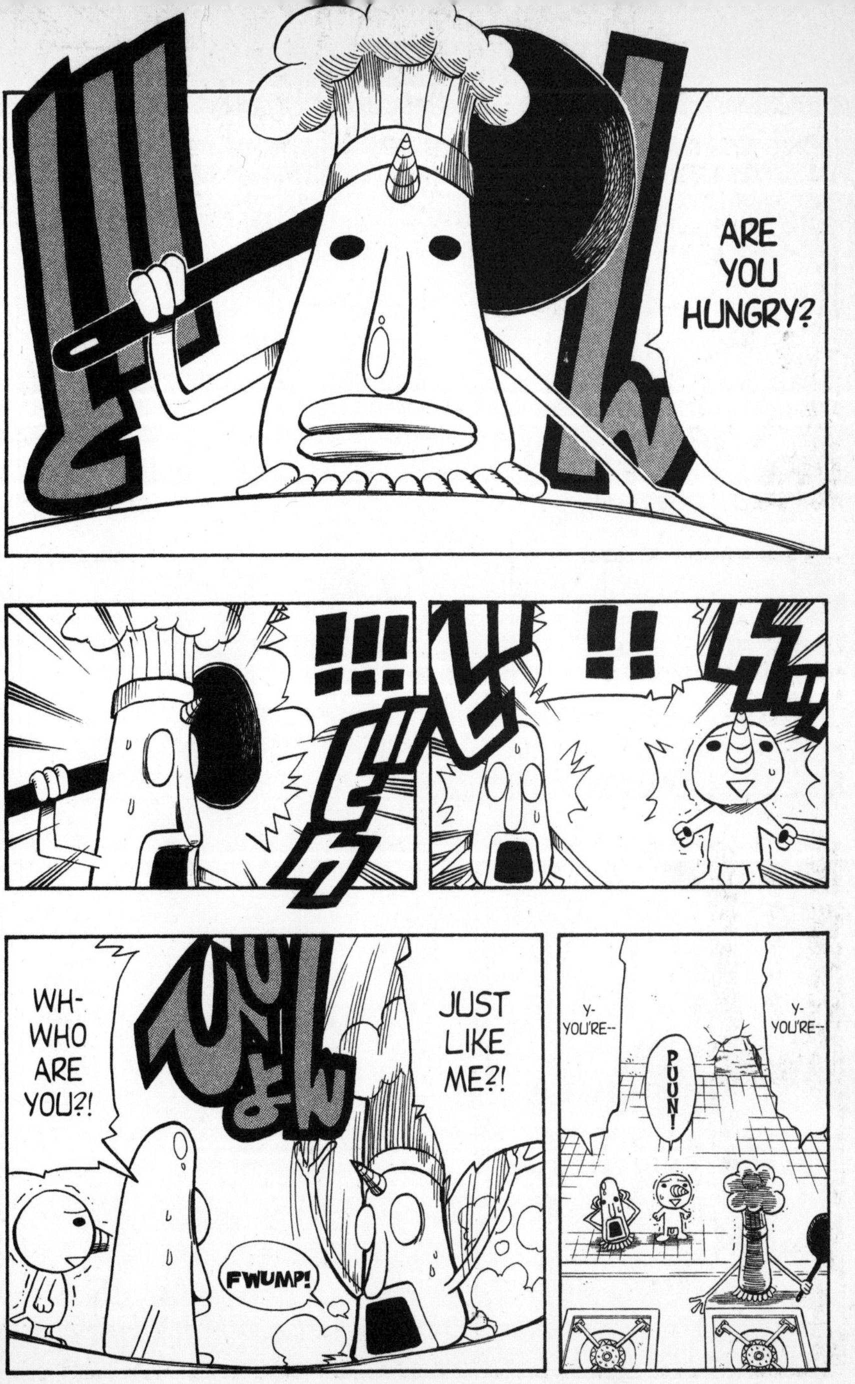

ARE YOU HUNGRY?
!!
!!!
Y- YOU'RE--
PUUN!
Y- YOU'RE--
JUST LIKE ME?!
WH- WHO ARE YOU?!
FWUMP!

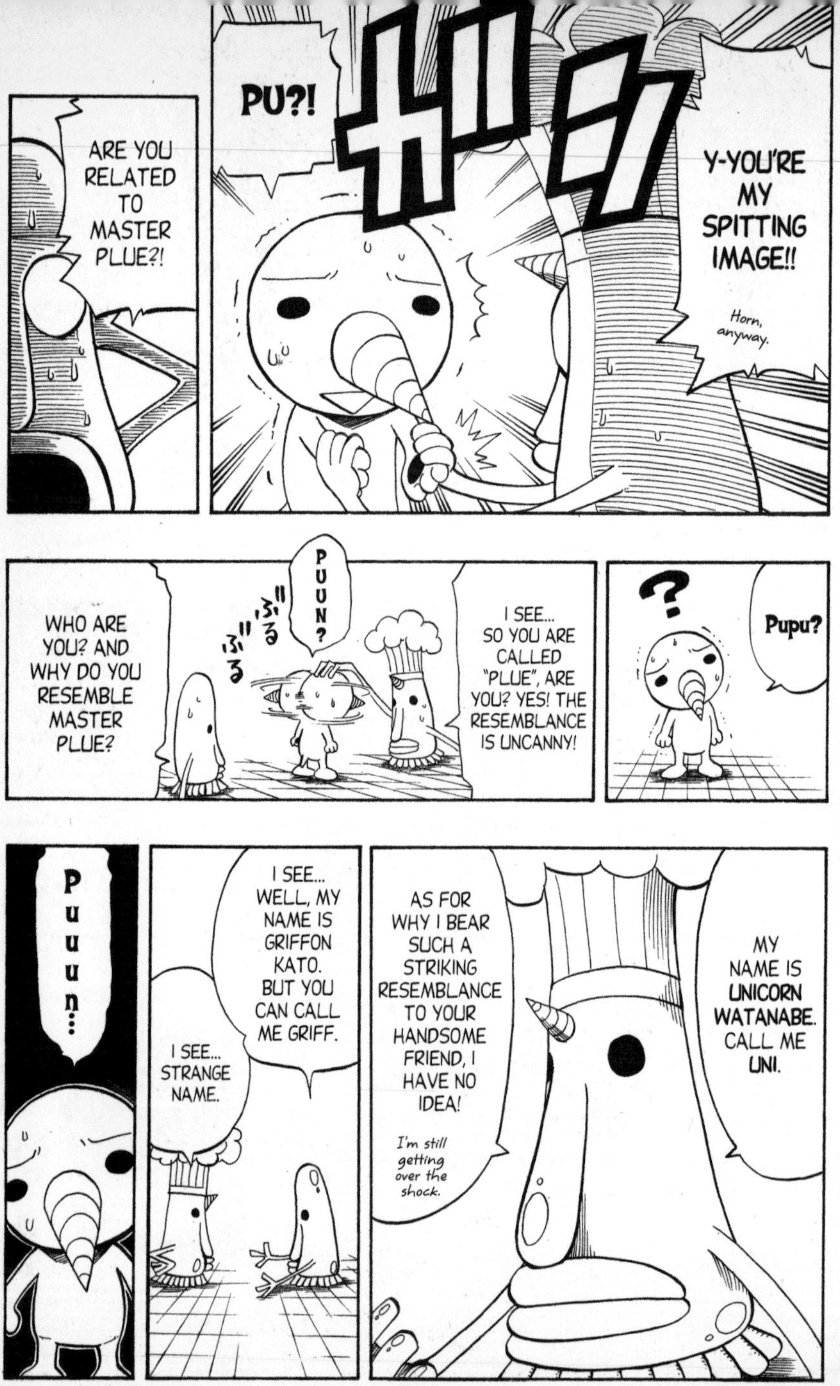
Y-YOU'RE MY SPITTING IMAGE!!
Horn, anyway.
PU?!
ARE YOU RELATED TO MASTER PLUE?!
Pupu?
I SEE... SO YOU ARE CALLED "PLUE", ARE YOU? YES! THE RESEMBLANCE IS UNCANNY!
PUUN?
ぶるぶる
WHO ARE YOU? AND WHY DO YOU RESEMBLE MASTER PLUE?
MY NAME IS UNICORN WATANABE. CALL ME UNI.
AS FOR WHY I BEAR SUCH A STRIKING RESEMBLANCE TO YOUR HANDSOME FRIEND, I HAVE NO IDEA!
I'm still getting over the shock.
I SEE... WELL, MY NAME IS GRIFFON KATO. BUT YOU CAN CALL ME GRIFF.
I SEE... STRANGE NAME.
Puuun...

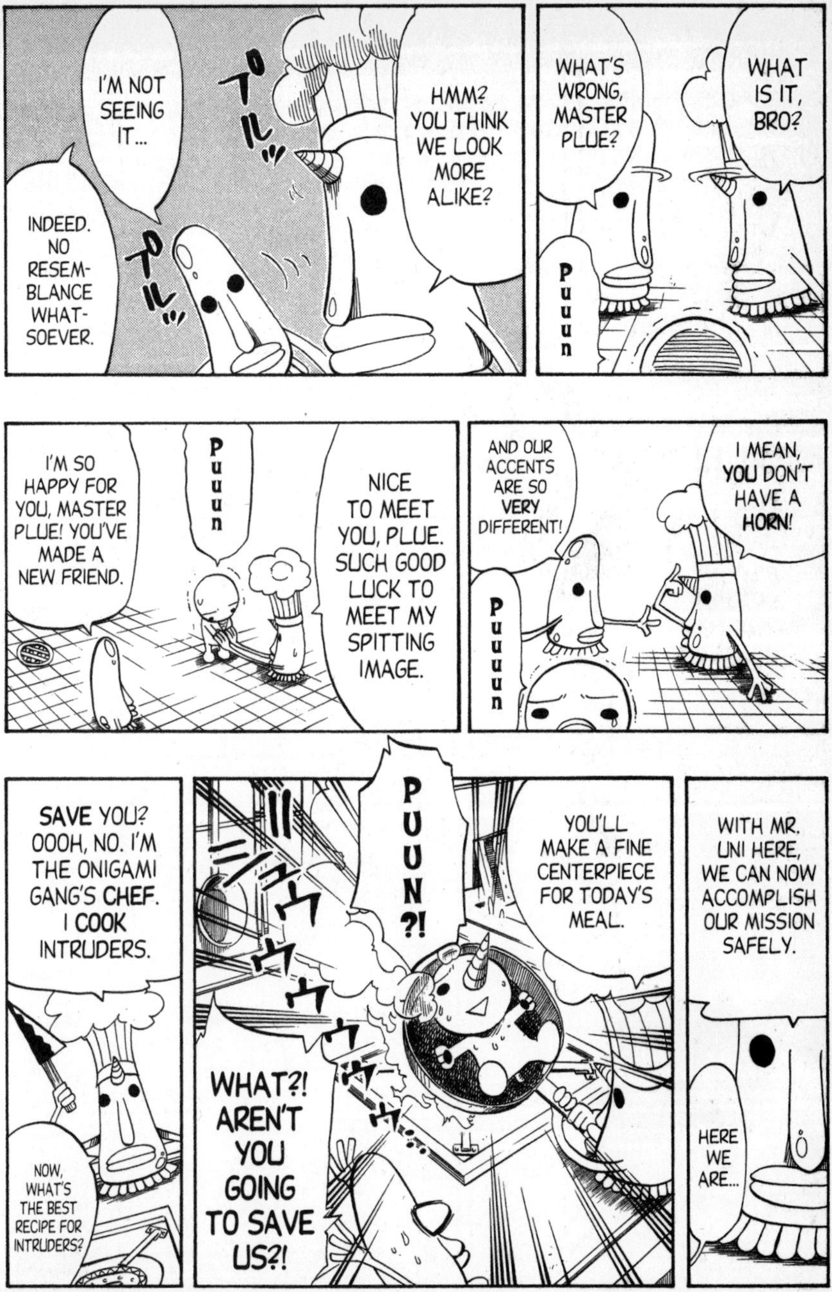
WHAT IS IT, BRO?
WHAT'S WRONG, MASTER PLUE?
Puuun
HMM? YOU THINK WE LOOK MORE ALIKE?
プルッ
I'M NOT SEEING IT...
プルッ
INDEED. NO RESEMBLANCE WHATSOEVER.
I MEAN, **YOU** DON'T HAVE A **HORN**!
AND OUR ACCENTS ARE SO **VERY** DIFFERENT!
Puuuun
NICE TO MEET YOU, PLUE. SUCH GOOD LUCK TO MEET MY SPITTING IMAGE.
Puuun
I'M SO HAPPY FOR YOU, MASTER PLUE! YOU'VE MADE A NEW FRIEND.
WITH MR. UNI HERE, WE CAN NOW ACCOMPLISH OUR MISSION SAFELY.
HERE WE ARE...
YOU'LL MAKE A FINE CENTERPIECE FOR TODAY'S MEAL.
PUUN?!
WHAT?! AREN'T YOU GOING TO SAVE US?!
SAVE YOU? OOOH, NO. I'M THE ONIGAMI GANG'S **CHEF**. I **COOK** INTRUDERS.
NOW, WHAT'S THE BEST RECIPE FOR INTRUDERS?

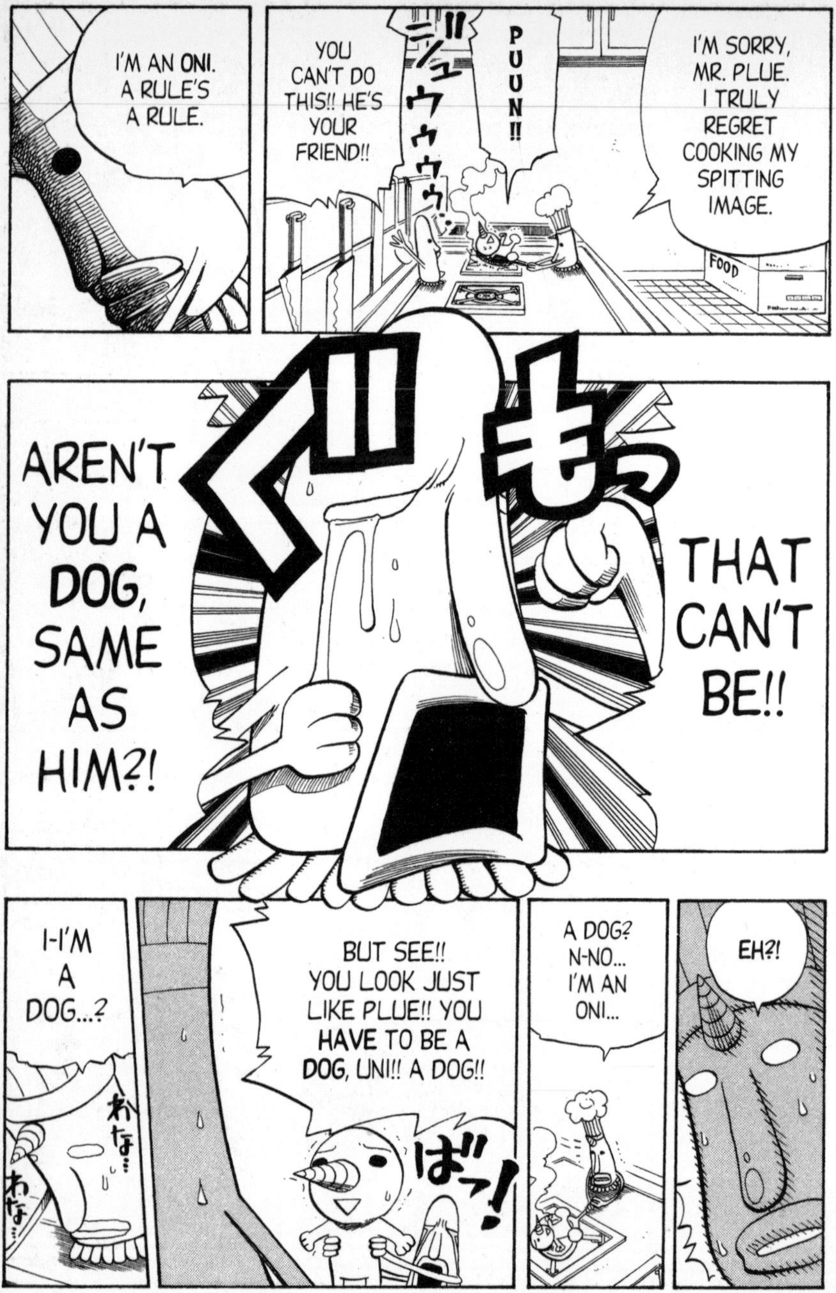

I'M SORRY, MR. PLUE. I TRULY REGRET COOKING MY SPITTING IMAGE.
FOOD
PUUN!!
ジュウウウウ
YOU CAN'T DO THIS!! HE'S YOUR FRIEND!!
I'M AN ONI. A RULE'S A RULE.
THAT CAN'T BE!!
ぐもっ
AREN'T YOU A DOG, SAME AS HIM?!
EH?!
A DOG? N-NO... I'M AN ONI...
BUT SEE!! YOU LOOK JUST LIKE PLUE!! YOU HAVE TO BE A DOG, UNI!! A DOG!!
ばっ!
I-I'M A DOG...?
わな…
わな…

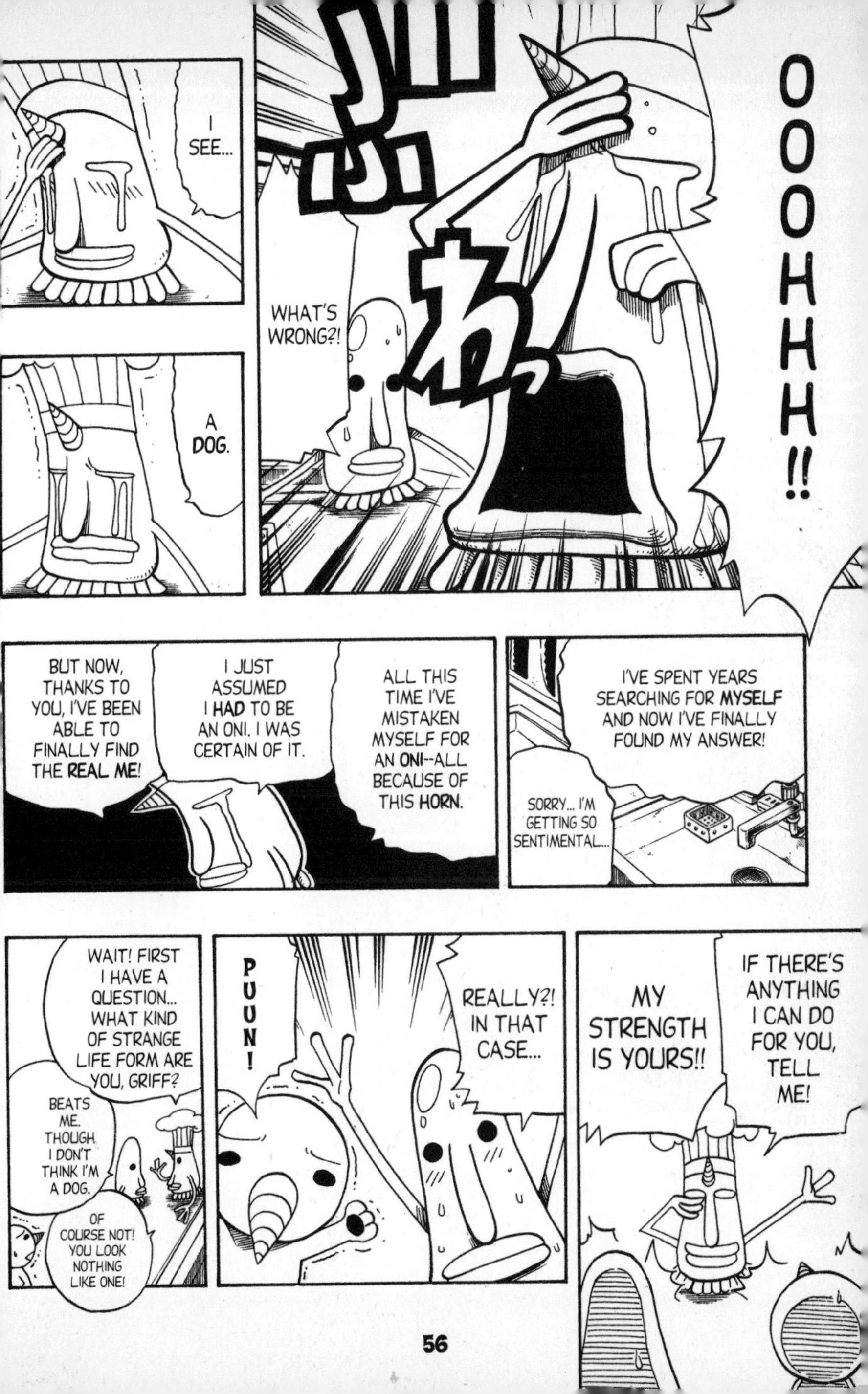
OOOOHHH!!
WHAT'S WRONG?!
I SEE...
A DOG.
I'VE SPENT YEARS SEARCHING FOR MYSELF AND NOW I'VE FINALLY FOUND MY ANSWER!
SORRY... I'M GETTING SO SENTIMENTAL...
ALL THIS TIME I'VE MISTAKEN MYSELF FOR AN ONI--ALL BECAUSE OF THIS HORN.
I JUST ASSUMED I HAD TO BE AN ONI. I WAS CERTAIN OF IT.
BUT NOW, THANKS TO YOU, I'VE BEEN ABLE TO FINALLY FIND THE REAL ME!
IF THERE'S ANYTHING I CAN DO FOR YOU, TELL ME!
MY STRENGTH IS YOURS!!
REALLY?! IN THAT CASE...
PUUN!
WAIT! FIRST I HAVE A QUESTION... WHAT KIND OF STRANGE LIFE FORM ARE YOU, GRIFF?
BEATS ME. THOUGH I DON'T THINK I'M A DOG.
OF COURSE NOT! YOU LOOK NOTHING LIKE ONE!

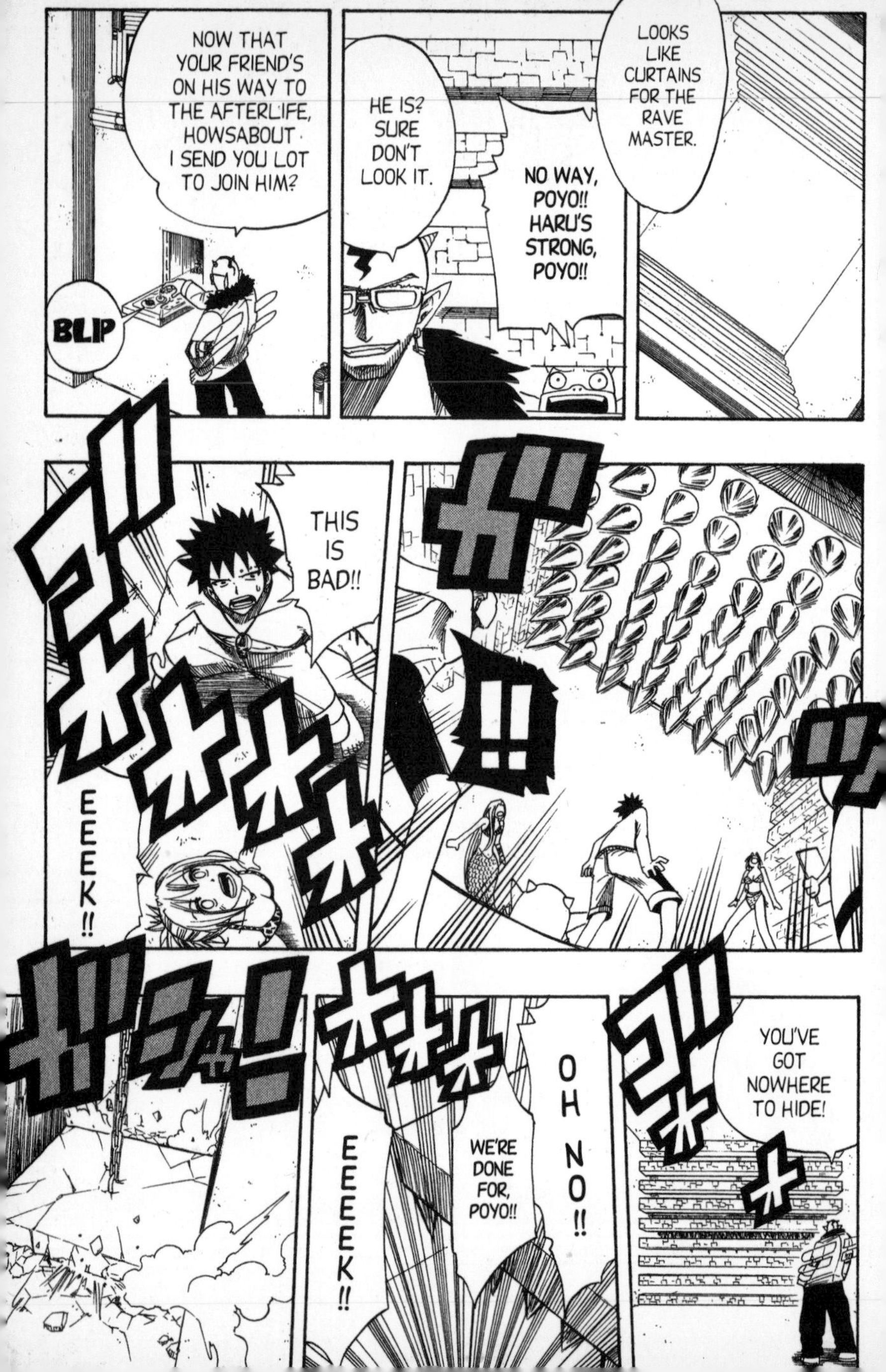
LOOKS LIKE CURTAINS FOR THE RAVE MASTER.
NO WAY, POYO!! HARU'S STRONG, POYO!!
HE IS? SURE DON'T LOOK IT.
NOW THAT YOUR FRIEND'S ON HIS WAY TO THE AFTERLIFE, HOWSABOUT I SEND YOU LOT TO JOIN HIM?
BLIP
!!
THIS IS BAD!!
EEEEK!!
YOU'VE GOT NOWHERE TO HIDE!
OH NO!!
WE'RE DONE FOR, POYO!!
EEEEEK!!

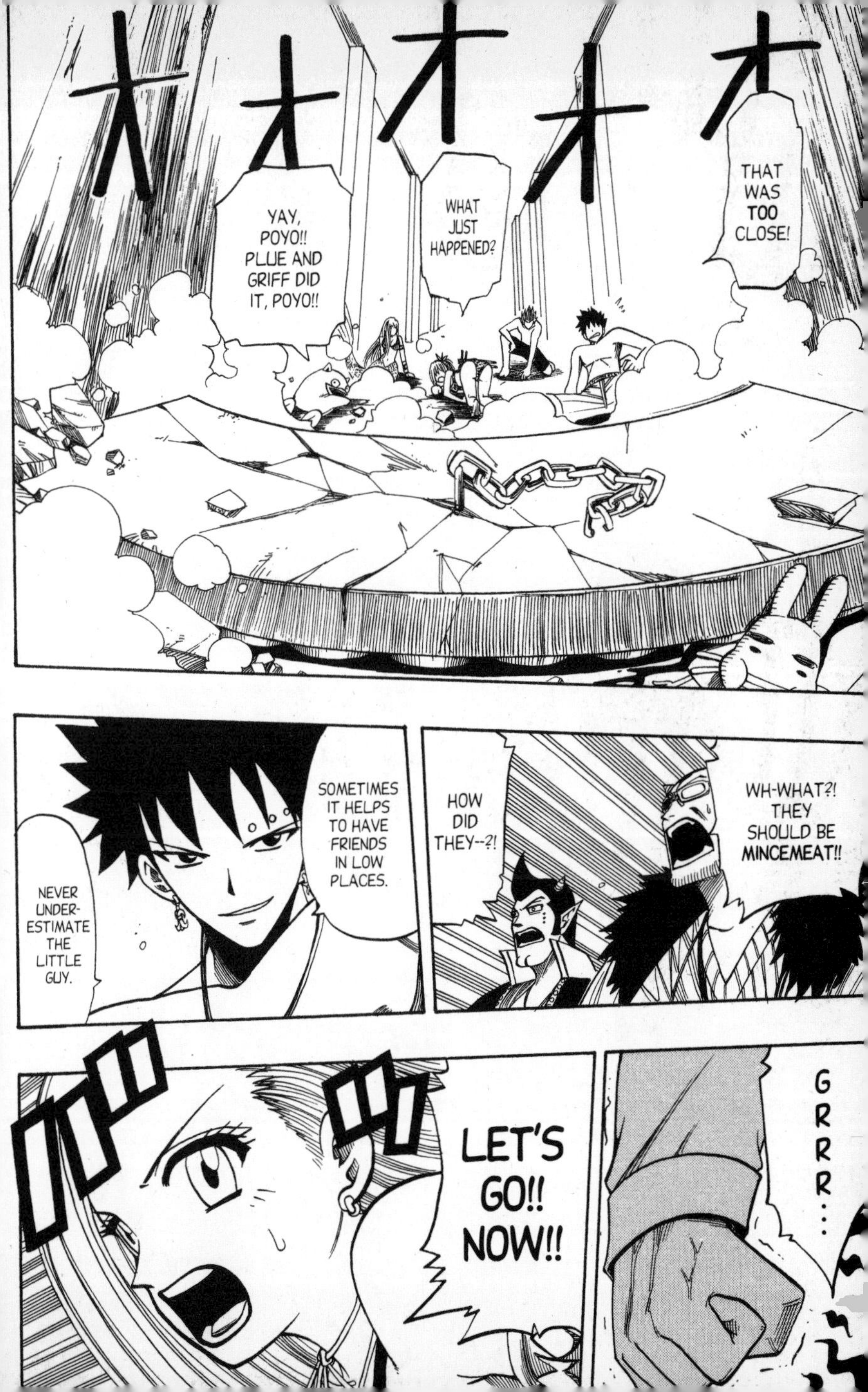

オオオオオ
THAT WAS TOO CLOSE!
WHAT JUST HAPPENED?
YAY, POYO!! PLUE AND GRIFF DID IT, POYO!!
WH-WHAT?! THEY SHOULD BE MINCEMEAT!!
HOW DID THEY--?!
SOMETIMES IT HELPS TO HAVE FRIENDS IN LOW PLACES.
NEVER UNDER-ESTIMATE THE LITTLE GUY.
GRRR...
LET'S GO!! NOW!!

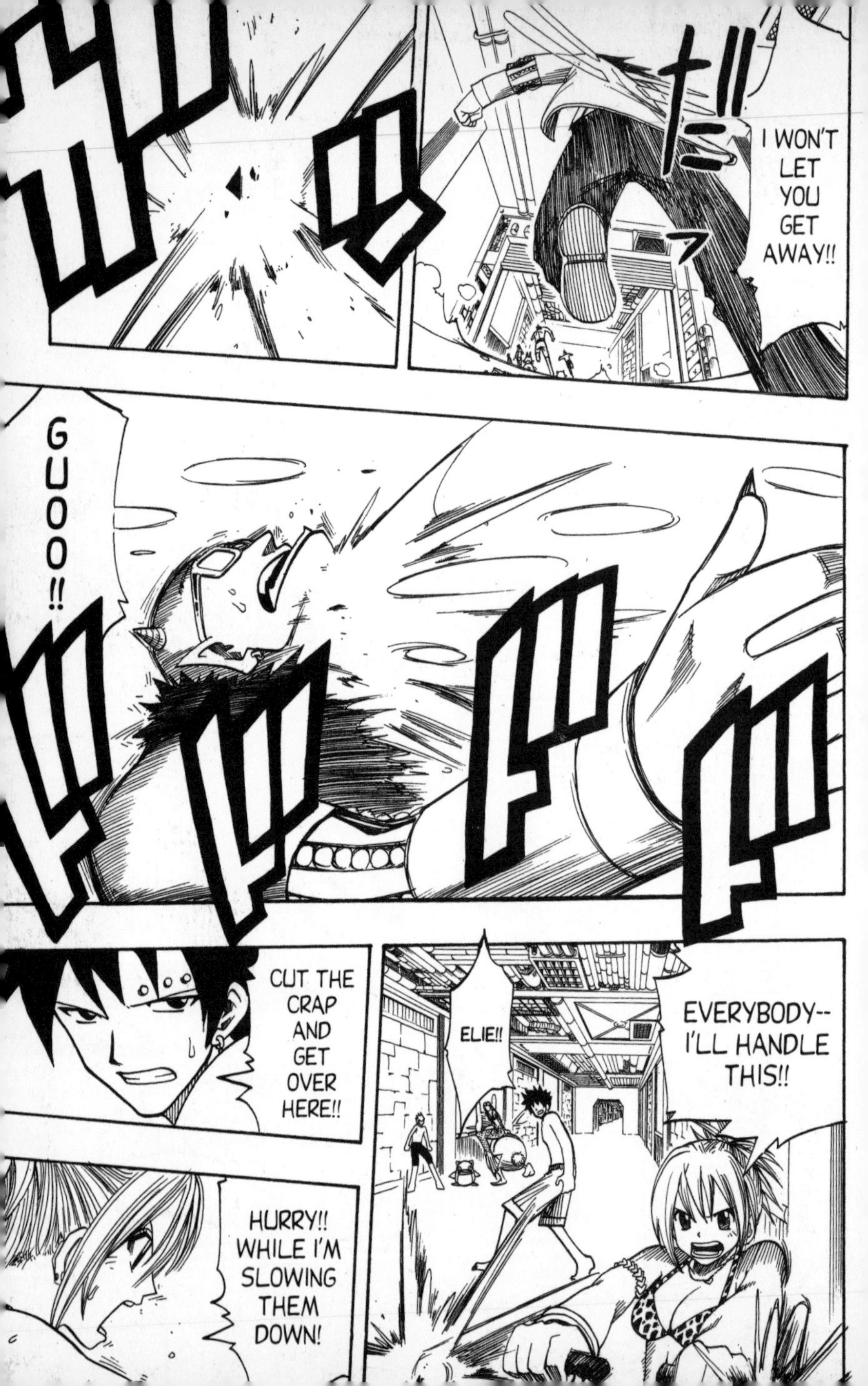
I WON'T LET YOU GET AWAY!!
GUOOO!!
EVERYBODY-- I'LL HANDLE THIS!!
ELIE!!
CUT THE CRAP AND GET OVER HERE!!
HURRY!! WHILE I'M SLOWING THEM DOWN!

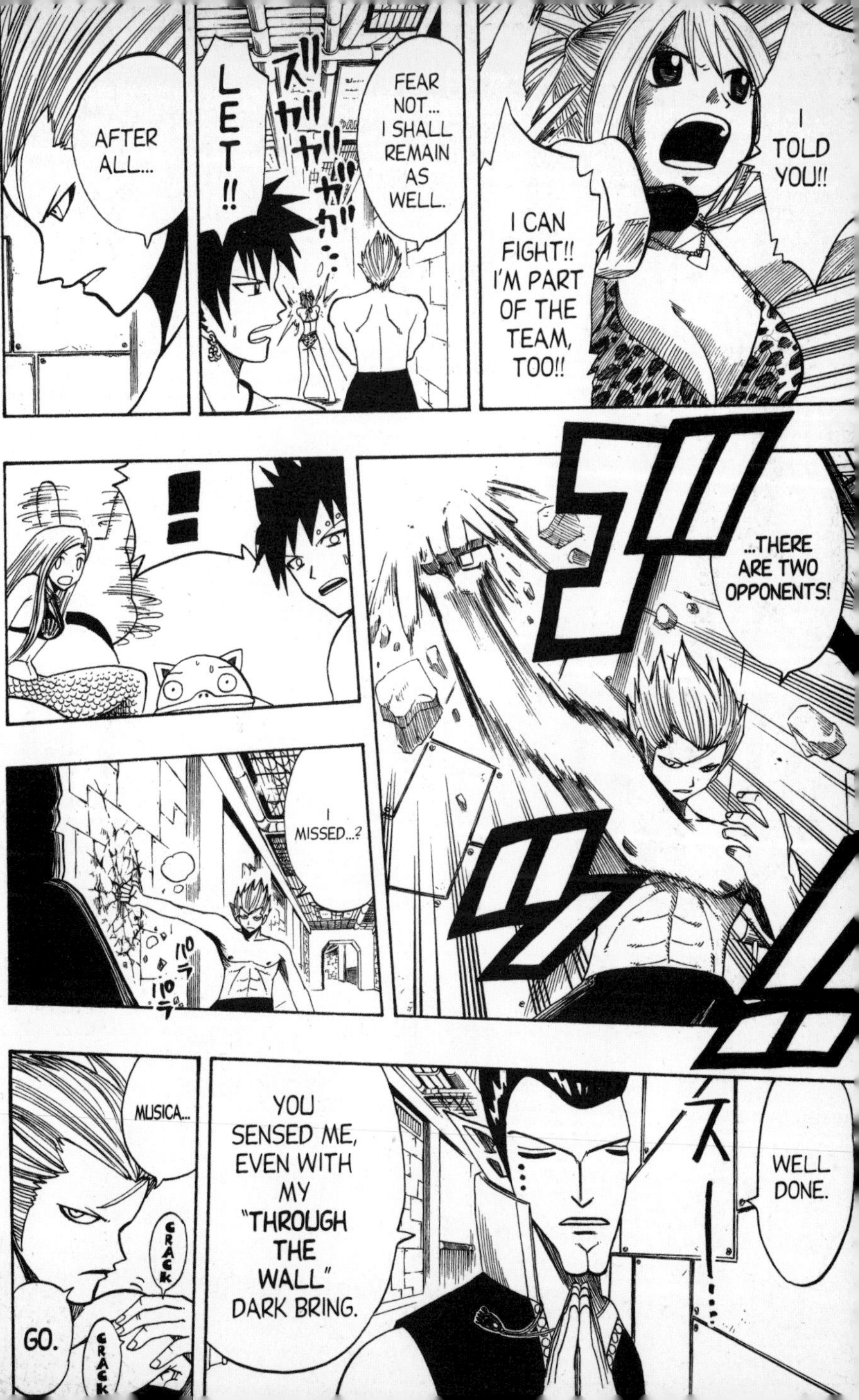
I TOLD YOU!!
I CAN FIGHT!! I'M PART OF THE TEAM, TOO!!
FEAR NOT... I SHALL REMAIN AS WELL.
LET!!
AFTER ALL...
...THERE ARE TWO OPPONENTS!
!
I MISSED...?
WELL DONE.
YOU SENSED ME, EVEN WITH MY "THROUGH THE WALL" DARK BRING.
MUSICA...
CRACK
GO.
CRACK

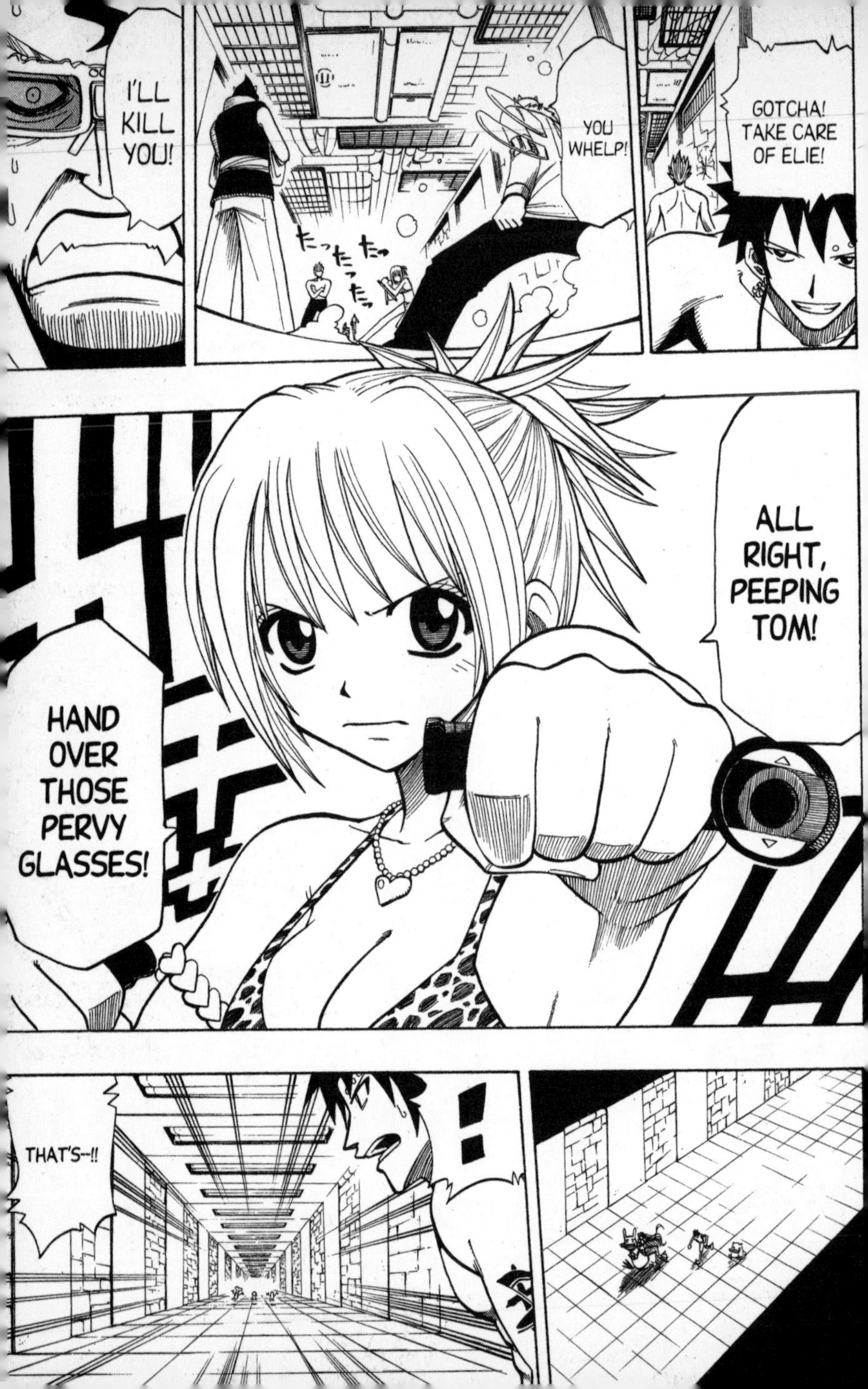
GOTCHA! TAKE CARE OF ELIE!
YOU WHELP!
たっ たっ たっ たっ
I'LL KILL YOU!
ALL RIGHT, PEEPING TOM!
HAND OVER THOSE PERVY GLASSES!
THAT'S--!!

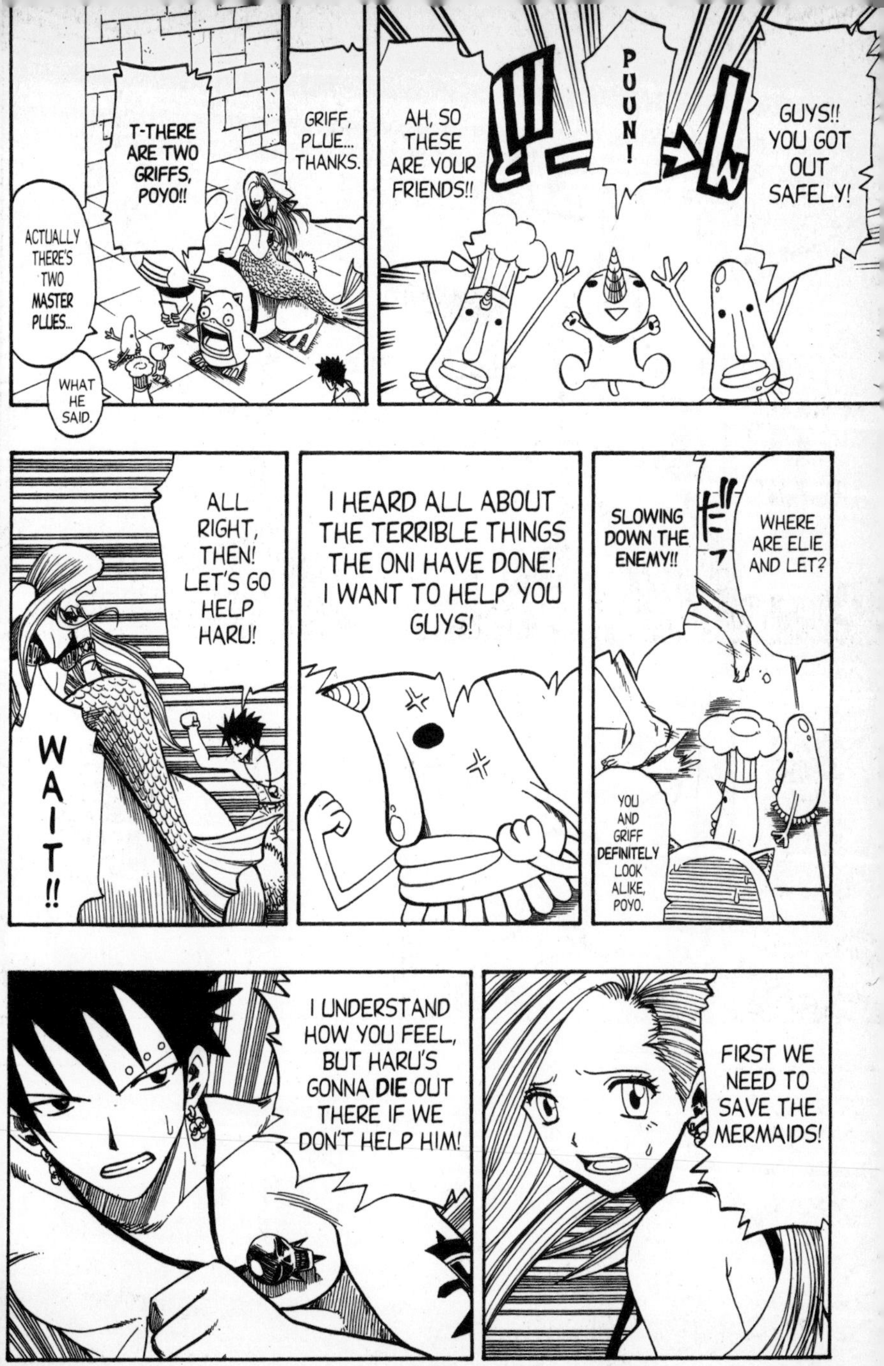
GUYS!! YOU GOT OUT SAFELY!
PUUN!
AH, SO THESE ARE YOUR FRIENDS!!
GRIFF, PLUE... THANKS.
T-THERE ARE TWO GRIFFS, POYO!!
ACTUALLY THERE'S TWO MASTER PLUES...
WHAT HE SAID.
WHERE ARE ELIE AND LET?
SLOWING DOWN THE ENEMY!!
YOU AND GRIFF DEFINITELY LOOK ALIKE, POYO.
I HEARD ALL ABOUT THE TERRIBLE THINGS THE ONI HAVE DONE! I WANT TO HELP YOU GUYS!
ALL RIGHT, THEN! LET'S GO HELP HARU!
WAIT!!
FIRST WE NEED TO SAVE THE MERMAIDS!
I UNDERSTAND HOW YOU FEEL, BUT HARU'S GONNA DIE OUT THERE IF WE DON'T HELP HIM!

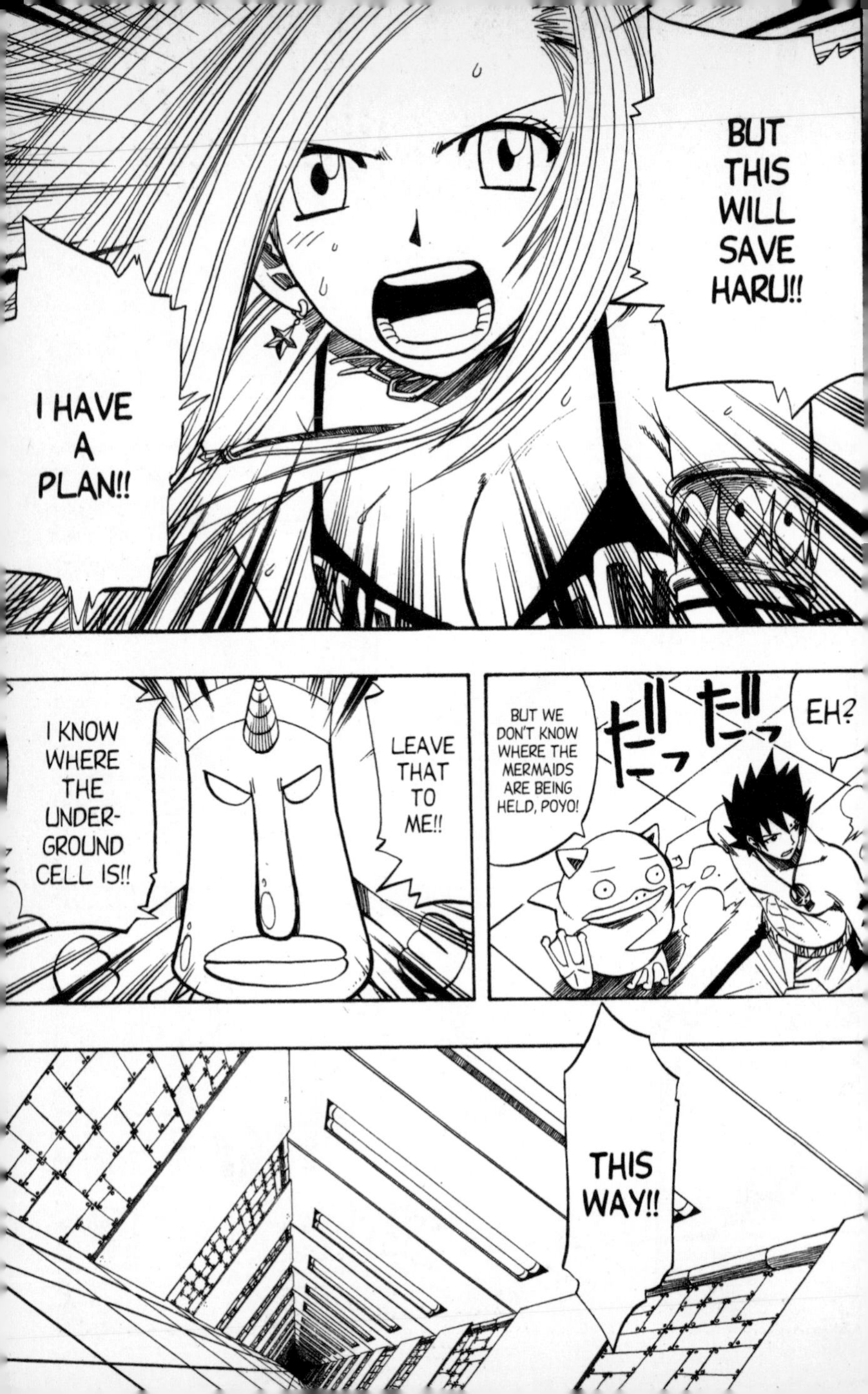
BUT THIS WILL SAVE HARU!!
I HAVE A PLAN!!
EH?
だっ だっ
BUT WE DON'T KNOW WHERE THE MERMAIDS ARE BEING HELD, POYO!
LEAVE THAT TO ME!!
I KNOW WHERE THE UNDER-GROUND CELL IS!!
THIS WAY!!

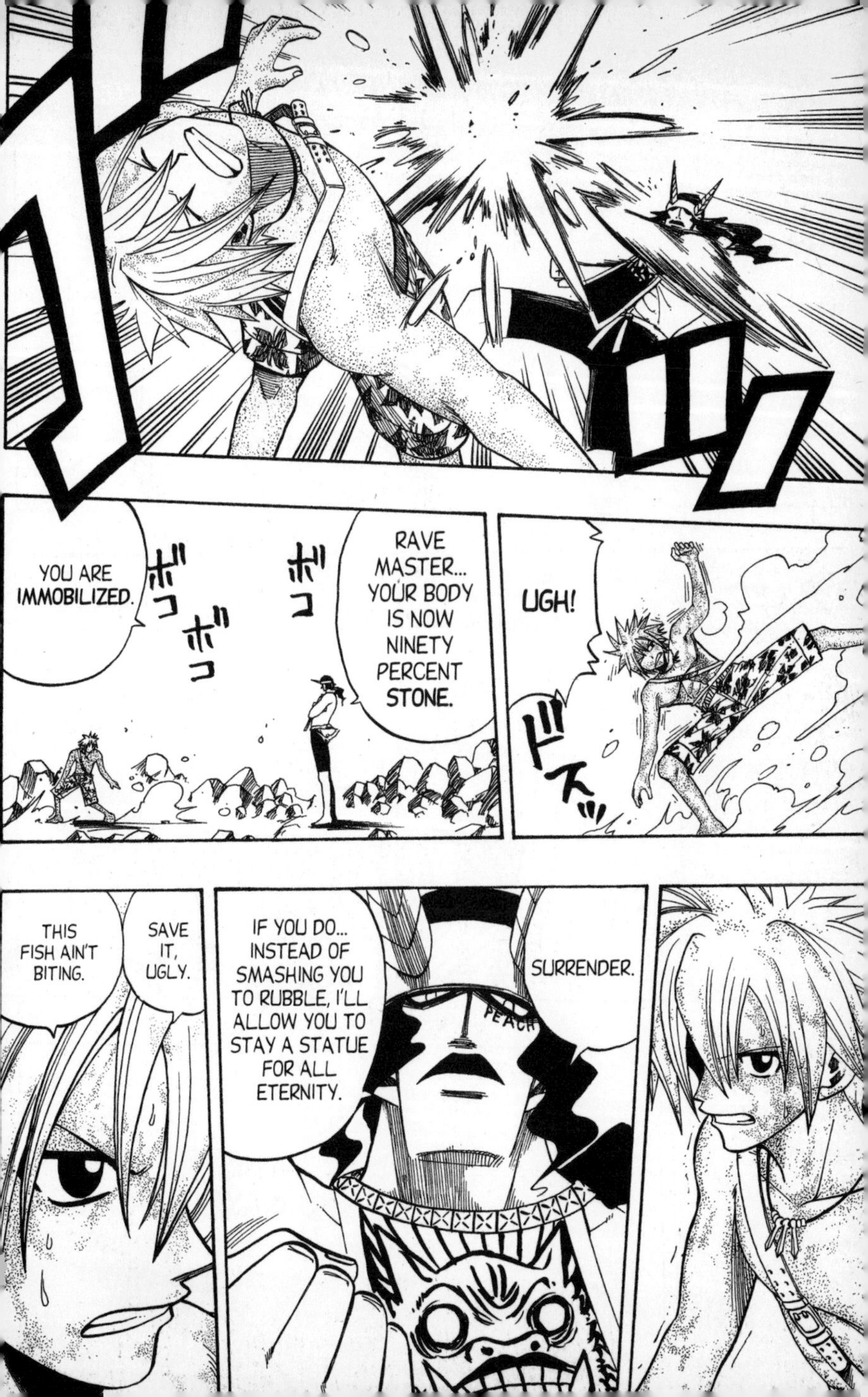

UGH!
ドスッ
RAVE MASTER... YOUR BODY IS NOW NINETY PERCENT STONE.
ボコ
ボコ
ボコ
YOU ARE IMMOBILIZED.
SURRENDER.
IF YOU DO... INSTEAD OF SMASHING YOU TO RUBBLE, I'LL ALLOW YOU TO STAY A STATUE FOR ALL ETERNITY.
PEACH
SAVE IT, UGLY.
THIS FISH AIN'T BITING.

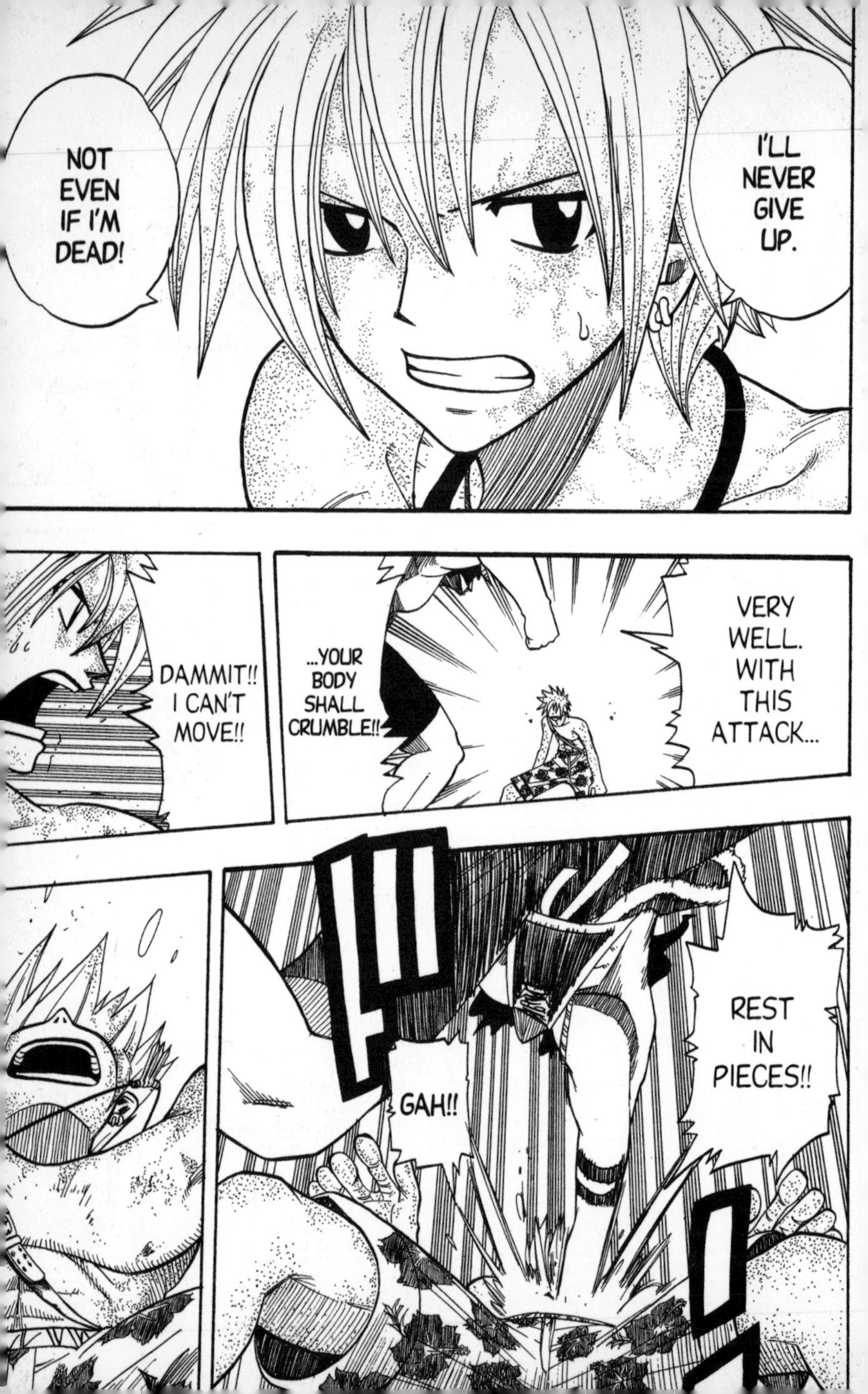
I'LL NEVER GIVE UP.
NOT EVEN IF I'M DEAD!
VERY WELL. WITH THIS ATTACK...
...YOUR BODY SHALL CRUMBLE!!
DAMMIT!! I CAN'T MOVE!!
REST IN PIECES!!
GAH!!

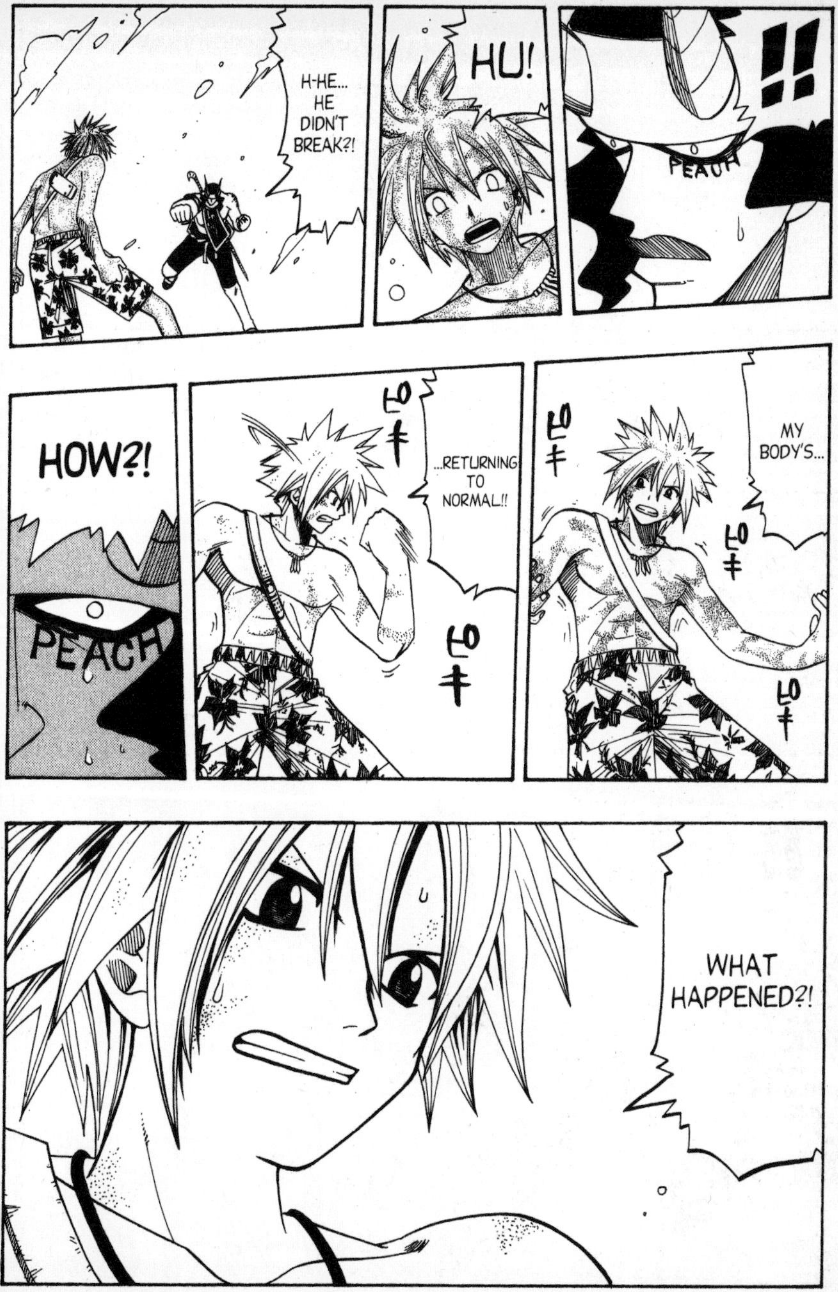
!!
PEACH
HU!
H-HE... HE DIDN'T BREAK?!
ピキ
MY BODY'S...
ピキ
ピキ
ピキ
...RETURNING TO NORMAL!!
ピキ
HOW?!
PEACH
WHAT HAPPENED?!

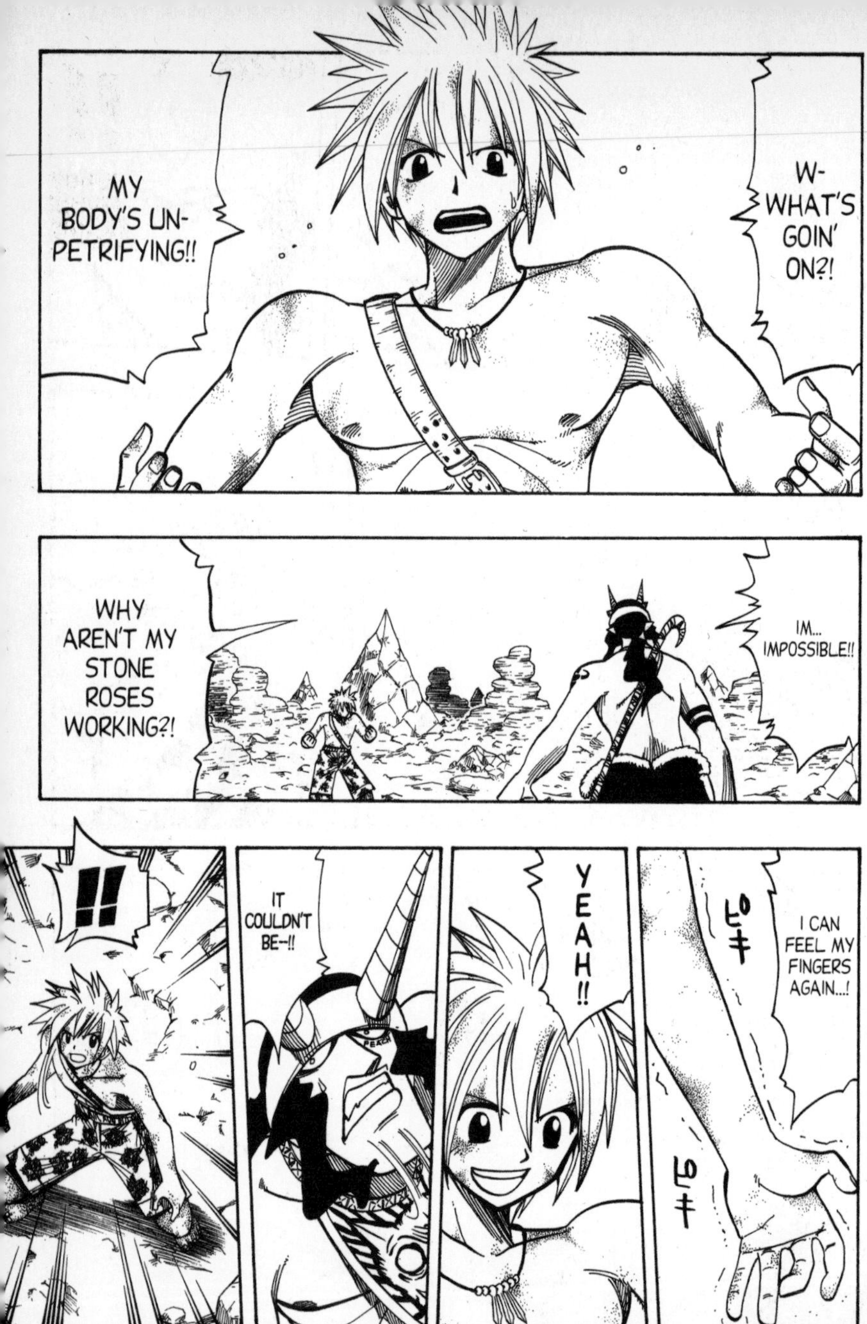
W-
WHAT'S GOIN' ON?!
MY BODY'S UN-PETRIFYING!!
IM... IMPOSSIBLE!!
WHY AREN'T MY STONE ROSES WORKING?!
ピキ
ピキ
I CAN FEEL MY FINGERS AGAIN...!
YEAH!!
IT COULDN'T BE--!!
!!

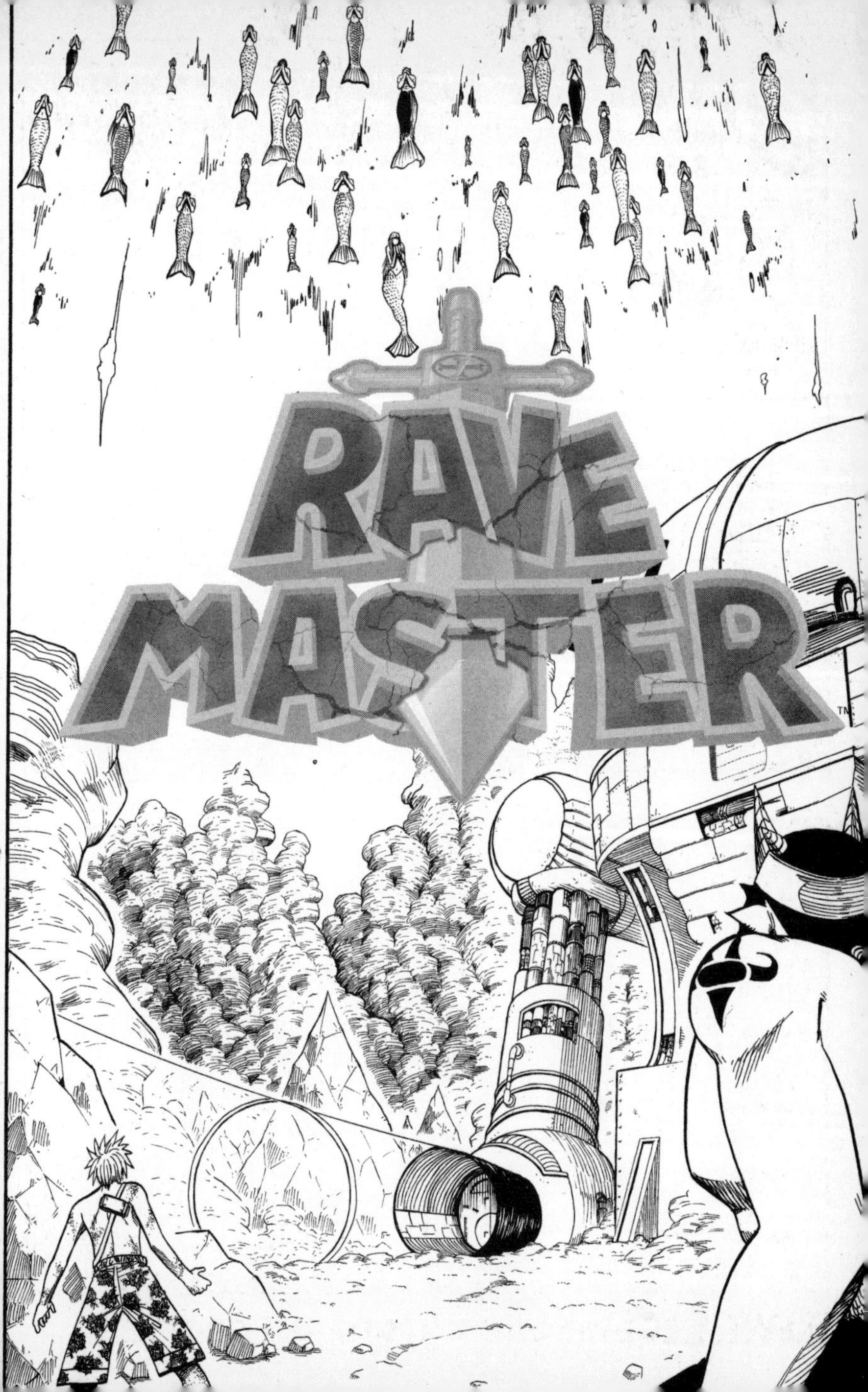
RAVE
MASTER™

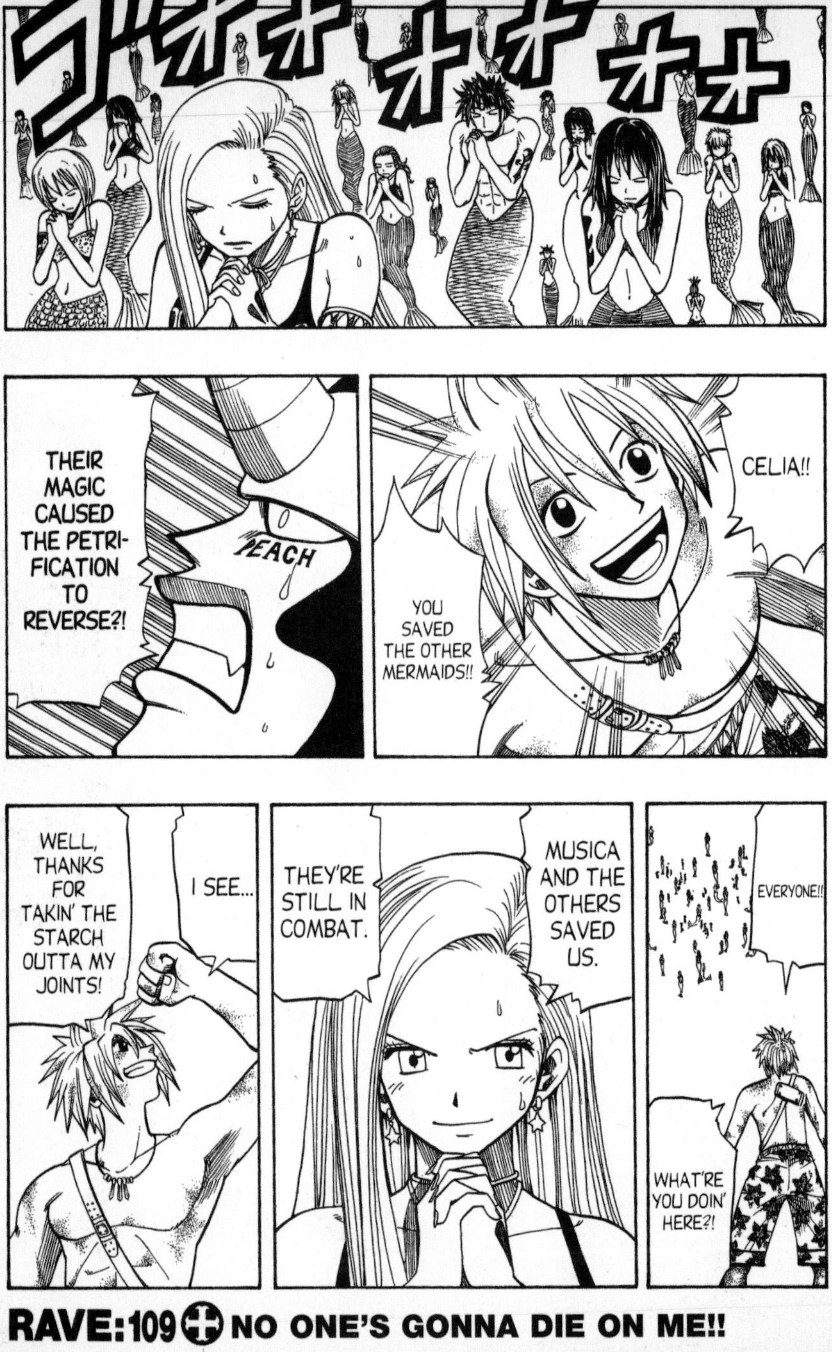
ゴオオオオオオ
CELIA!!
YOU SAVED THE OTHER MERMAIDS!!
THEIR MAGIC CAUSED THE PETRIFICATION TO REVERSE?!
PEACH
EVERYONE!!
WHAT'RE YOU DOIN' HERE?!
MUSICA AND THE OTHERS SAVED US.
THEY'RE STILL IN COMBAT.
I SEE...
WELL, THANKS FOR TAKIN' THE STARCH OUTTA MY JOINTS!

RAVE:109 NO ONE'S GONNA DIE ON ME!!

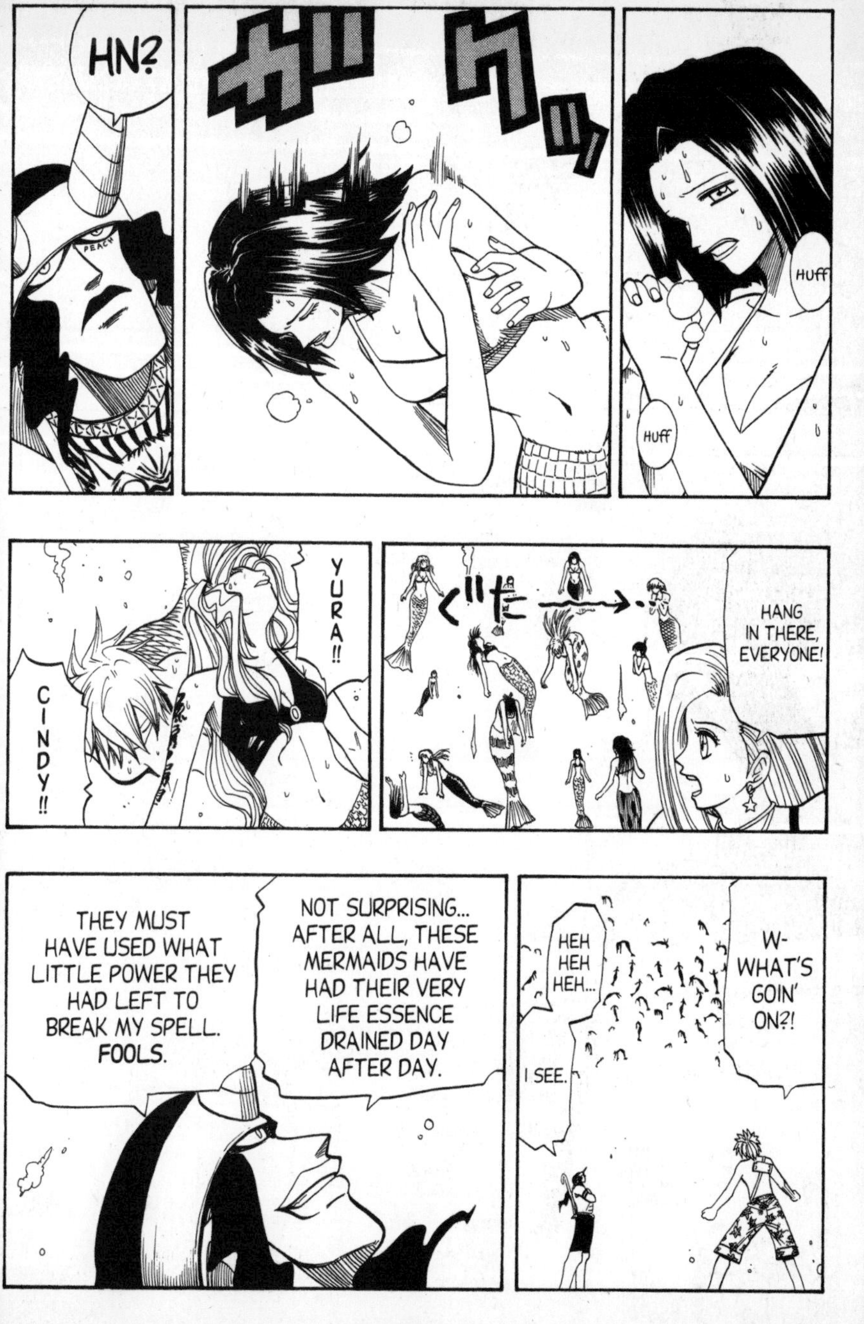
HUFF
HUFF
HN?
HANG IN THERE, EVERYONE!
YURA!!
CINDY!!
W- WHAT'S GOIN' ON?!
HEH HEH HEH...
I SEE.
NOT SURPRISING... AFTER ALL, THESE MERMAIDS HAVE HAD THEIR VERY LIFE ESSENCE DRAINED DAY AFTER DAY.
THEY MUST HAVE USED WHAT LITTLE POWER THEY HAD LEFT TO BREAK MY SPELL. FOOLS.

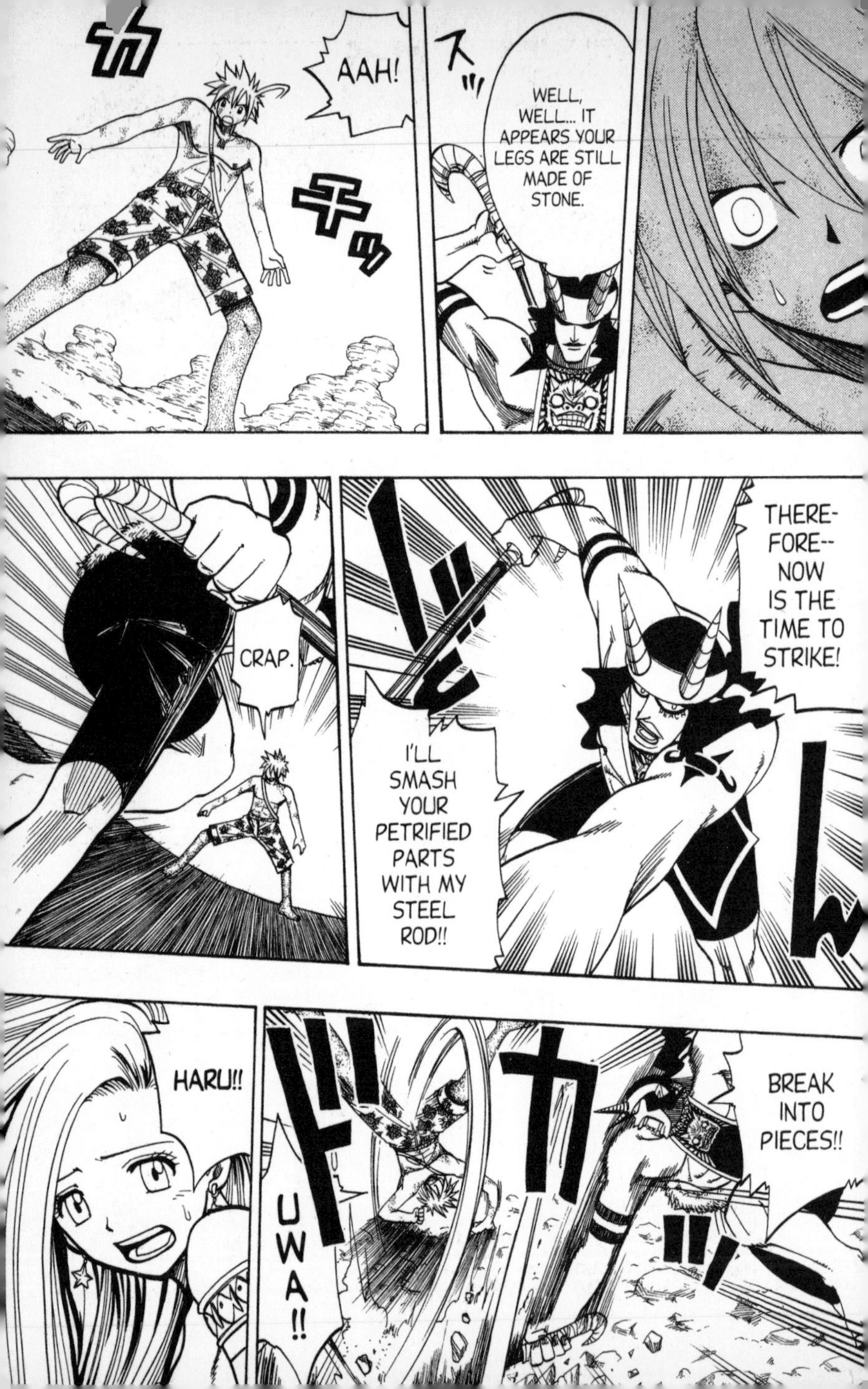
WELL, WELL... IT APPEARS YOUR LEGS ARE STILL MADE OF STONE.
AAH!
THERE-FORE-- NOW IS THE TIME TO STRIKE!
I'LL SMASH YOUR PETRIFIED PARTS WITH MY STEEL ROD!!
CRAP.
BREAK INTO PIECES!!
ドカ!!
UWA!!
HARU!!

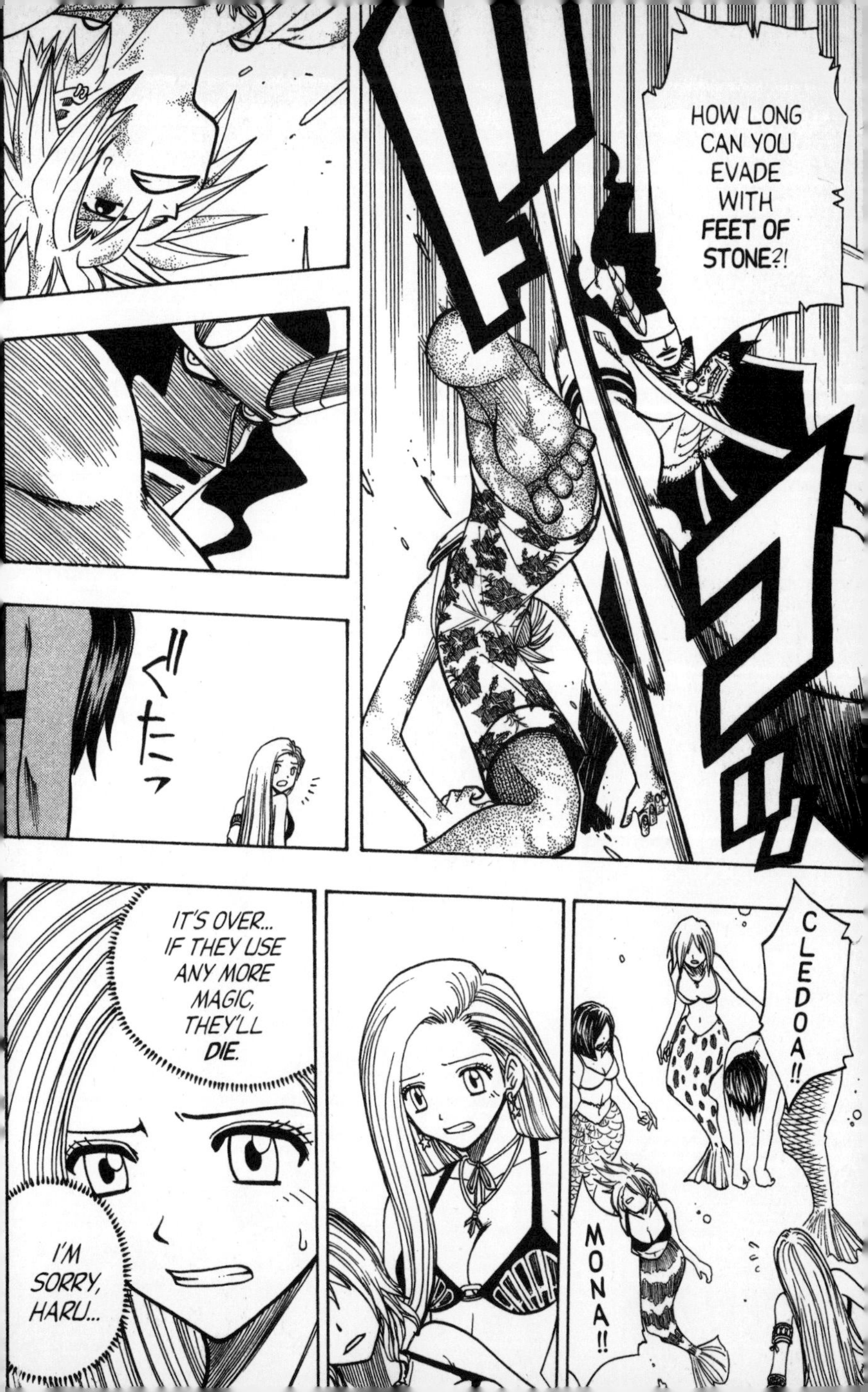
HOW LONG CAN YOU EVADE WITH **FEET OF STONE**?!
CLEDOA!!
MONA!!
IT'S OVER... IF THEY USE ANY MORE MAGIC, THEY'LL **DIE**.
I'M SORRY, HARU...

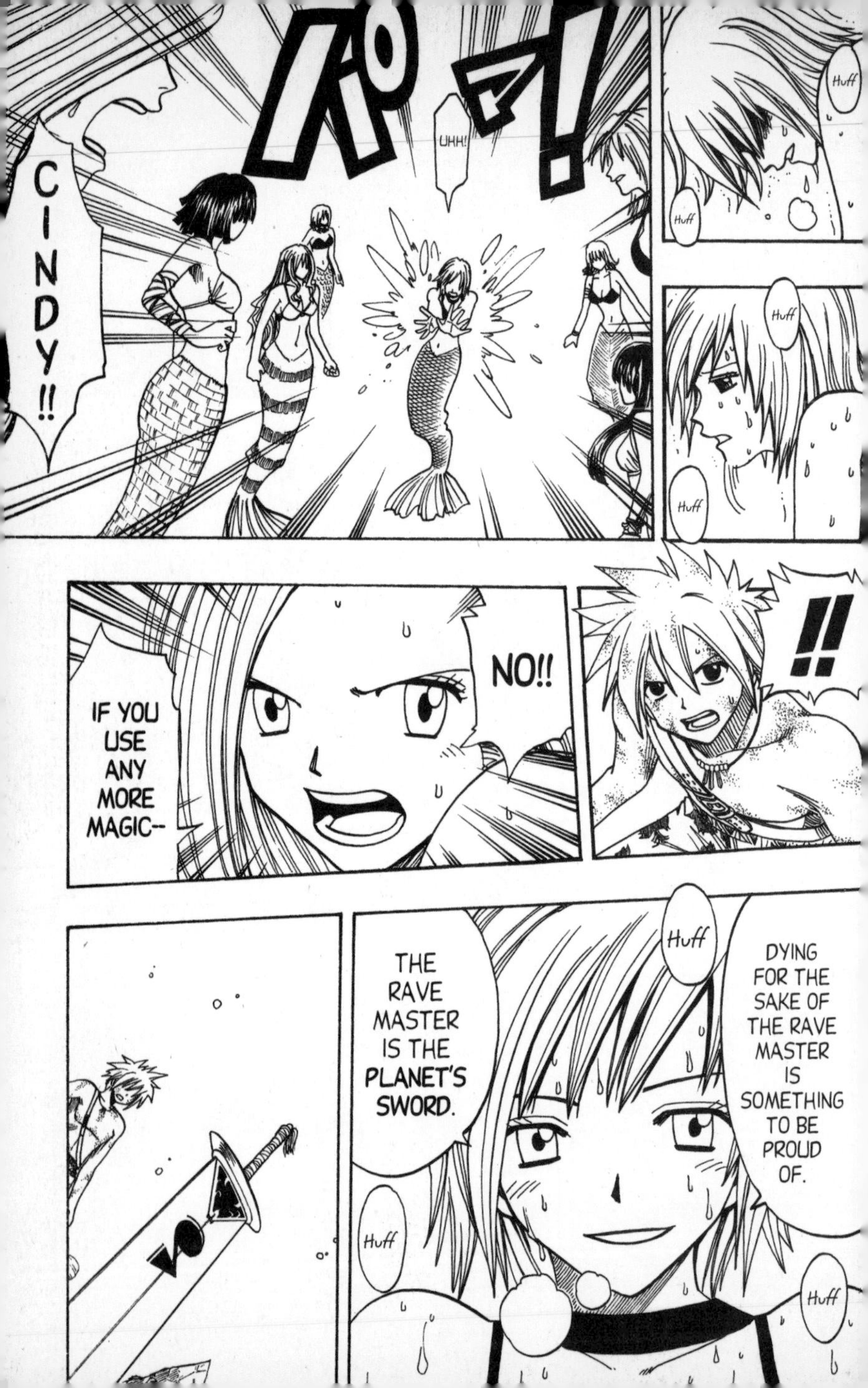

Huff
Huff
Huff
Huff
パッ!
UHH!
CINDY!!
!!
NO!!
IF YOU USE ANY MORE MAGIC--
Huff
DYING FOR THE SAKE OF THE RAVE MASTER IS SOMETHING TO BE PROUD OF.
THE RAVE MASTER IS THE PLANET'S SWORD.
Huff
Huff

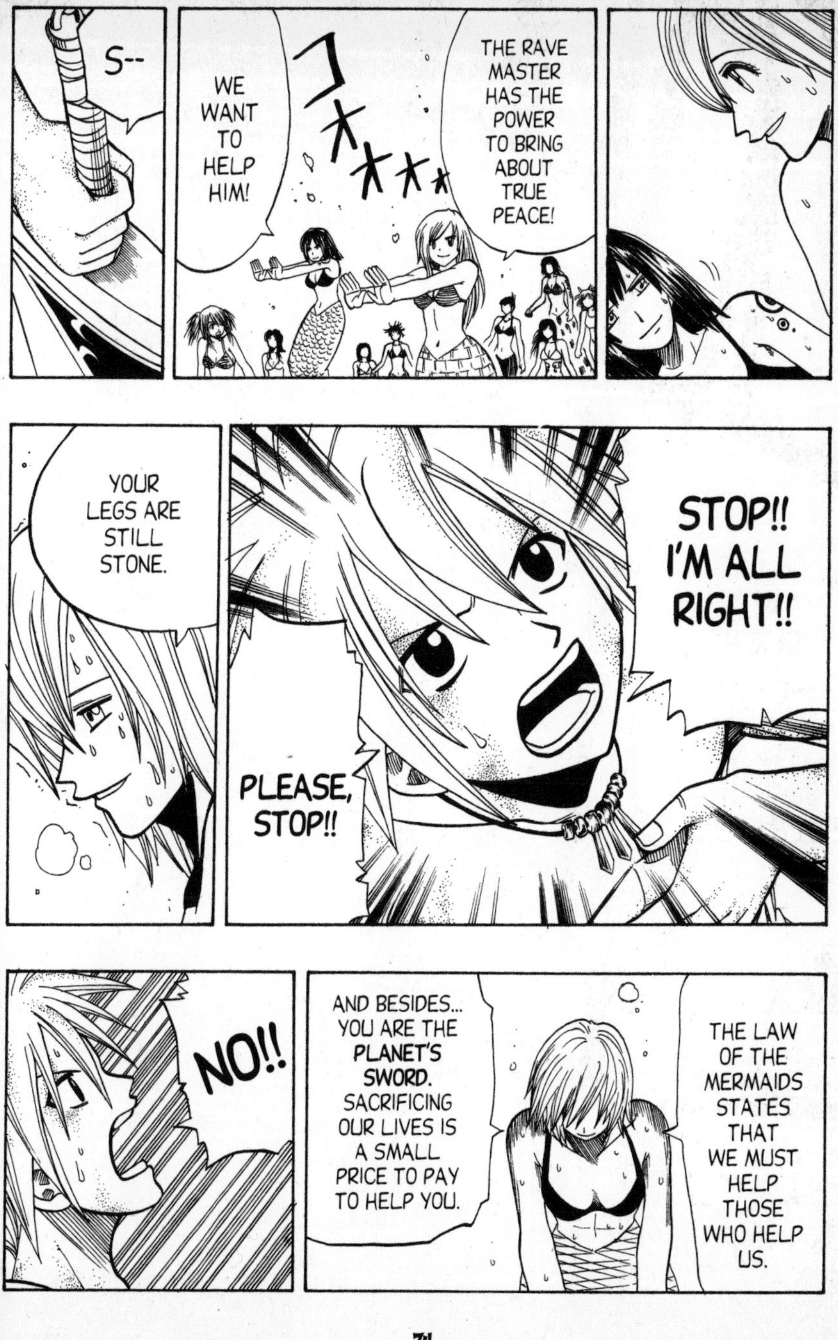
THE RAVE MASTER HAS THE POWER TO BRING ABOUT TRUE PEACE!
WE WANT TO HELP HIM!
S--
STOP!! I'M ALL RIGHT!!
PLEASE, STOP!!
YOUR LEGS ARE STILL STONE.
THE LAW OF THE MERMAIDS STATES THAT WE MUST HELP THOSE WHO HELP US.
AND BESIDES... YOU ARE THE PLANET'S SWORD. SACRIFICING OUR LIVES IS A SMALL PRICE TO PAY TO HELP YOU.
NO!!

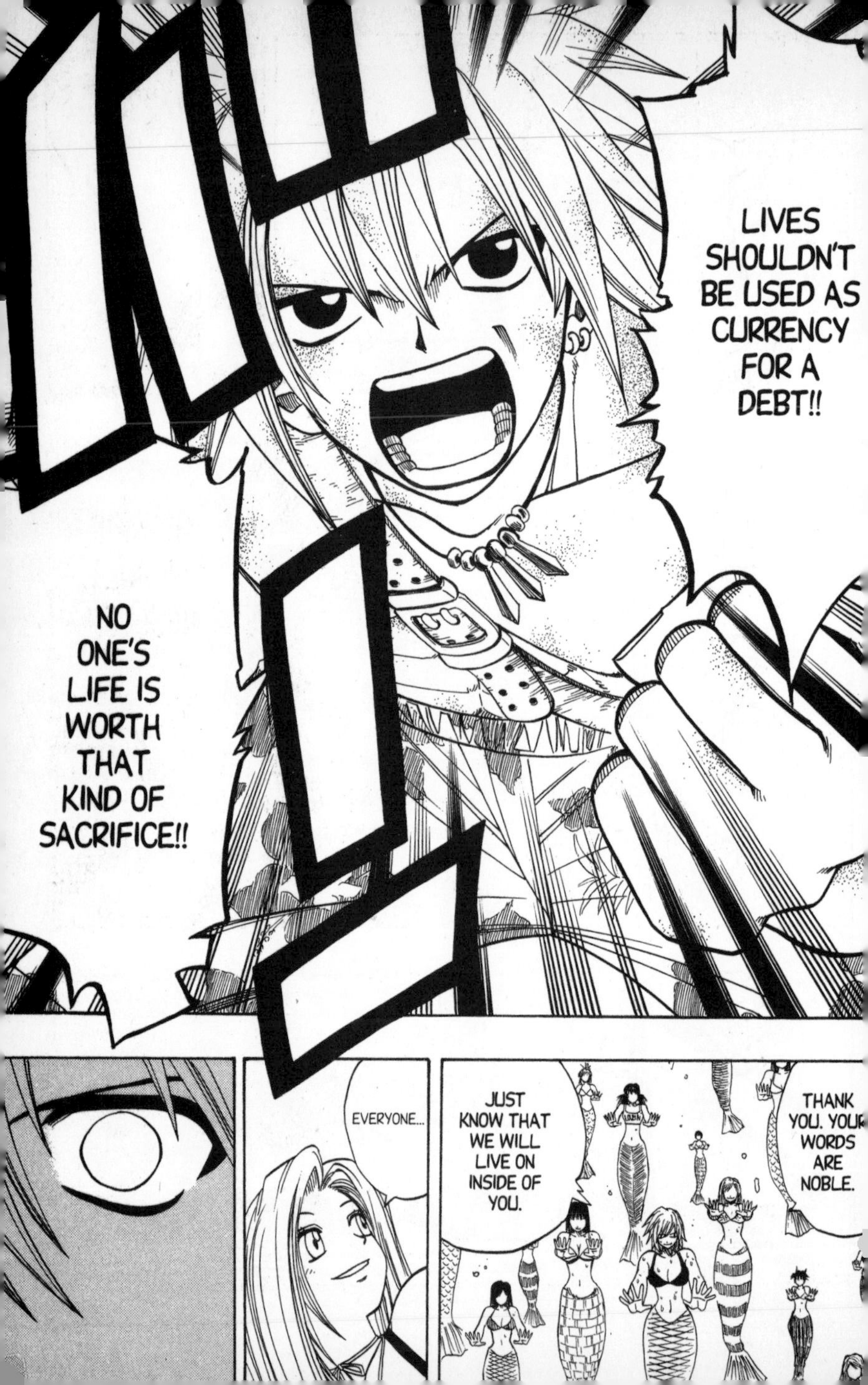
LIVES SHOULDN'T BE USED AS CURRENCY FOR A DEBT!!
NO ONE'S LIFE IS WORTH THAT KIND OF SACRIFICE!!
THANK YOU. YOUR WORDS ARE NOBLE.
JUST KNOW THAT WE WILL LIVE ON INSIDE OF YOU.
EVERYONE...

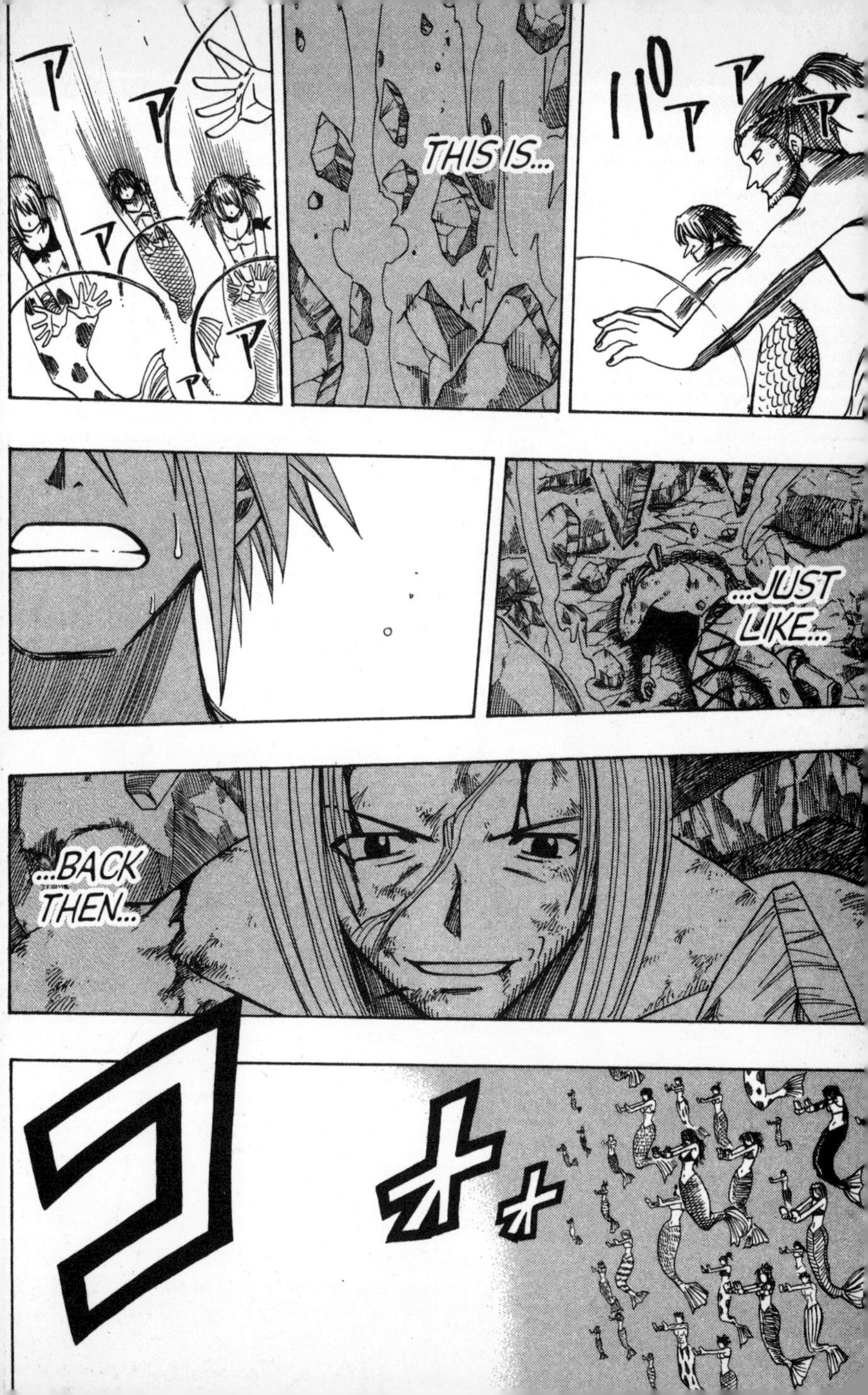
THIS IS...
...JUST LIKE...
...BACK THEN...

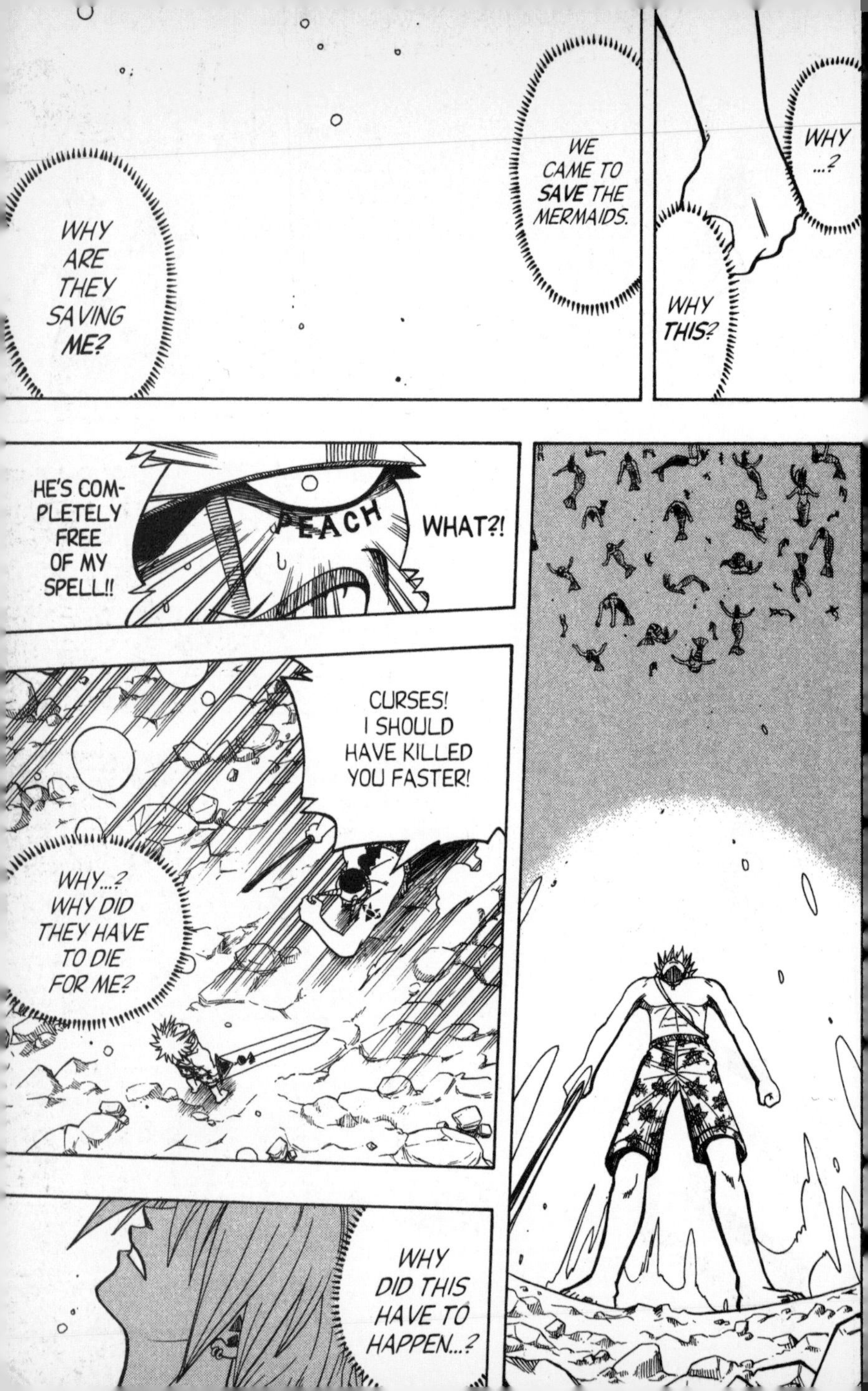
WHY ...?
WHY THIS?
WE CAME TO SAVE THE MERMAIDS.
WHY ARE THEY SAVING ME?
WHAT?!
PEACH
HE'S COM-PLETELY FREE OF MY SPELL!!
CURSES! I SHOULD HAVE KILLED YOU FASTER!
WHY...? WHY DID THEY HAVE TO DIE FOR ME?
WHY DID THIS HAVE TO HAPPEN...?

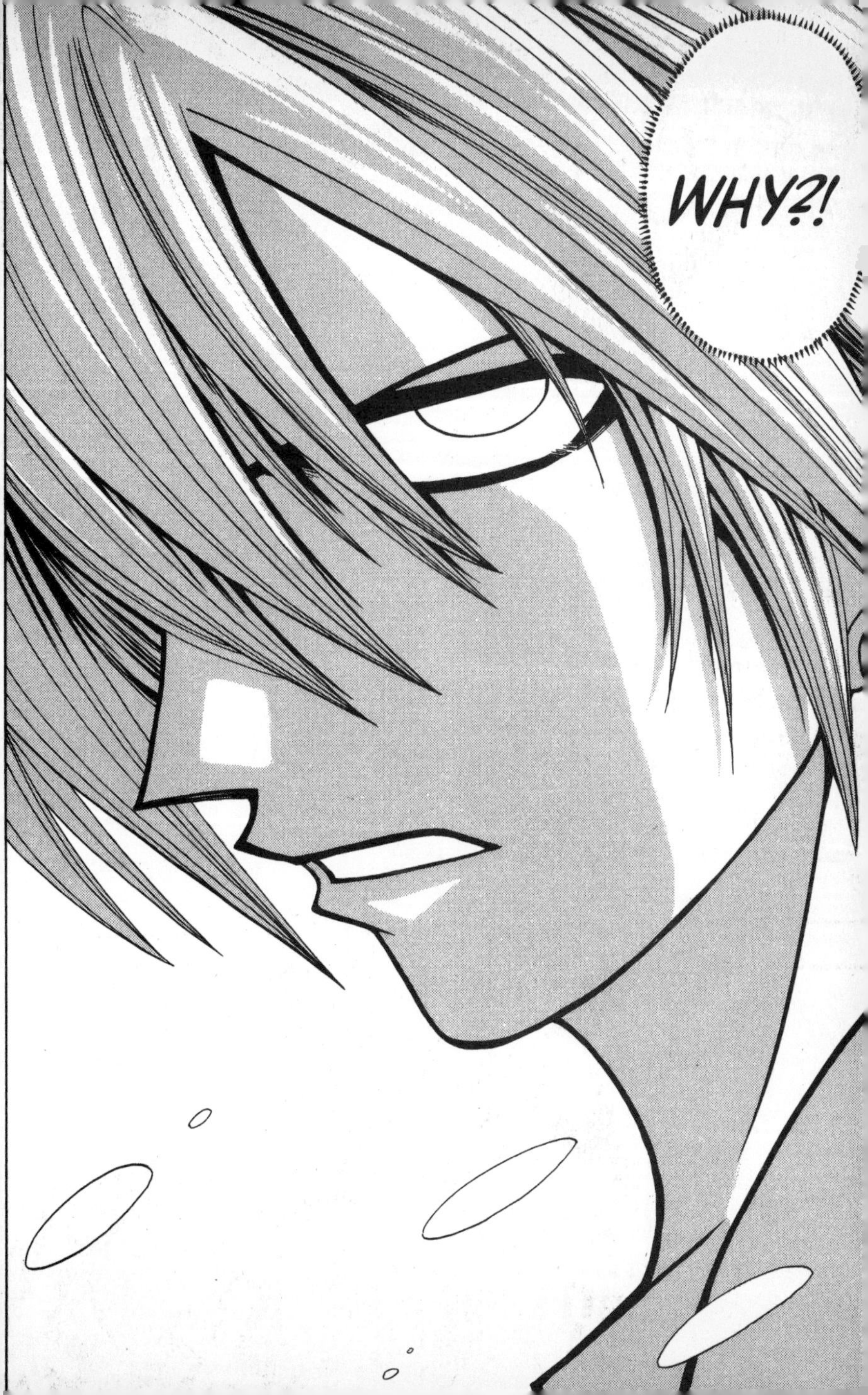
WHY?!

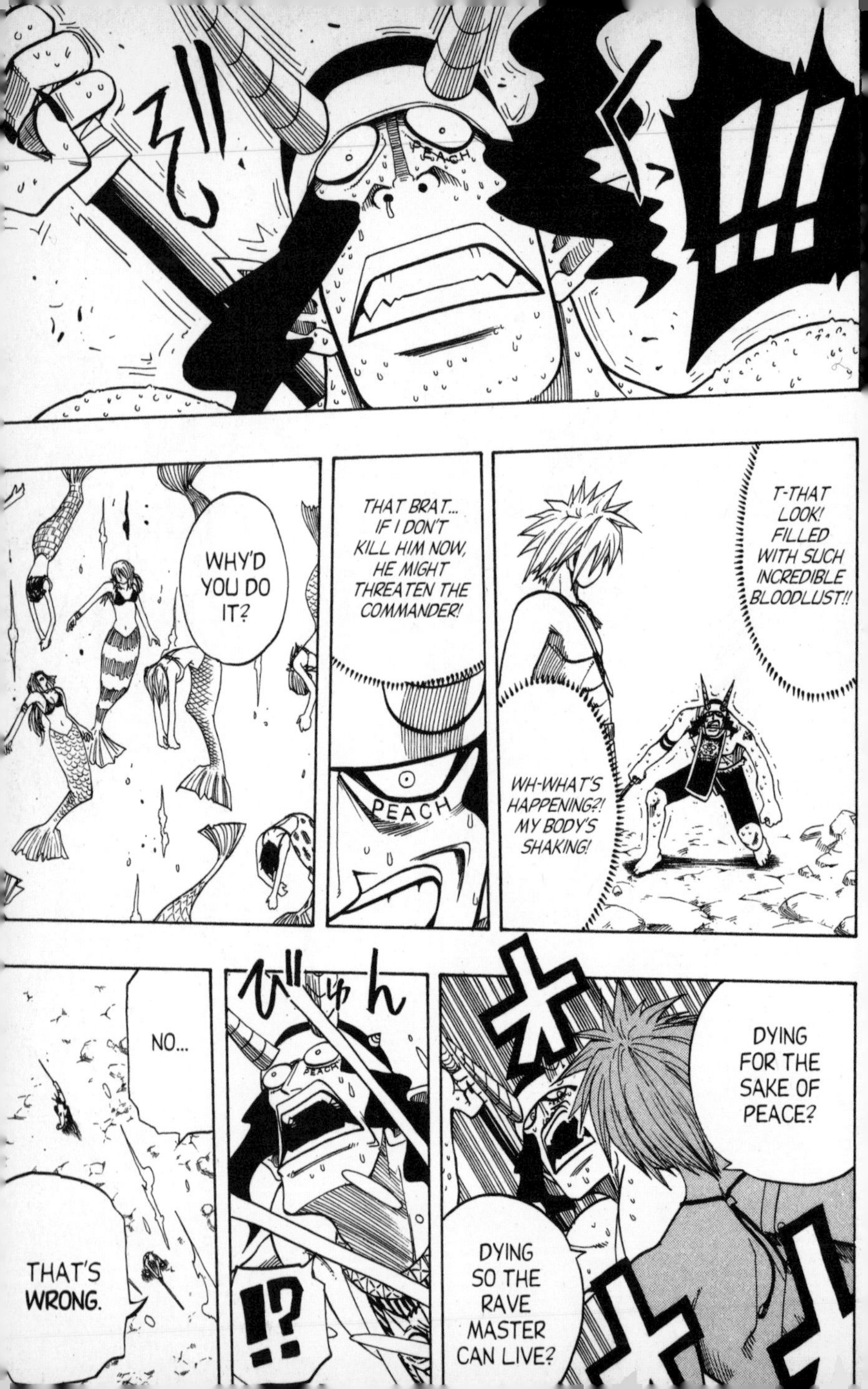
!!!
PEACH
T-THAT LOOK! FILLED WITH SUCH INCREDIBLE BLOODLUST!!
WH-WHAT'S HAPPENING?! MY BODY'S SHAKING!
THAT BRAT... IF I DON'T KILL HIM NOW, HE MIGHT THREATEN THE COMMANDER!
PEACH
WHY'D YOU DO IT?
DYING FOR THE SAKE OF PEACE?
DYING SO THE RAVE MASTER CAN LIVE?
びゅん
PEACH
!?
NO...
THAT'S WRONG.

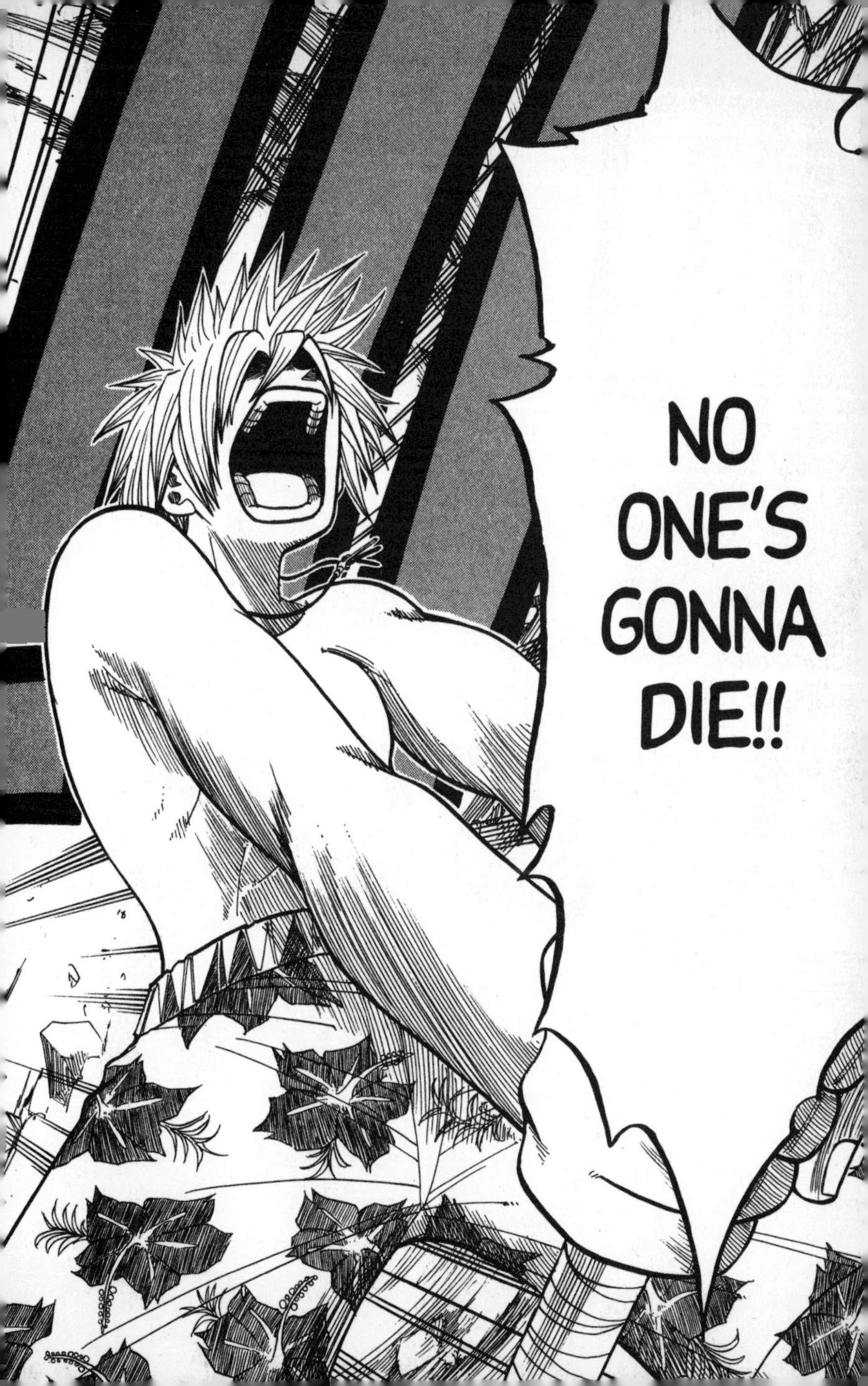
NO ONE'S GONNA DIE!!

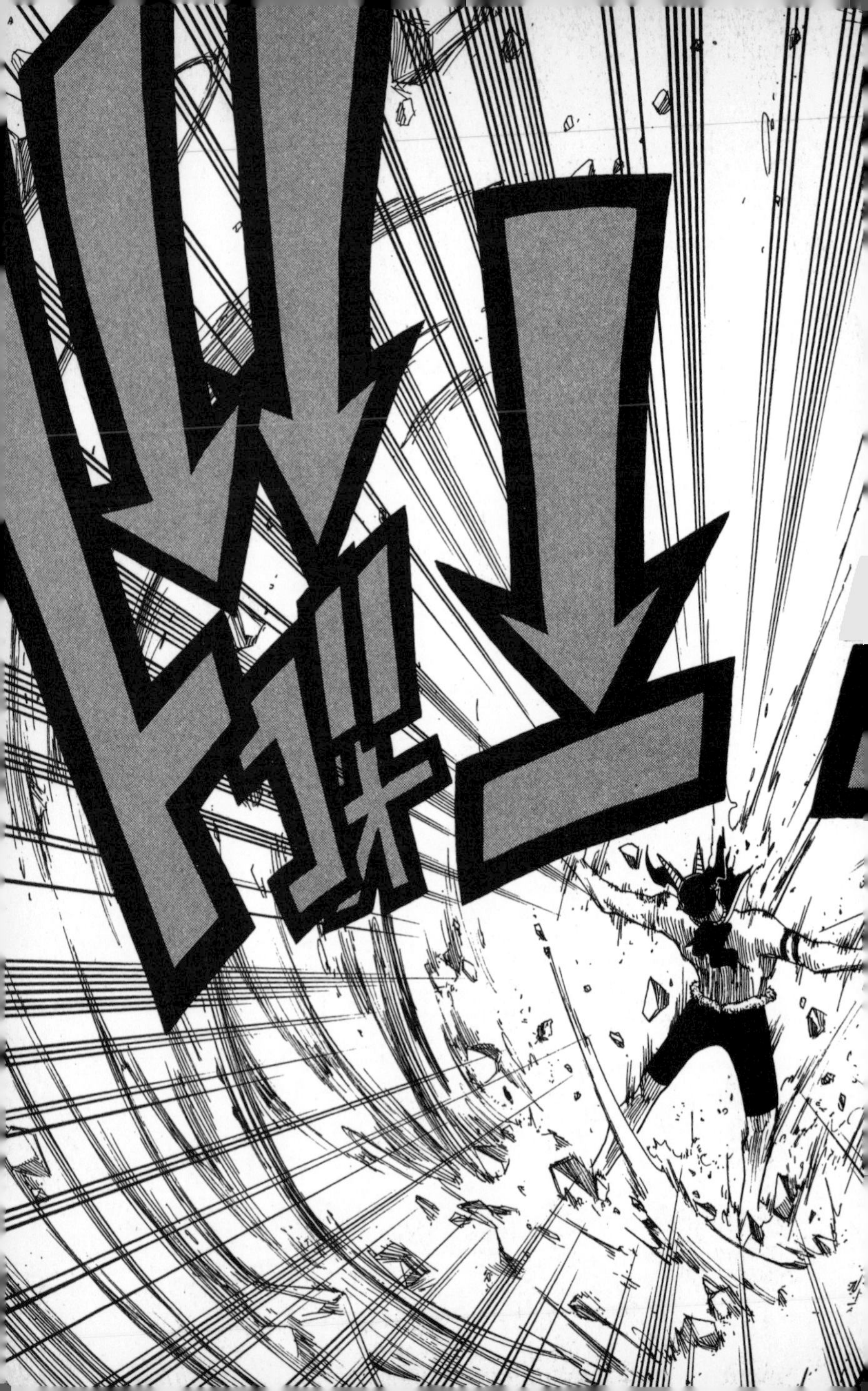

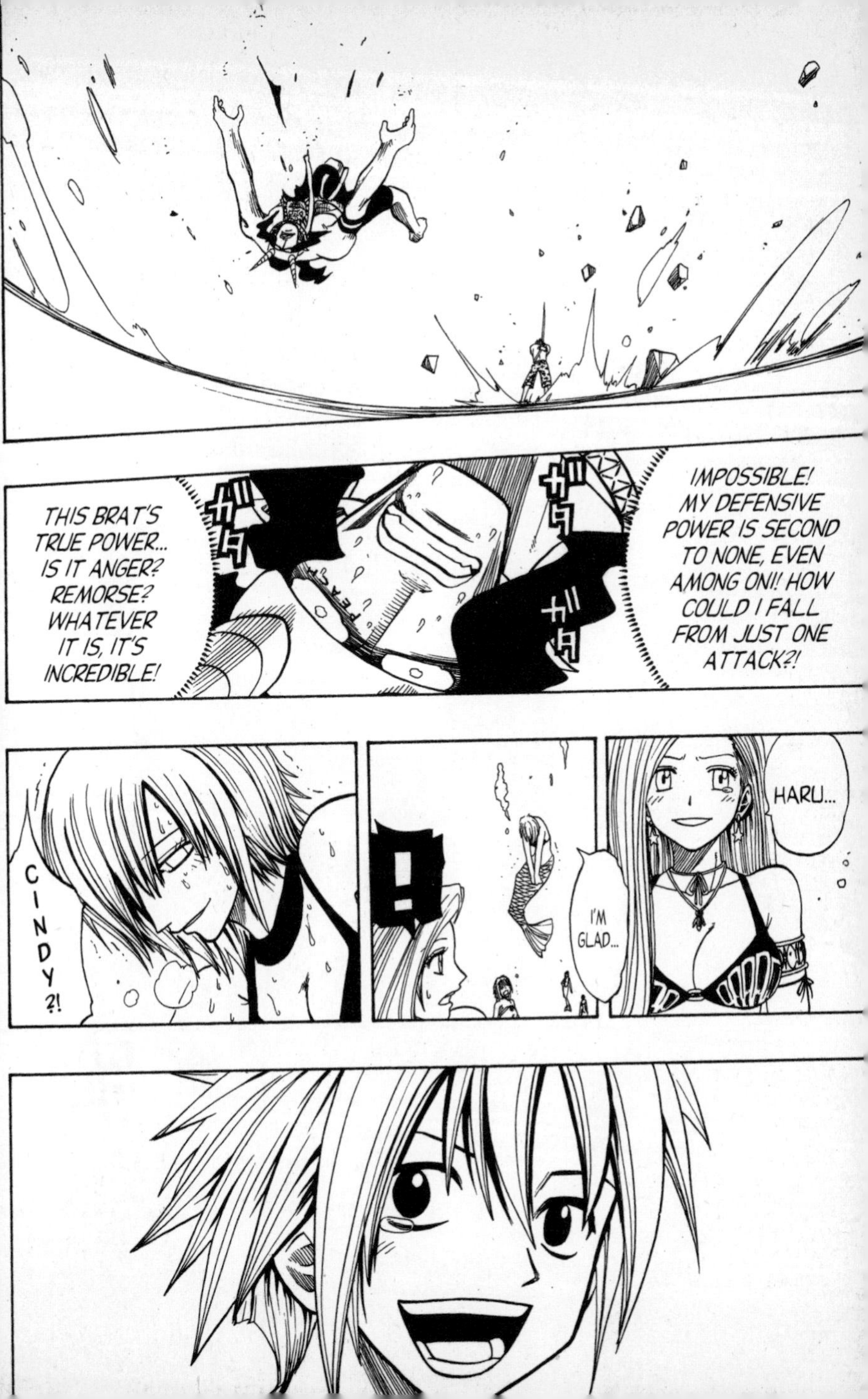
IMPOSSIBLE! MY DEFENSIVE POWER IS SECOND TO NONE, EVEN AMONG ONI! HOW COULD I FALL FROM JUST ONE ATTACK?!
ガタ
ガタ
ガタ
THIS BRAT'S TRUE POWER... IS IT ANGER? REMORSE? WHATEVER IT IS, IT'S INCREDIBLE!
HARU...
I'M GLAD...
!
CINDY?!

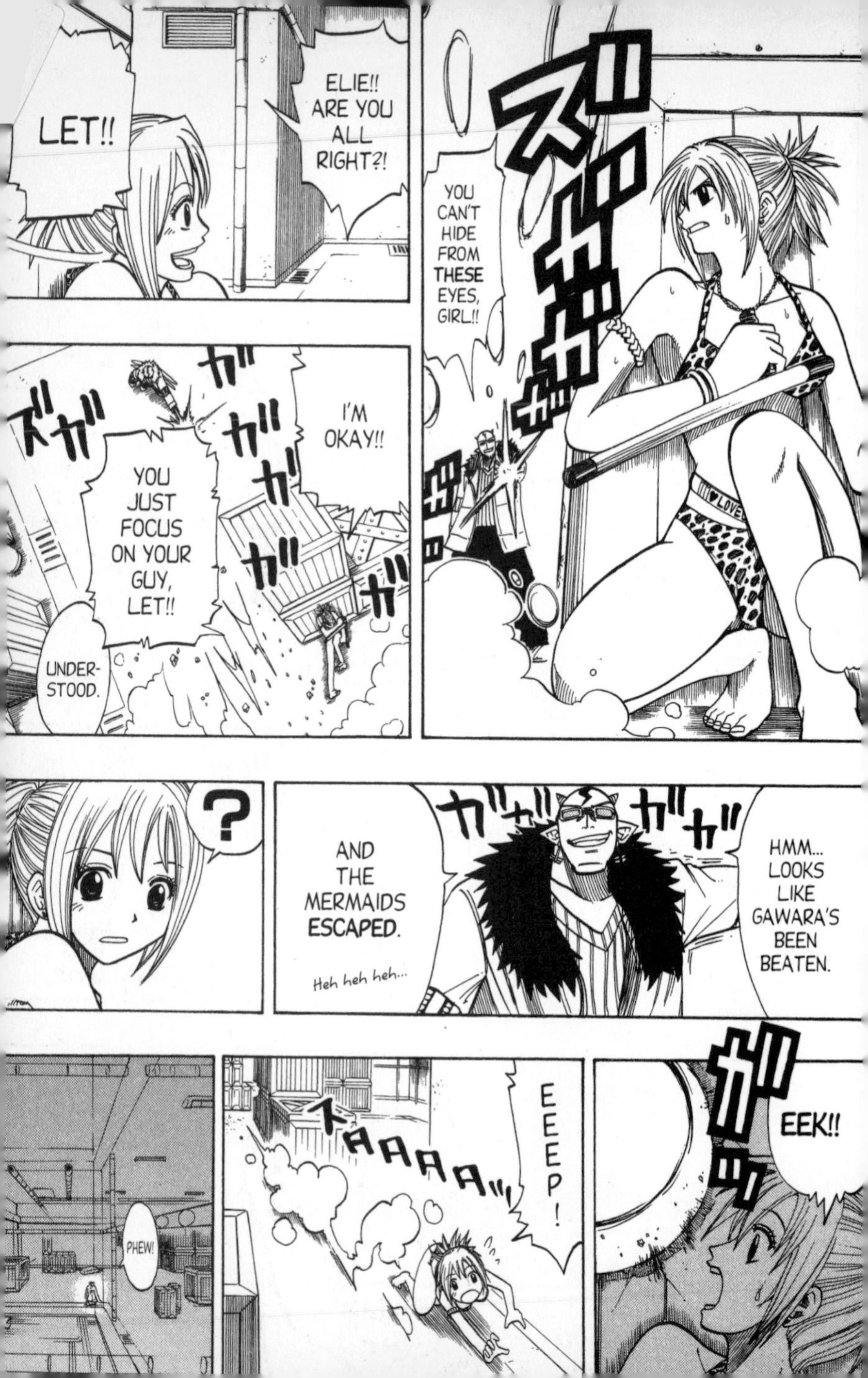
YOU CAN'T HIDE FROM THESE EYES, GIRL!!
ELIE!! ARE YOU ALL RIGHT?!
LET!!
I'M OKAY!!
YOU JUST FOCUS ON YOUR GUY, LET!!
UNDERSTOOD.
HMM... LOOKS LIKE GAWARA'S BEEN BEATEN.
AND THE MERMAIDS ESCAPED.
Heh heh heh...
?
EEK!!
EEEP!
AAAAA
PHEW!

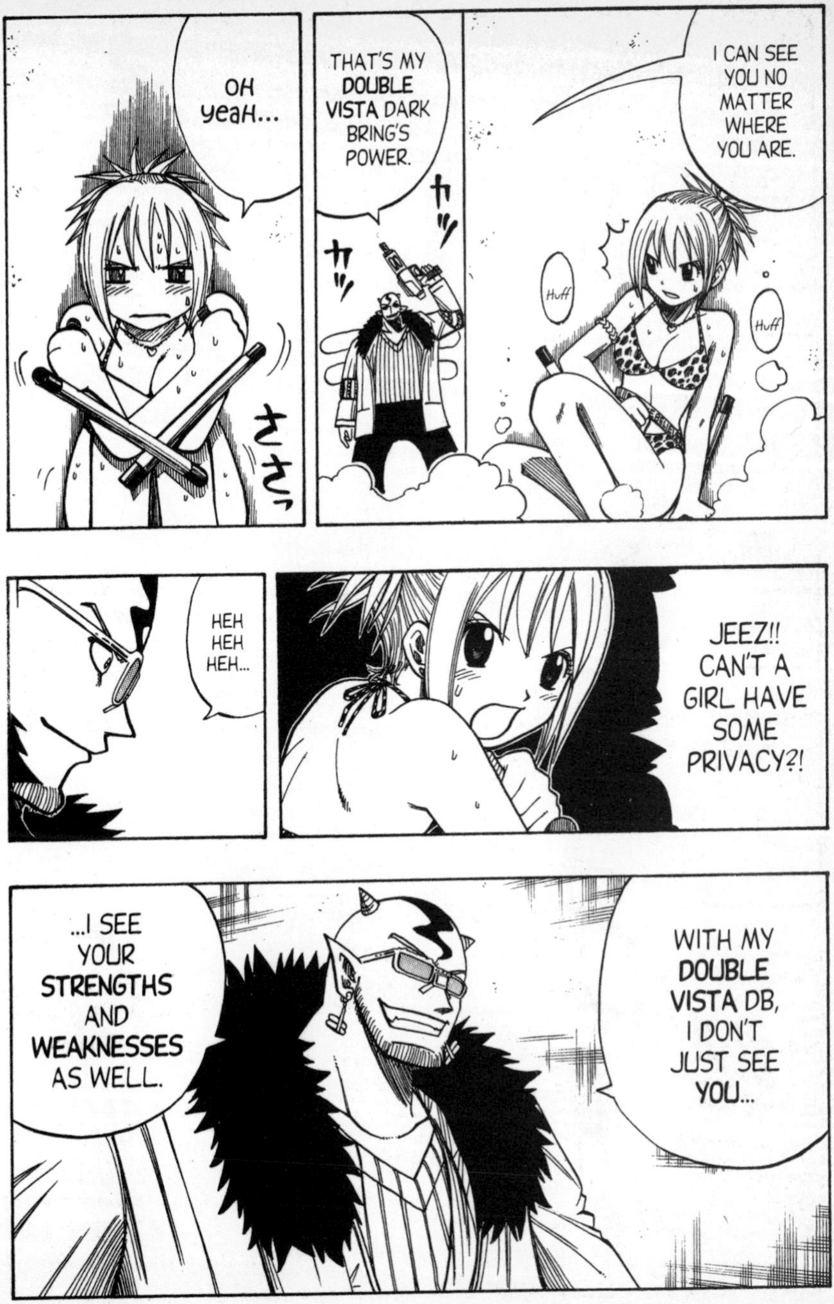
I CAN SEE YOU NO MATTER WHERE YOU ARE.
Huff
Huff
THAT'S MY DOUBLE VISTA DARK BRING'S POWER.
カッ
カッ
OH yeaH...
ささっ
JEEZ!! CAN'T A GIRL HAVE SOME PRIVACY?!
HEH HEH HEH...
WITH MY DOUBLE VISTA DB, I DON'T JUST SEE YOU...
...I SEE YOUR STRENGTHS AND WEAKNESSES AS WELL.

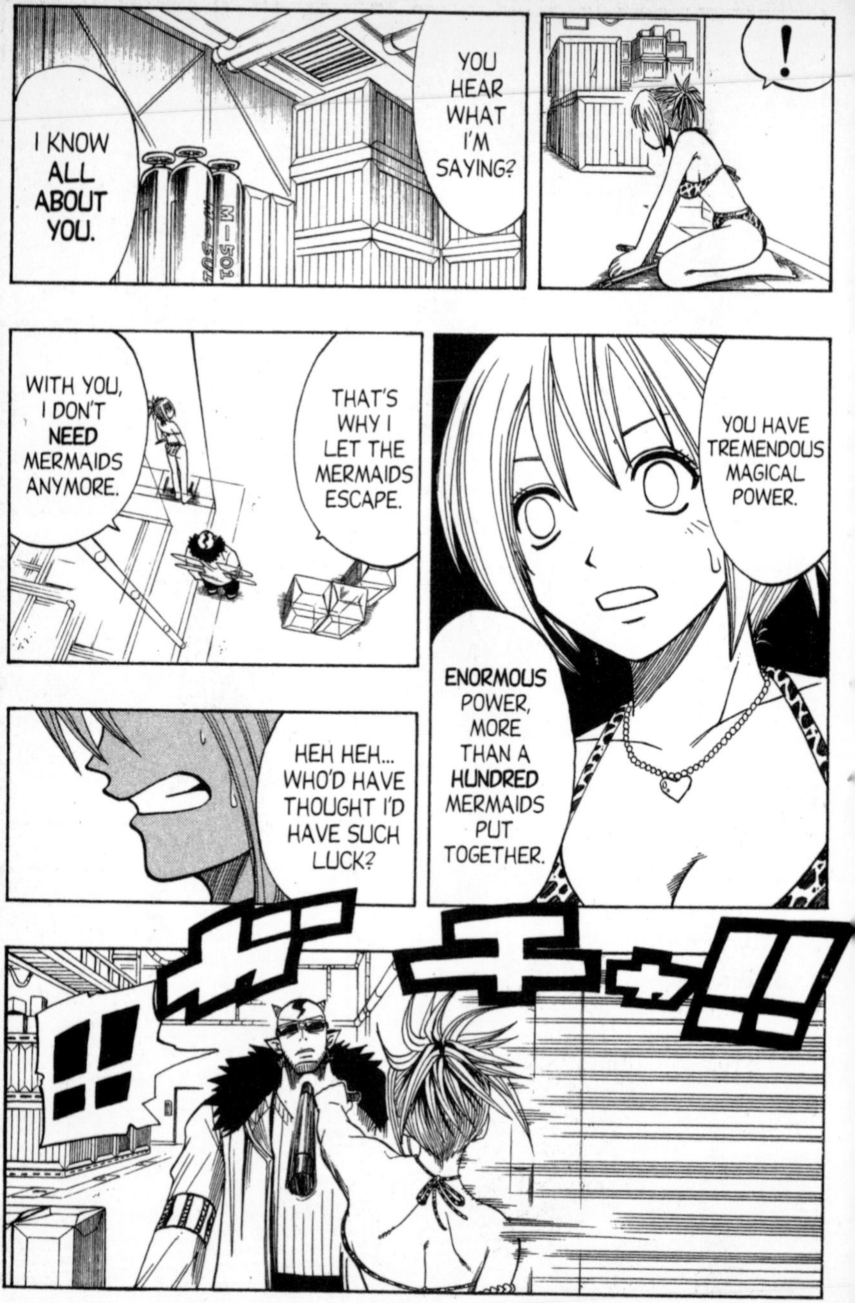

!
YOU HEAR WHAT I'M SAYING?
I KNOW **ALL ABOUT YOU.**
M-501
YOU HAVE TREMENDOUS MAGICAL POWER.
ENORMOUS POWER, MORE THAN A **HUNDRED** MERMAIDS PUT TOGETHER.
THAT'S WHY I LET THE MERMAIDS ESCAPE.
WITH YOU, I DON'T **NEED** MERMAIDS ANYMORE.
HEH HEH... WHO'D HAVE THOUGHT I'D HAVE SUCH LUCK?

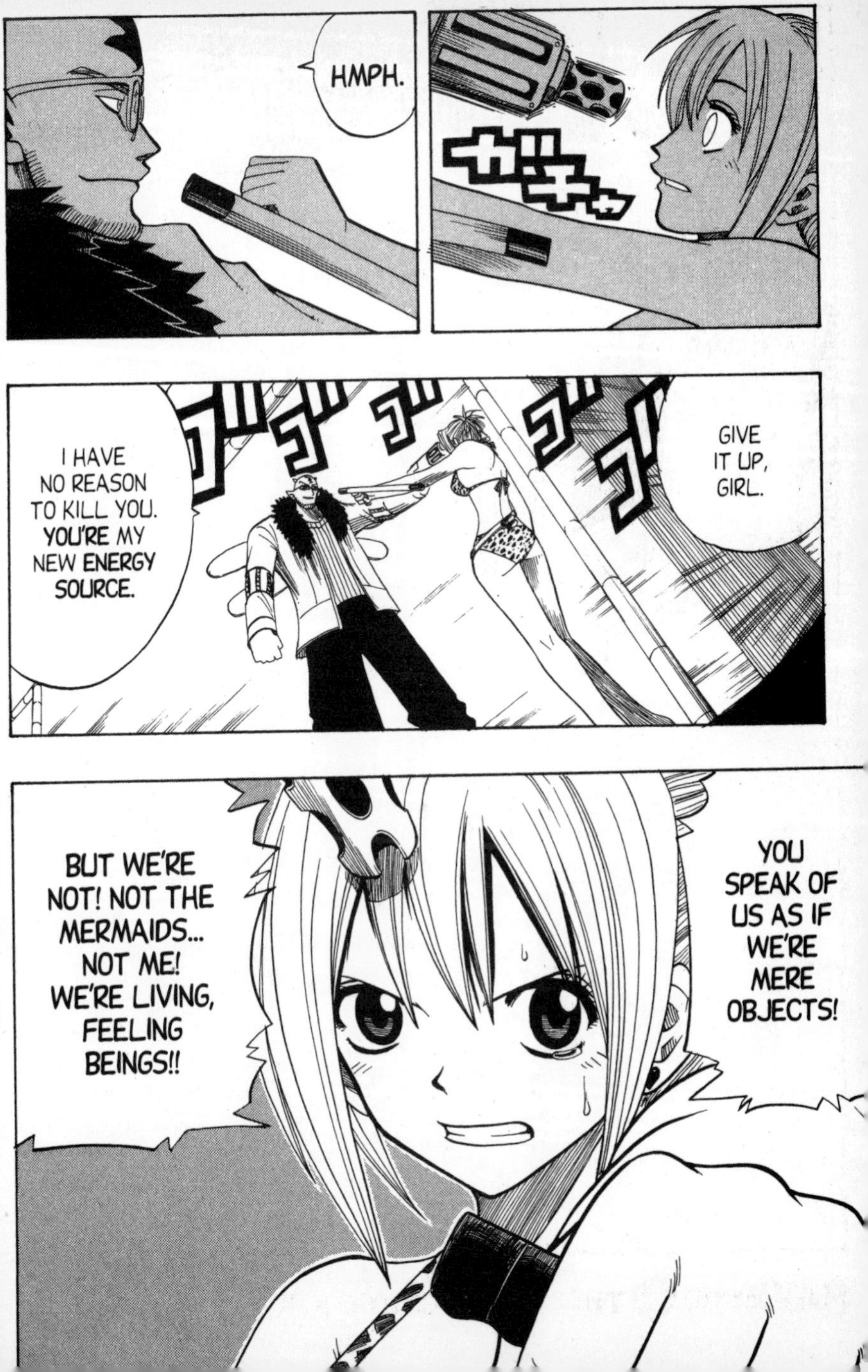
ガチャ
HMPH.
GIVE IT UP, GIRL.
I HAVE NO REASON TO KILL YOU. YOU'RE MY NEW ENERGY SOURCE.
YOU SPEAK OF US AS IF WE'RE MERE OBJECTS!
BUT WE'RE NOT! NOT THE MERMAIDS... NOT ME! WE'RE LIVING, FEELING BEINGS!!

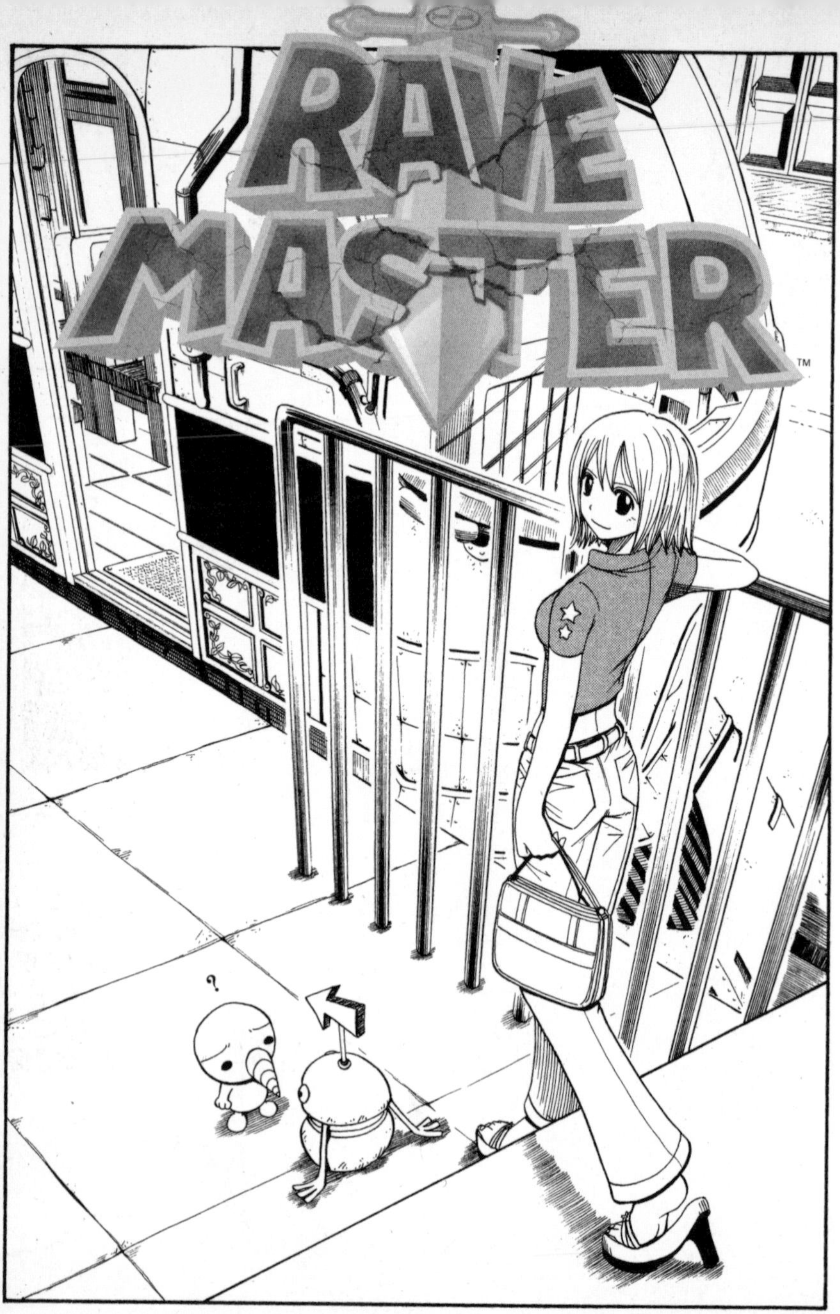
RAVE MASTER™
?

RAVE:110 THE TWO DEMON KINGS

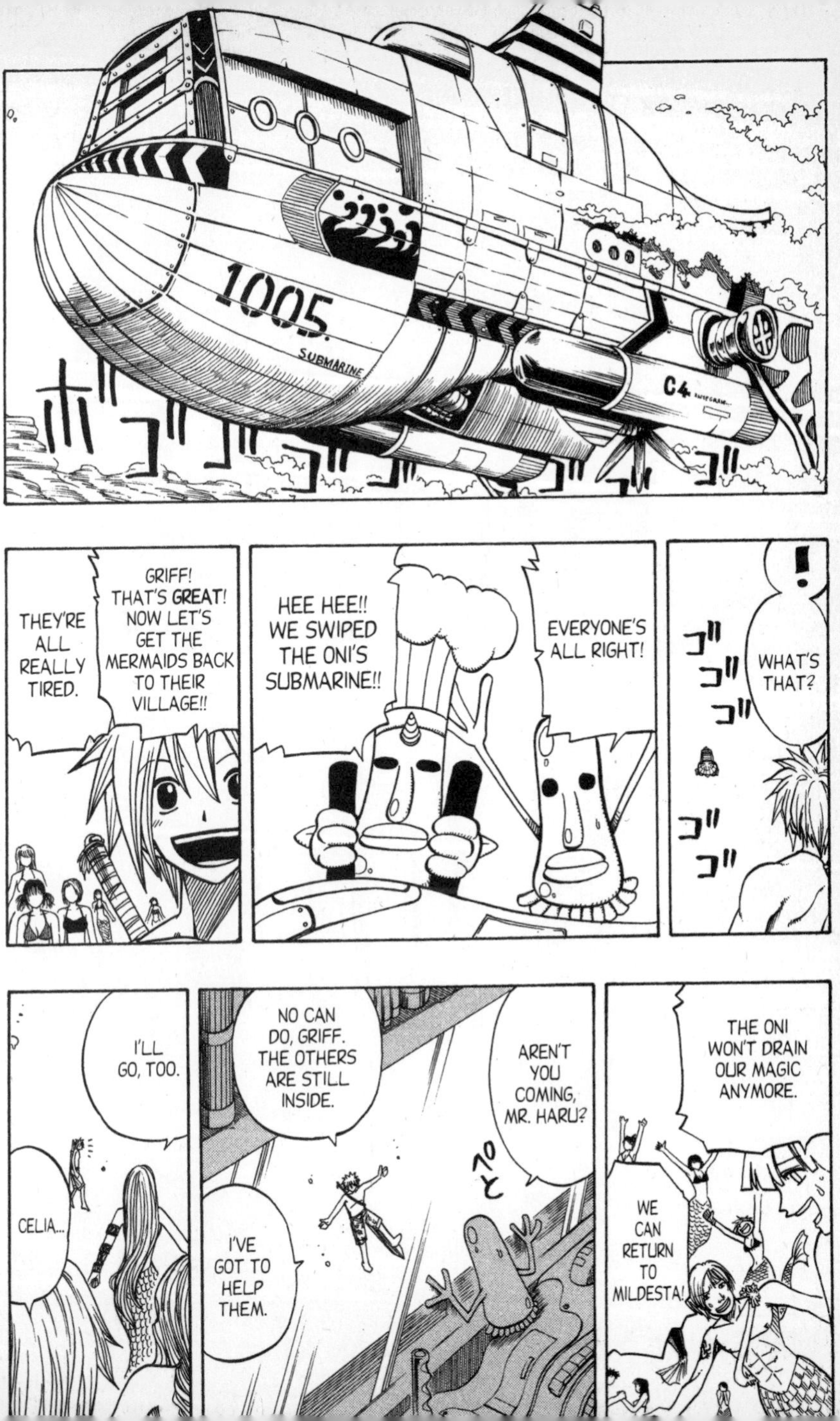
1005.
SUBMARINE
C4
!
WHAT'S THAT?
EVERYONE'S ALL RIGHT!
HEE HEE!! WE SWIPED THE ONI'S SUBMARINE!!
GRIFF! THAT'S **GREAT**! NOW LET'S GET THE MERMAIDS BACK TO THEIR VILLAGE!!
THEY'RE ALL REALLY TIRED.
THE ONI WON'T DRAIN OUR MAGIC ANYMORE.
WE CAN RETURN TO MILDESTA!
AREN'T YOU COMING, MR. HARU?
NO CAN DO, GRIFF. THE OTHERS ARE STILL INSIDE.
I'VE GOT TO HELP THEM.
I'LL GO, TOO.
CELIA...

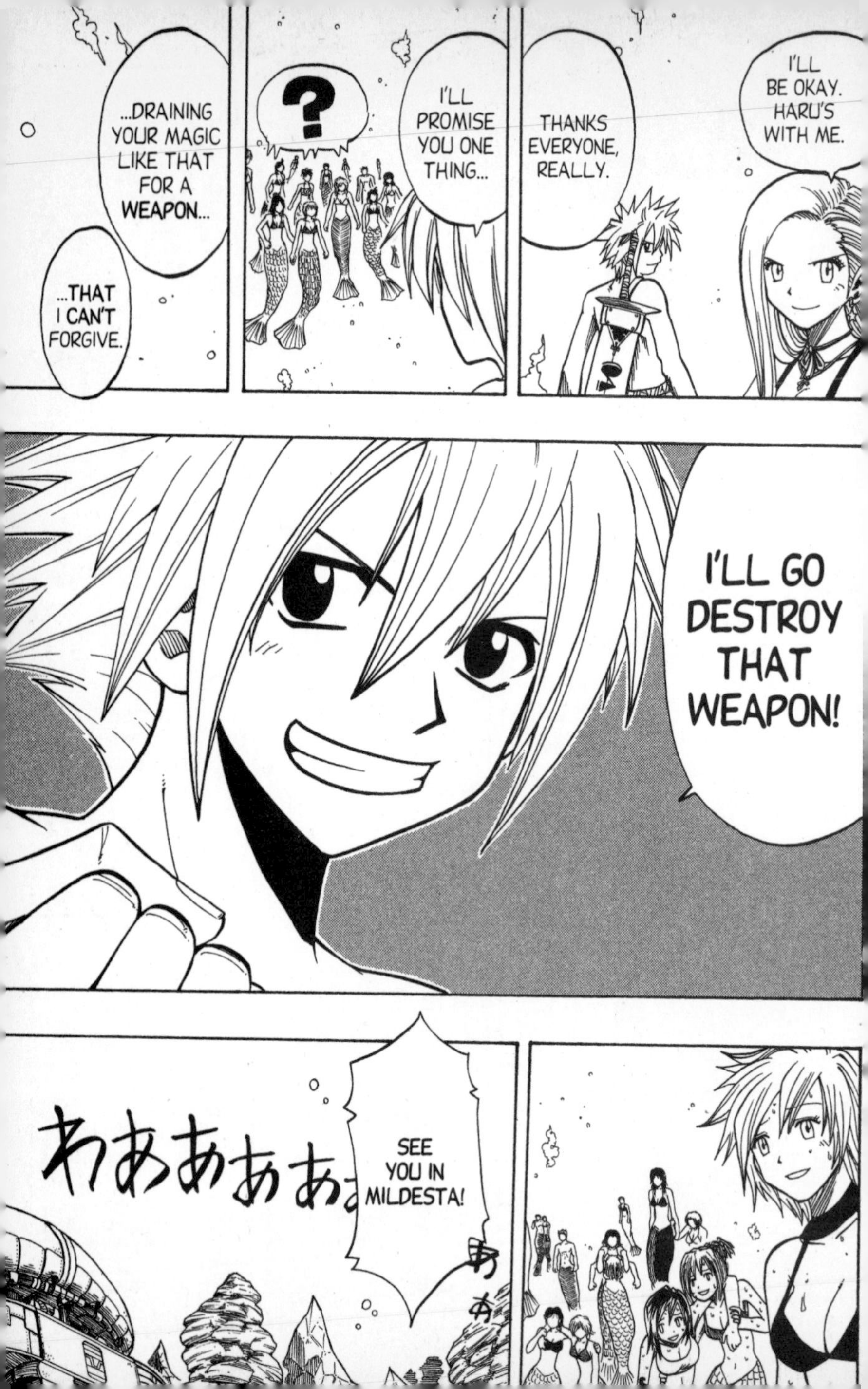
I'LL BE OKAY. HARU'S WITH ME.
THANKS EVERYONE, REALLY.
?
I'LL PROMISE YOU ONE THING...
...DRAINING YOUR MAGIC LIKE THAT FOR A WEAPON...
...THAT I CAN'T FORGIVE.
I'LL GO DESTROY THAT WEAPON!
SEE YOU IN MILDESTA!
わあああああ
ああ

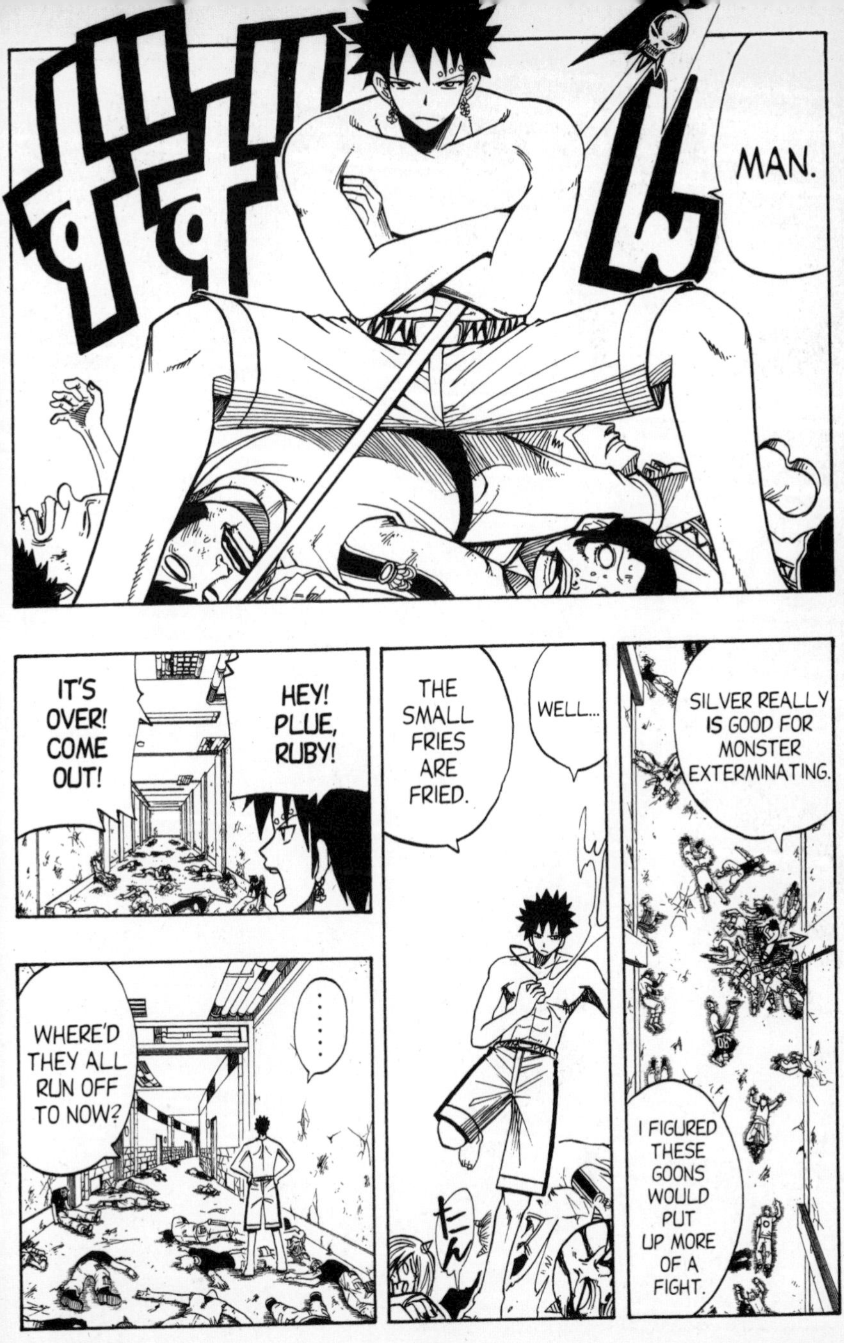
MAN.
SILVER REALLY IS GOOD FOR MONSTER EXTERMINATING.
I FIGURED THESE GOONS WOULD PUT UP MORE OF A FIGHT.
WELL...
THE SMALL FRIES ARE FRIED.
HEY! PLUE, RUBY!
IT'S OVER! COME OUT!
......
WHERE'D THEY ALL RUN OFF TO NOW?

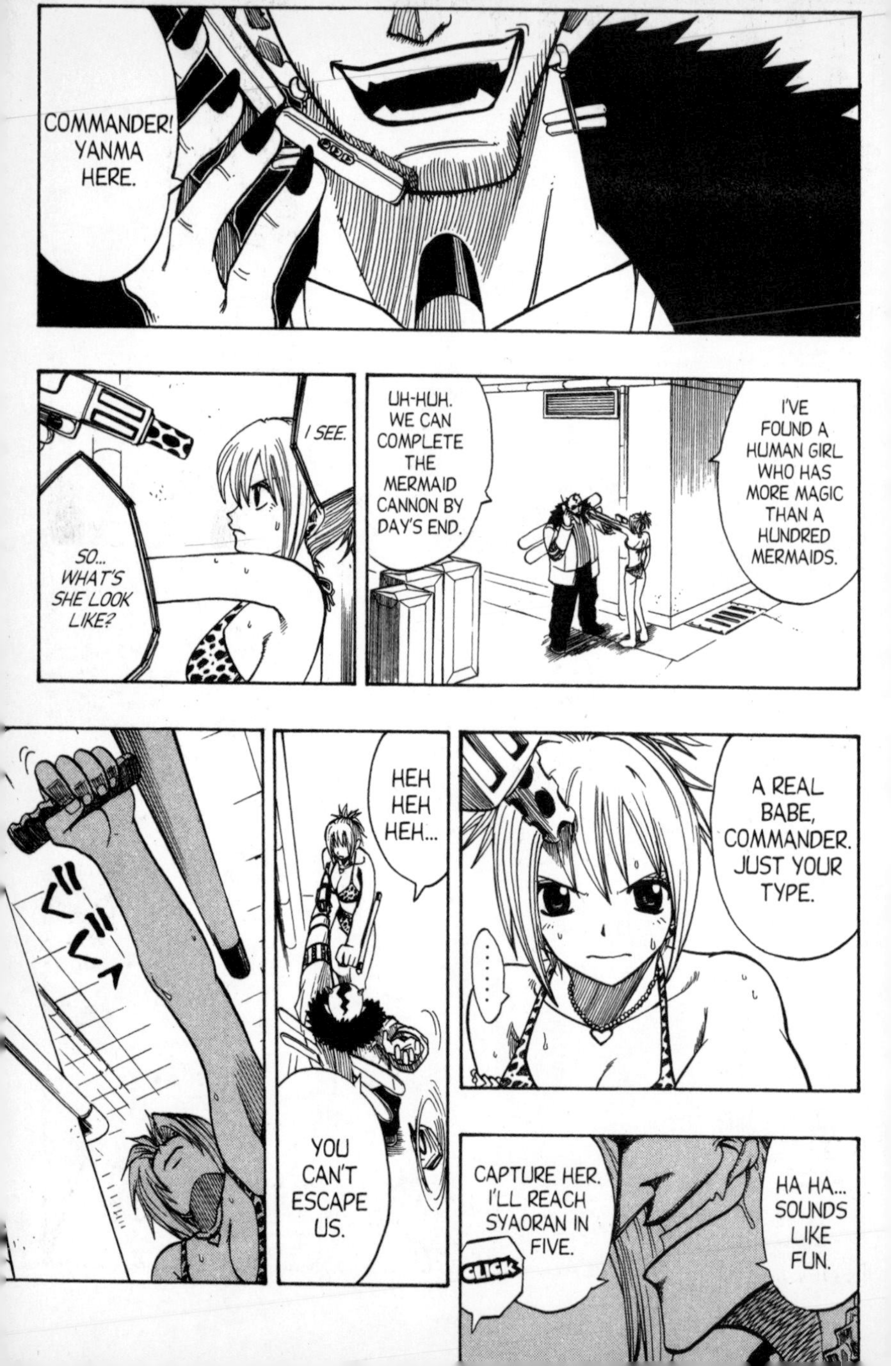

COMMANDER! YANMA HERE.
I'VE FOUND A HUMAN GIRL WHO HAS MORE MAGIC THAN A HUNDRED MERMAIDS.
UH-HUH. WE CAN COMPLETE THE MERMAID CANNON BY DAY'S END.
I SEE.
SO... WHAT'S SHE LOOK LIKE?
A REAL BABE, COMMANDER. JUST YOUR TYPE.
......
HA HA... SOUNDS LIKE FUN.
CAPTURE HER. I'LL REACH SYAORAN IN FIVE.
CLICK
HEH HEH HEH...
YOU CAN'T ESCAPE US.

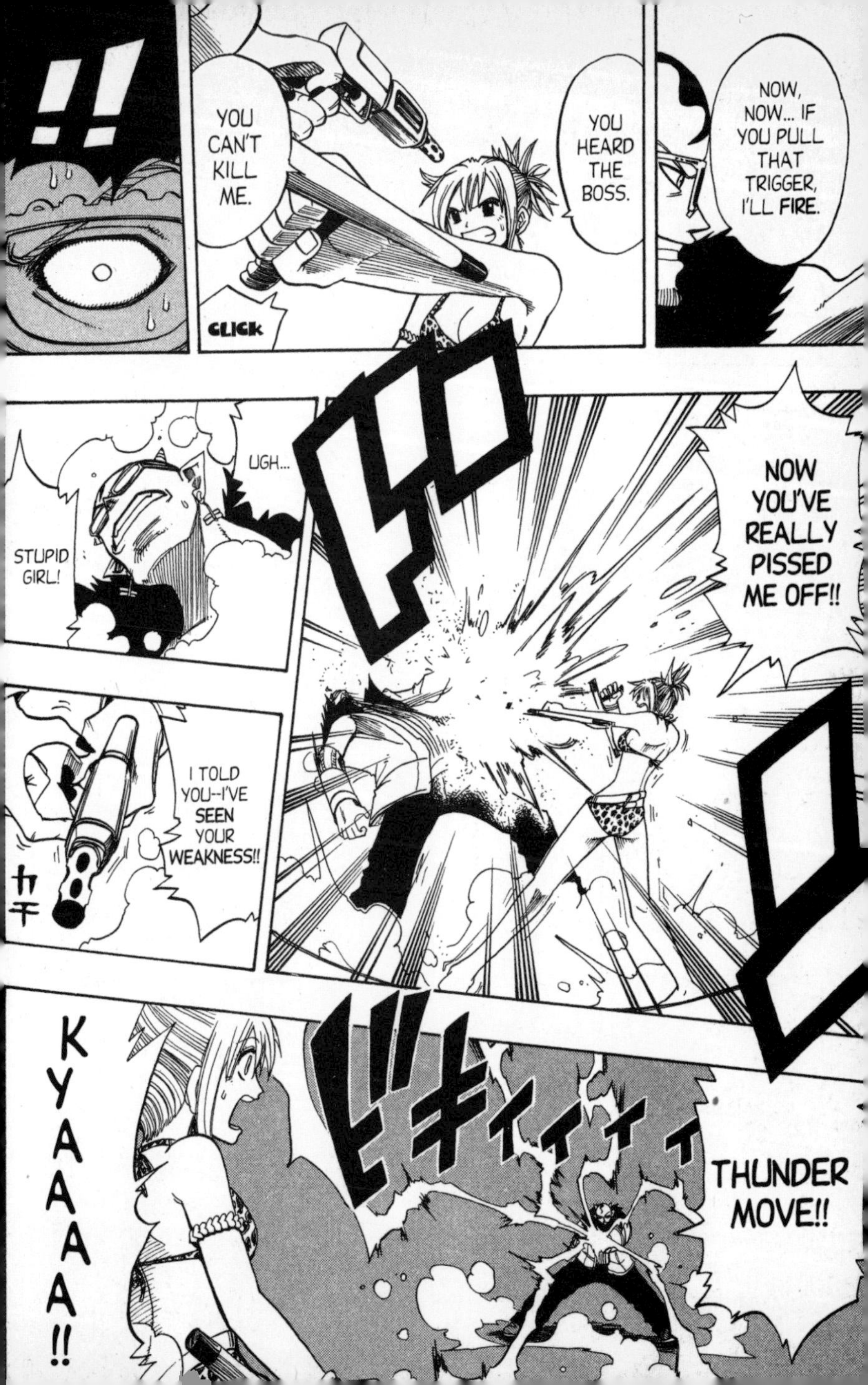
NOW, NOW... IF YOU PULL THAT TRIGGER, I'LL FIRE.
YOU HEARD THE BOSS.
YOU CAN'T KILL ME.
CLICK
!!
NOW YOU'VE REALLY PISSED ME OFF!!
UGH...
STUPID GIRL!
I TOLD YOU--I'VE SEEN YOUR WEAKNESS!!
カチ
THUNDER MOVE!!
KYAAAAA!!

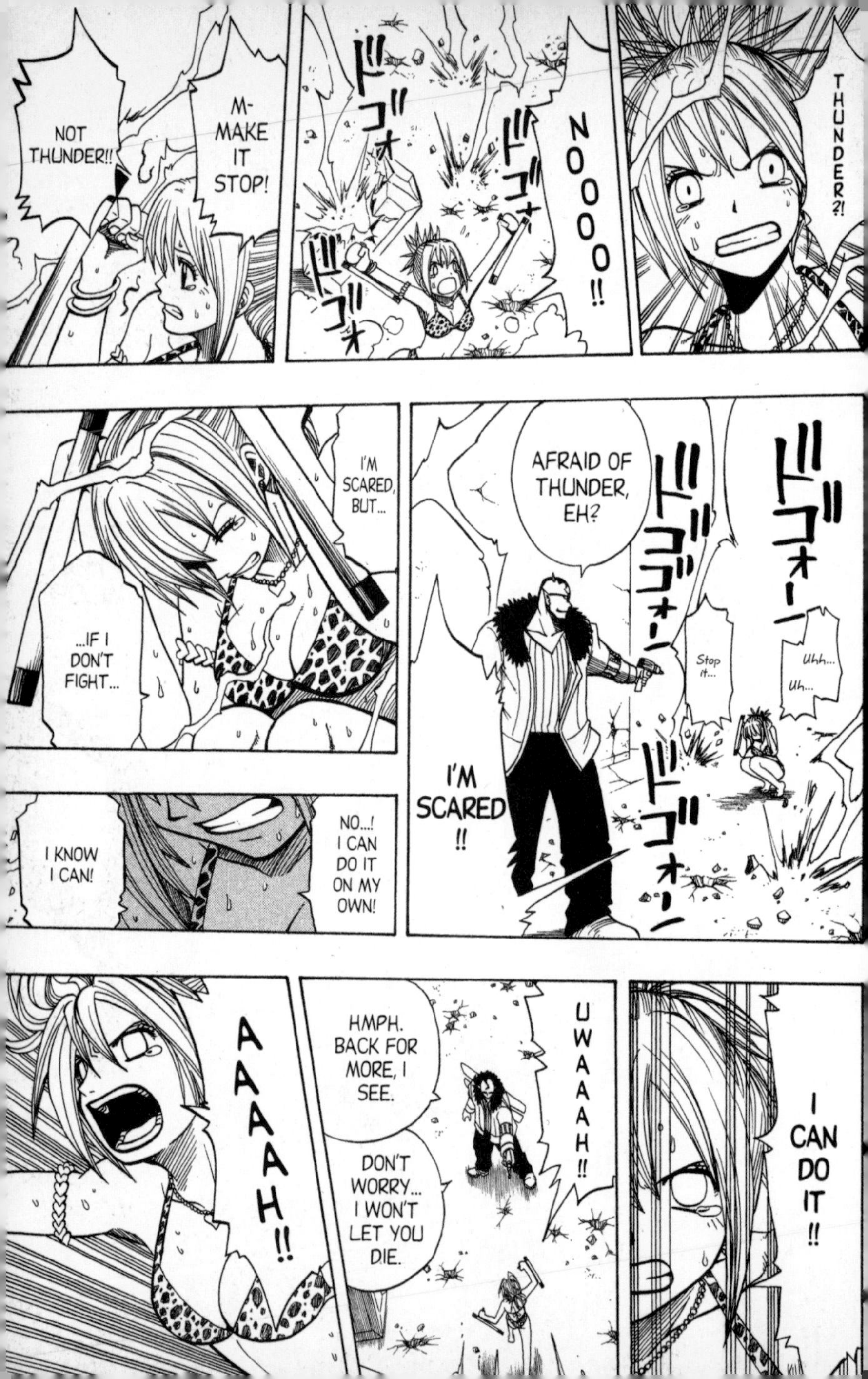
THUNDER?!
ドゴォ
ドゴォ
ドゴォ
NOOOOO!!
M- MAKE IT STOP!
NOT THUNDER!!
ドゴォーン
ドゴゴォーン
Uhh... Uh...
Stop it...
AFRAID OF THUNDER, EH?
ドゴォーン
I'M SCARED!!
I'M SCARED, BUT...
...IF I DON'T FIGHT...
NO...! I CAN DO IT ON MY OWN!
I KNOW I CAN!
I CAN DO IT!!
UWAAAAH!!
HMPH. BACK FOR MORE, I SEE.
DON'T WORRY... I WON'T LET YOU DIE.
AAAAH!!

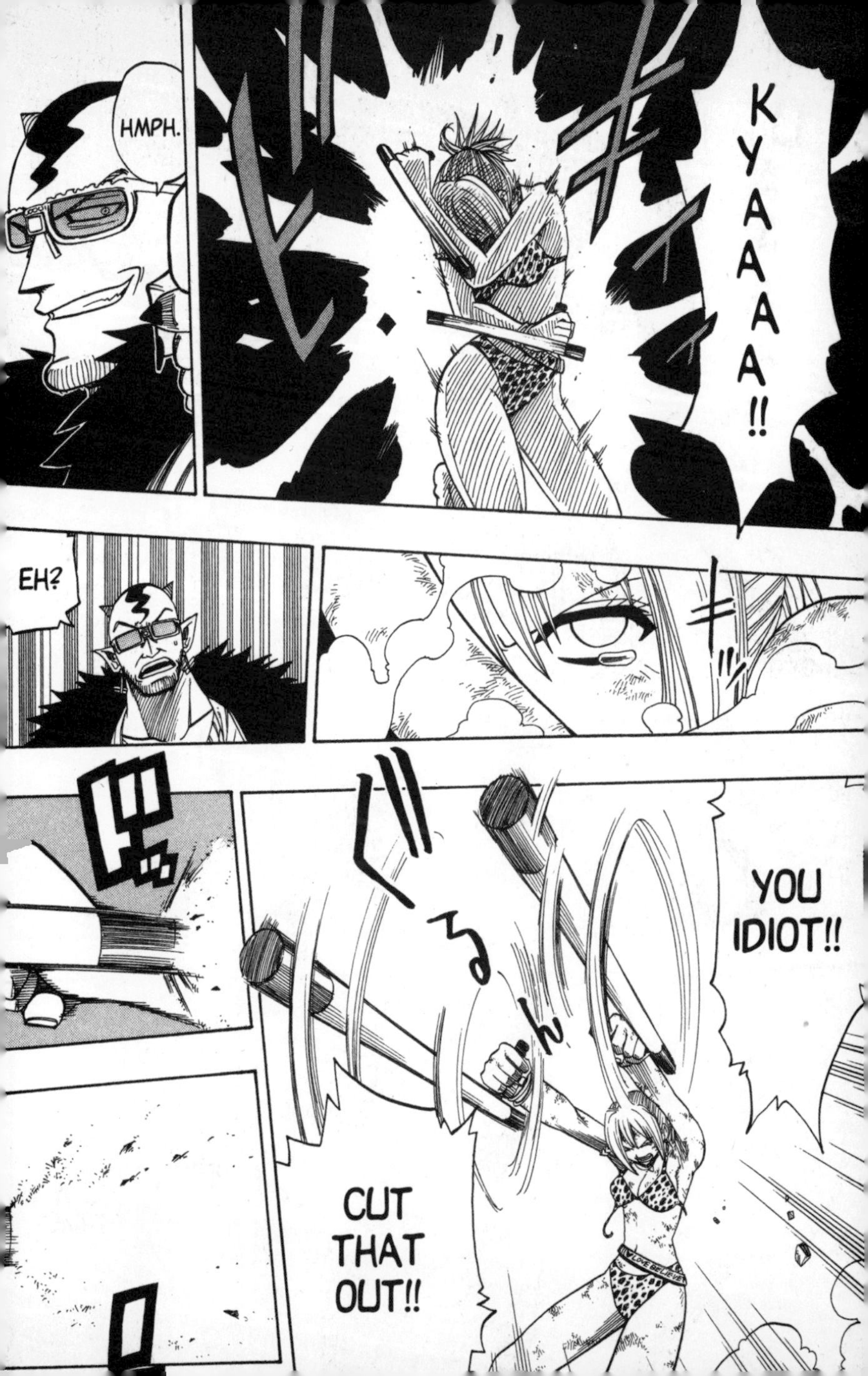
KYAAAAA!!
HMPH.
EH?
YOU IDIOT!!
CUT THAT OUT!!

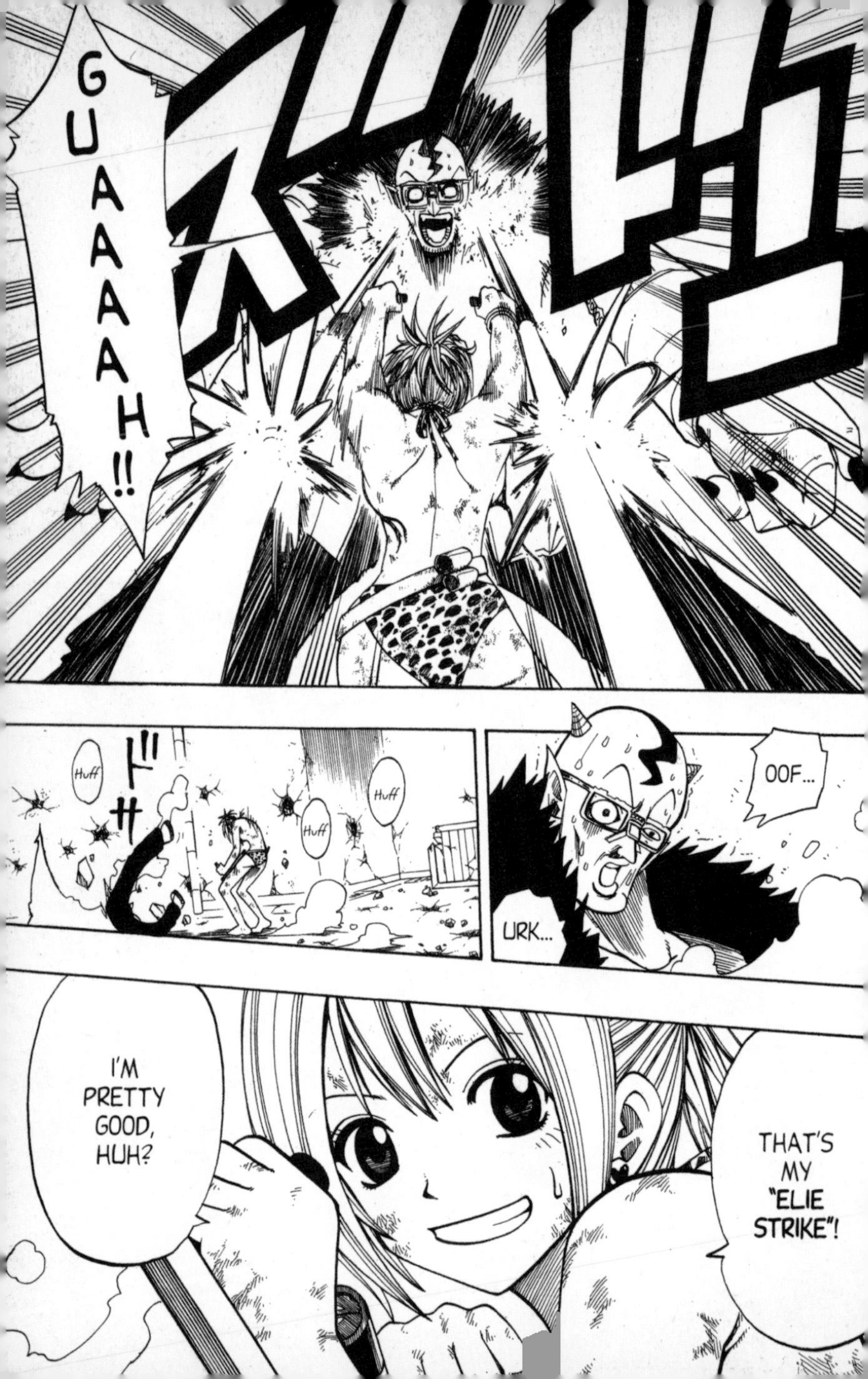
GUAAAAH!!
OOF...
URK...
Huff
Huff
Huff
THAT'S MY "ELIE STRIKE"!
I'M PRETTY GOOD, HUH?

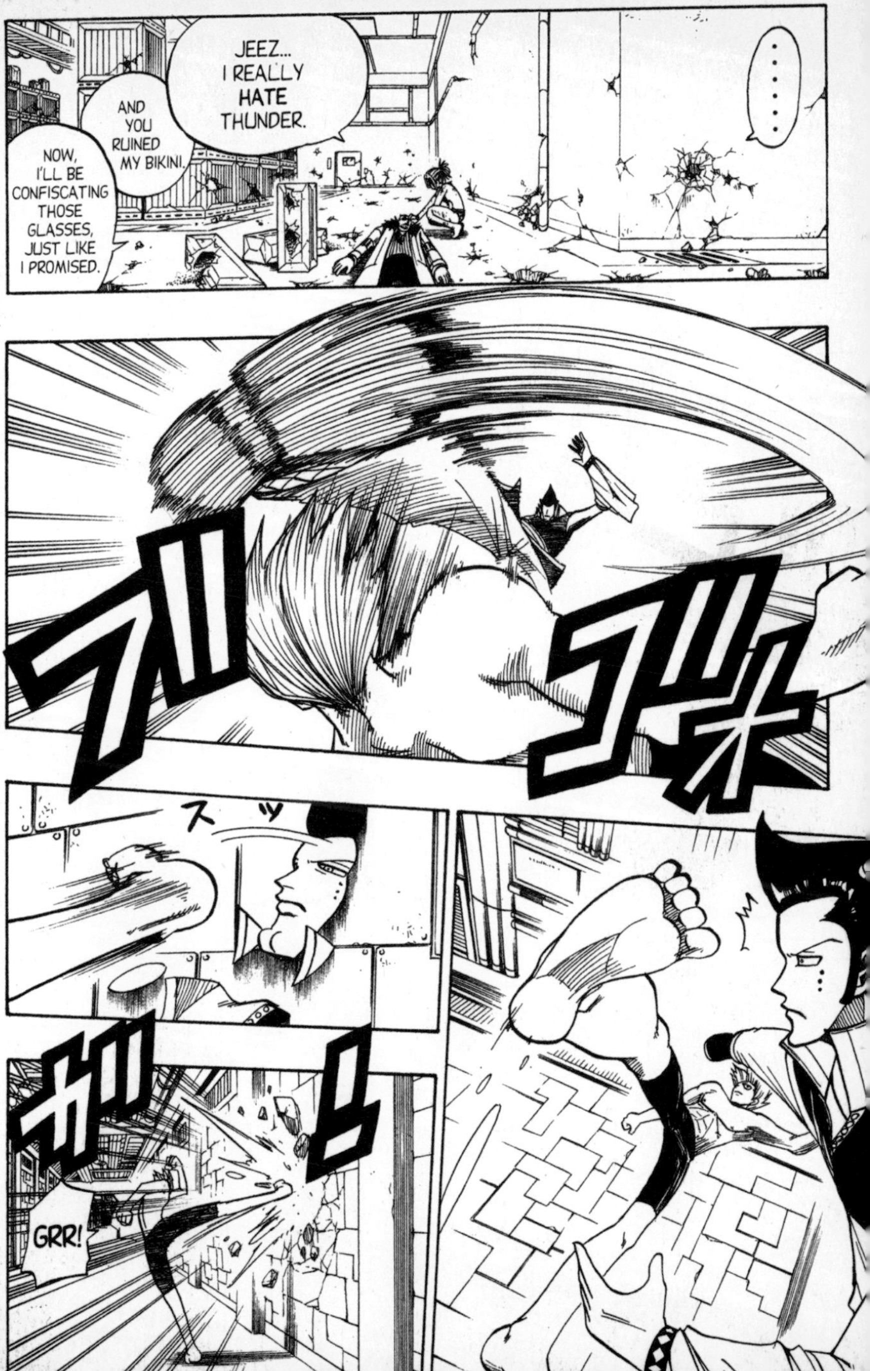
......
JEEZ... I REALLY HATE THUNDER.
AND YOU RUINED MY BIKINI.
NOW, I'LL BE CONFISCATING THOSE GLASSES, JUST LIKE I PROMISED.
スッ
GRR!

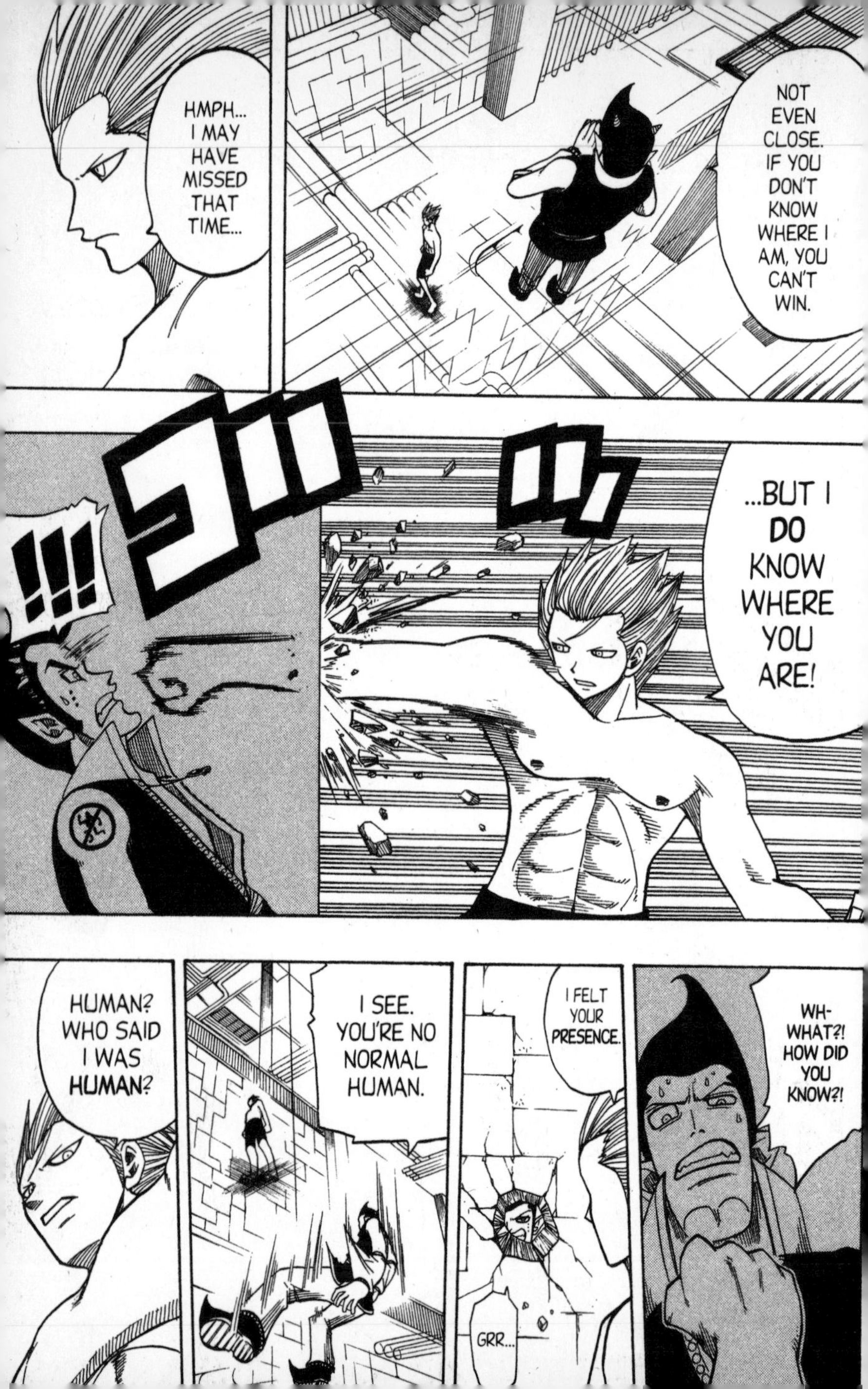
NOT EVEN CLOSE. IF YOU DON'T KNOW WHERE I AM, YOU CAN'T WIN.
HMPH... I MAY HAVE MISSED THAT TIME...
...BUT I **DO** KNOW WHERE YOU ARE!
!!!
WH-WHAT?! HOW DID YOU KNOW?!
I FELT YOUR PRESENCE.
GRR...
I SEE. YOU'RE NO NORMAL HUMAN.
HUMAN? WHO SAID I WAS **HUMAN**?

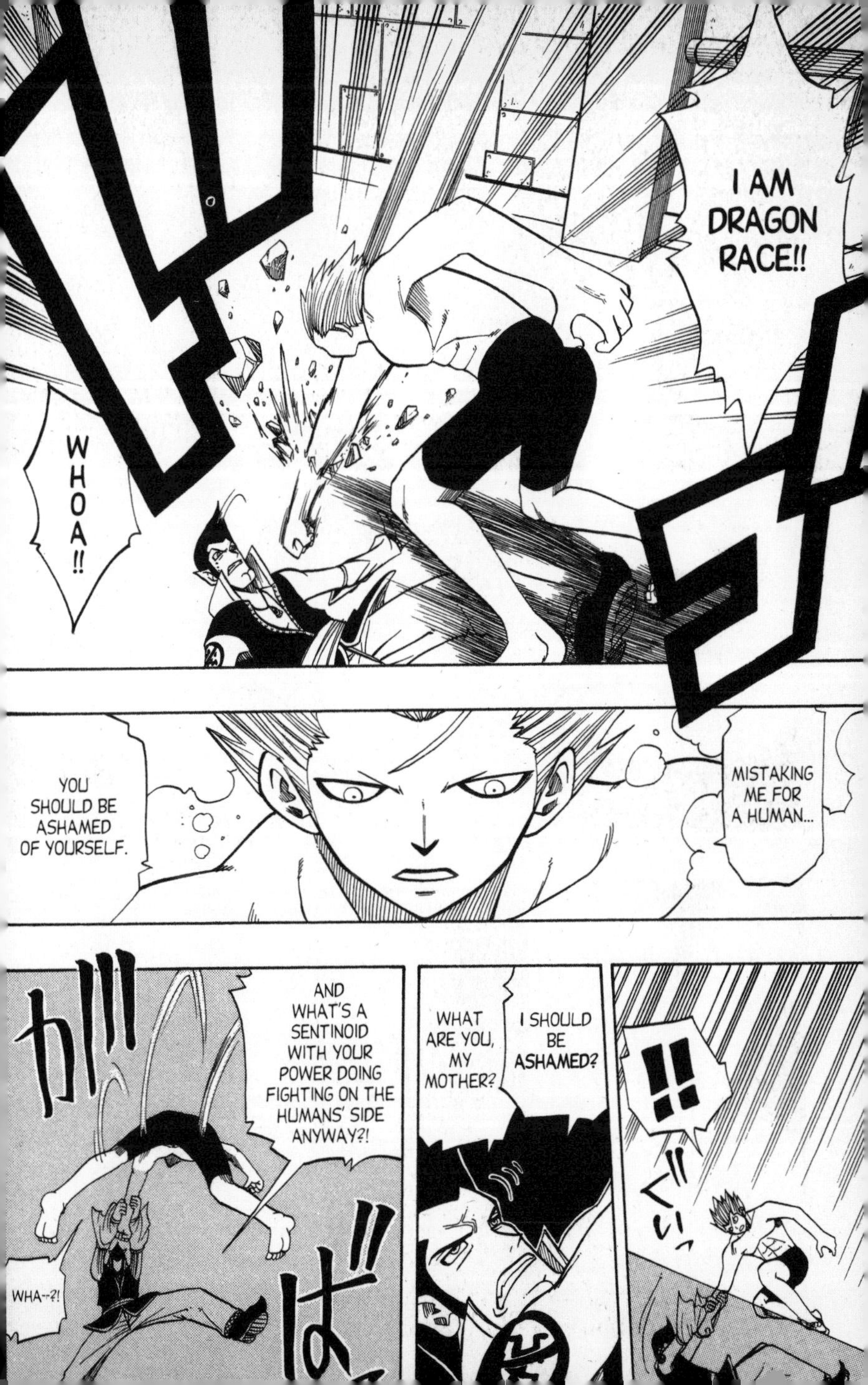

I AM DRAGON RACE!!
WHOA!!
MISTAKING ME FOR A HUMAN...
YOU SHOULD BE ASHAMED OF YOURSELF.
!!
I SHOULD BE ASHAMED?
WHAT ARE YOU, MY MOTHER?
AND WHAT'S A SENTINOID WITH YOUR POWER DOING FIGHTING ON THE HUMANS' SIDE ANYWAY?!
WHA--?!

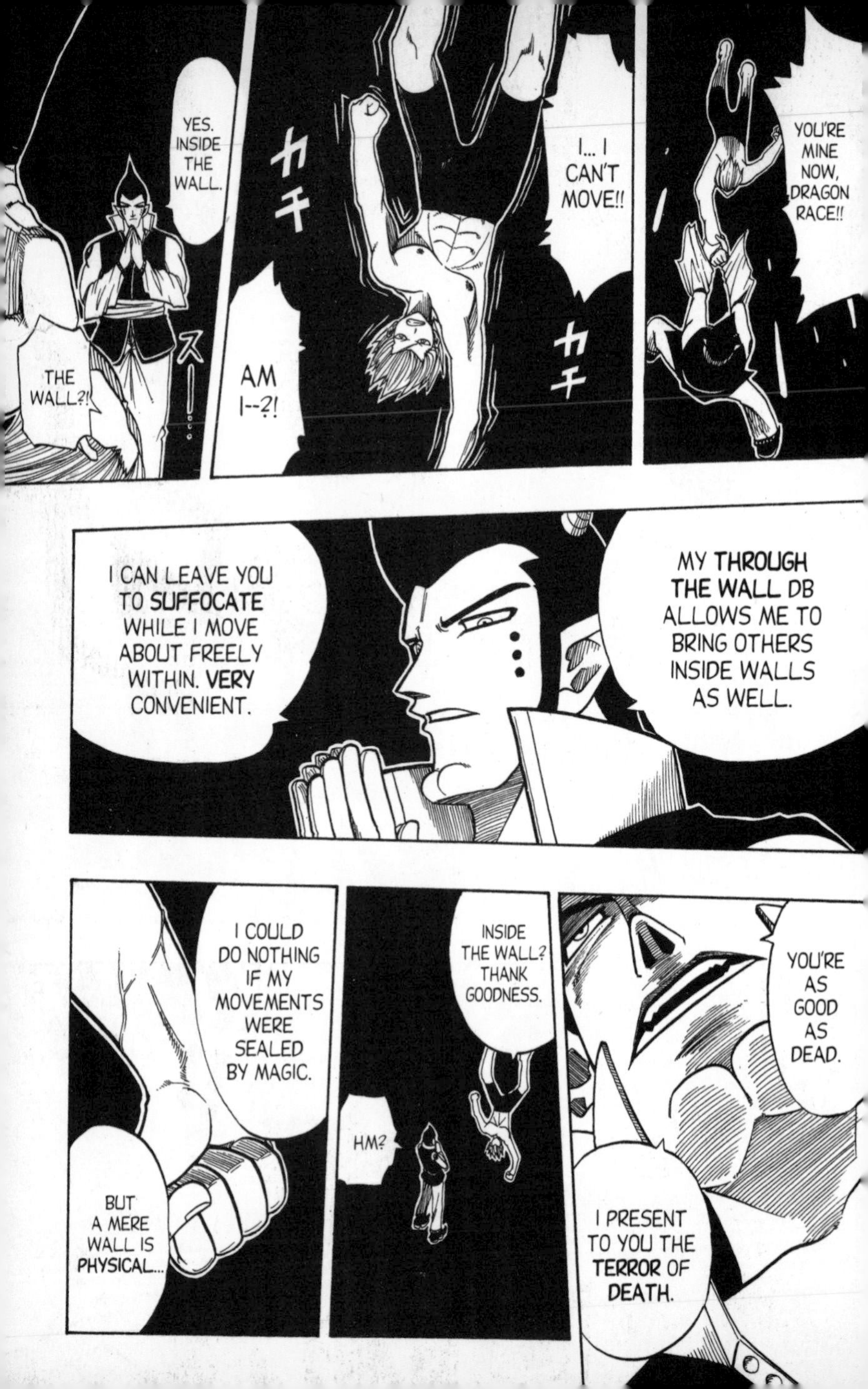

YOU'RE MINE NOW, DRAGON RACE!!
I... I CAN'T MOVE!!
カチ
カチ
AM I--?!
YES. INSIDE THE WALL.
スー…
THE WALL?!
MY **THROUGH THE WALL** DB ALLOWS ME TO BRING OTHERS INSIDE WALLS AS WELL.
I CAN LEAVE YOU TO **SUFFOCATE** WHILE I MOVE ABOUT FREELY WITHIN. **VERY** CONVENIENT.
YOU'RE AS GOOD AS DEAD.
I PRESENT TO YOU THE **TERROR** OF **DEATH.**
INSIDE THE WALL? THANK GOODNESS.
HM?
I COULD DO NOTHING IF MY MOVEMENTS WERE SEALED BY MAGIC.
BUT A MERE WALL IS **PHYSICAL...**

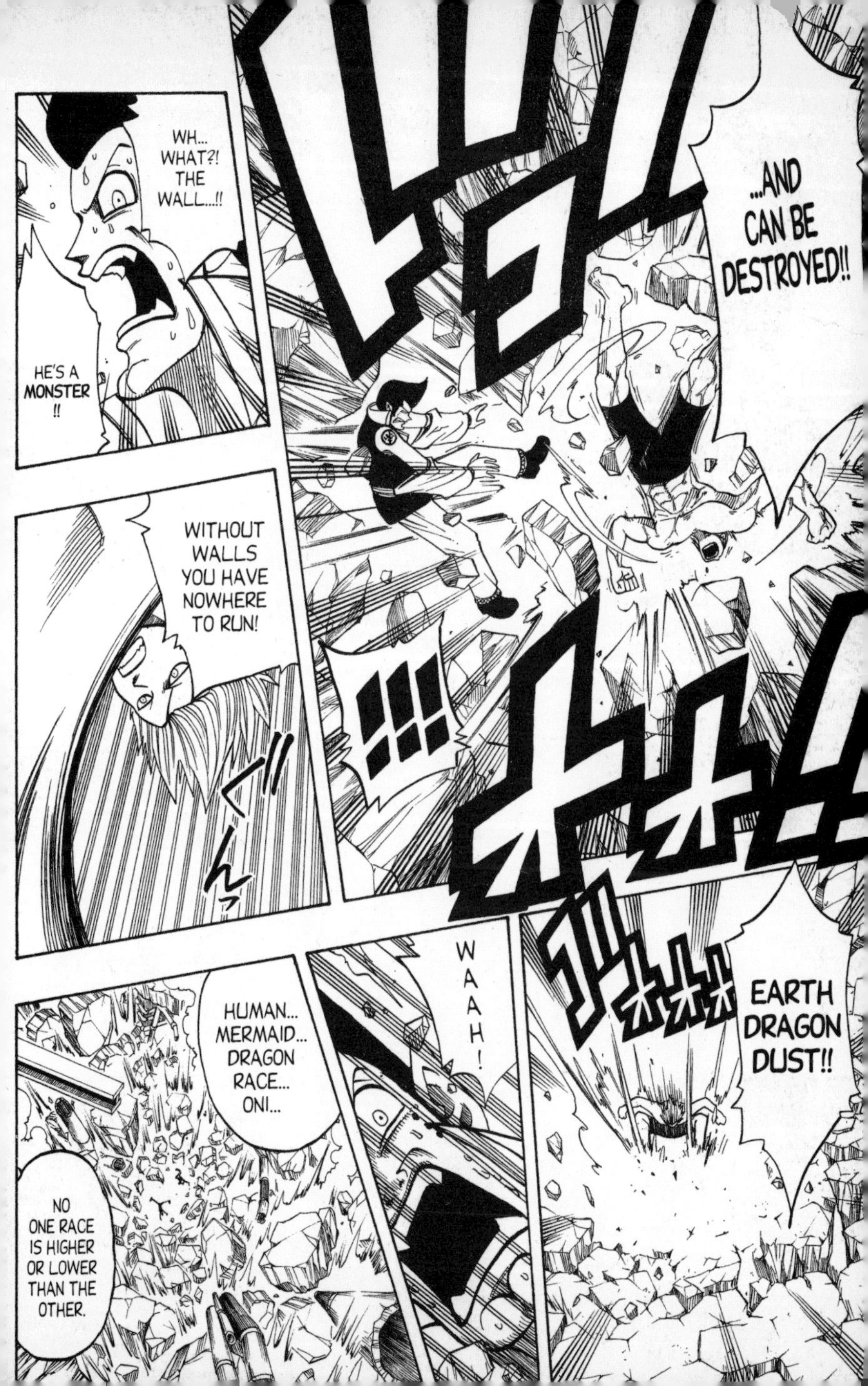
...AND CAN BE DESTROYED!!
!!!
WH... WHAT?! THE WALL...!!
HE'S A MONSTER !!
WITHOUT WALLS YOU HAVE NOWHERE TO RUN!
EARTH DRAGON DUST!!
WAAH!
HUMAN... MERMAID... DRAGON RACE... ONI...
NO ONE RACE IS HIGHER OR LOWER THAN THE OTHER.

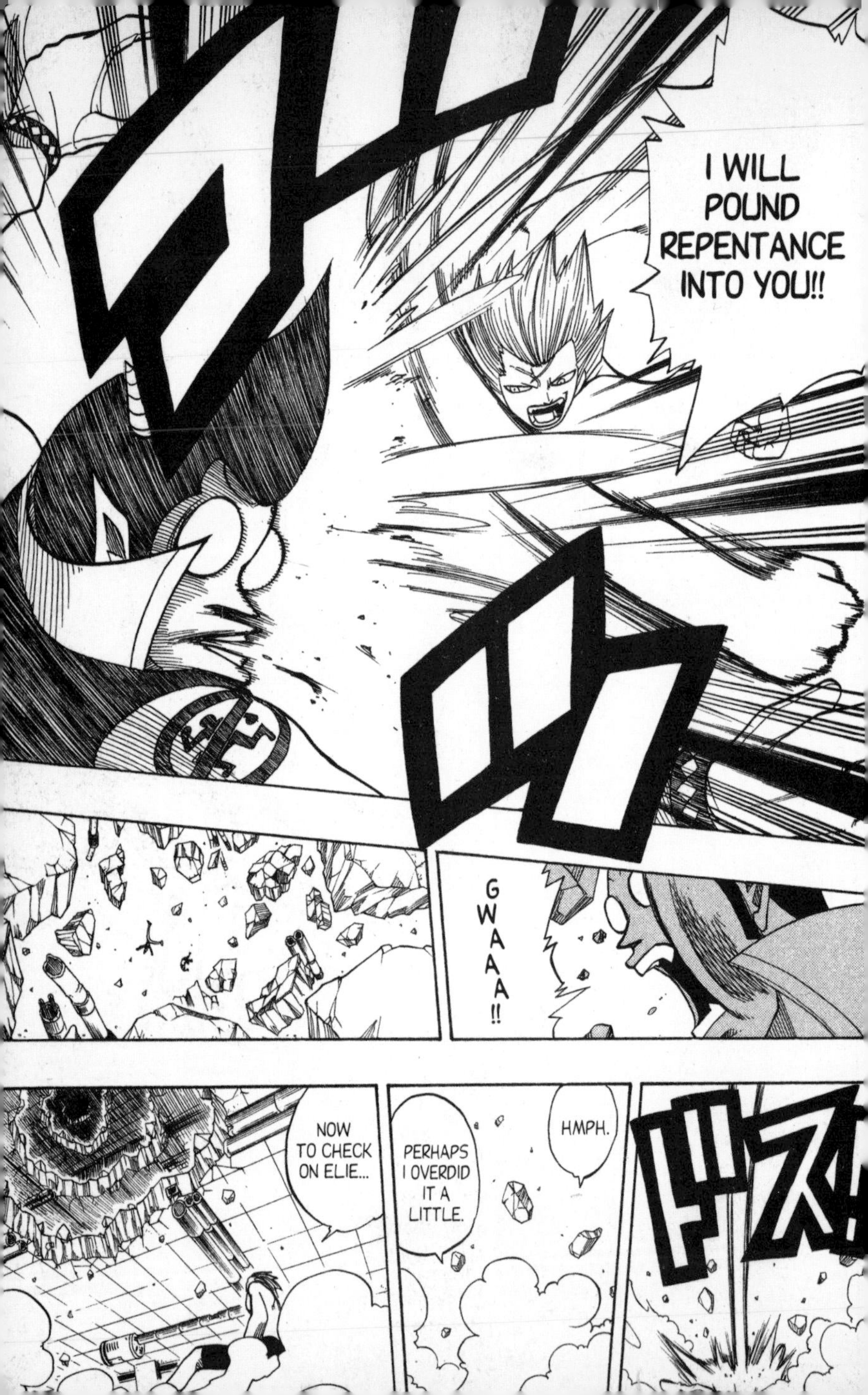
I WILL POUND REPENTANCE INTO YOU!!
GWAAAA!!
HMPH.
PERHAPS I OVERDID IT A LITTLE.
NOW TO CHECK ON ELIE...

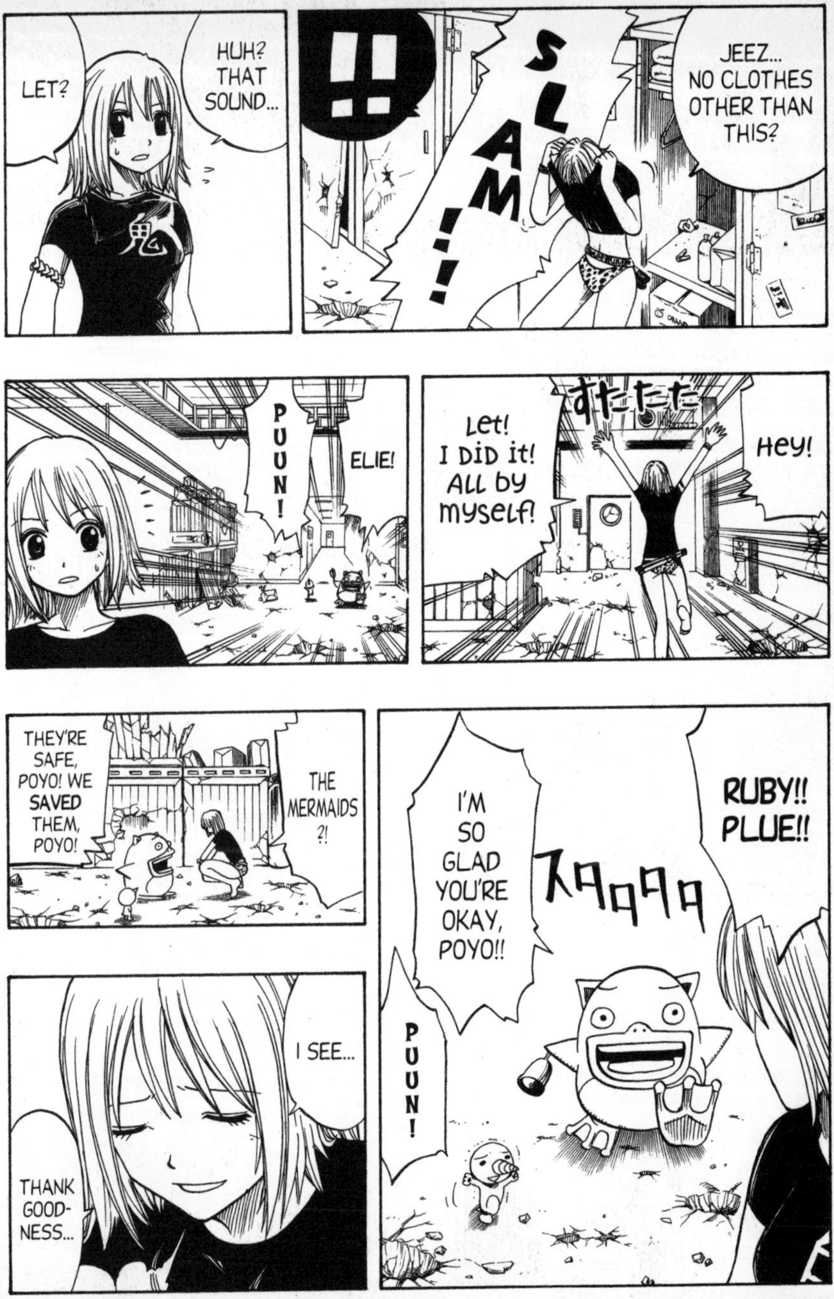
JEEZ... NO CLOTHES OTHER THAN THIS?
SLAM!!!
!!
HUH? THAT SOUND...
LET?
Hey!
すたたた
Let! I DID it! ALL by myself!
ELIE!
PUUN!
RUBY!! PLUE!!
スタタタタ
I'M SO GLAD YOU'RE OKAY, POYO!!
PUUN!
THE MERMAIDS?!
THEY'RE SAFE, POYO! WE SAVED THEM, POYO!
I SEE...
THANK GOOD-NESS...

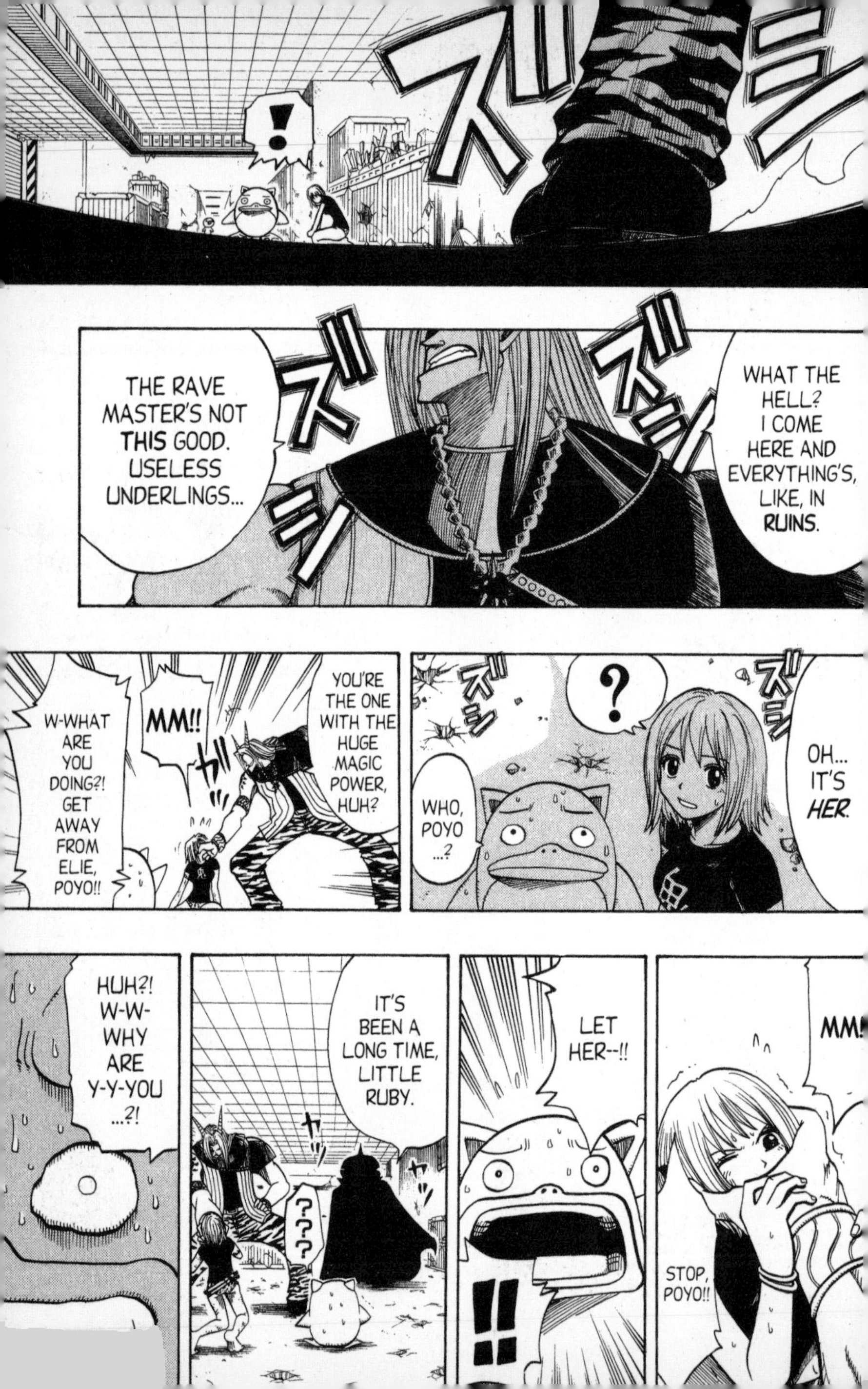
!
WHAT THE HELL? I COME HERE AND EVERYTHING'S, LIKE, IN RUINS.
THE RAVE MASTER'S NOT THIS GOOD. USELESS UNDERLINGS...
OH... IT'S HER.
?
WHO, POYO ...?
YOU'RE THE ONE WITH THE HUGE MAGIC POWER, HUH?
MM!!
W-WHAT ARE YOU DOING?! GET AWAY FROM ELIE, POYO!!
MM!
STOP, POYO!!
LET HER--!!
!!
IT'S BEEN A LONG TIME, LITTLE RUBY.
???
HUH?! W-W-WHY ARE Y-Y-YOU ...?!

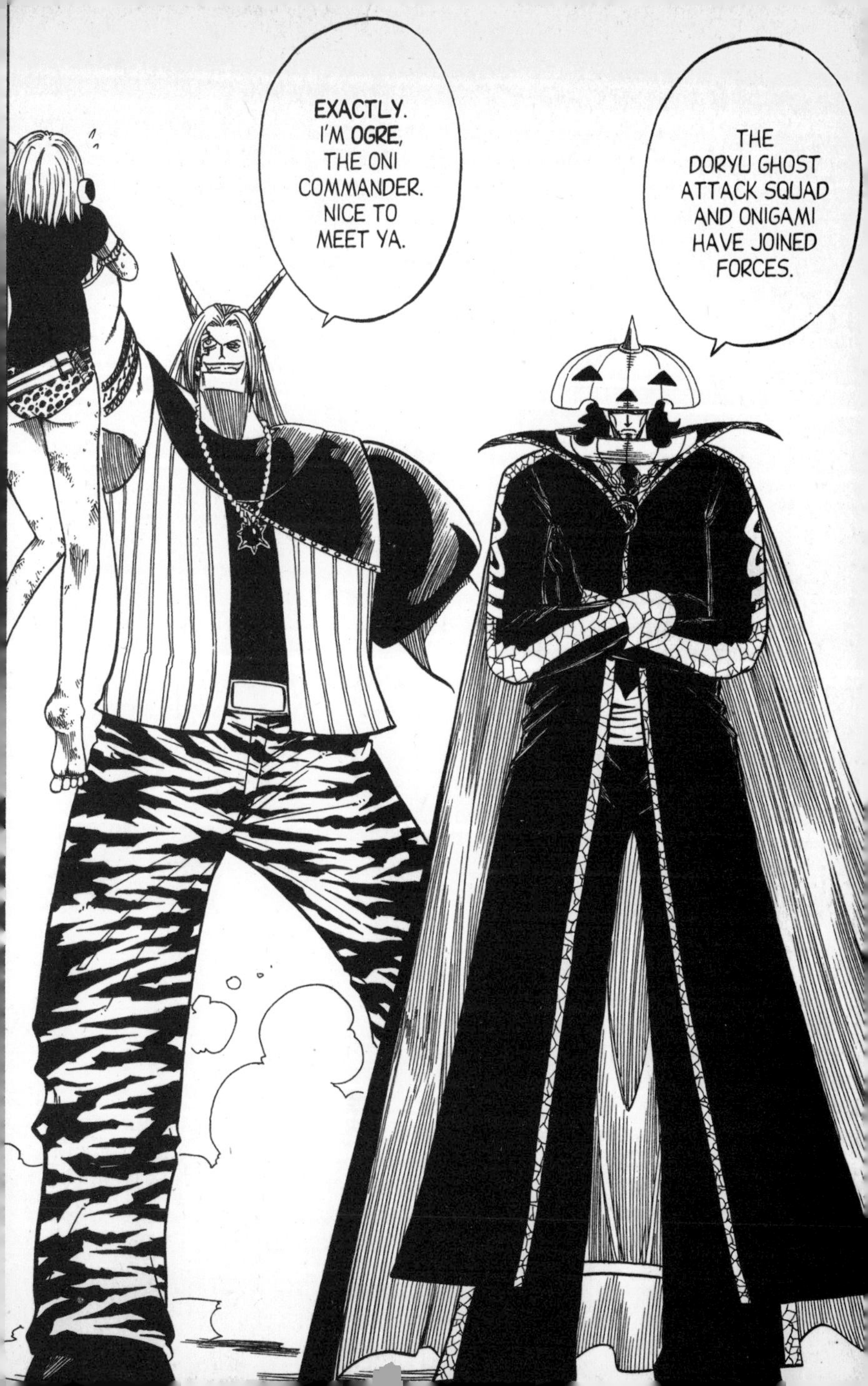
THE DORYU GHOST ATTACK SQUAD AND ONIGAMI HAVE JOINED FORCES.
EXACTLY. I'M OGRE, THE ONI COMMANDER. NICE TO MEET YA.

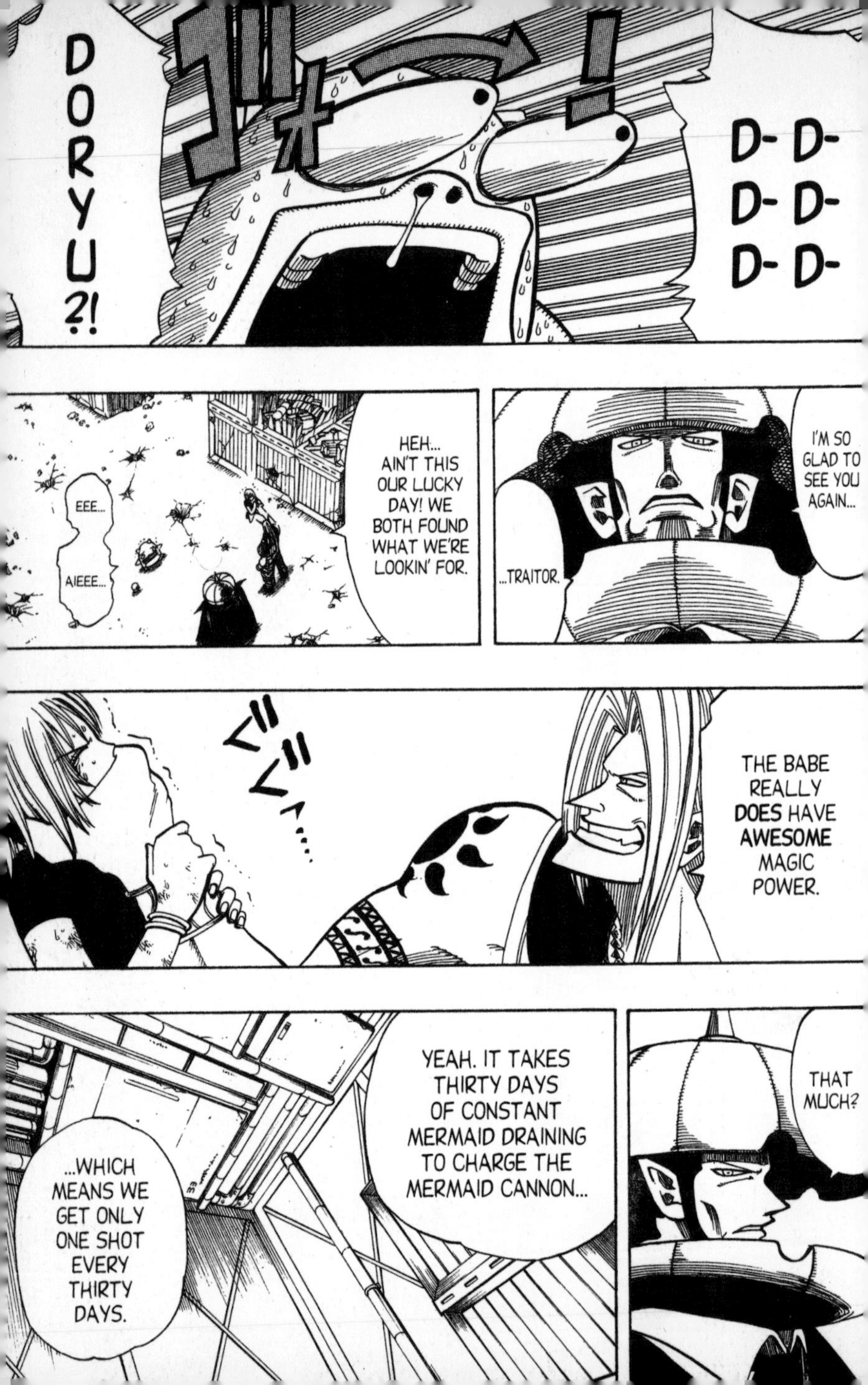
D- D-
D- D-
D- D-
DORYU?!
I'M SO GLAD TO SEE YOU AGAIN...
...TRAITOR.
HEH... AIN'T THIS OUR LUCKY DAY! WE BOTH FOUND WHAT WE'RE LOOKIN' FOR.
EEE...
AIEEE...
THE BABE REALLY **DOES** HAVE **AWESOME** MAGIC POWER.
THAT MUCH?
YEAH. IT TAKES THIRTY DAYS OF CONSTANT MERMAID DRAINING TO CHARGE THE MERMAID CANNON...
...WHICH MEANS WE GET ONLY ONE SHOT EVERY THIRTY DAYS.

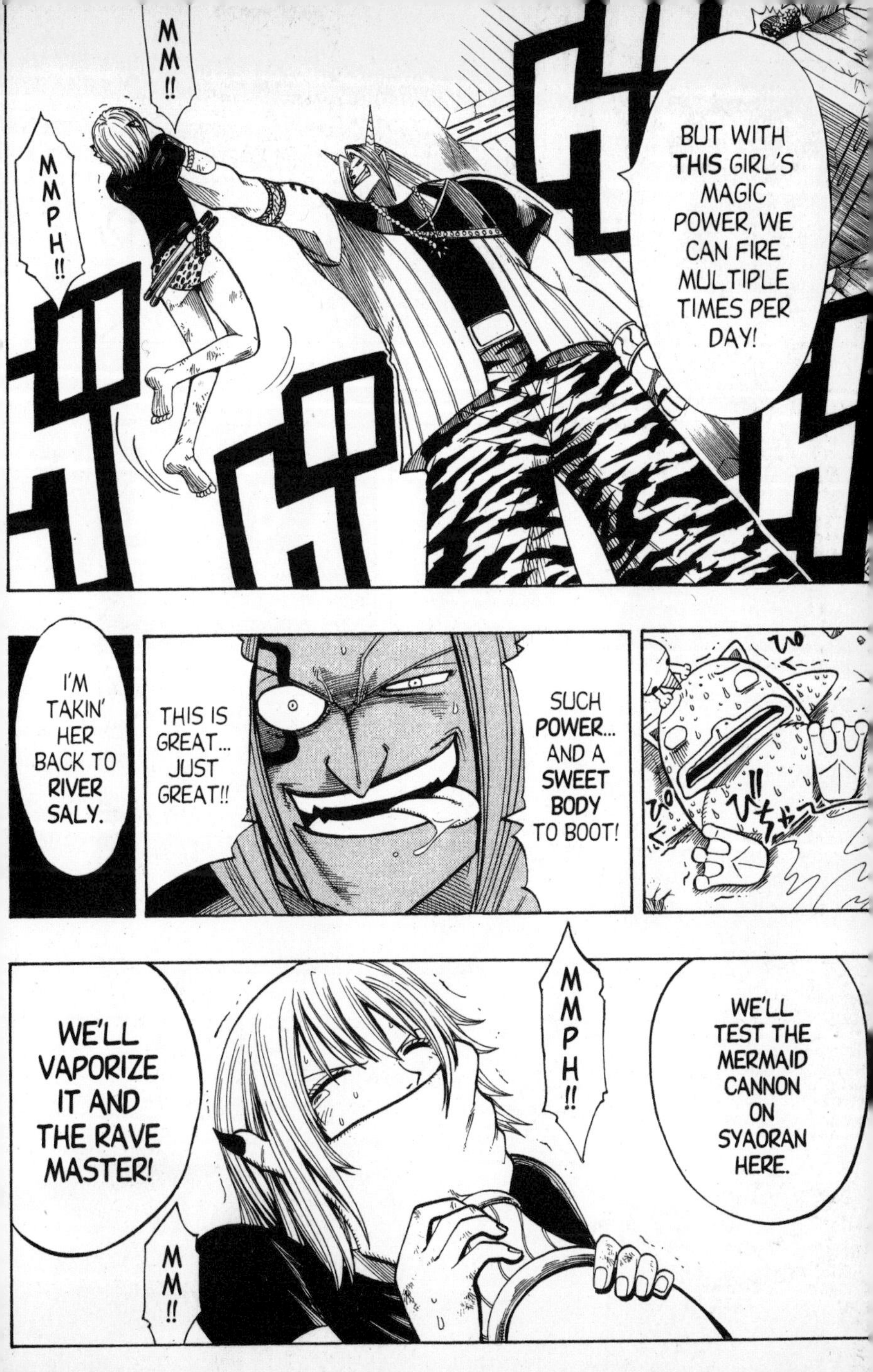
BUT WITH THIS GIRL'S MAGIC POWER, WE CAN FIRE MULTIPLE TIMES PER DAY!
MM!!
MMPH!!
SUCH POWER... AND A SWEET BODY TO BOOT!
THIS IS GREAT... JUST GREAT!!
I'M TAKIN' HER BACK TO RIVER SALY.
WE'LL TEST THE MERMAID CANNON ON SYAORAN HERE.
MMPH!!
WE'LL VAPORIZE IT AND THE RAVE MASTER!
MM!!

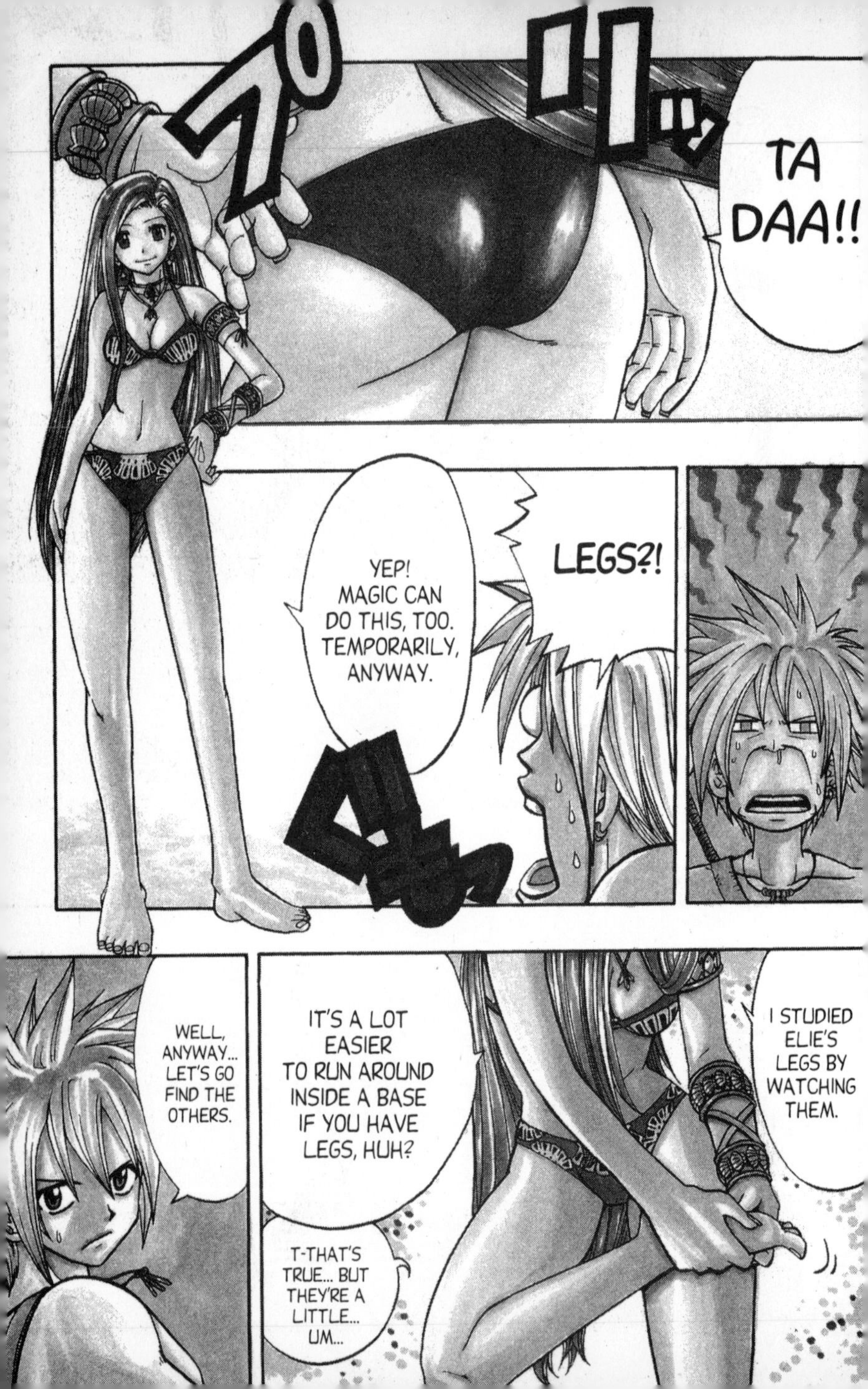
TA DAA!!
LEGS?!
YEP! MAGIC CAN DO THIS, TOO. TEMPORARILY, ANYWAY.
I STUDIED ELIE'S LEGS BY WATCHING THEM.
IT'S A LOT EASIER TO RUN AROUND INSIDE A BASE IF YOU HAVE LEGS, HUH?
T-THAT'S TRUE... BUT THEY'RE A LITTLE... UM...
WELL, ANYWAY... LET'S GO FIND THE OTHERS.

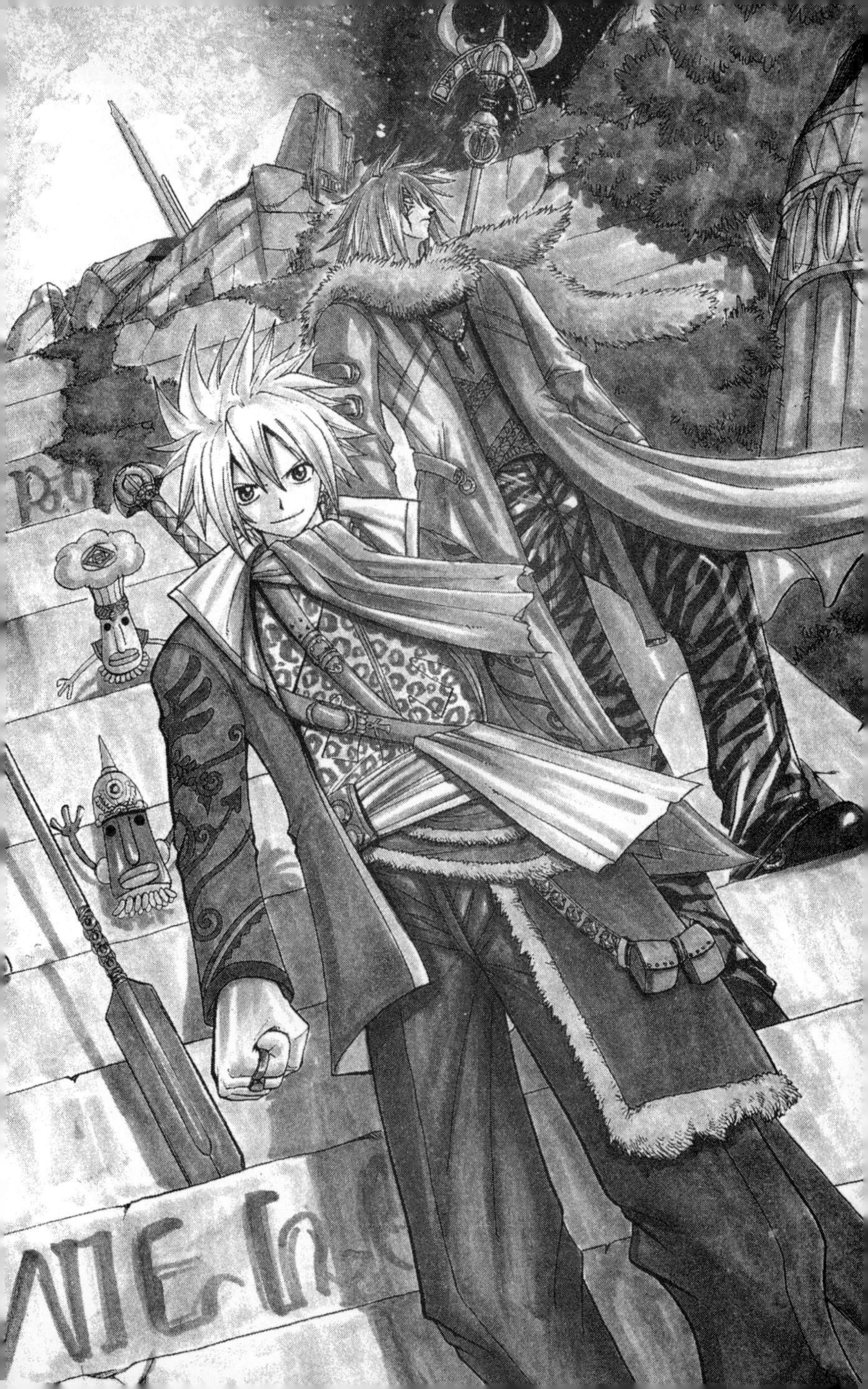

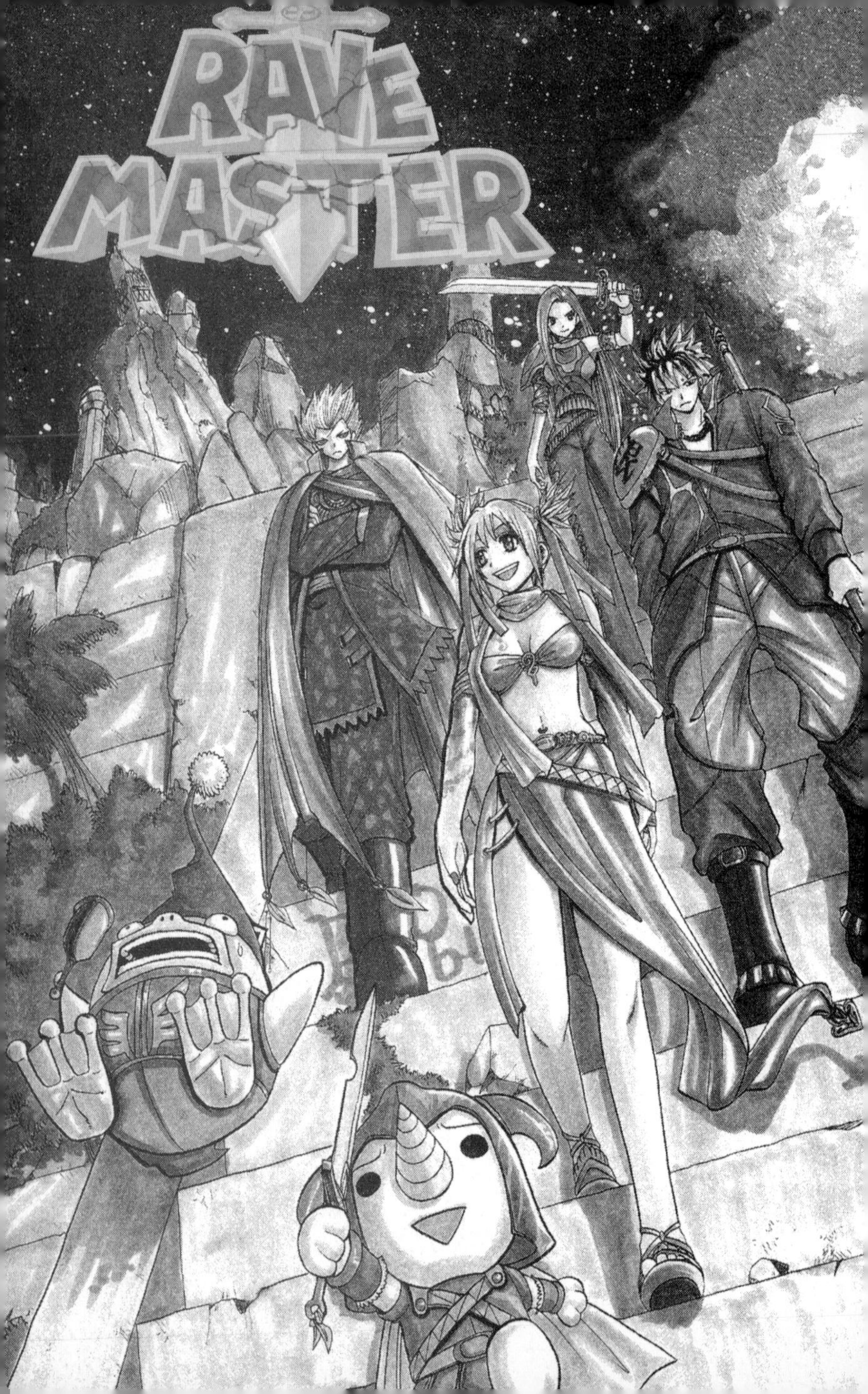
RAVE MASTER

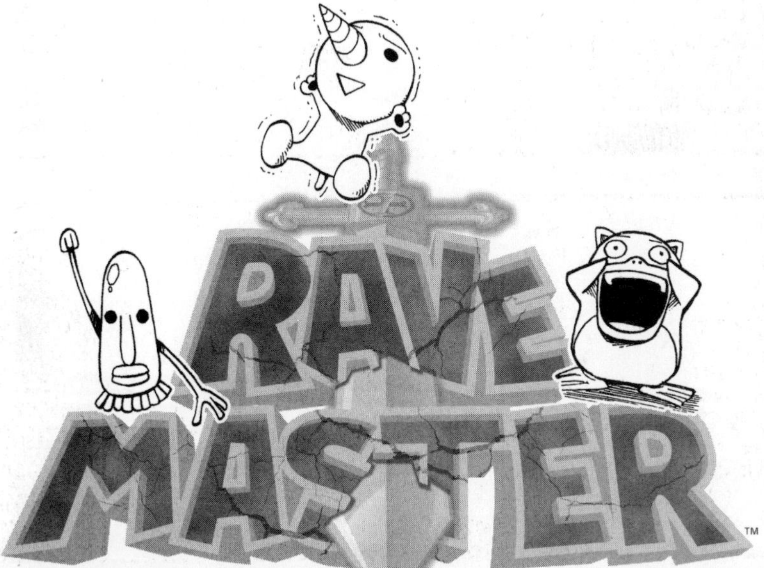
RAVE MASTER™

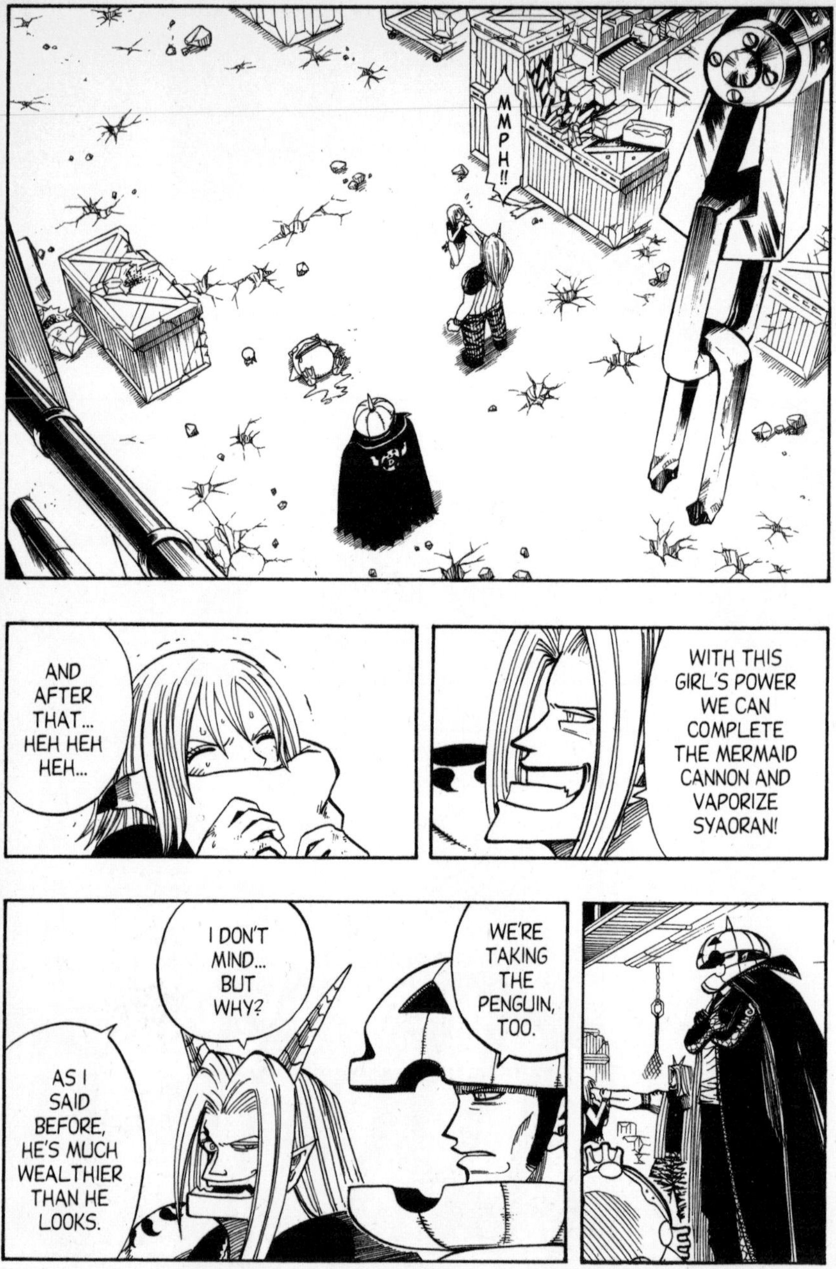
MMPH!!
WITH THIS GIRL'S POWER WE CAN COMPLETE THE MERMAID CANNON AND VAPORIZE SYAORAN!
AND AFTER THAT... HEH HEH HEH...
WE'RE TAKING THE PENGUIN, TOO.
I DON'T MIND... BUT WHY?
AS I SAID BEFORE, HE'S MUCH WEALTHIER THAN HE LOOKS.

RAVE:111 ✠ DESPAIR REPEATED?!

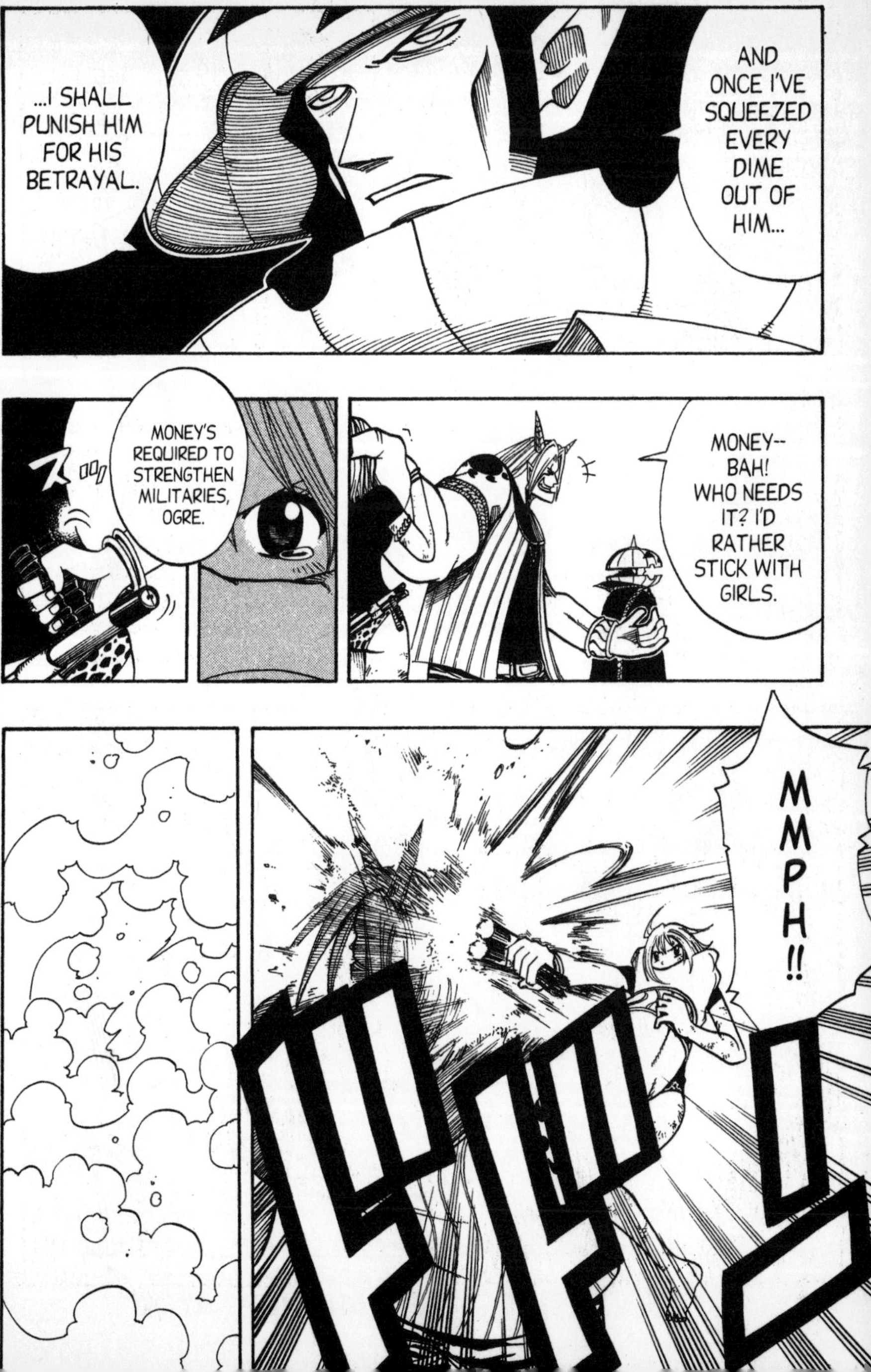
AND ONCE I'VE SQUEEZED EVERY DIME OUT OF HIM...
...I SHALL PUNISH HIM FOR HIS BETRAYAL.
MONEY-- BAH! WHO NEEDS IT? I'D RATHER STICK WITH GIRLS.
MONEY'S REQUIRED TO STRENGTHEN MILITARIES, OGRE.
MMPH!!

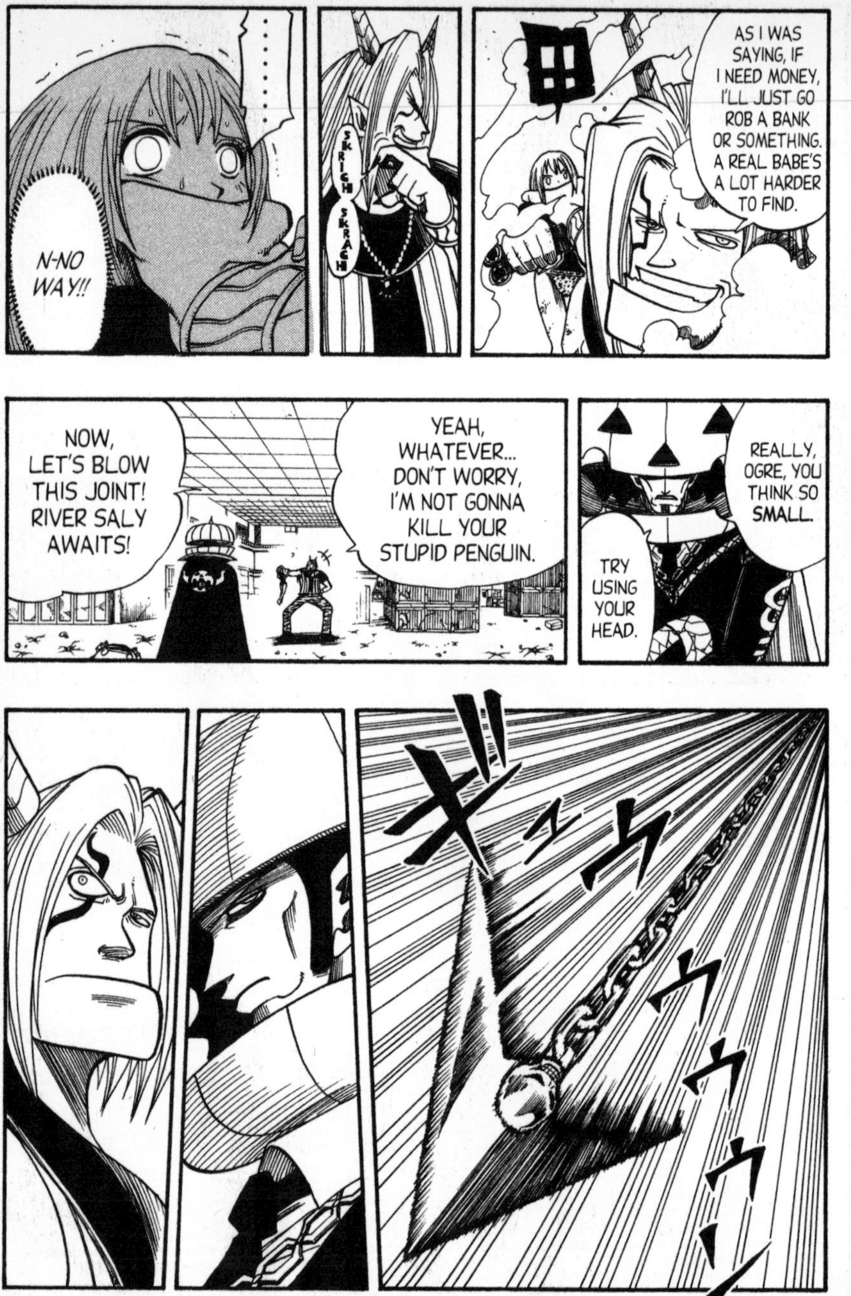
AS I WAS SAYING, IF I NEED MONEY, I'LL JUST GO ROB A BANK OR SOMETHING. A REAL BABE'S A LOT HARDER TO FIND.
SKRICH
SKRACH
N-NO WAY!!
REALLY, OGRE, YOU THINK SO SMALL.
TRY USING YOUR HEAD.
YEAH, WHATEVER... DON'T WORRY, I'M NOT GONNA KILL YOUR STUPID PENGUIN.
NOW, LET'S BLOW THIS JOINT! RIVER SALY AWAITS!
ギュウウウウン

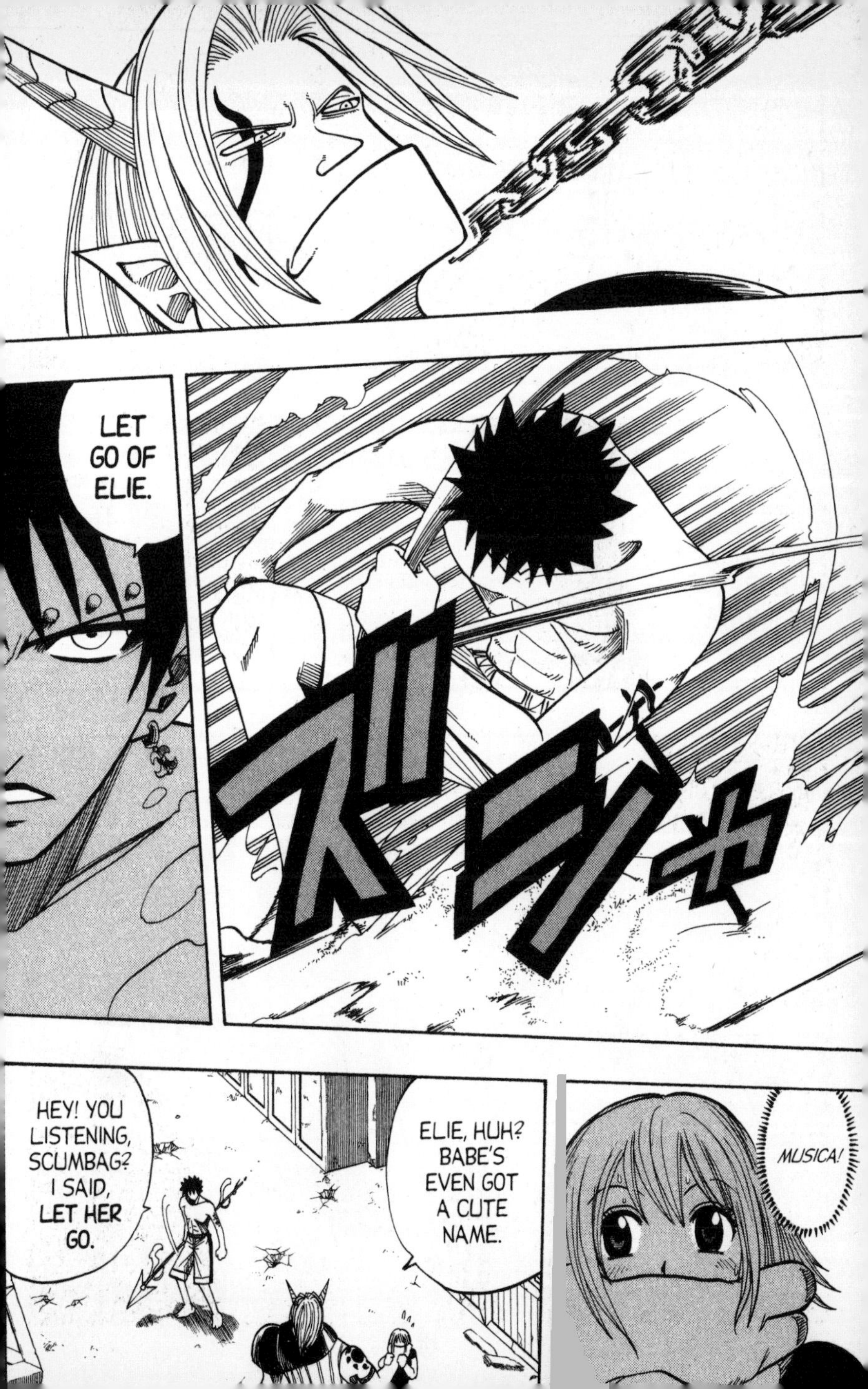
LET GO OF ELIE.
MUSICA!
ELIE, HUH? BABE'S EVEN GOT A CUTE NAME.
HEY! YOU LISTENING, SCUMBAG? I SAID, LET HER GO.

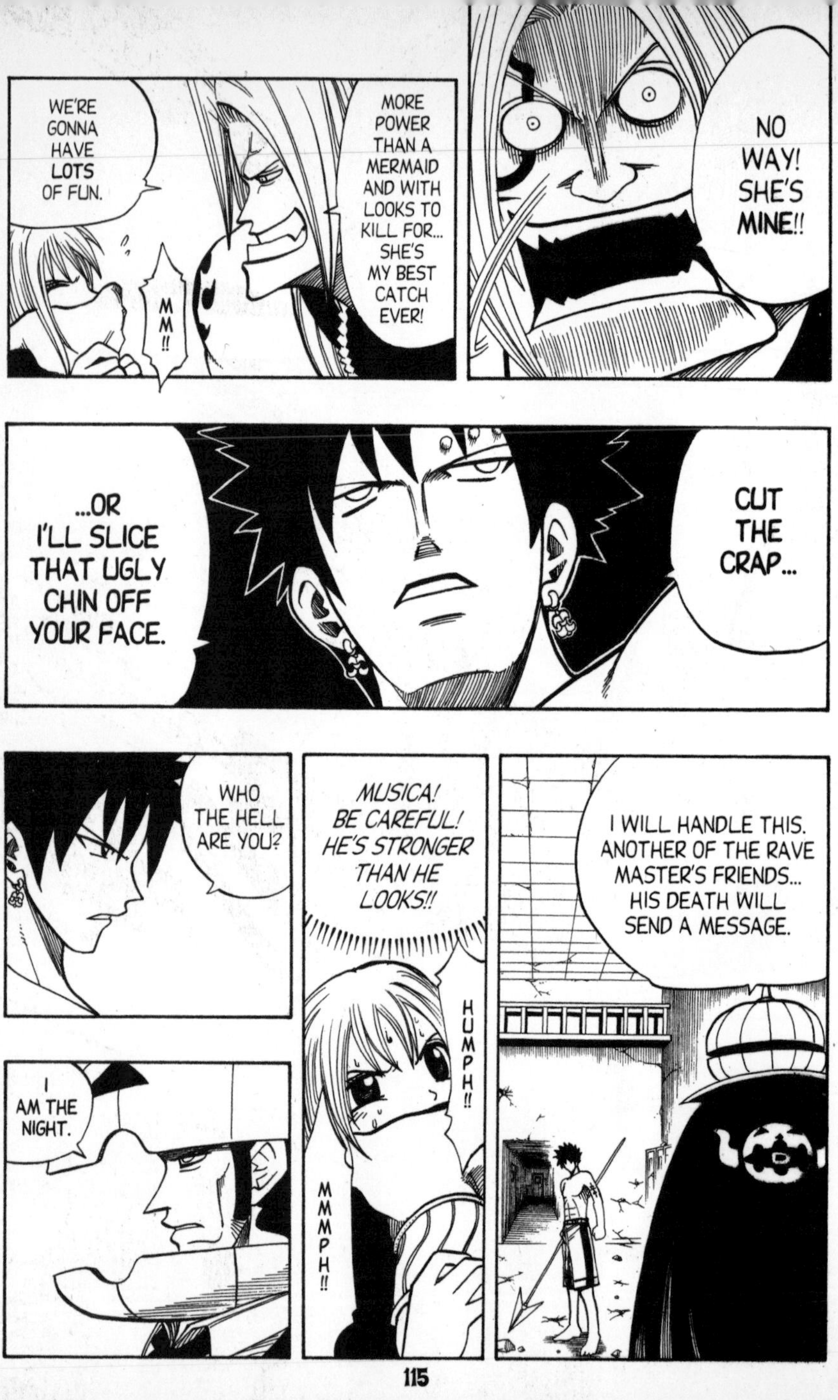
NO WAY! SHE'S MINE!!
MORE POWER THAN A MERMAID AND WITH LOOKS TO KILL FOR... SHE'S MY BEST CATCH EVER!
WE'RE GONNA HAVE LOTS OF FUN.
MM!!
CUT THE CRAP...
...OR I'LL SLICE THAT UGLY CHIN OFF YOUR FACE.
I WILL HANDLE THIS. ANOTHER OF THE RAVE MASTER'S FRIENDS... HIS DEATH WILL SEND A MESSAGE.
MUSICA! BE CAREFUL! HE'S STRONGER THAN HE LOOKS!!
HUMPH!!
MMMPH!!
WHO THE HELL ARE YOU?
I AM THE NIGHT.

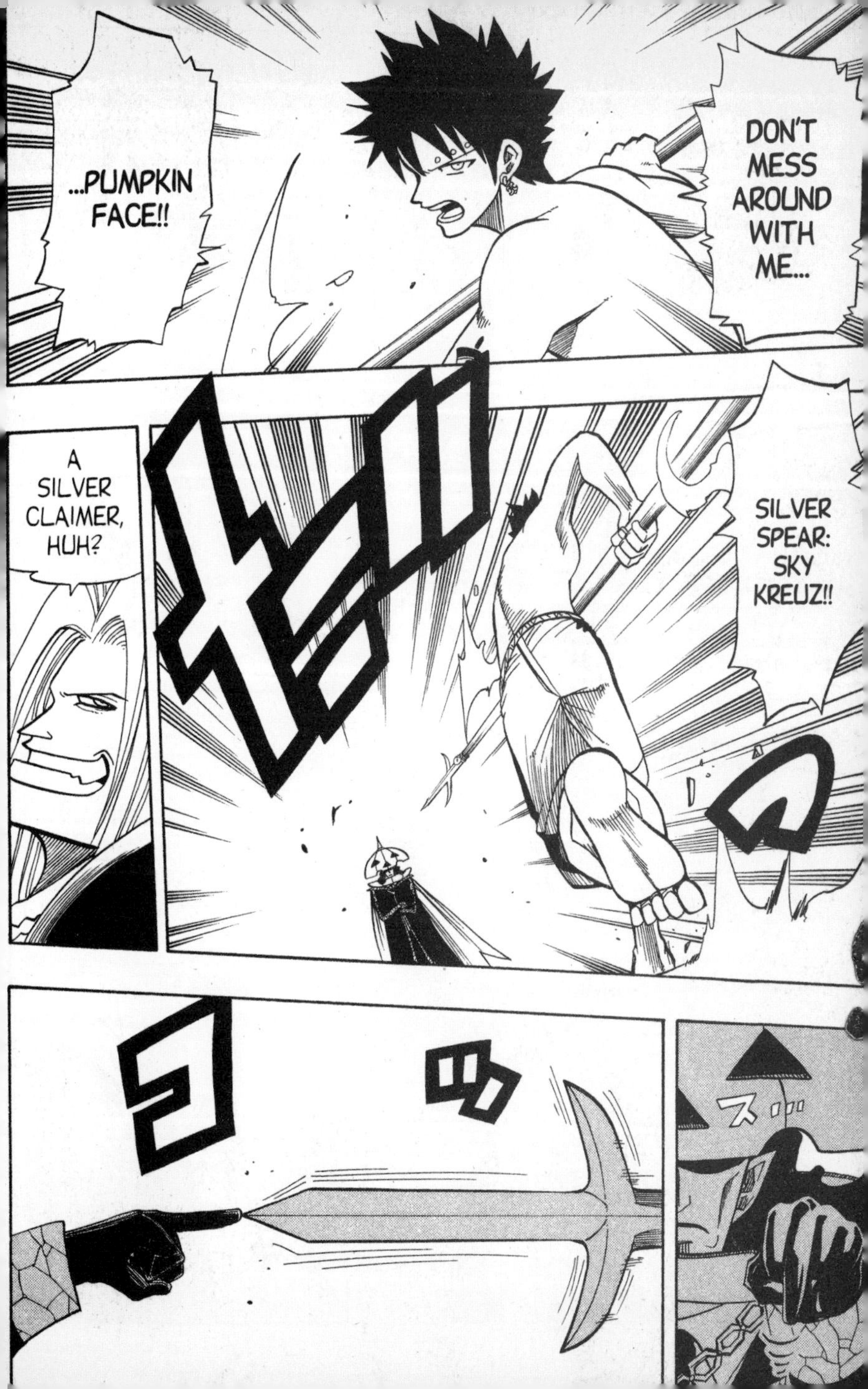
DON'T MESS AROUND WITH ME...
...PUMPKIN FACE!!
SILVER SPEAR: SKY KREUZ!!
A SILVER CLAIMER, HUH?

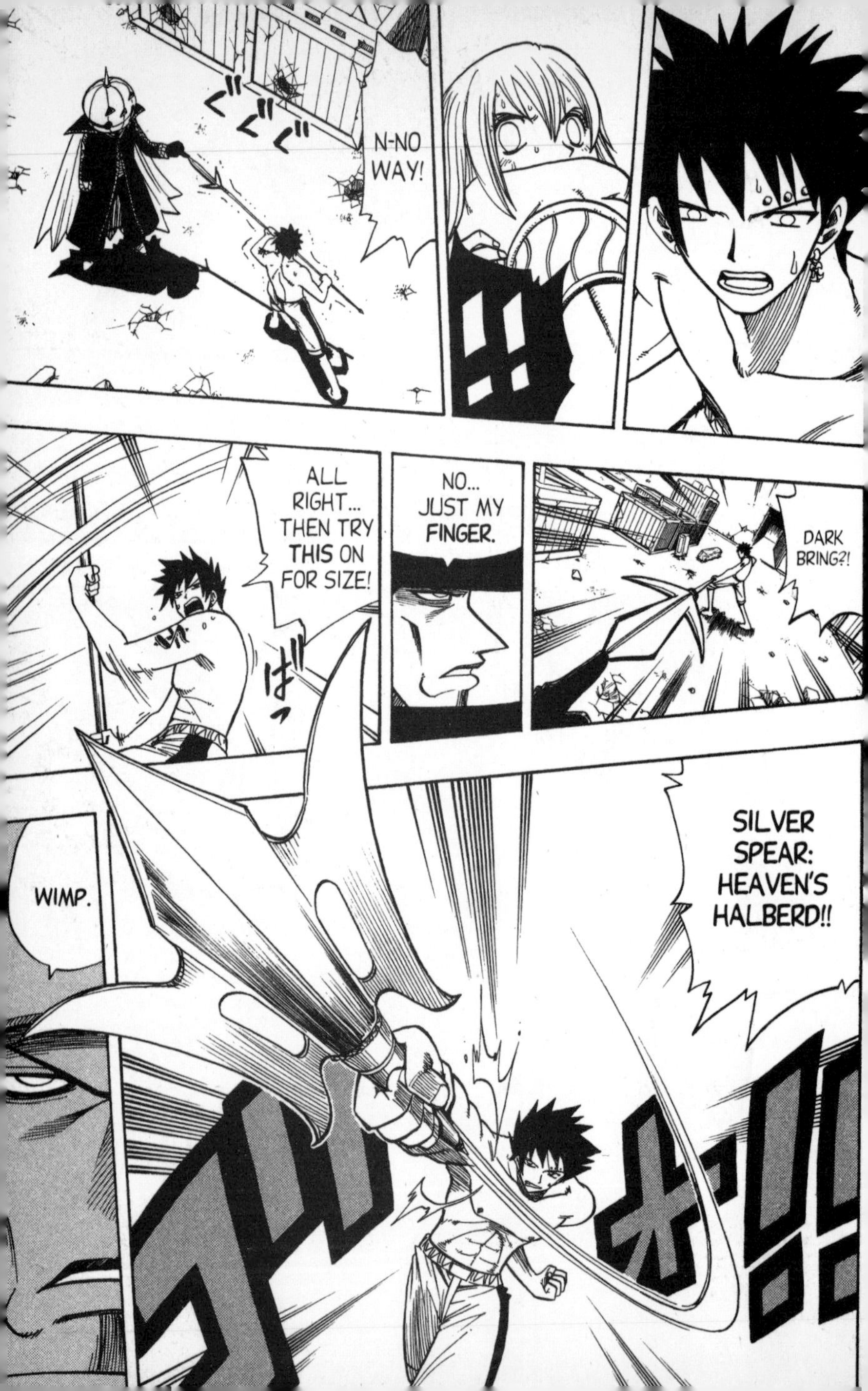
N-NO WAY!
ぐぐぐ
DARK BRING?!
NO... JUST MY FINGER.
ALL RIGHT... THEN TRY THIS ON FOR SIZE!
ばっ
SILVER SPEAR: HEAVEN'S HALBERD!!
WIMP.

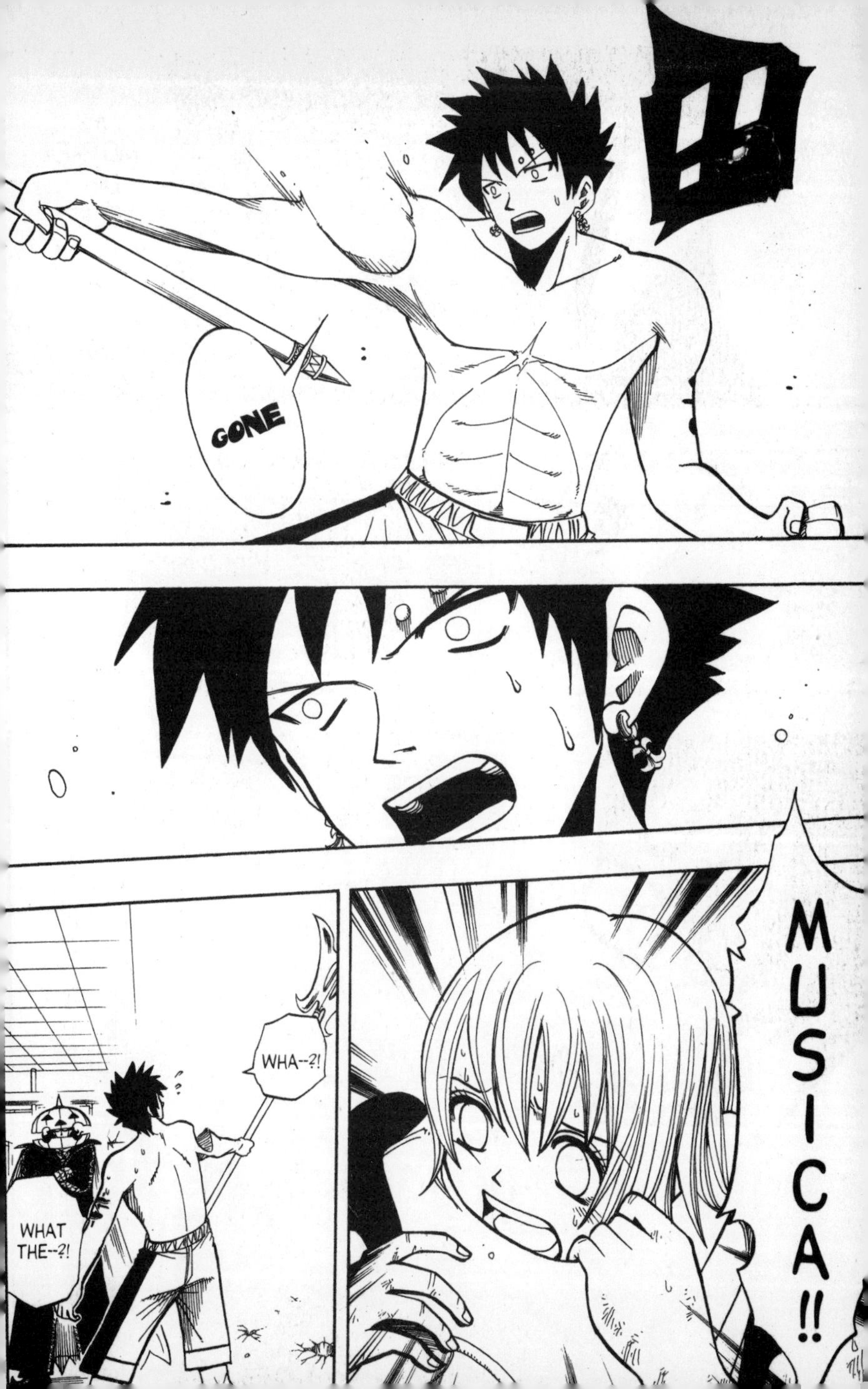
GONE
MUSICA!!
WHA--?!
WHAT THE--?!

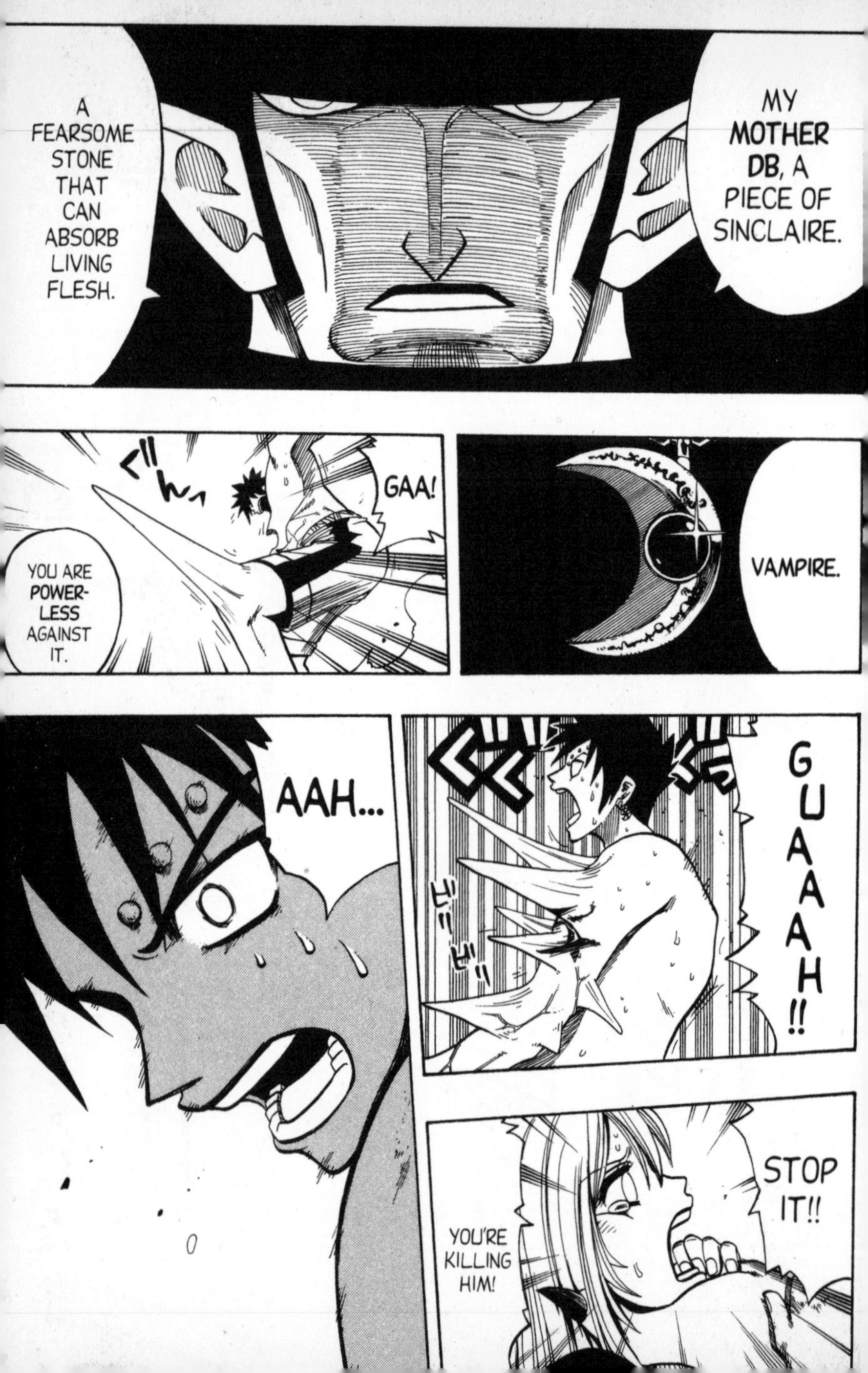
MY MOTHER DB, A PIECE OF SINCLAIRE.
A FEARSOME STONE THAT CAN ABSORB LIVING FLESH.
VAMPIRE.
GAA!
YOU ARE POWERLESS AGAINST IT.
GUAAAAH!!
STOP IT!!
YOU'RE KILLING HIM!
AAH...

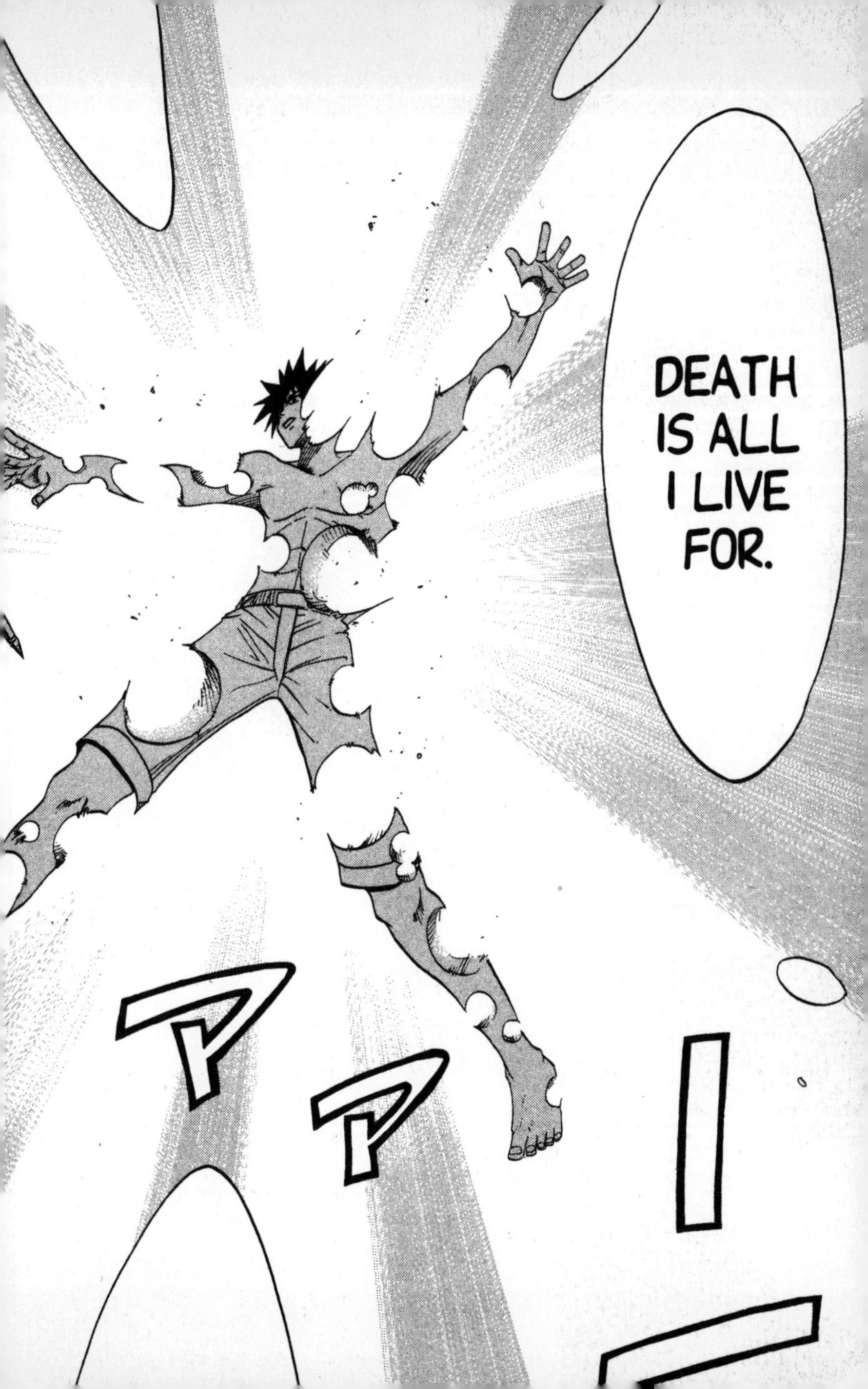
DEATH IS ALL I LIVE FOR.
アアー

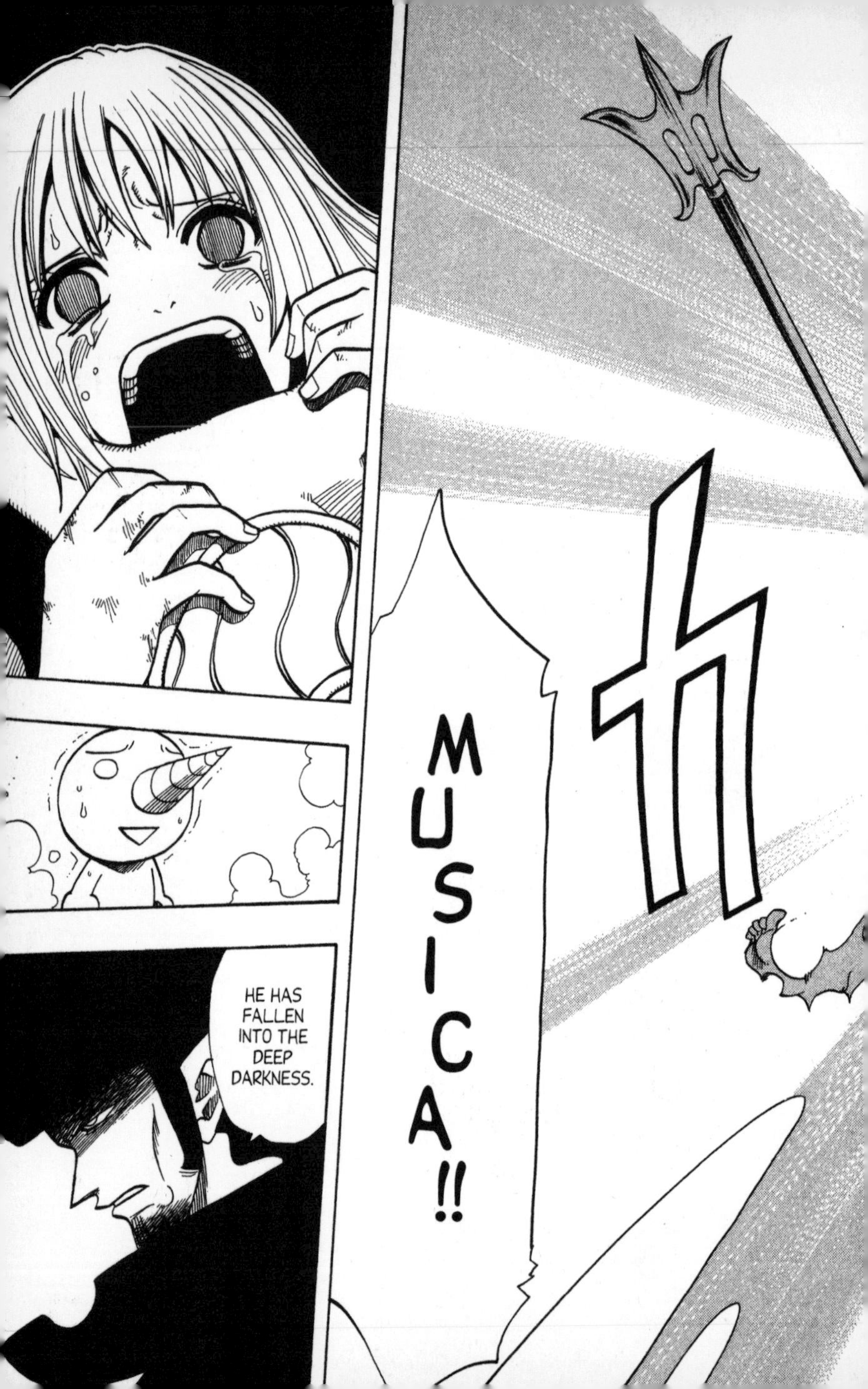
MUSICA!!
カ
HE HAS FALLEN INTO THE DEEP DARKNESS.

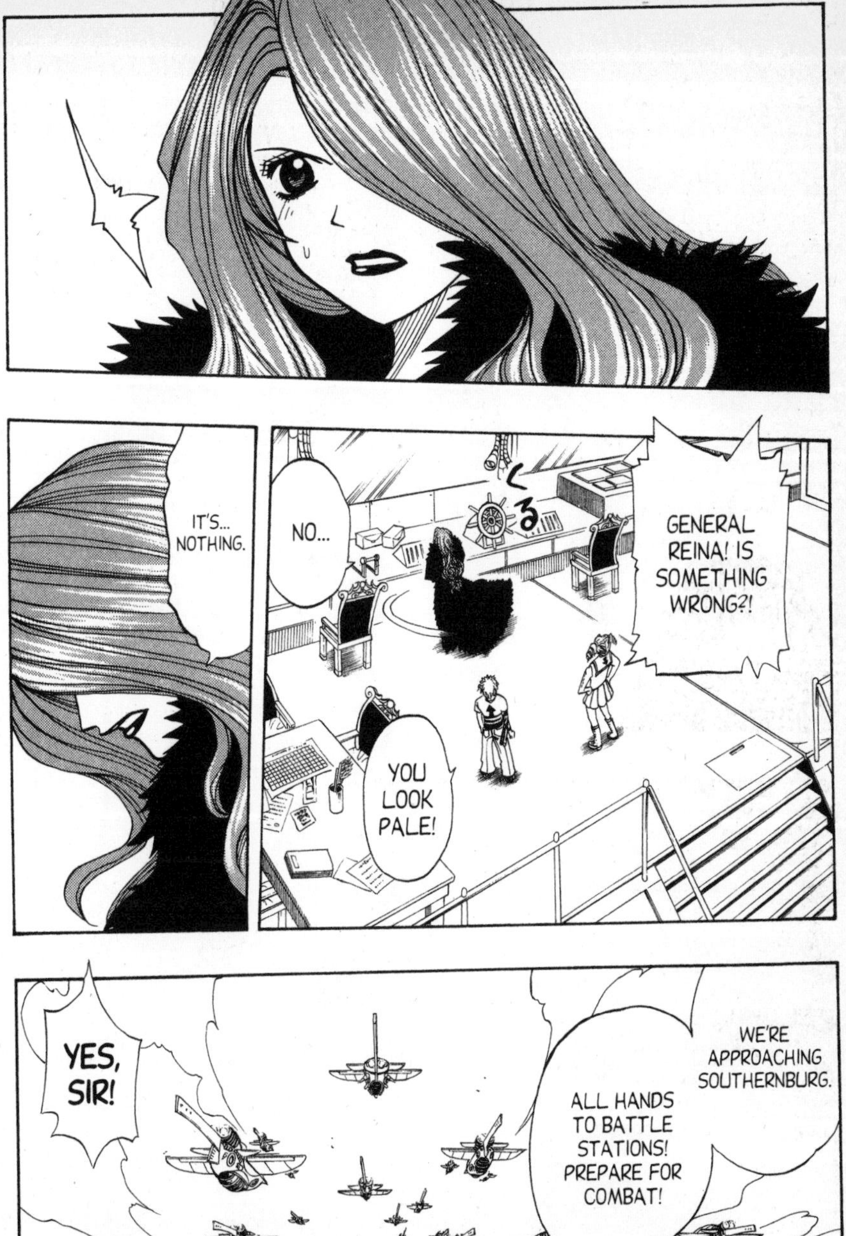
GENERAL REINA! IS SOMETHING WRONG?!
くる
NO...
YOU LOOK PALE!
IT'S... NOTHING.
WE'RE APPROACHING SOUTHERNBURG.
ALL HANDS TO BATTLE STATIONS! PREPARE FOR COMBAT!
YES, SIR!

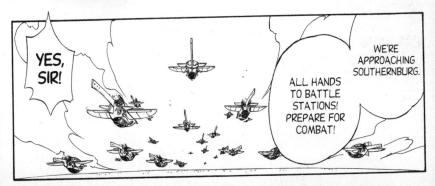

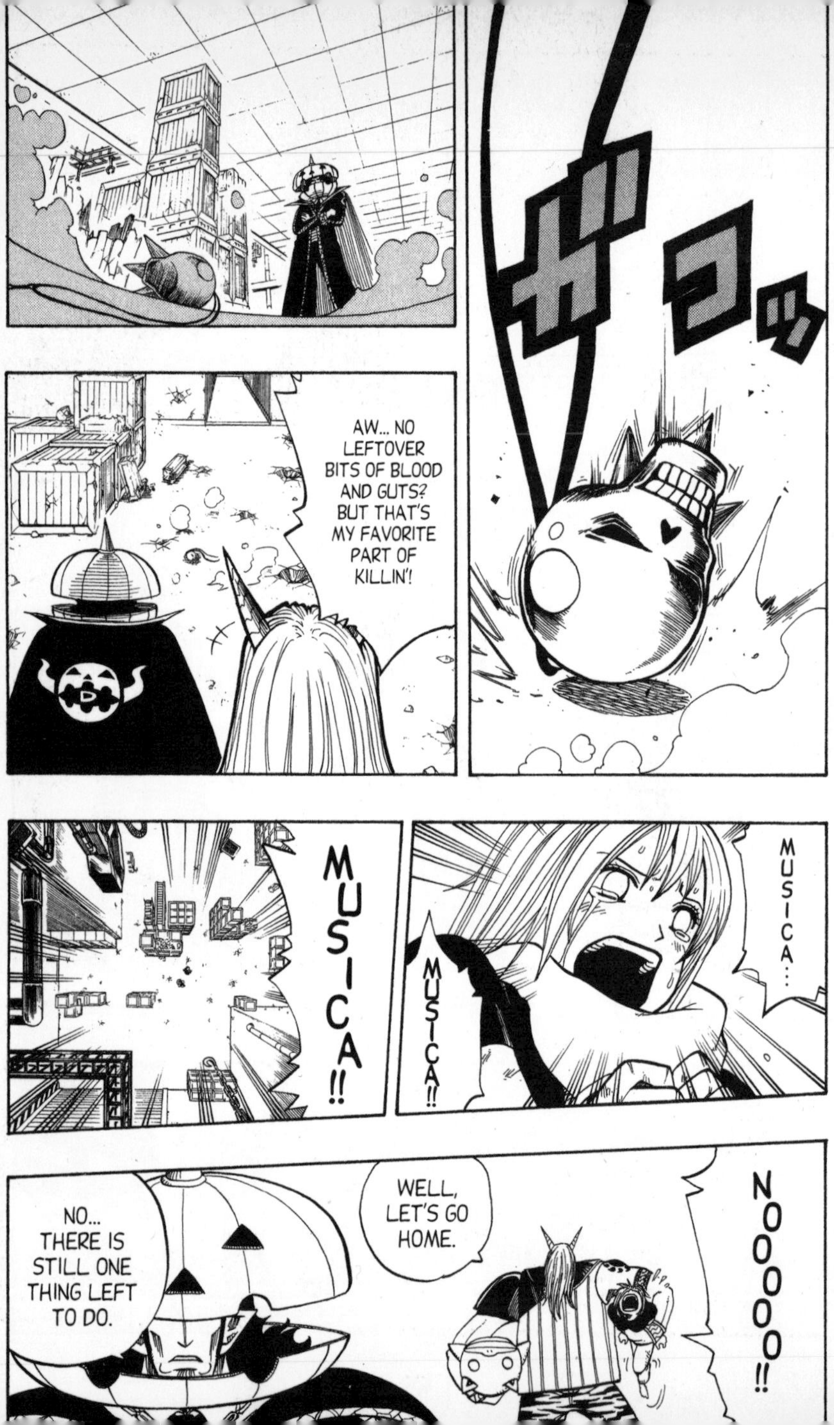
ガコッ
AW... NO LEFTOVER BITS OF BLOOD AND GUTS? BUT THAT'S MY FAVORITE PART OF KILLIN'!
MUSICA...
MUSICA!!
MUSICA!!
NOOOOO!!
WELL, LET'S GO HOME.
NO... THERE IS STILL ONE THING LEFT TO DO.

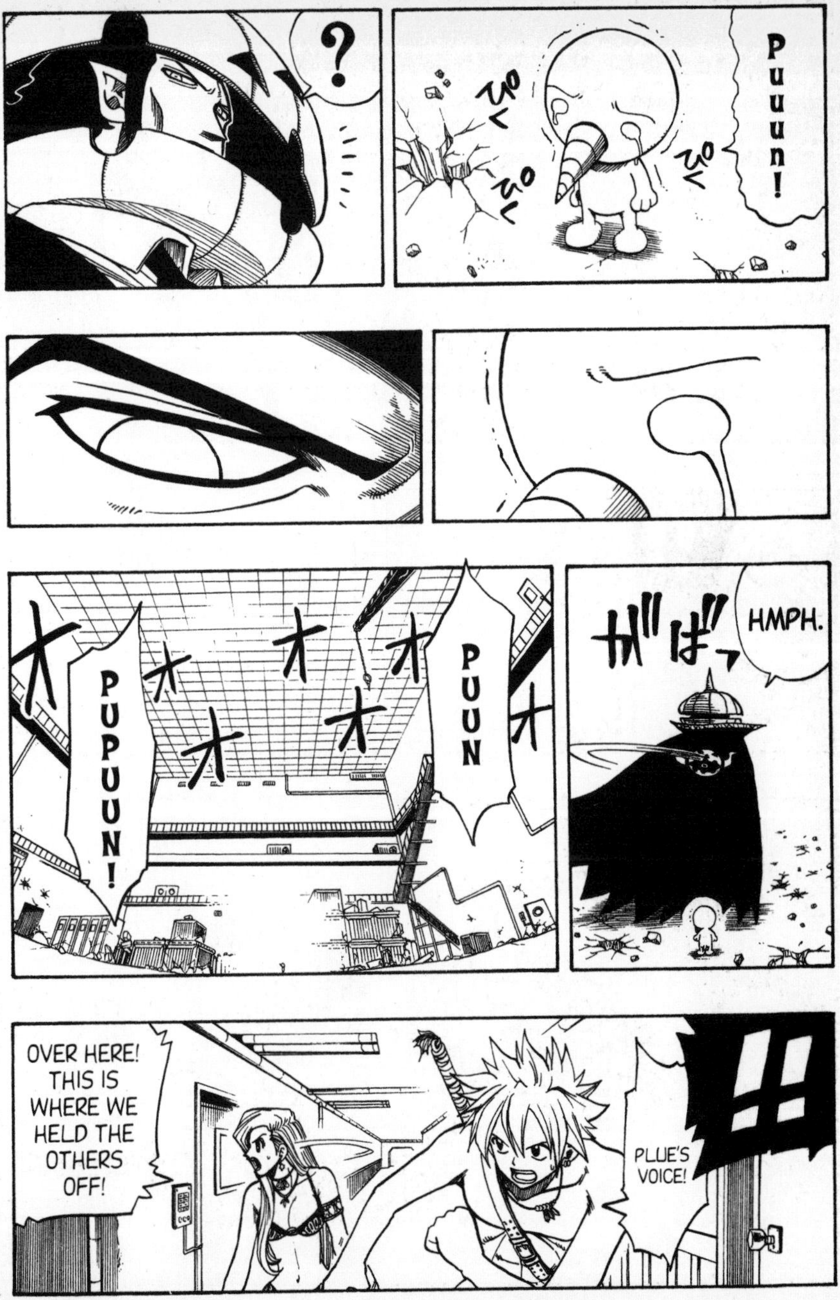

Puuun!
ぴく
ぴく
ぴく
?
HMPH.
がばっ
PUUN
PUPUUN!
!!
PLUE'S VOICE!
OVER HERE! THIS IS WHERE WE HELD THE OTHERS OFF!

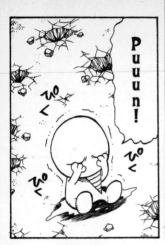

Puuun!

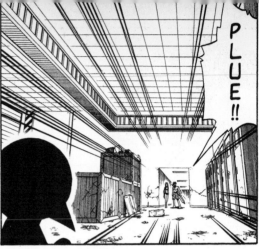

PLUE!!

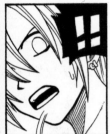

!!

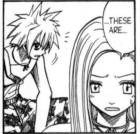

...THESE ARE...

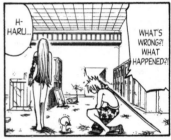

H-HARU...

WHAT'S WRONG?! WHAT HAPPENED?!

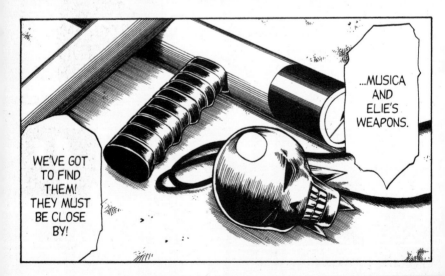

...MUSICA AND ELIE'S WEAPONS.

WE'VE GOT TO FIND THEM! THEY MUST BE CLOSE BY!

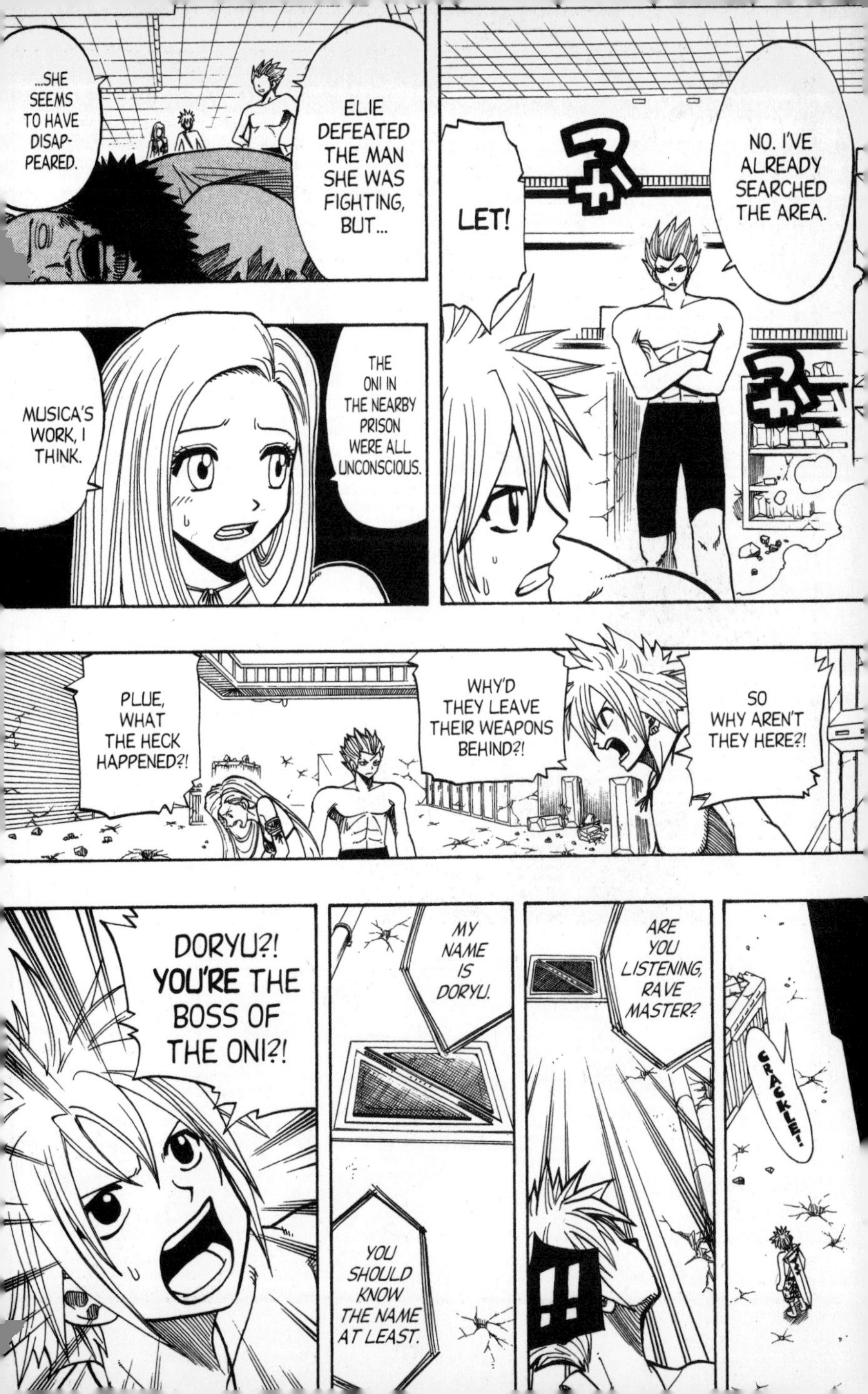
LET!
NO. I'VE ALREADY SEARCHED THE AREA.
ELIE DEFEATED THE MAN SHE WAS FIGHTING, BUT...
...SHE SEEMS TO HAVE DISAPPEARED.
THE ONI IN THE NEARBY PRISON WERE ALL UNCONSCIOUS.
MUSICA'S WORK, I THINK.
SO WHY AREN'T THEY HERE?!
WHY'D THEY LEAVE THEIR WEAPONS BEHIND?!
PLUE, WHAT THE HECK HAPPENED?!
CRACKLE!
ARE YOU LISTENING, RAVE MASTER?
MY NAME IS DORYU.
YOU SHOULD KNOW THE NAME AT LEAST.
DORYU?! **YOU'RE** THE BOSS OF THE ONI?!

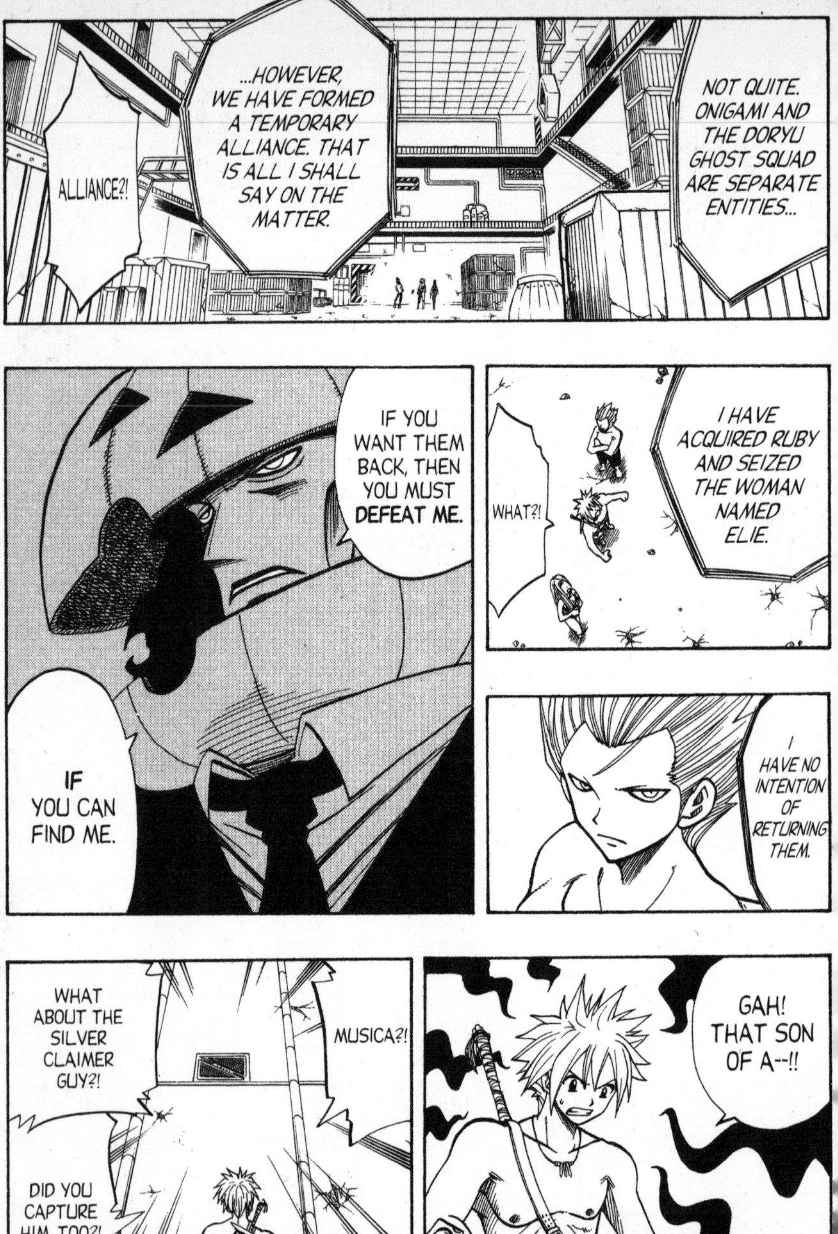
NOT QUITE. ONIGAMI AND THE DORYU GHOST SQUAD ARE SEPARATE ENTITIES...
...HOWEVER, WE HAVE FORMED A TEMPORARY ALLIANCE. THAT IS ALL I SHALL SAY ON THE MATTER.
ALLIANCE?!
I HAVE ACQUIRED RUBY AND SEIZED THE WOMAN NAMED ELIE.
WHAT?!
I HAVE NO INTENTION OF RETURNING THEM.
IF YOU WANT THEM BACK, THEN YOU MUST DEFEAT ME.
IF YOU CAN FIND ME.
GAH! THAT SON OF A--!!
MUSICA?!
WHAT ABOUT THE SILVER CLAIMER GUY?!
DID YOU CAPTURE HIM, TOO?!

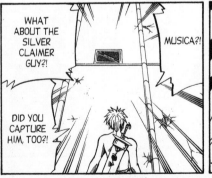

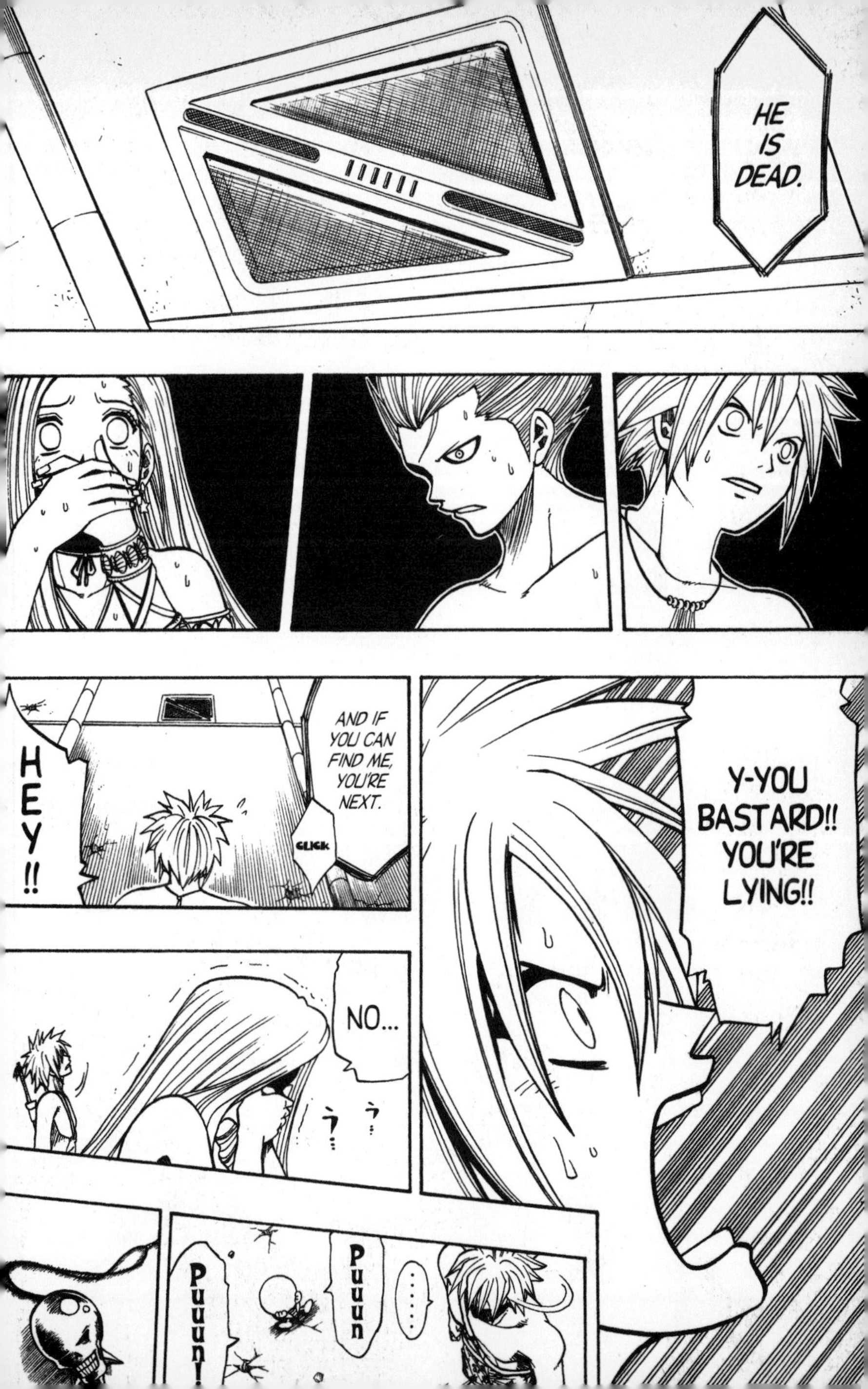
HE IS DEAD.
Y-YOU BASTARD!! YOU'RE LYING!!
AND IF YOU CAN FIND ME, YOU'RE NEXT.
CLICK
HEY!!
NO...
う
う
......
Puuun
Puuun!

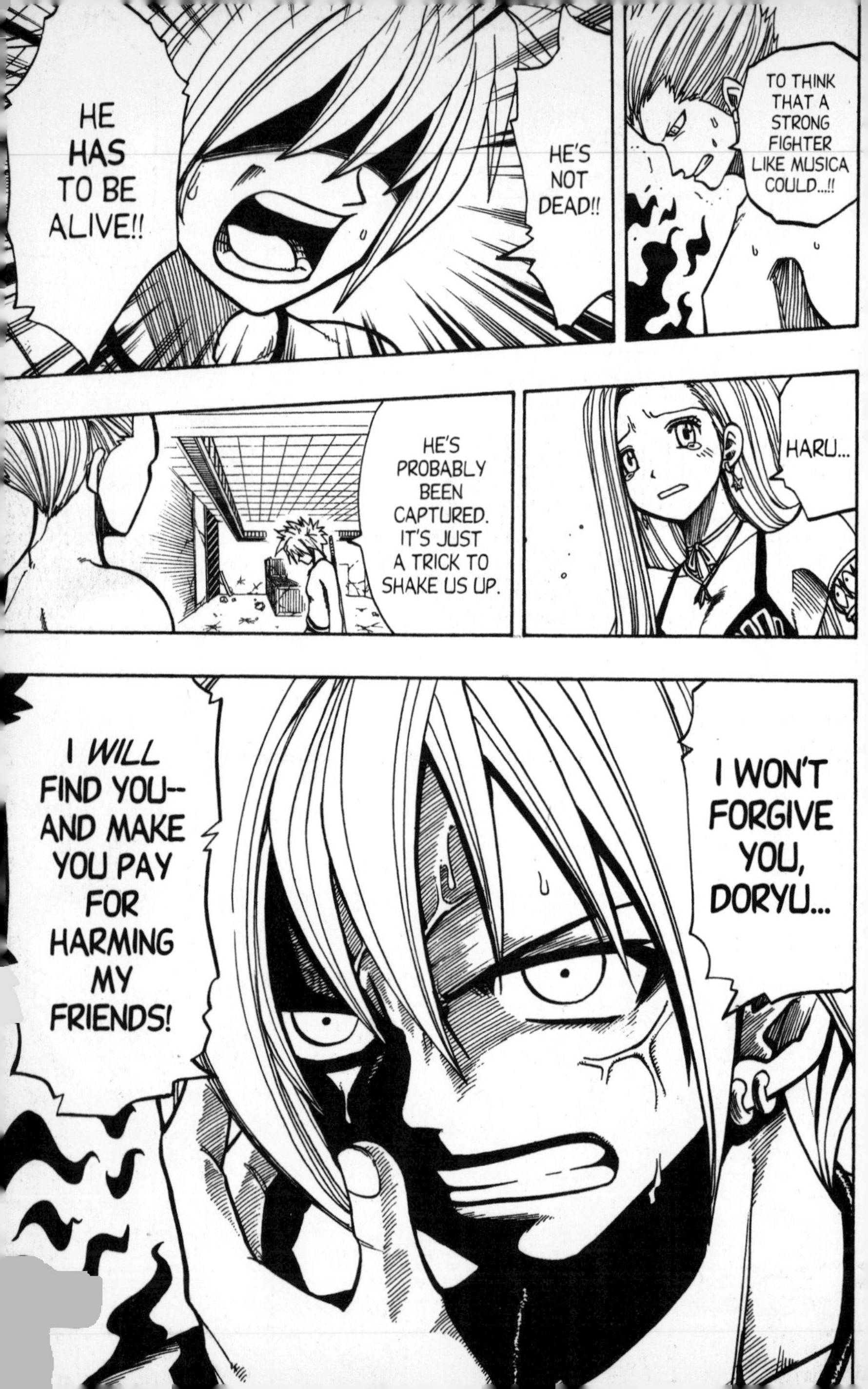
TO THINK THAT A STRONG FIGHTER LIKE MUSICA COULD...!!
HE'S NOT DEAD!!
HE HAS TO BE ALIVE!!
HARU...
HE'S PROBABLY BEEN CAPTURED. IT'S JUST A TRICK TO SHAKE US UP.
I WON'T FORGIVE YOU, DORYU...
I WILL FIND YOU-- AND MAKE YOU PAY FOR HARMING MY FRIENDS!

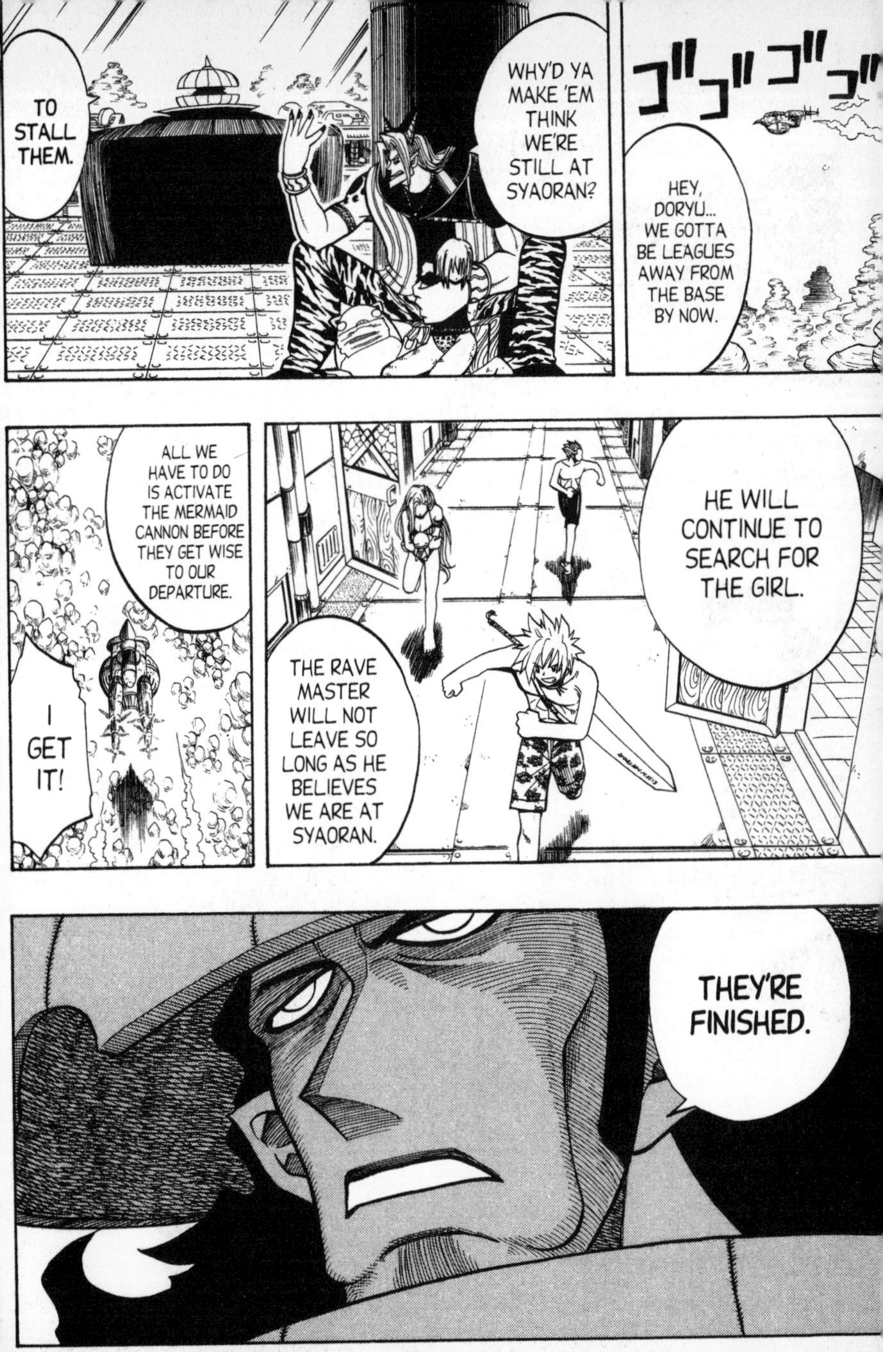
ゴゴゴゴ
HEY, DORYU... WE GOTTA BE LEAGUES AWAY FROM THE BASE BY NOW.
WHY'D YA MAKE 'EM THINK WE'RE STILL AT SYAORAN?
TO STALL THEM.
HE WILL CONTINUE TO SEARCH FOR THE GIRL.
THE RAVE MASTER WILL NOT LEAVE SO LONG AS HE BELIEVES WE ARE AT SYAORAN.
ALL WE HAVE TO DO IS ACTIVATE THE MERMAID CANNON BEFORE THEY GET WISE TO OUR DEPARTURE.
I GET IT!
THEY'RE FINISHED.

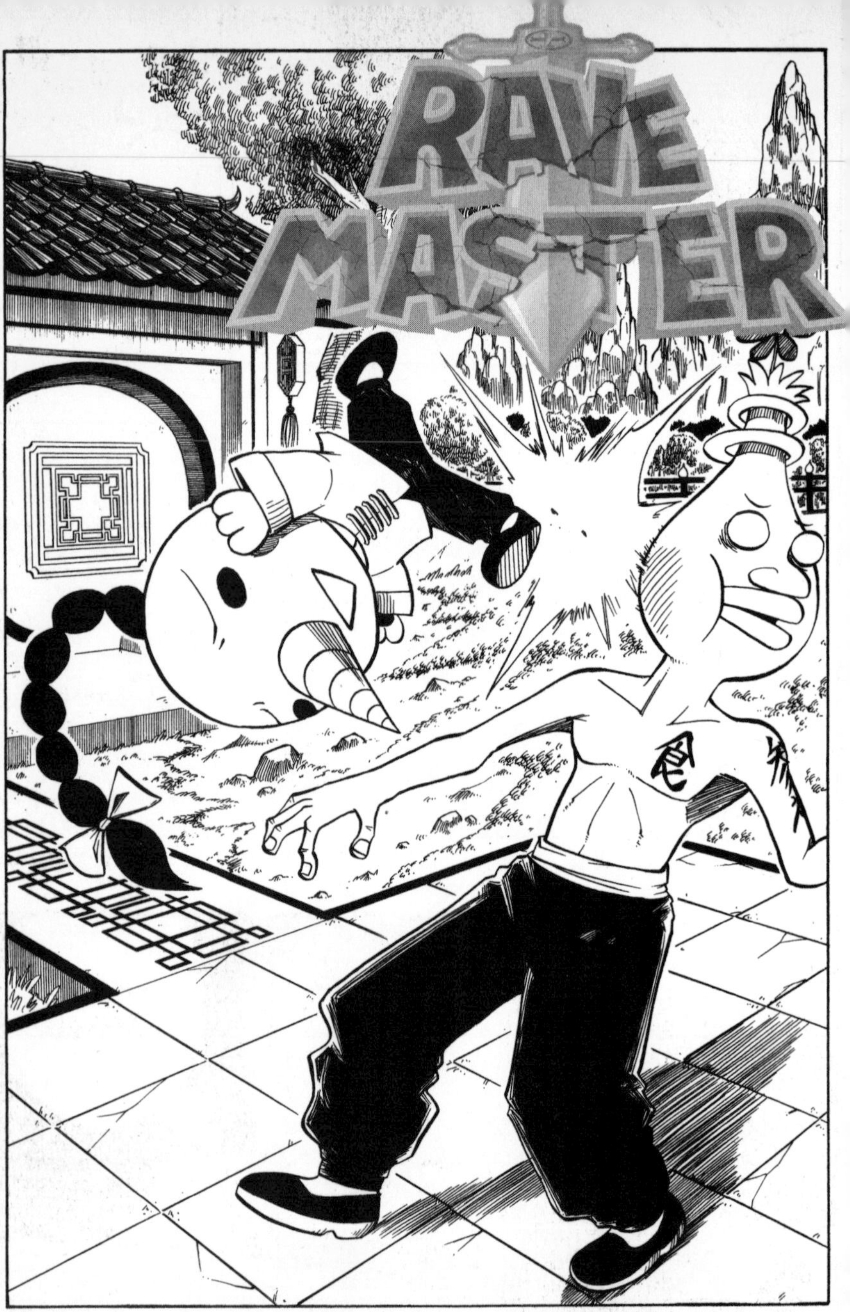
RAVE MASTER

RAVE:112 THE POWER OF SORROW

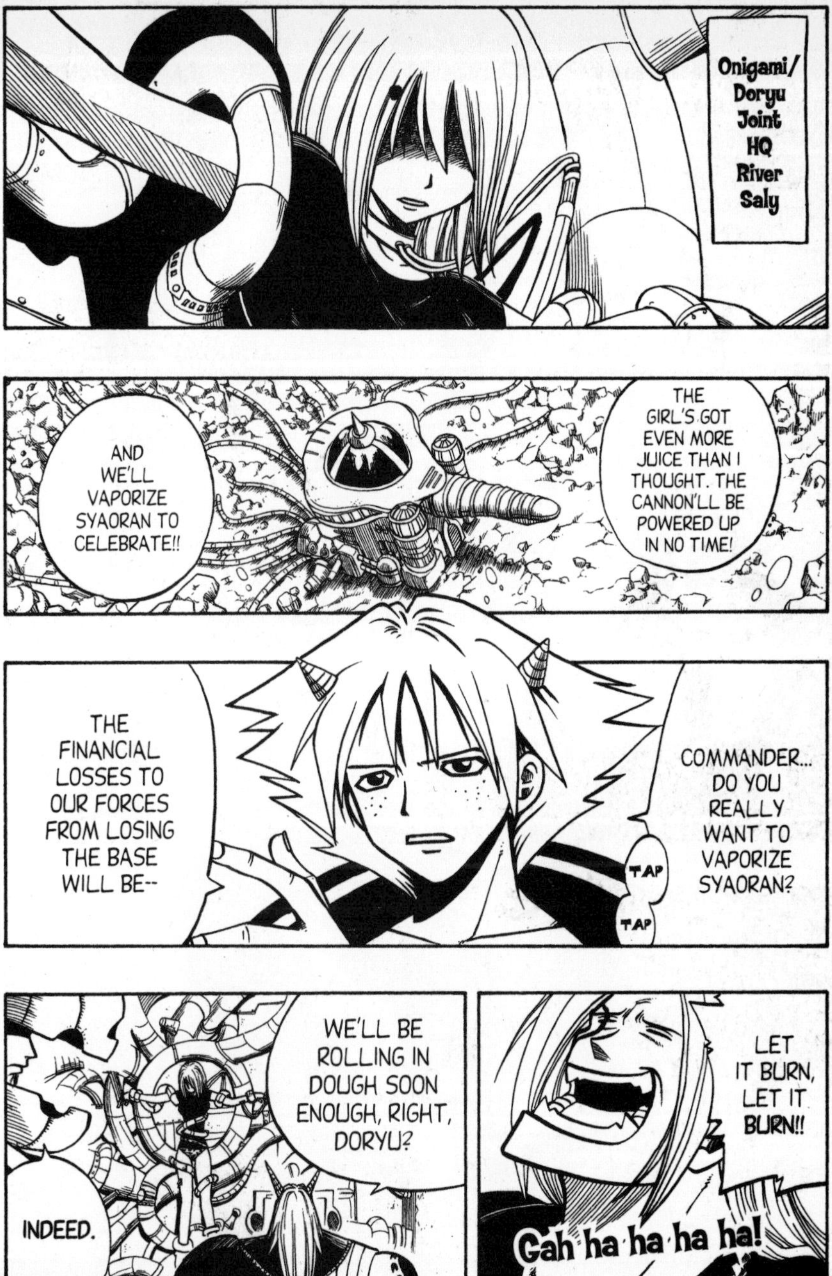
Onigami/Doryu Joint HQ River Saly
THE GIRL'S GOT EVEN MORE JUICE THAN I THOUGHT. THE CANNON'LL BE POWERED UP IN NO TIME!
AND WE'LL VAPORIZE SYAORAN TO CELEBRATE!!
COMMANDER... DO YOU REALLY WANT TO VAPORIZE SYAORAN?
TAP
TAP
THE FINANCIAL LOSSES TO OUR FORCES FROM LOSING THE BASE WILL BE--
LET IT BURN, LET IT BURN!!
Gah ha ha ha ha!
WE'LL BE ROLLING IN DOUGH SOON ENOUGH, RIGHT, DORYU?
INDEED.

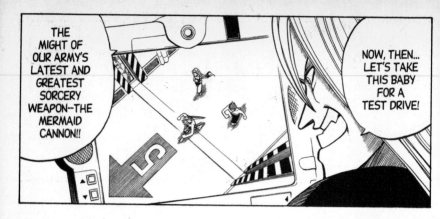

NOW, THEN... LET'S TAKE THIS BABY FOR A TEST DRIVE!
THE MIGHT OF OUR ARMY'S LATEST AND GREATEST SORCERY WEAPON--THE MERMAID CANNON!!
PREPARE THE CANNON!
YES, SIR!
ARE YOU SURE IT IS SUFFICIENT TO DESTROY SYAORAN? WE CAN'T RISK THE RAVE MASTER GETTING AWAY.
OH, IT'S SUFFICIENT, ALL RIGHT. THIS CANNON USES MAGICAL ENERGY AS ITS POWER SOURCE.
TAP
TAP
TAP
TAP
TAP
TAP
TAP
TAP
IT'S MUCH MORE POWERFUL AND RELIABLE THAN PHYSICAL ATTACKS. *AND* IT FUNCTIONS COMPLETELY DIFFERENTLY FROM CONVENTIONAL WEAPONS.
TAP
DIFFERENT HOW?
YOU MAY FIND IT HARD TO BELIEVE...
...BUT IT...

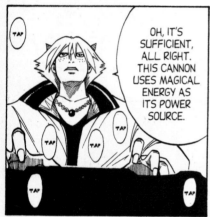

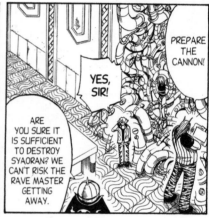

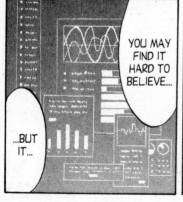

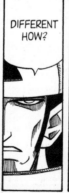

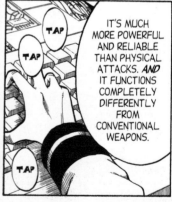

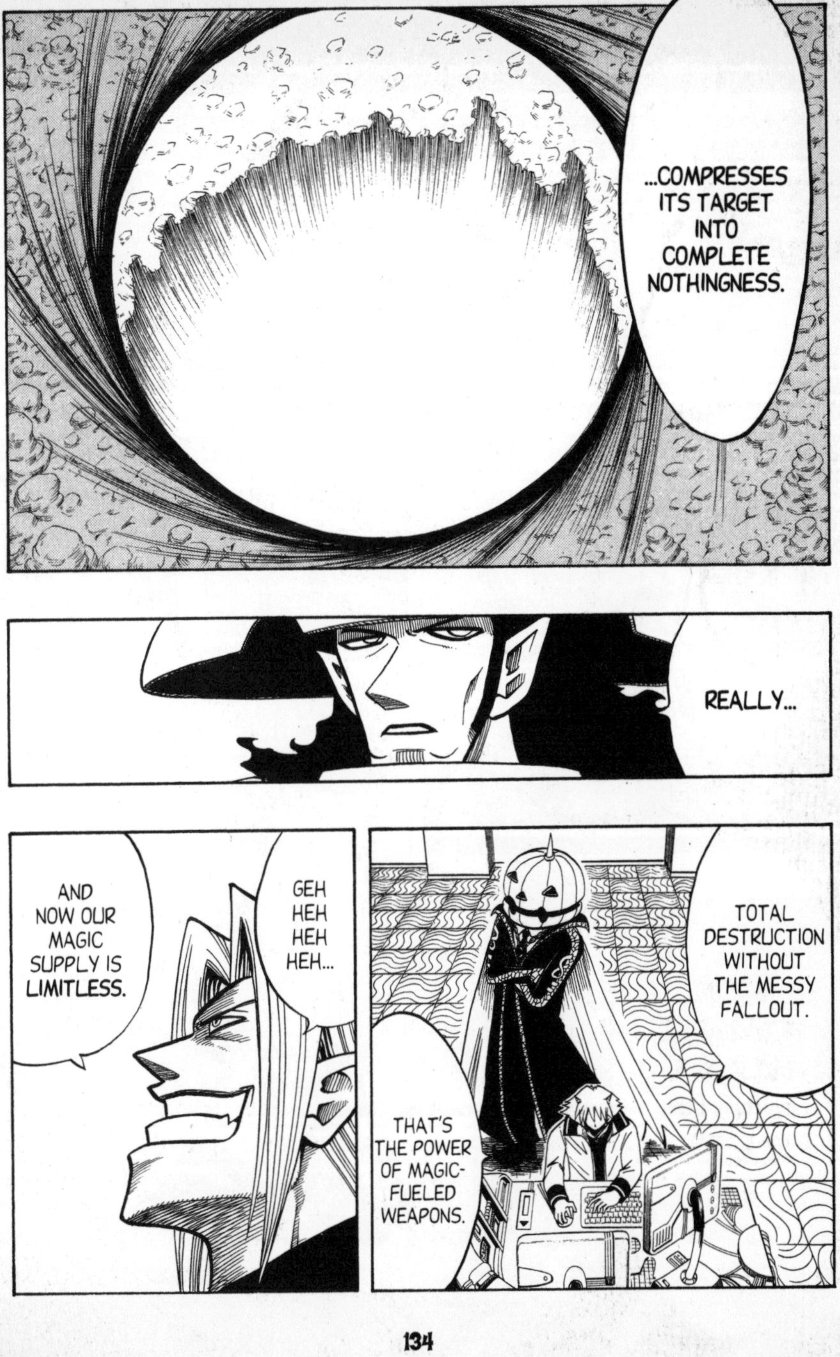
...COMPRESSES ITS TARGET INTO COMPLETE NOTHINGNESS.
REALLY...
TOTAL DESTRUCTION WITHOUT THE MESSY FALLOUT.
THAT'S THE POWER OF MAGIC-FUELED WEAPONS.
GEH HEH HEH HEH...
AND NOW OUR MAGIC SUPPLY IS **LIMITLESS.**

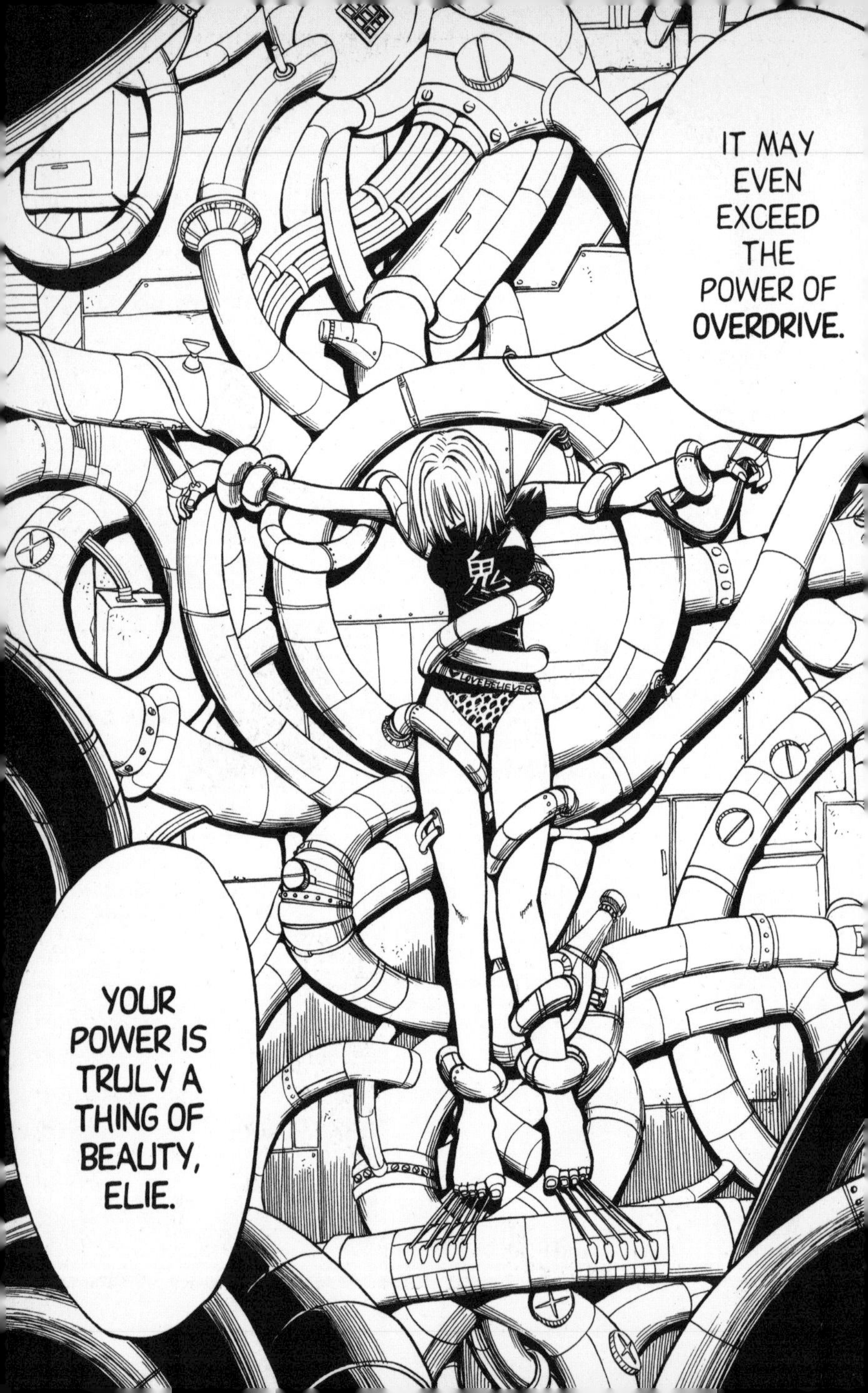
IT MAY EVEN EXCEED THE POWER OF OVERDRIVE.
YOUR POWER IS TRULY A THING OF BEAUTY, ELIE.

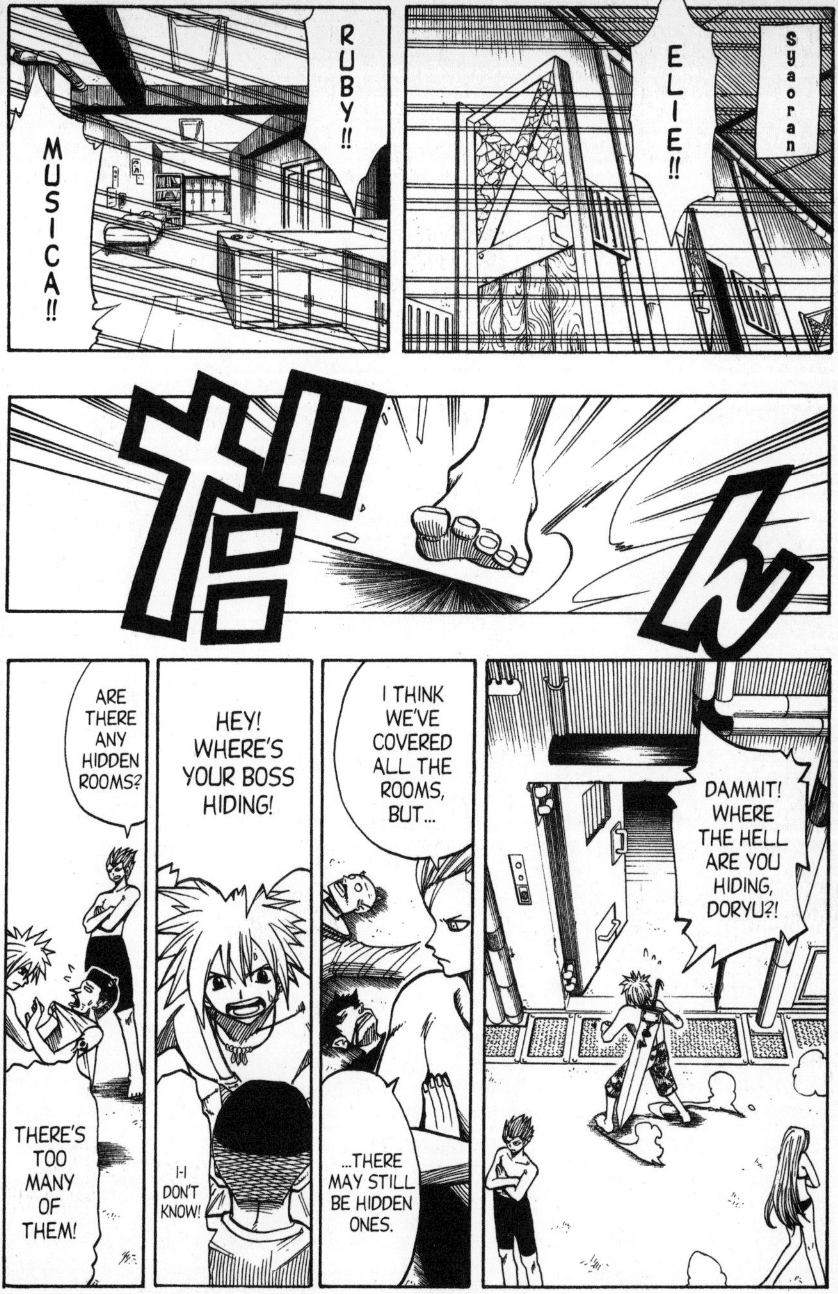
syaoran
ELIE!!
RUBY!!
MUSICA!!
DAMMIT! WHERE THE HELL ARE YOU HIDING, DORYU?!
I THINK WE'VE COVERED ALL THE ROOMS, BUT...
...THERE MAY STILL BE HIDDEN ONES.
HEY! WHERE'S YOUR BOSS HIDING!
I-I DON'T KNOW!
ARE THERE ANY HIDDEN ROOMS?
THERE'S TOO MANY OF THEM!

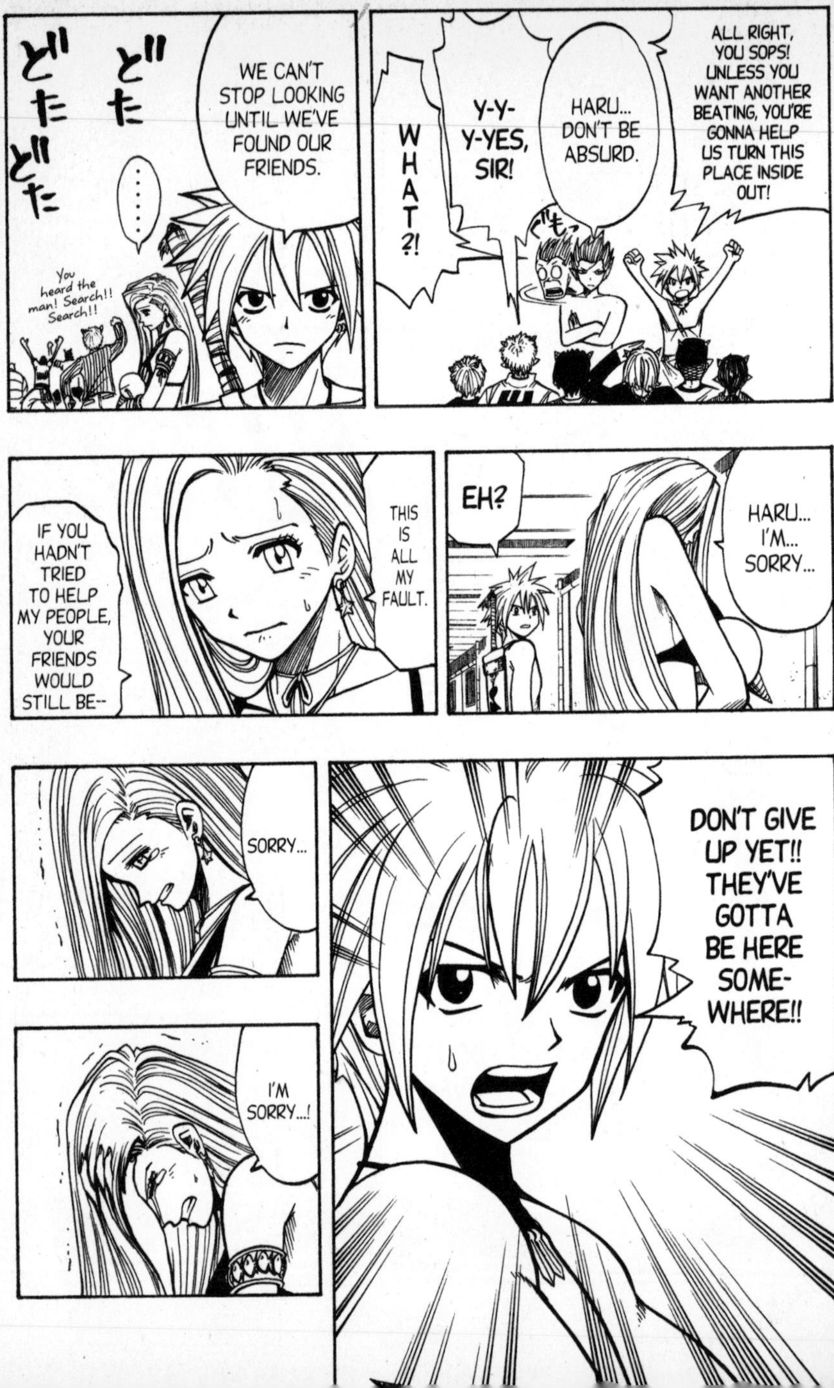
ALL RIGHT, YOU SOPS! UNLESS YOU WANT ANOTHER BEATING, YOU'RE GONNA HELP US TURN THIS PLACE INSIDE OUT!
HARU... DON'T BE ABSURD.
Y-Y-Y-YES, SIR!
WHAT?!
WE CAN'T STOP LOOKING UNTIL WE'VE FOUND OUR FRIENDS.
どたどたどた
......
You heard the man! Search!! Search!!
HARU... I'M... SORRY...
EH?
THIS IS ALL MY FAULT.
IF YOU HADN'T TRIED TO HELP MY PEOPLE, YOUR FRIENDS WOULD STILL BE--
DON'T GIVE UP YET!! THEY'VE GOTTA BE HERE SOME-WHERE!!
SORRY...
I'M SORRY...!

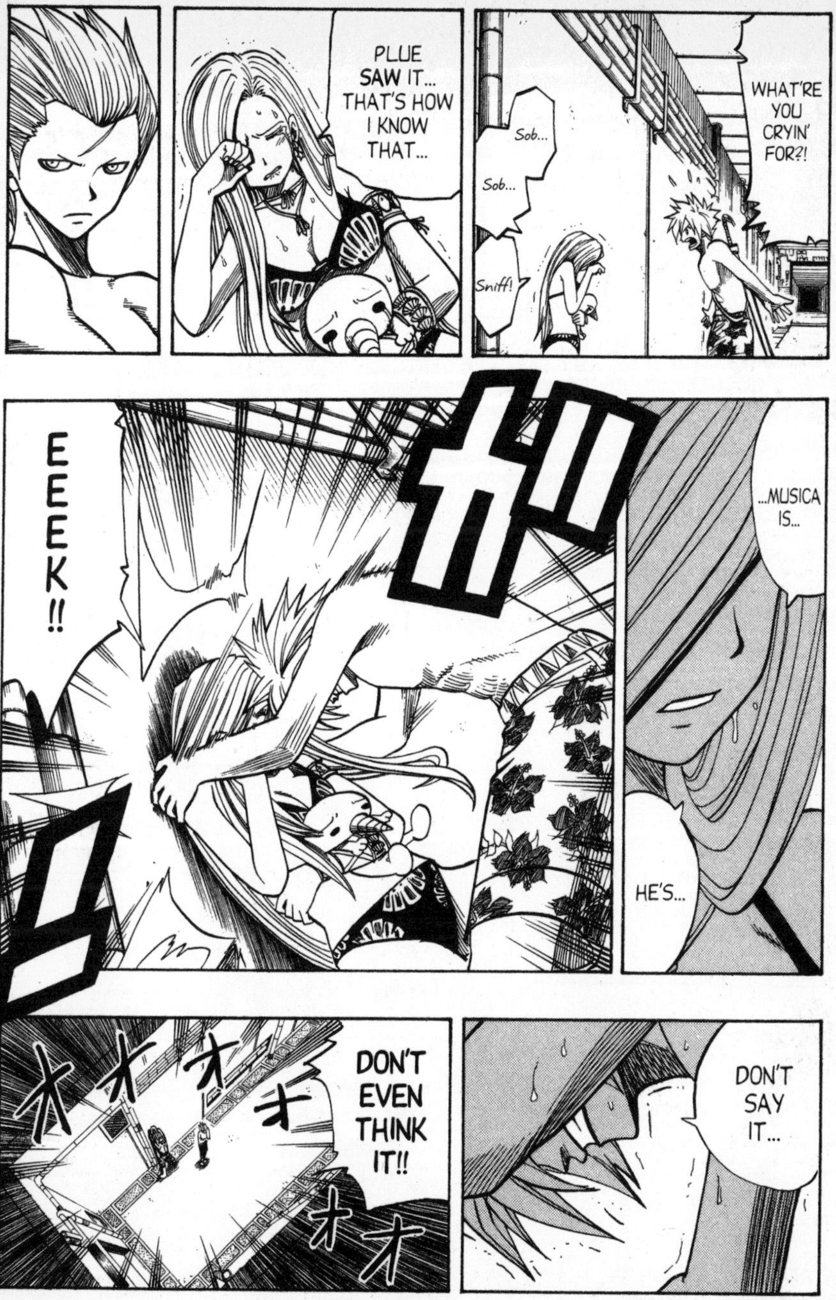
WHAT'RE YOU CRYIN' FOR?!
Sob...
Sob...
Sniff!
PLUE SAW IT... THAT'S HOW I KNOW THAT...
...MUSICA IS...
HE'S...
EEEEK!!
DON'T SAY IT...
DON'T EVEN THINK IT!!
オオオ
オオ

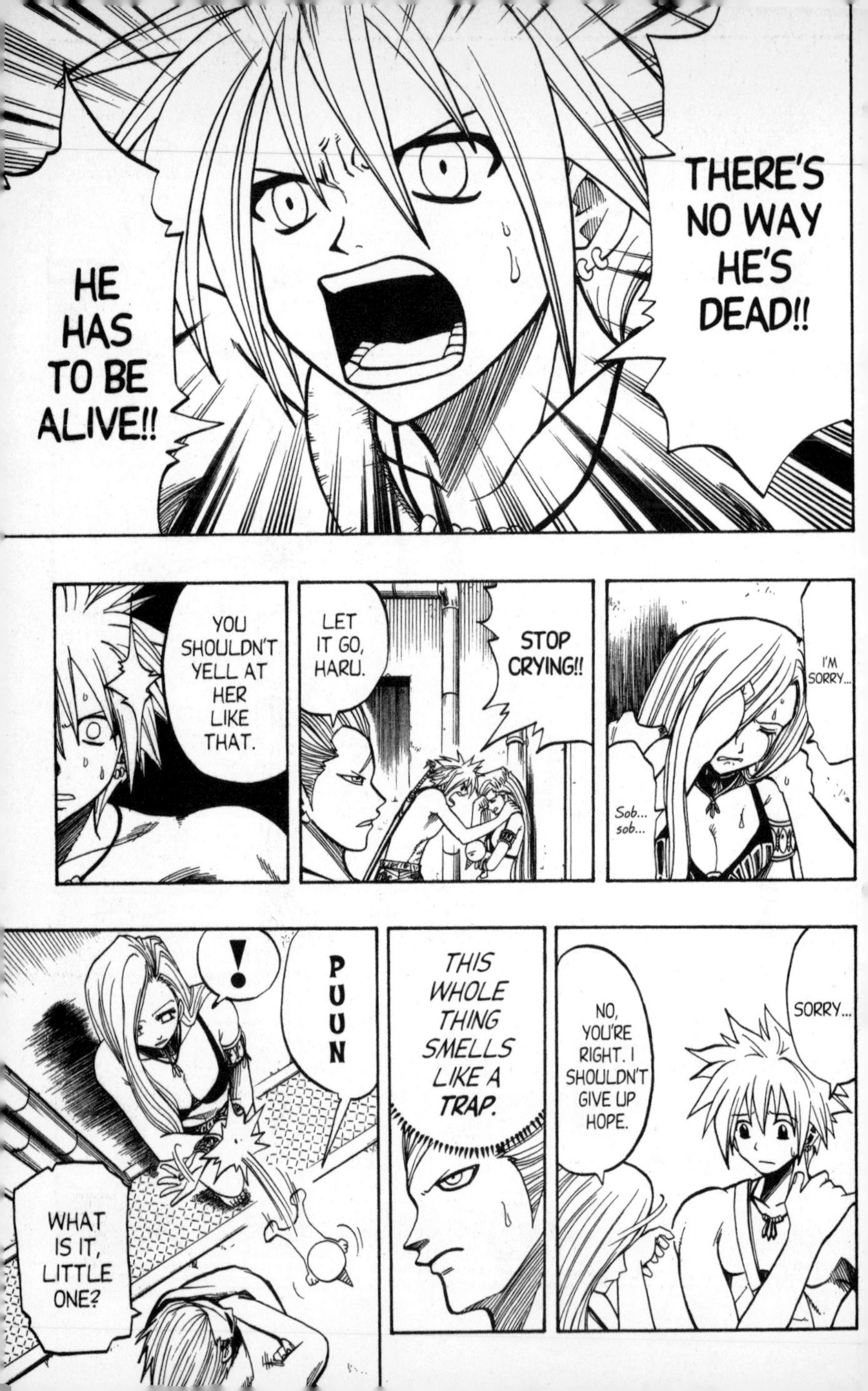
THERE'S NO WAY HE'S DEAD!!
HE HAS TO BE ALIVE!!
I'M SORRY...
Sob... sob...
STOP CRYING!!
LET IT GO, HARU.
YOU SHOULDN'T YELL AT HER LIKE THAT.
SORRY...
NO, YOU'RE RIGHT. I SHOULDN'T GIVE UP HOPE.
THIS WHOLE THING SMELLS LIKE A TRAP.
PUUN
!
WHAT IS IT, LITTLE ONE?

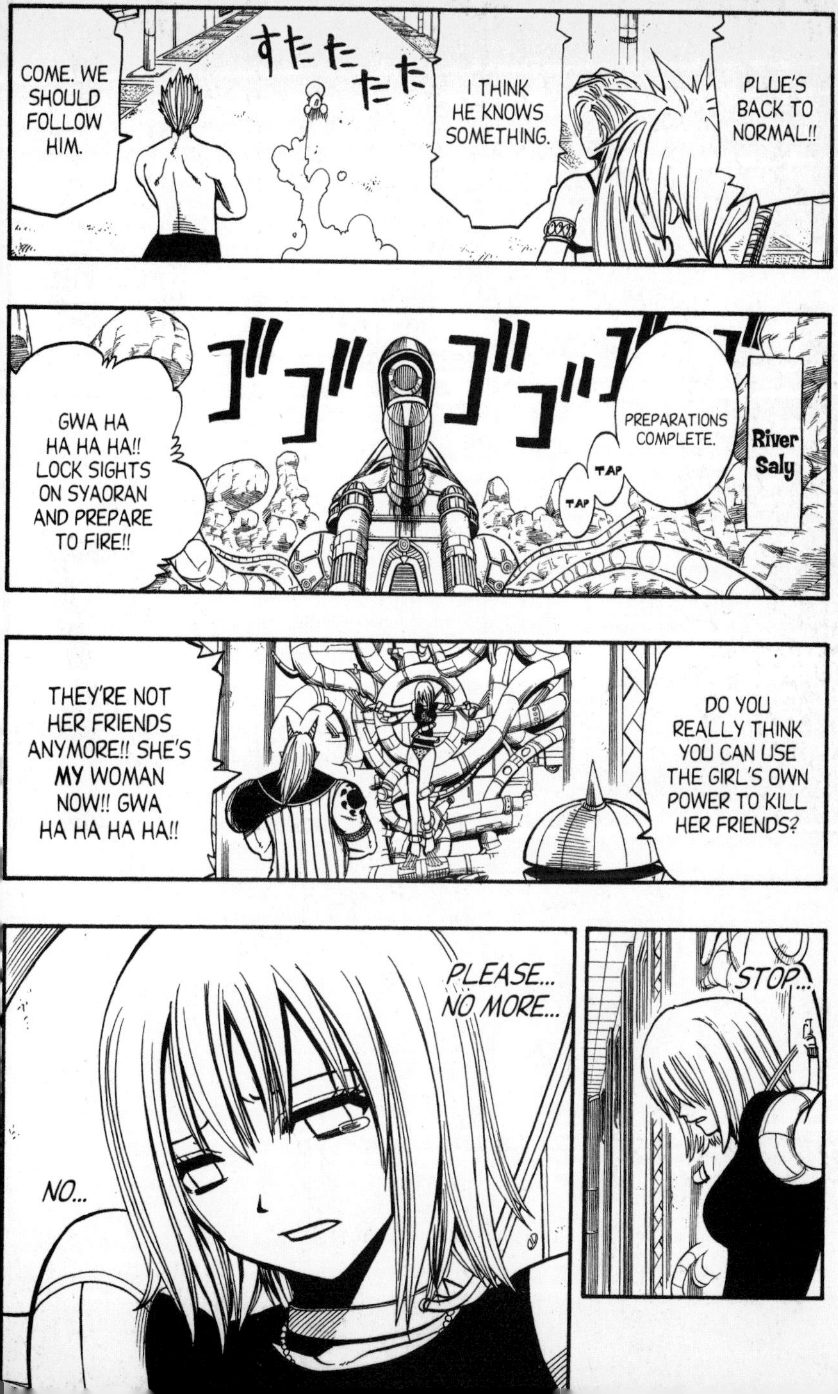
PLUE'S BACK TO NORMAL!!
I THINK HE KNOWS SOMETHING.
すたたたた
COME. WE SHOULD FOLLOW HIM.
River Saly
PREPARATIONS COMPLETE.
TAP
TAP
ゴゴゴゴゴ
GWA HA HA HA HA!! LOCK SIGHTS ON SYAORAN AND PREPARE TO FIRE!!
DO YOU REALLY THINK YOU CAN USE THE GIRL'S OWN POWER TO KILL HER FRIENDS?
THEY'RE NOT HER FRIENDS ANYMORE!! SHE'S MY WOMAN NOW!! GWA HA HA HA HA!!
STOP...
PLEASE... NO MORE...
NO...

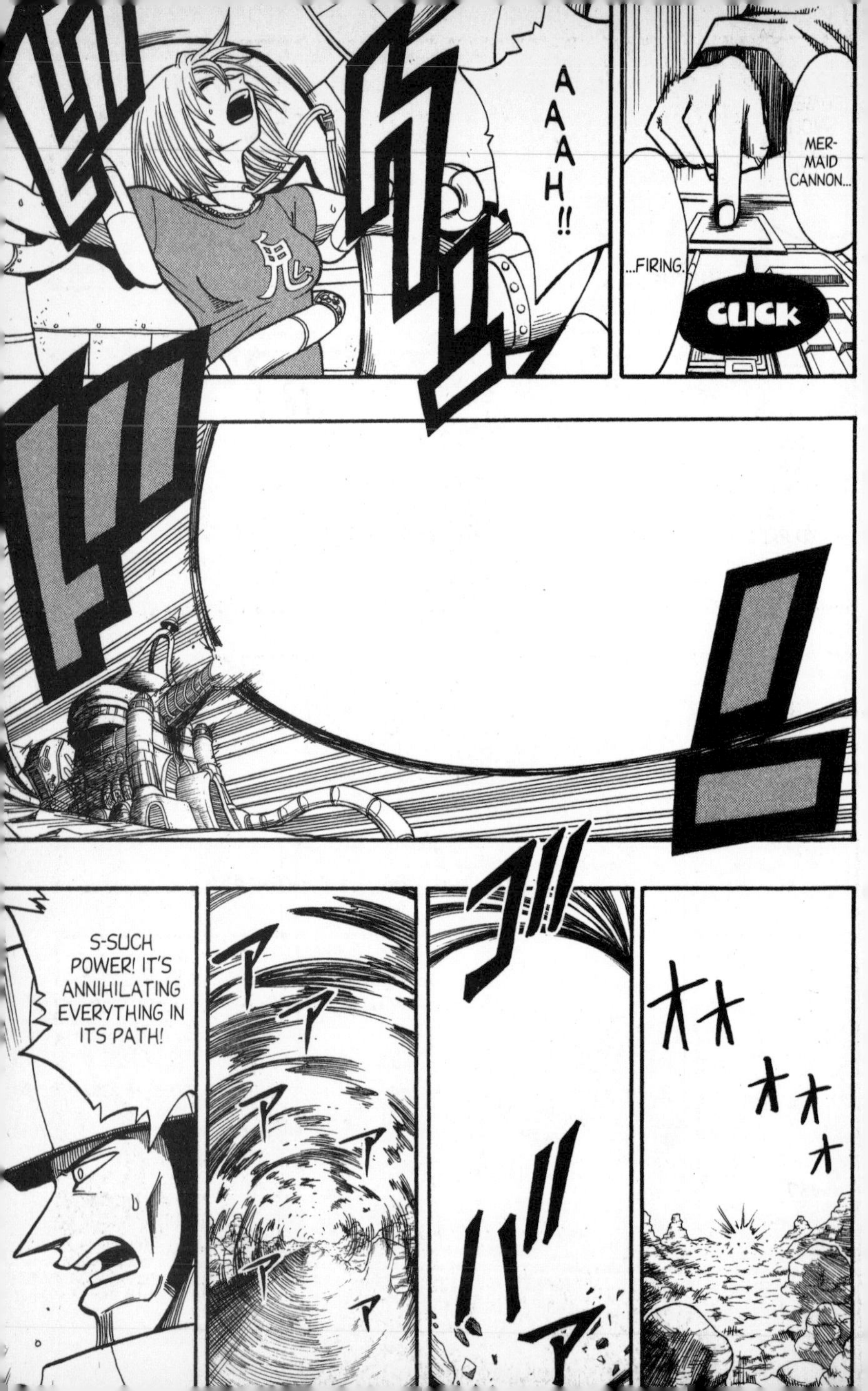
MER-MAID CANNON...
...FIRING.
CLICK
AAAH!!
S-SUCH POWER! IT'S ANNIHILATING EVERYTHING IN ITS PATH!

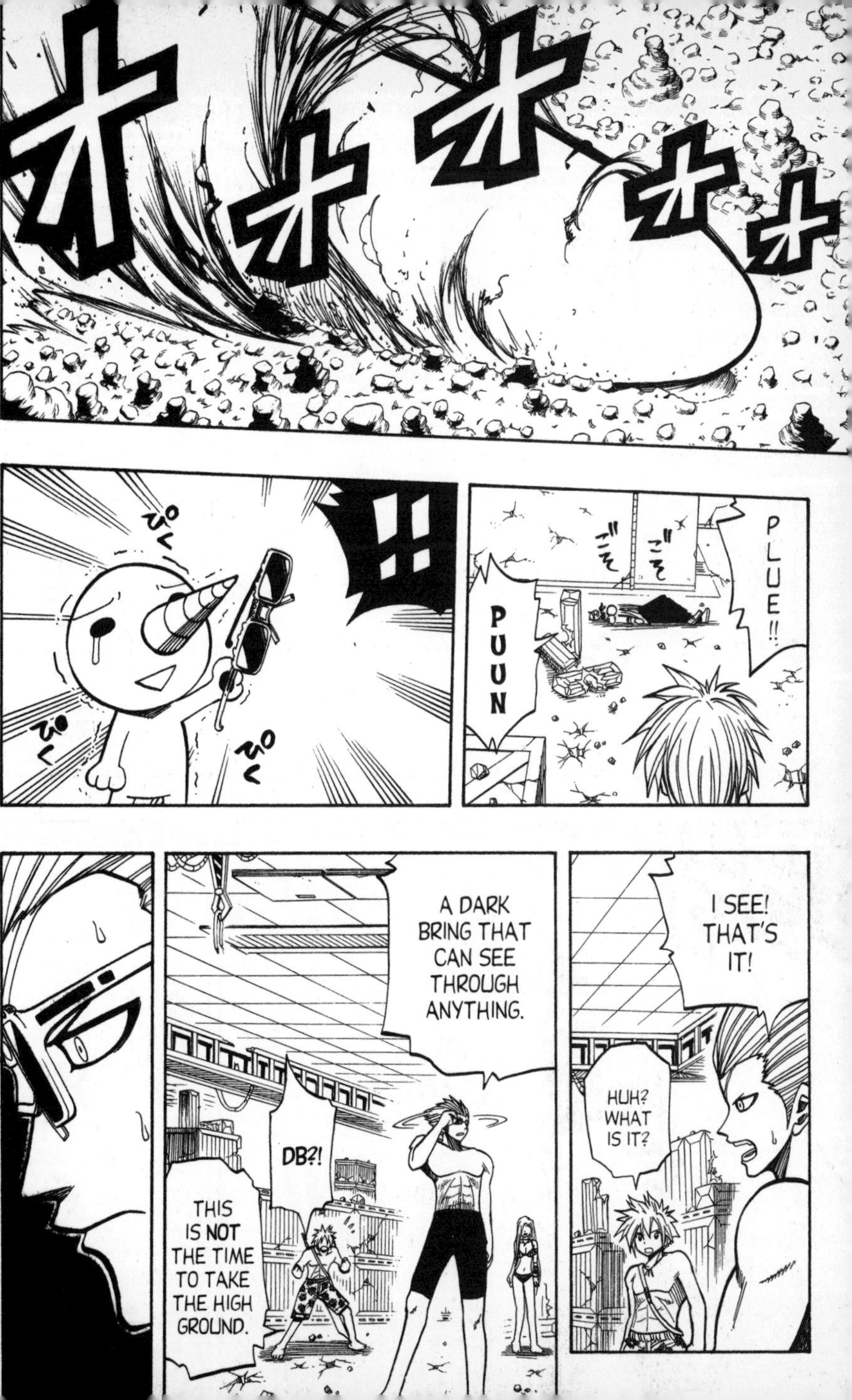

オオオォォ
PLUE!!
ごそ
ごそ
PUUN
!!
ぴく
ぴく
ぴく
I SEE! THAT'S IT!
HUH? WHAT IS IT?
A DARK BRING THAT CAN SEE THROUGH ANYTHING.
DB?!
THIS IS **NOT** THE TIME TO TAKE THE HIGH GROUND.

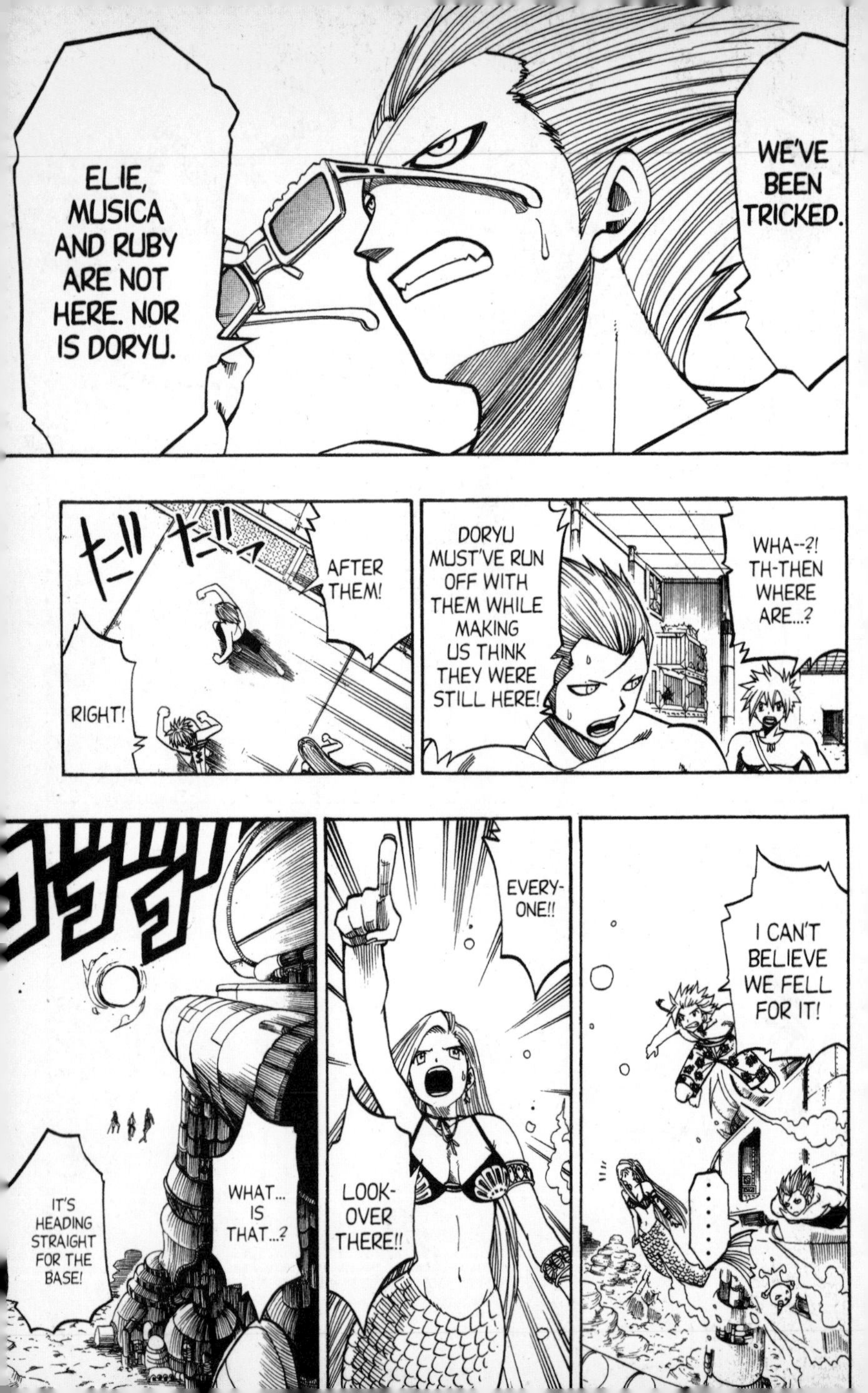
ELIE, MUSICA AND RUBY ARE NOT HERE. NOR IS DORYU.
WE'VE BEEN TRICKED.
WHA--?! TH-THEN WHERE ARE...?
DORYU MUST'VE RUN OFF WITH THEM WHILE MAKING US THINK THEY WERE STILL HERE!
AFTER THEM!
RIGHT!
I CAN'T BELIEVE WE FELL FOR IT!
......
EVERY-ONE!!
LOOK-OVER THERE!!
WHAT... IS THAT...?
IT'S HEADING STRAIGHT FOR THE BASE!

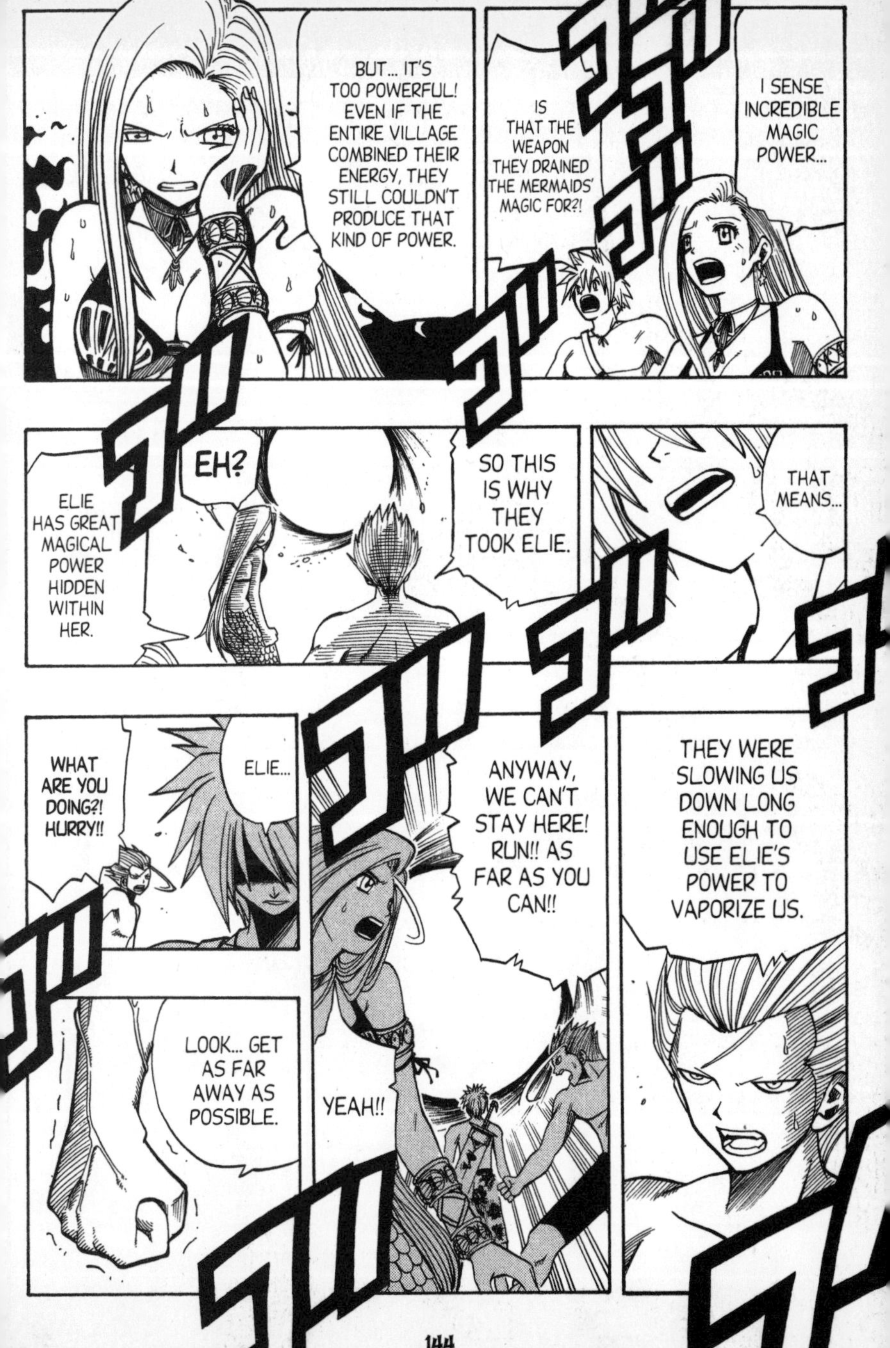
I SENSE INCREDIBLE MAGIC POWER...
IS THAT THE WEAPON THEY DRAINED THE MERMAIDS' MAGIC FOR?!
BUT... IT'S TOO POWERFUL! EVEN IF THE ENTIRE VILLAGE COMBINED THEIR ENERGY, THEY STILL COULDN'T PRODUCE THAT KIND OF POWER.
THAT MEANS...
SO THIS IS WHY THEY TOOK ELIE.
EH?
ELIE HAS GREAT MAGICAL POWER HIDDEN WITHIN HER.
THEY WERE SLOWING US DOWN LONG ENOUGH TO USE ELIE'S POWER TO VAPORIZE US.
ANYWAY, WE CAN'T STAY HERE! RUN!! AS FAR AS YOU CAN!!
YEAH!!
ELIE...
WHAT ARE YOU DOING?! HURRY!!
LOOK... GET AS FAR AWAY AS POSSIBLE.

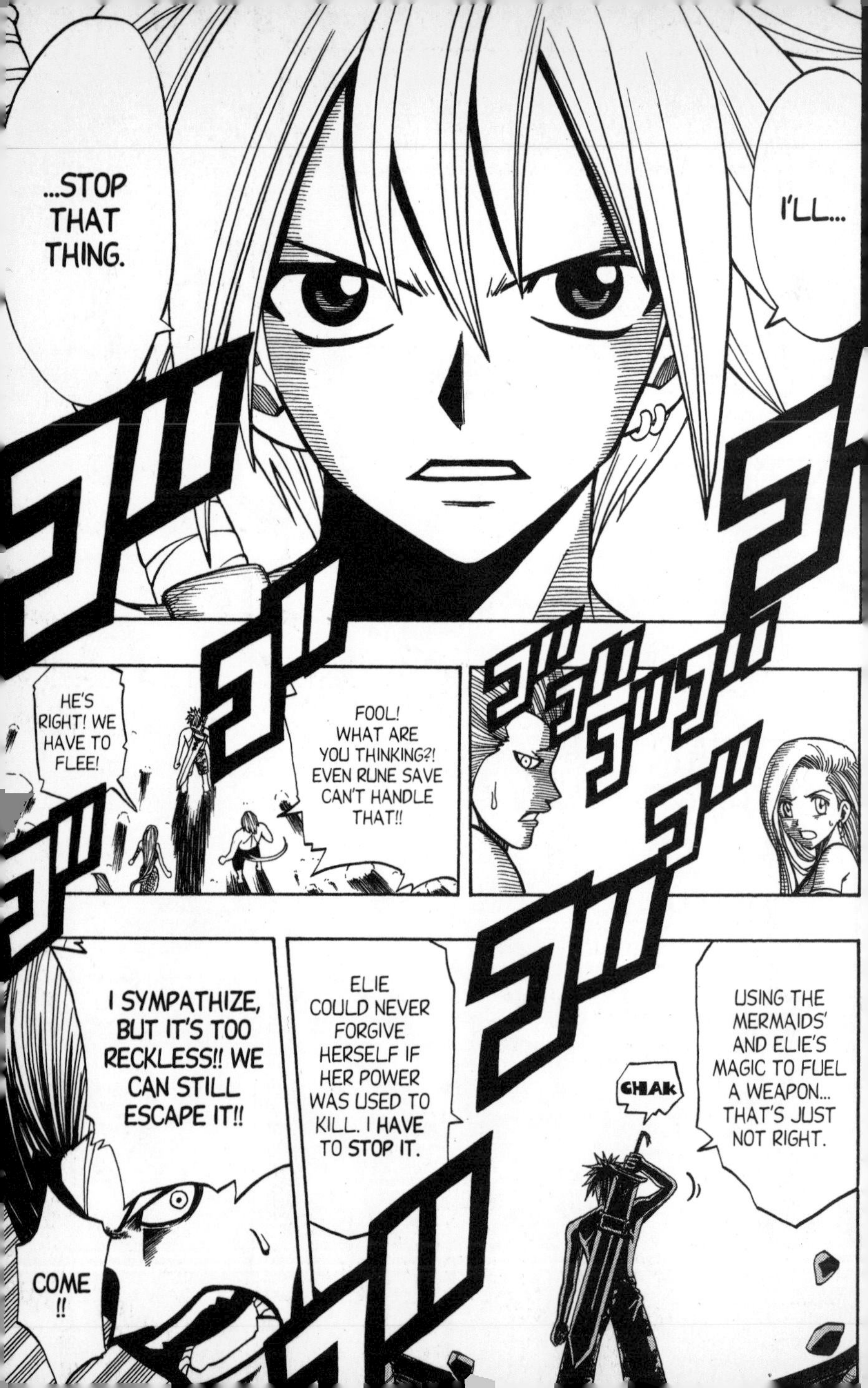
I'LL...
...STOP THAT THING.
FOOL! WHAT ARE YOU THINKING?! EVEN RUNE SAVE CAN'T HANDLE THAT!!
HE'S RIGHT! WE HAVE TO FLEE!
USING THE MERMAIDS' AND ELIE'S MAGIC TO FUEL A WEAPON... THAT'S JUST NOT RIGHT.
CHAK
ELIE COULD NEVER FORGIVE HERSELF IF HER POWER WAS USED TO KILL. I HAVE TO STOP IT.
I SYMPATHIZE, BUT IT'S TOO RECKLESS!! WE CAN STILL ESCAPE IT!!
COME !!

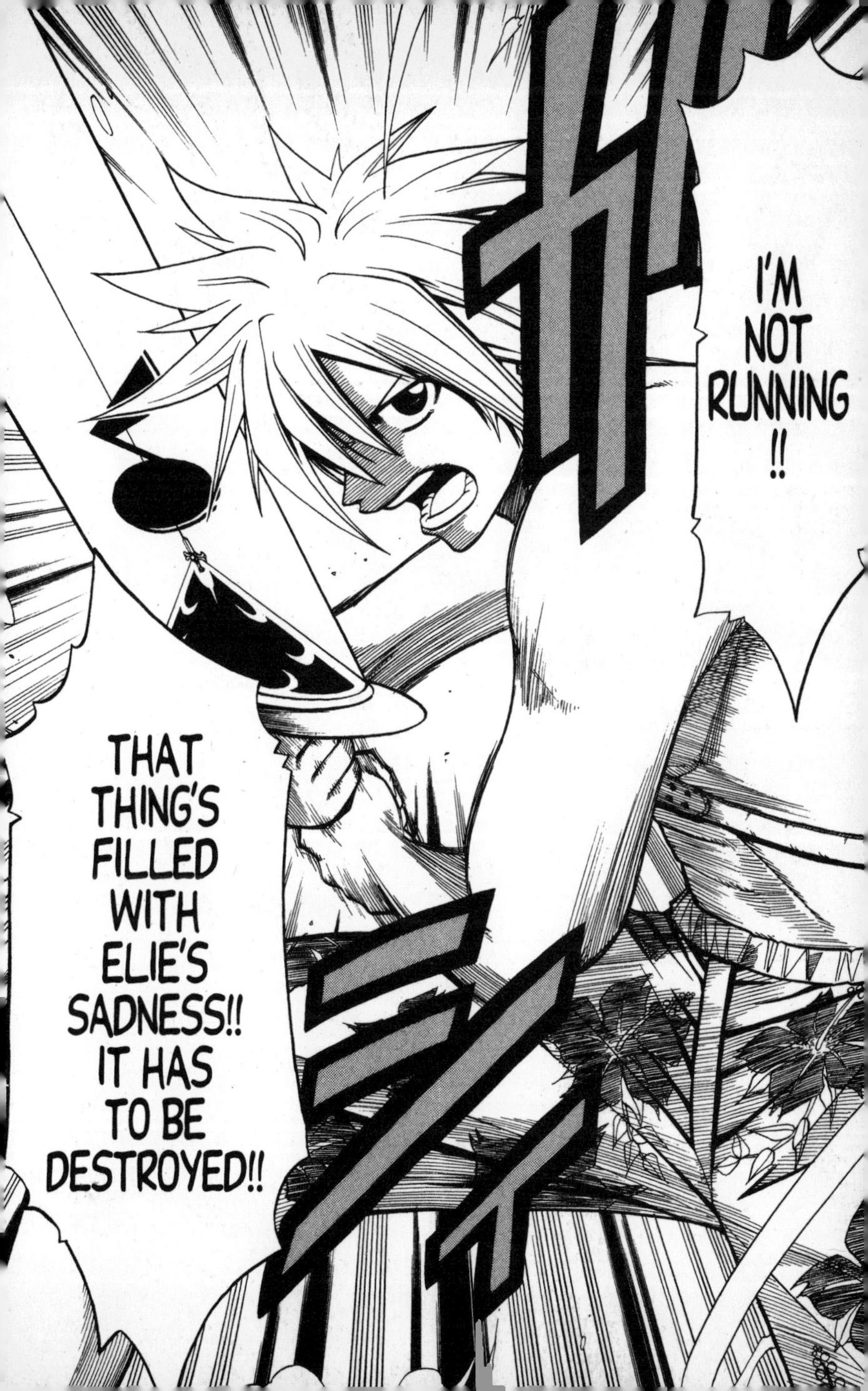
I'M NOT RUNNING!!
THAT THING'S FILLED WITH ELIE'S SADNESS!! IT HAS TO BE DESTROYED!!

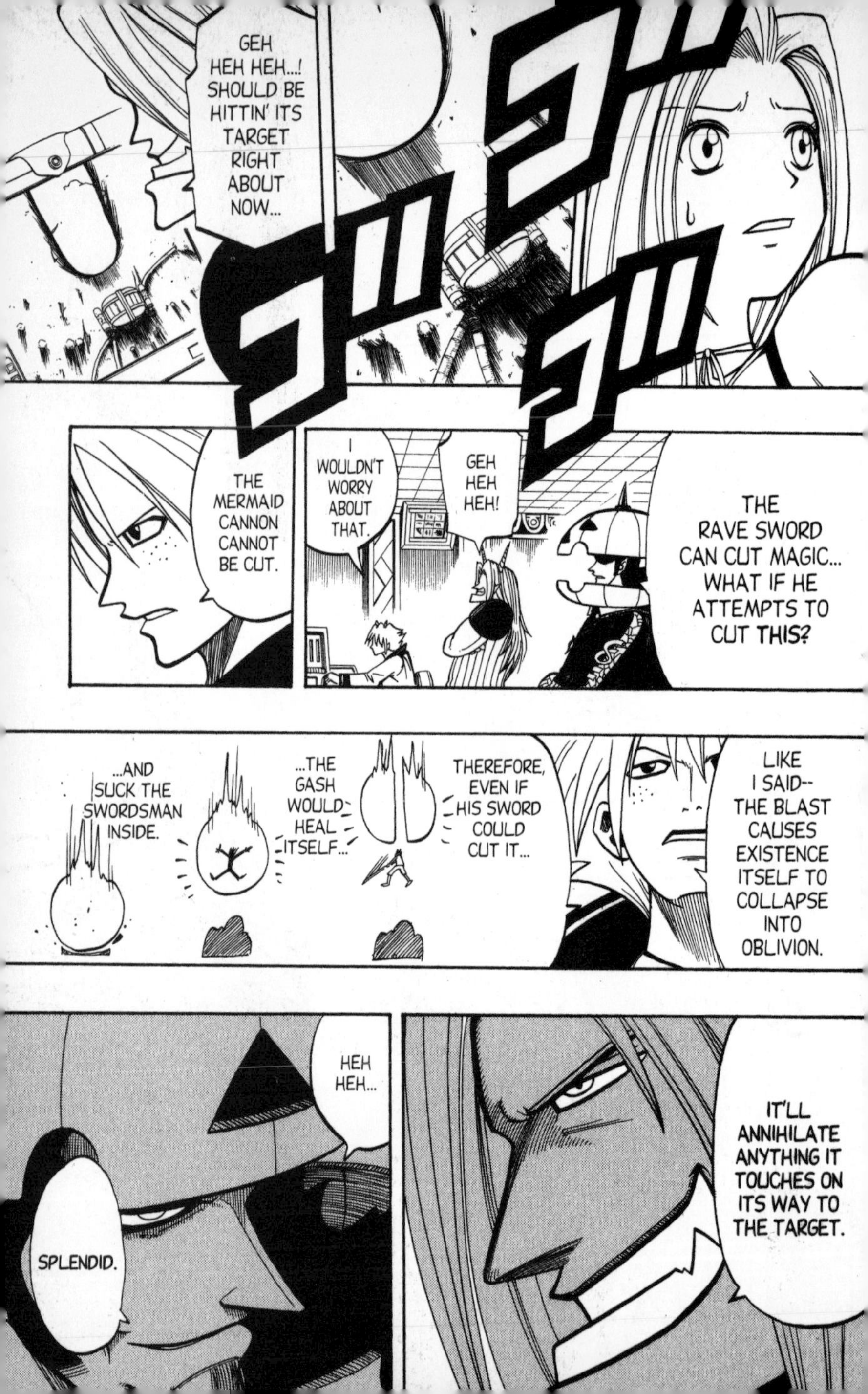
GEH HEH HEH...! SHOULD BE HITTIN' ITS TARGET RIGHT ABOUT NOW...
THE RAVE SWORD CAN CUT MAGIC... WHAT IF HE ATTEMPTS TO CUT THIS?
GEH HEH HEH!
I WOULDN'T WORRY ABOUT THAT.
THE MERMAID CANNON CANNOT BE CUT.
LIKE I SAID-- THE BLAST CAUSES EXISTENCE ITSELF TO COLLAPSE INTO OBLIVION.
THEREFORE, EVEN IF HIS SWORD COULD CUT IT...
...THE GASH WOULD HEAL ITSELF...
...AND SUCK THE SWORDSMAN INSIDE.
IT'LL ANNIHILATE ANYTHING IT TOUCHES ON ITS WAY TO THE TARGET.
HEH HEH...
SPLENDID.

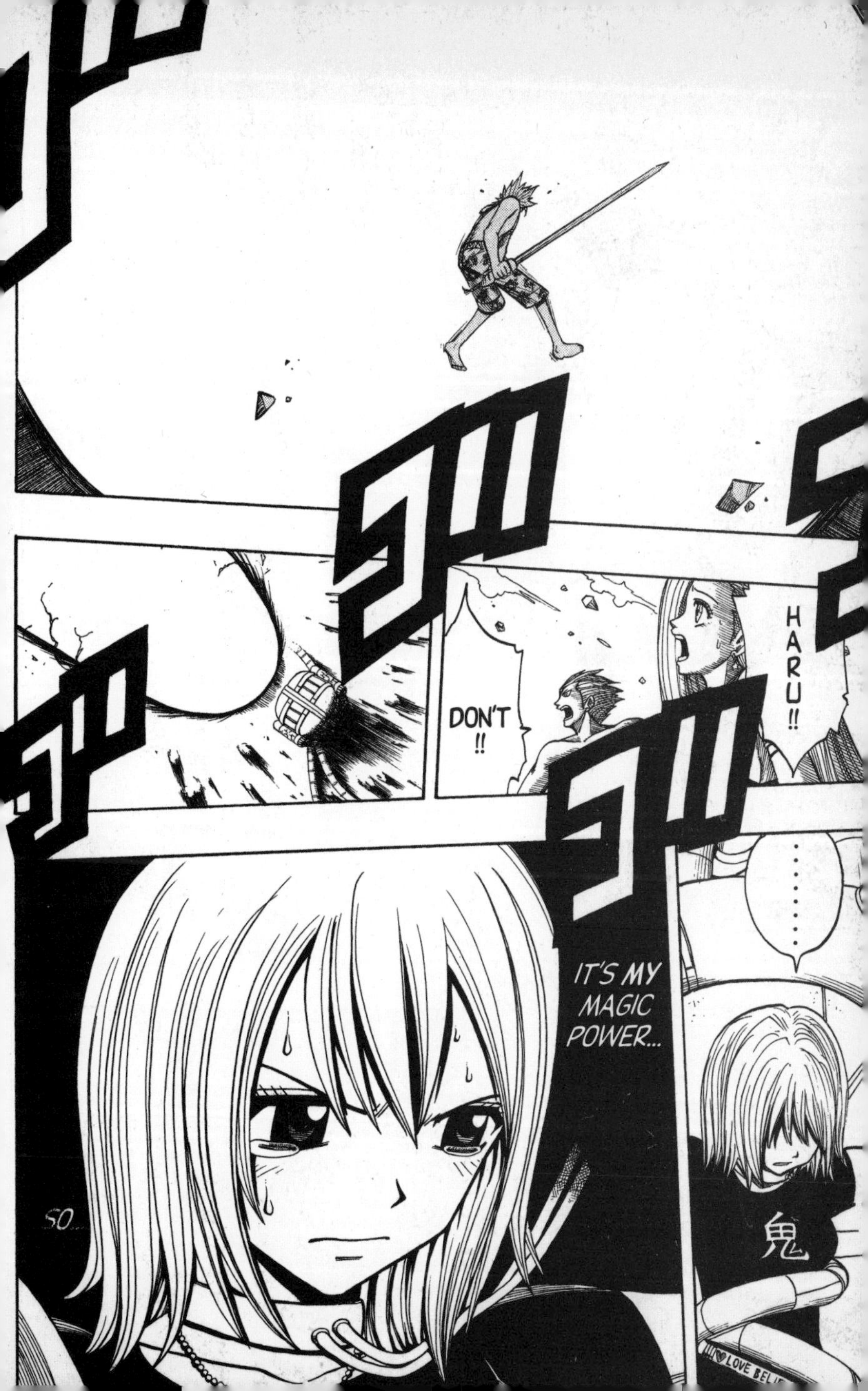
HARU!!
DON'T!!
......
IT'S MY MAGIC POWER...
SO...
♡LOVE BELIE

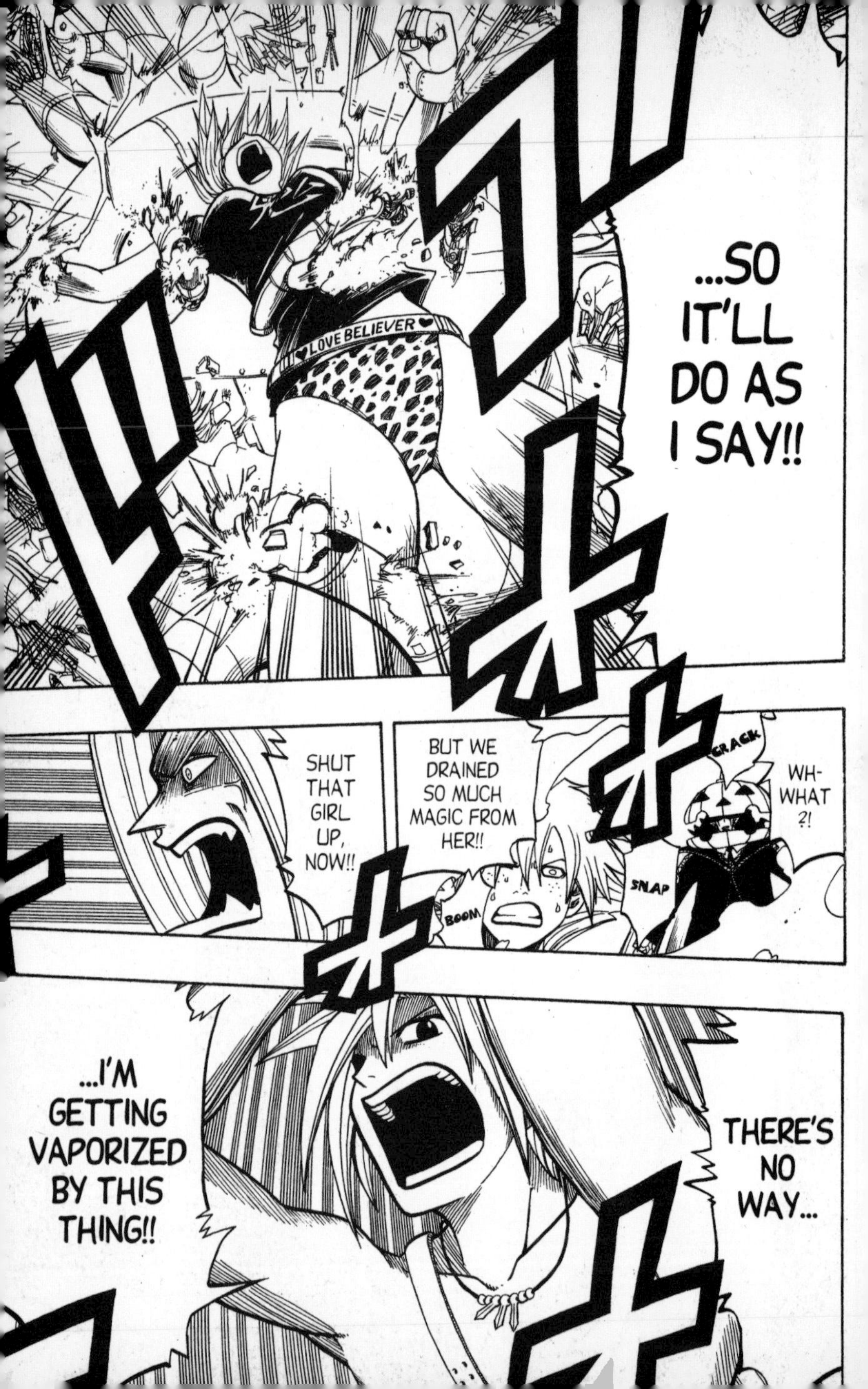

LOVE BELIEVER
...SO IT'LL DO AS I SAY!!
CRACK
WH-WHAT?!
BUT WE DRAINED SO MUCH MAGIC FROM HER!!
SNAP
BOOM
SHUT THAT GIRL UP, NOW!!
THERE'S NO WAY...
...I'M GETTING VAPORIZED BY THIS THING!!

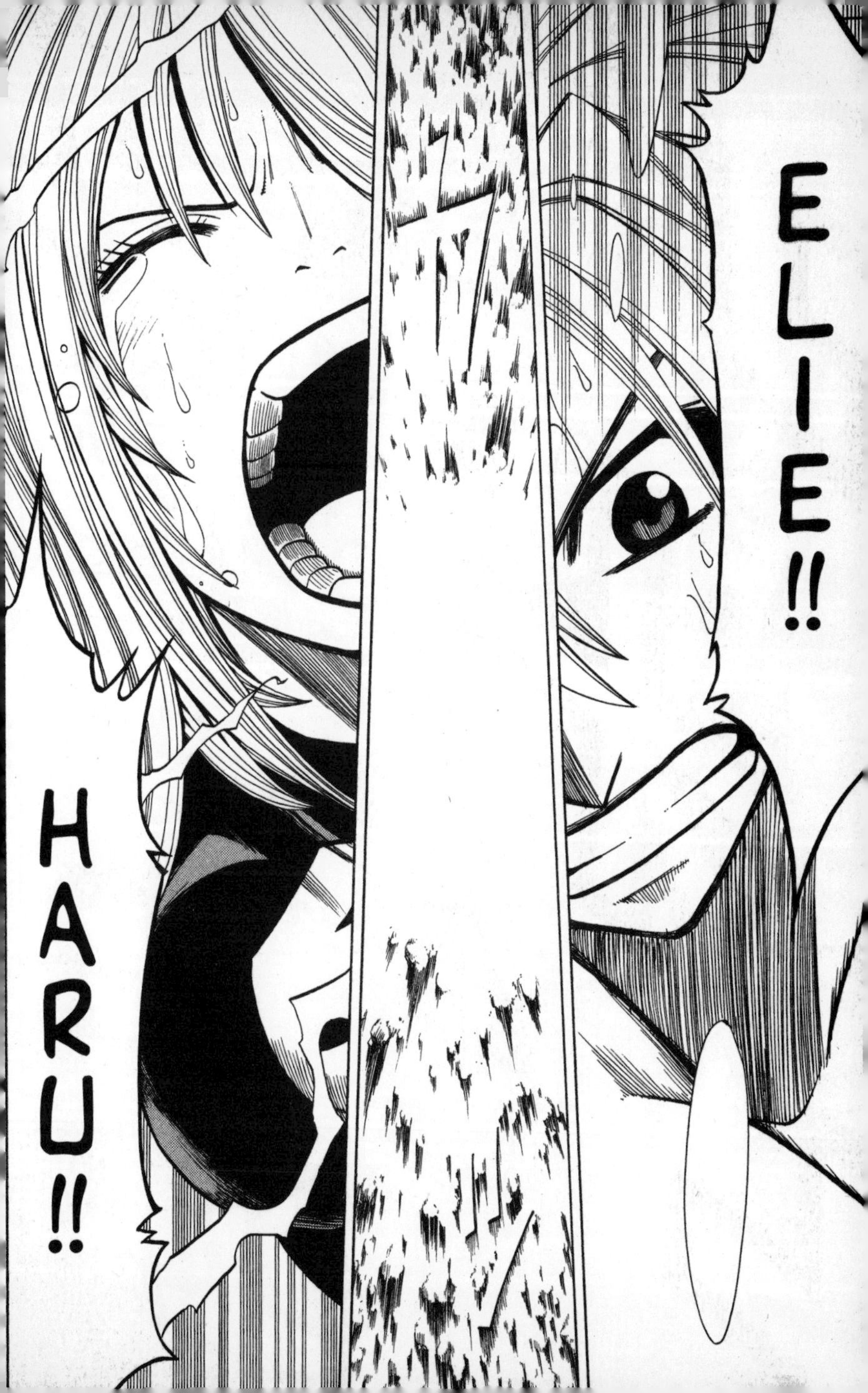
ELIE!!
HARU!!

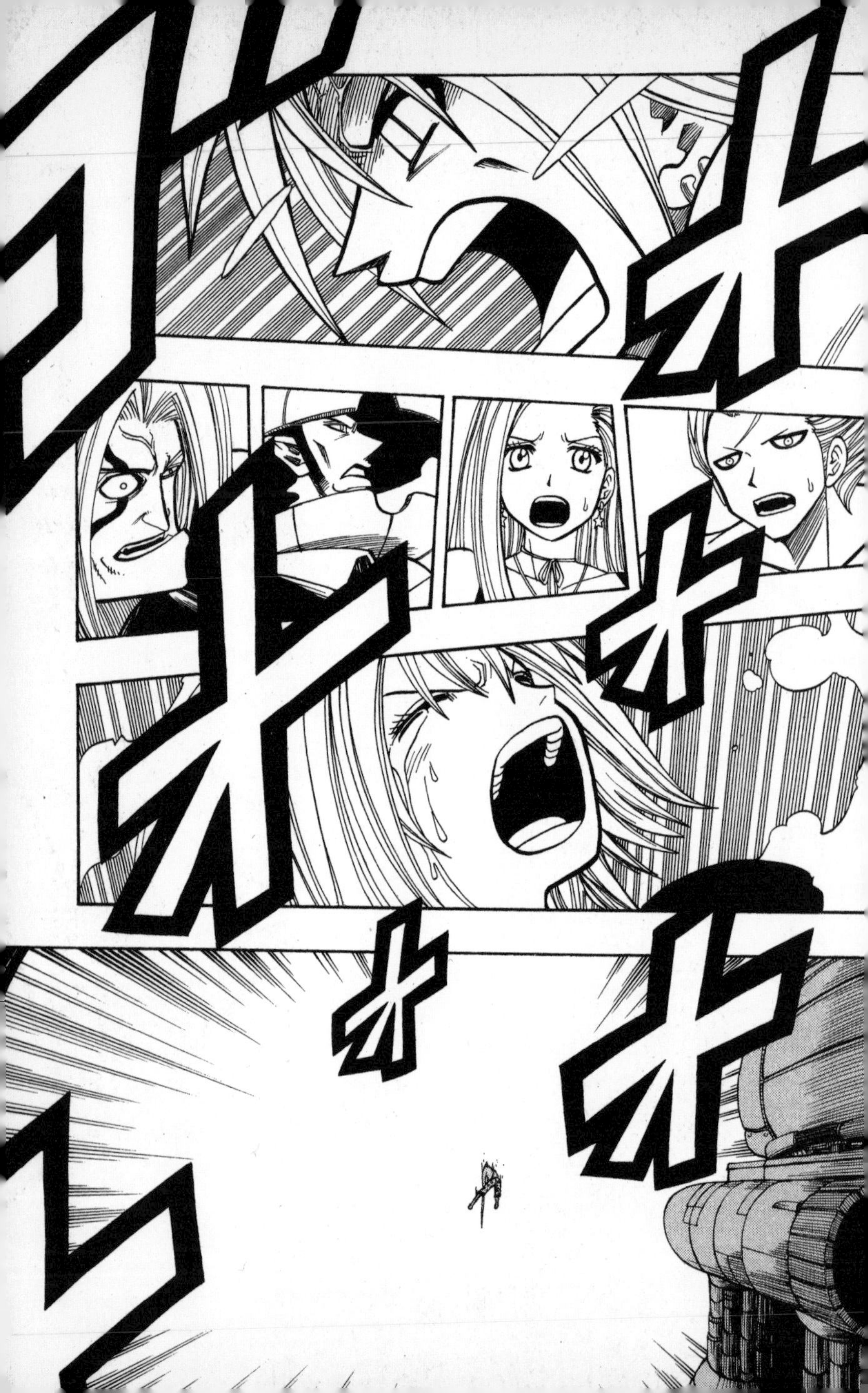

RAVE MASTER

RAVE:113 ✣ A THORNY DECISION

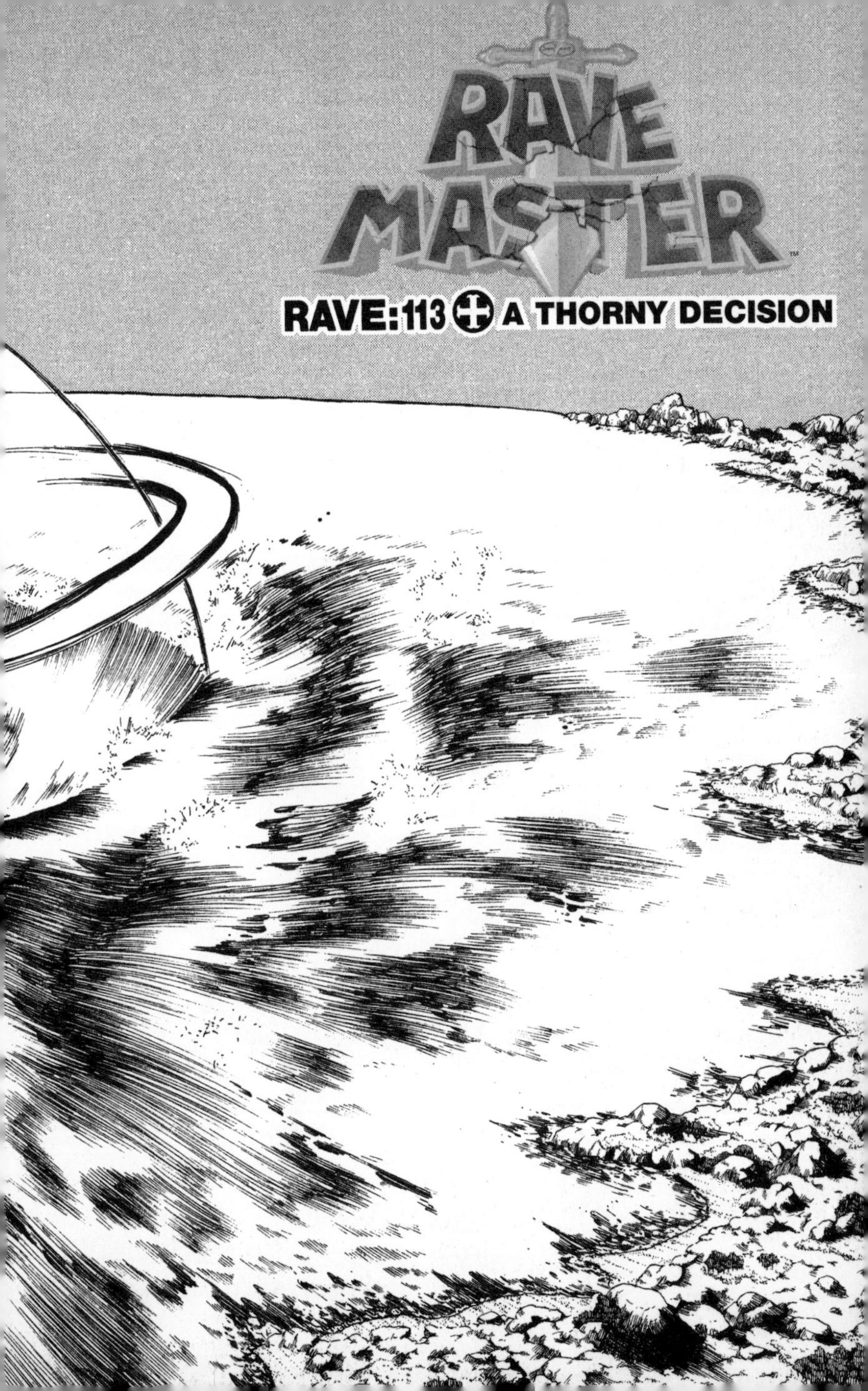

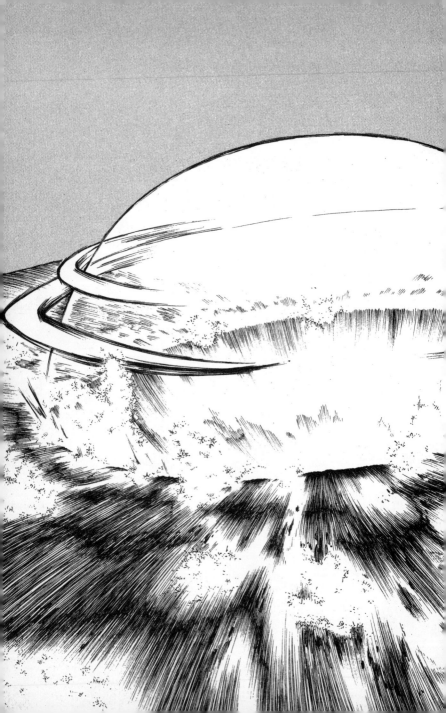

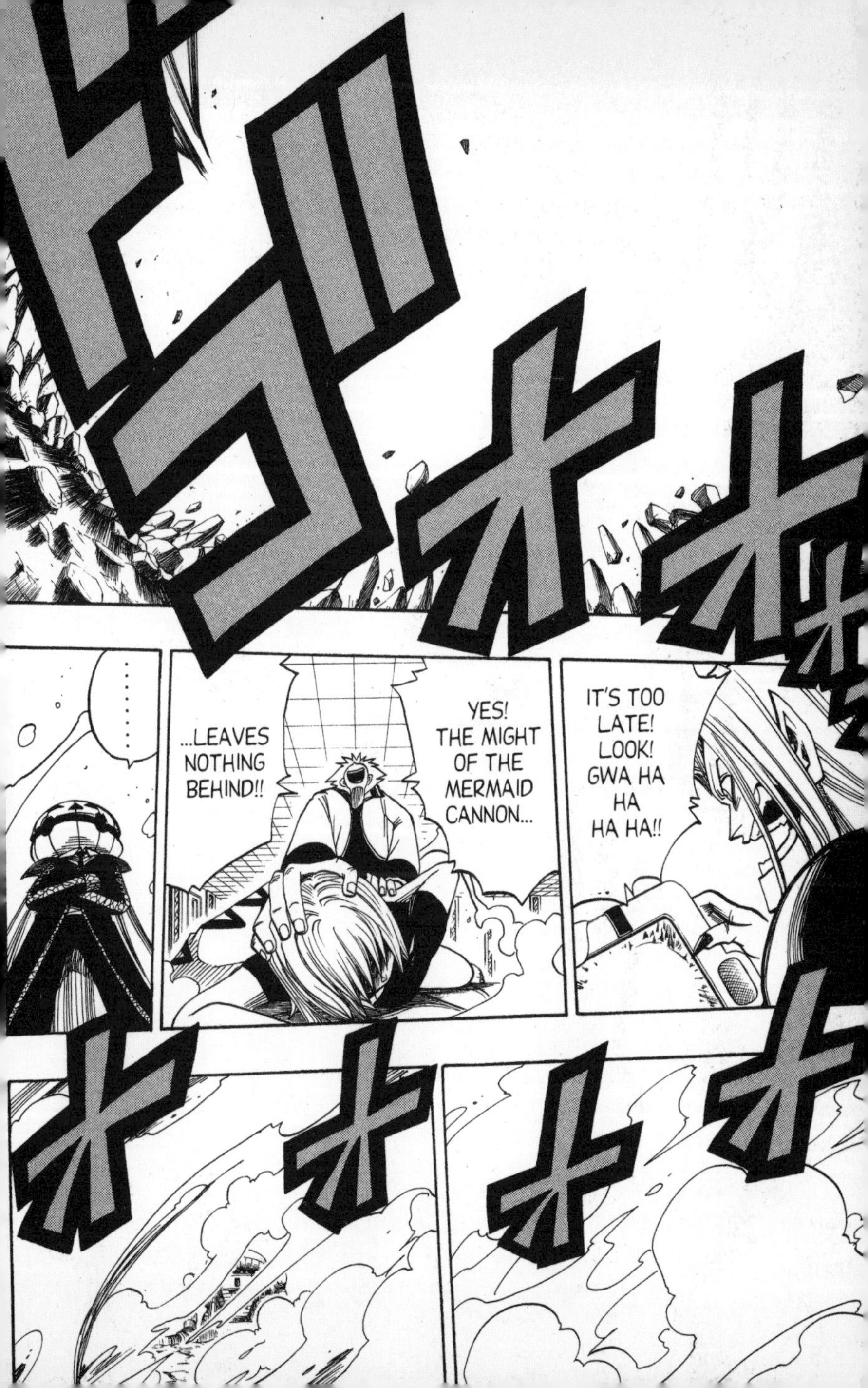
IT'S TOO LATE! LOOK! GWA HA HA HA HA!!
YES! THE MIGHT OF THE MERMAID CANNON...
...LEAVES NOTHING BEHIND!!
......

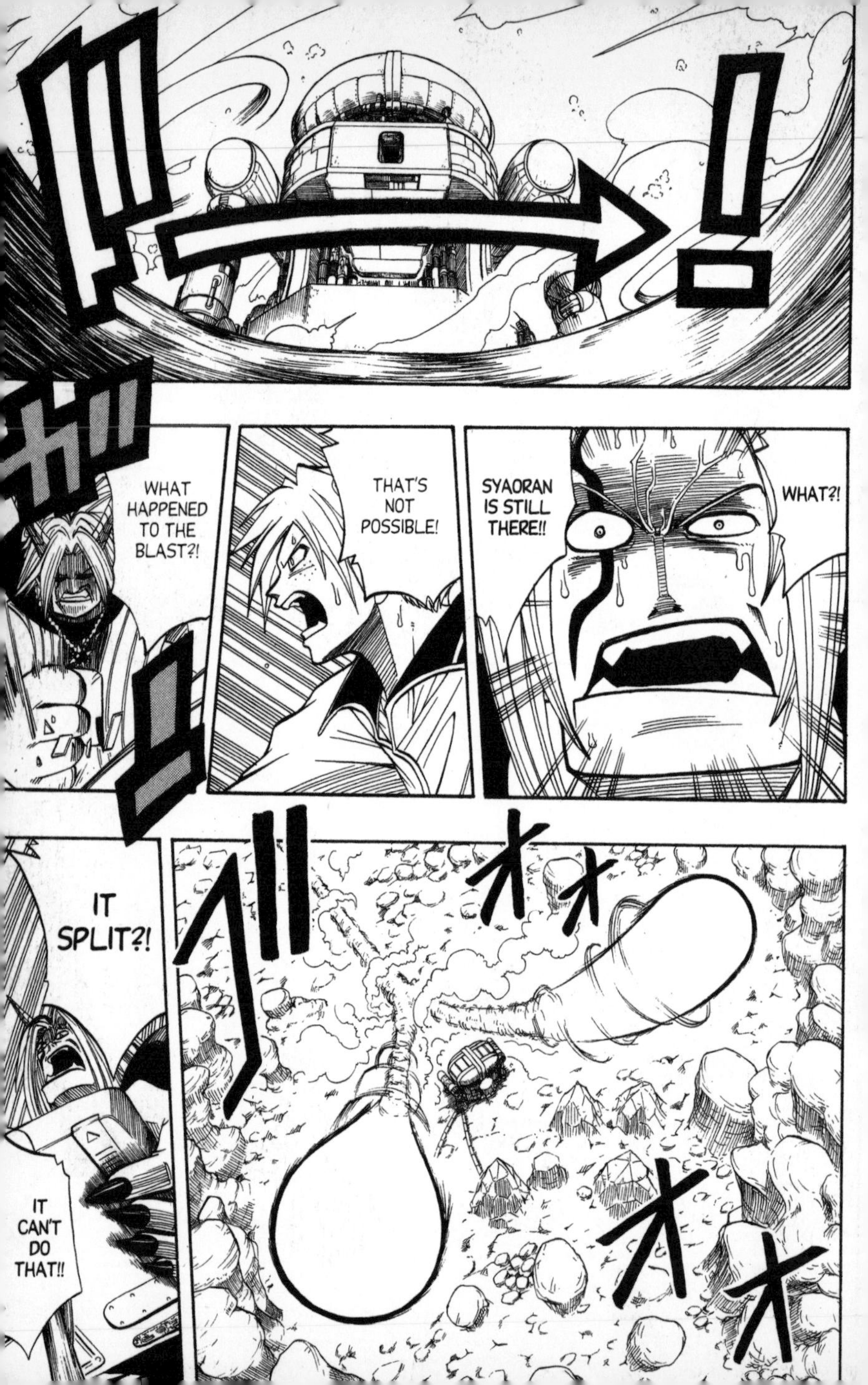
WHAT?!
SYAORAN IS STILL THERE!!
THAT'S NOT POSSIBLE!
WHAT HAPPENED TO THE BLAST?!
IT SPLIT?!
IT CAN'T DO THAT!!

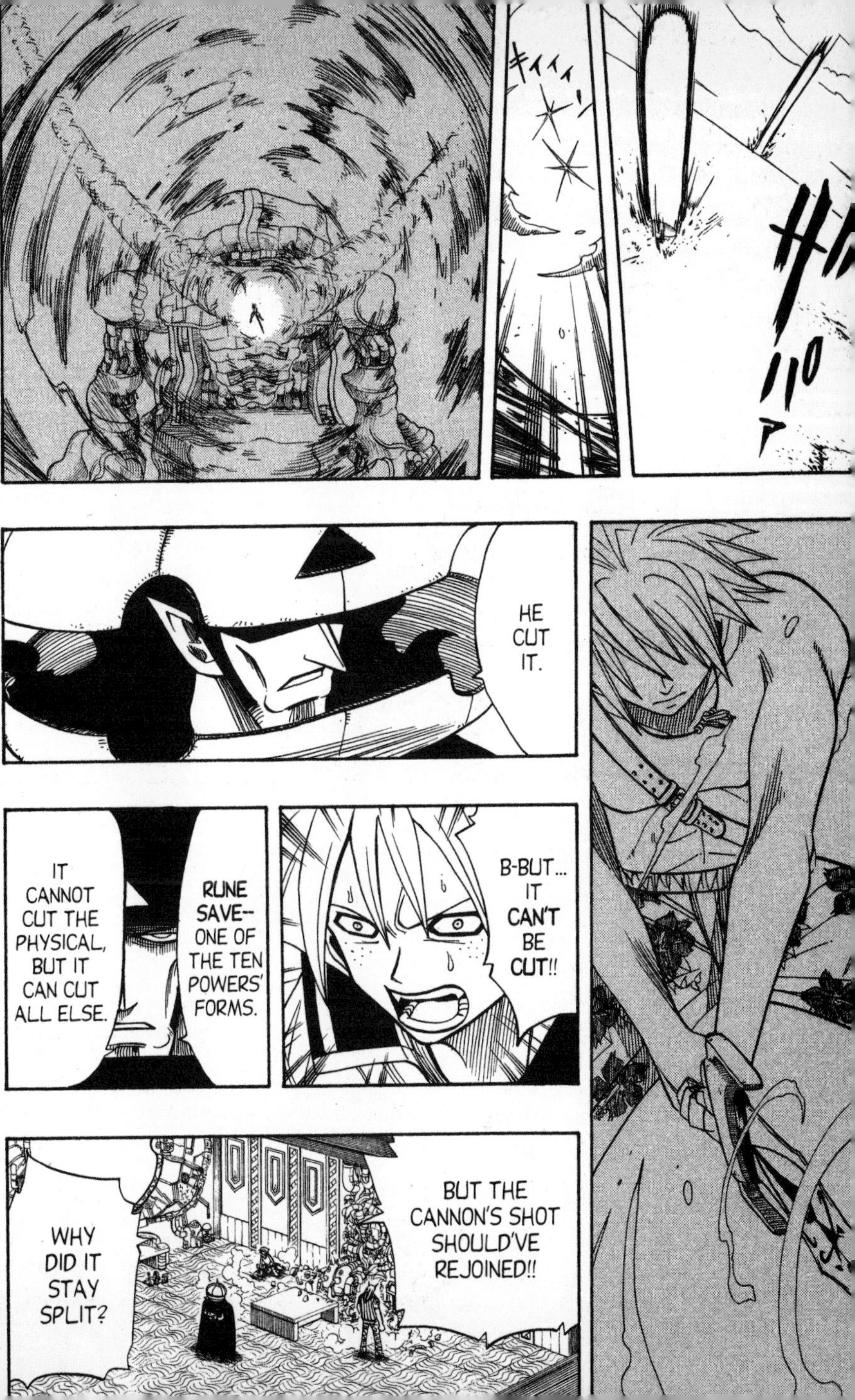
HE CUT IT.
B-BUT... IT CAN'T BE CUT!!
RUNE SAVE-- ONE OF THE TEN POWERS' FORMS.
IT CANNOT CUT THE PHYSICAL, BUT IT CAN CUT ALL ELSE.
BUT THE CANNON'S SHOT SHOULD'VE REJOINED!!
WHY DID IT STAY SPLIT?

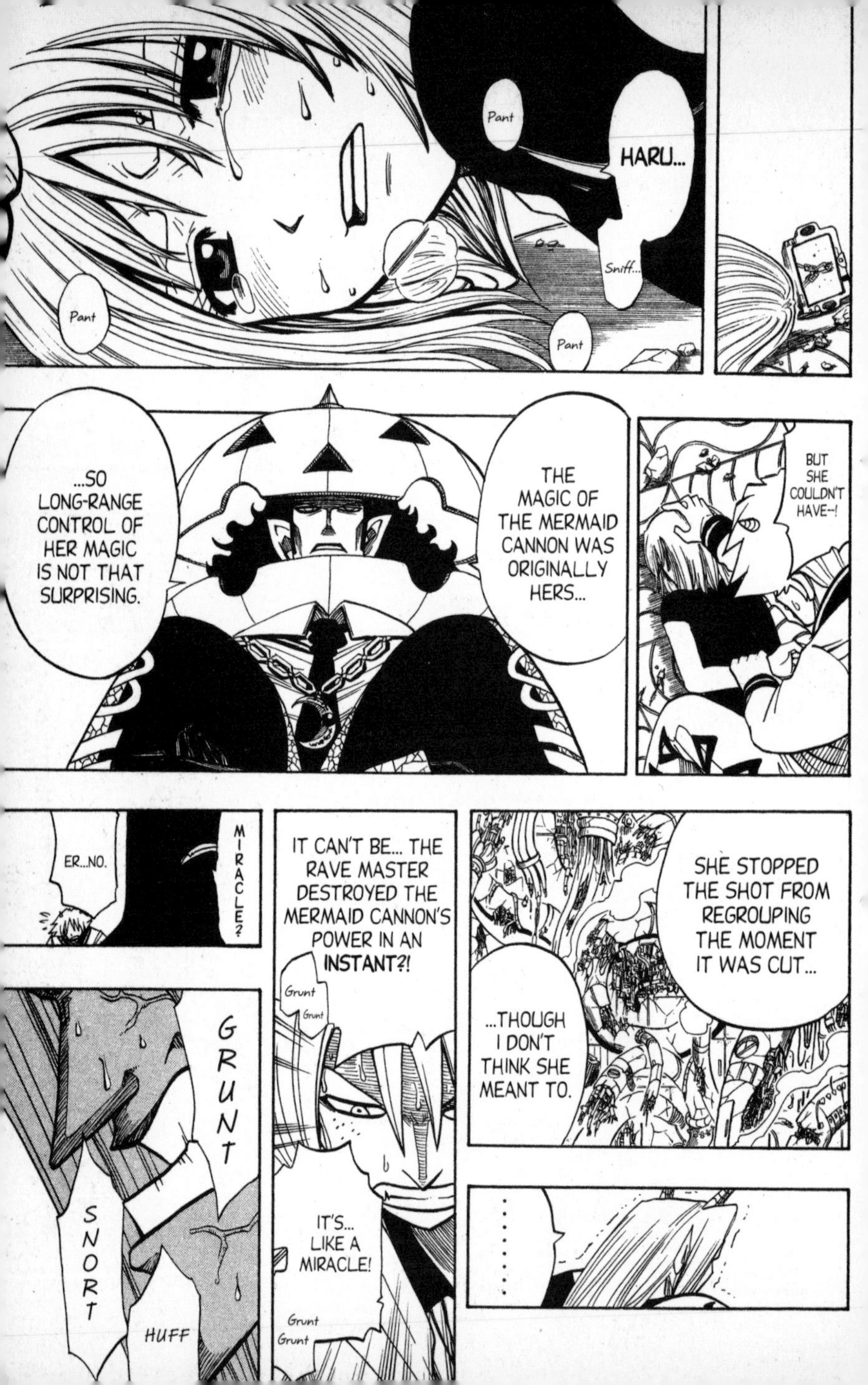
Pant
HARU...
Sniff...
Pant
Pant
BUT SHE COULDN'T HAVE--!
THE MAGIC OF THE MERMAID CANNON WAS ORIGINALLY HERS...
...SO LONG-RANGE CONTROL OF HER MAGIC IS NOT THAT SURPRISING.
SHE STOPPED THE SHOT FROM REGROUPING THE MOMENT IT WAS CUT...
...THOUGH I DON'T THINK SHE MEANT TO.
......
IT CAN'T BE... THE RAVE MASTER DESTROYED THE MERMAID CANNON'S POWER IN AN **INSTANT?!**
Grunt
Grunt
IT'S... LIKE A MIRACLE!
Grunt
Grunt
MIRACLE?
ER...NO.
GRUNT
SNORT
HUFF

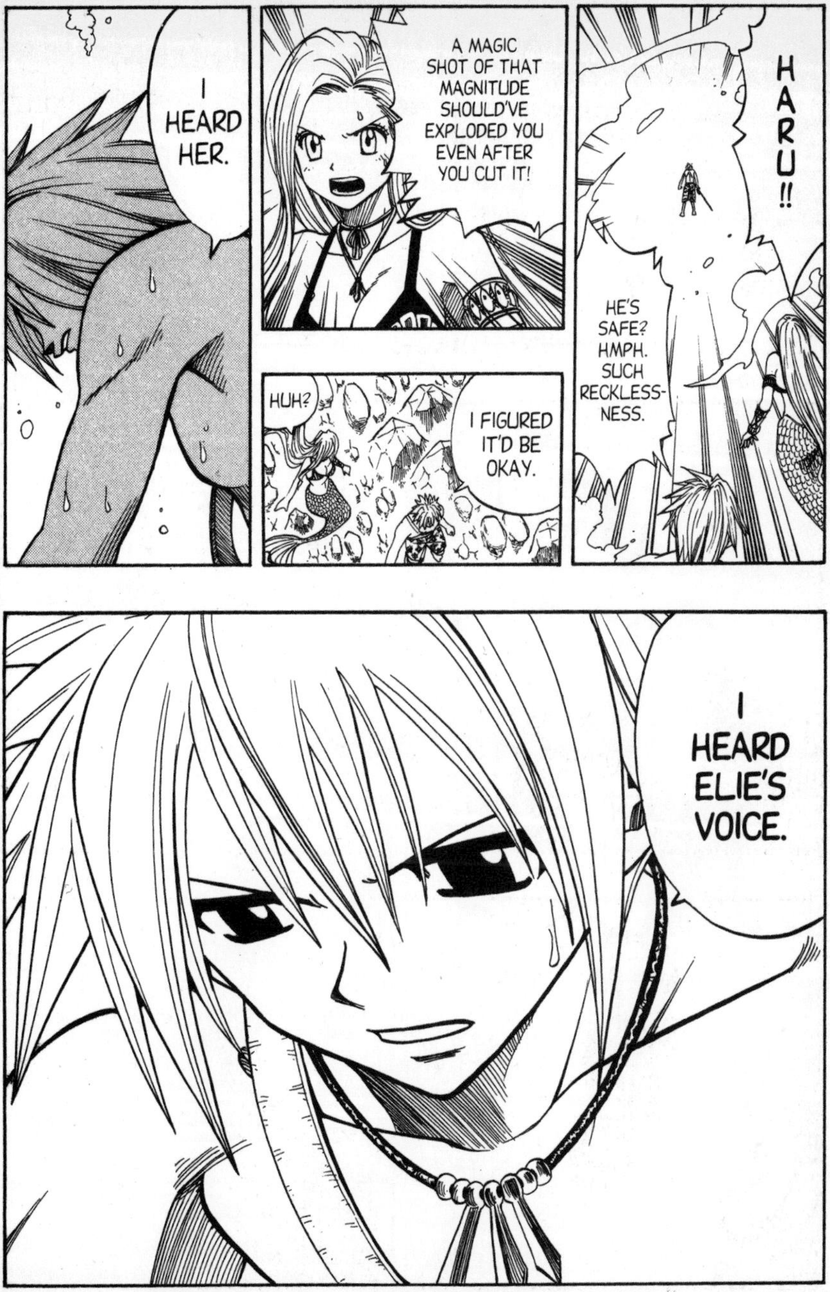
HARU!!
HE'S SAFE? HMPH. SUCH RECKLESS-NESS.
A MAGIC SHOT OF THAT MAGNITUDE SHOULD'VE EXPLODED YOU EVEN AFTER YOU CUT IT!
I FIGURED IT'D BE OKAY.
HUH?
I HEARD HER.
I HEARD ELIE'S VOICE.

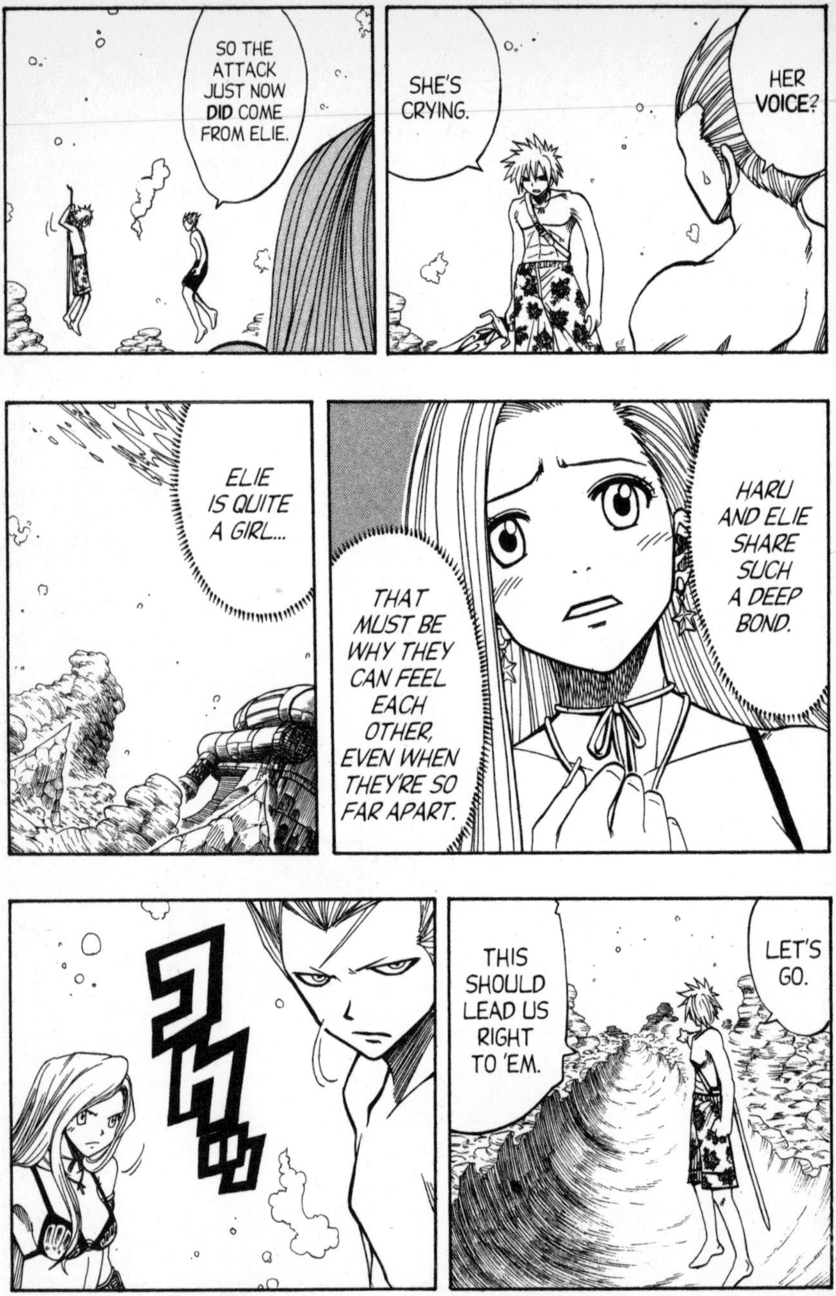
HER VOICE?
SHE'S CRYING.
SO THE ATTACK JUST NOW DID COME FROM ELIE.
HARU AND ELIE SHARE SUCH A DEEP BOND.
THAT MUST BE WHY THEY CAN FEEL EACH OTHER, EVEN WHEN THEY'RE SO FAR APART.
ELIE IS QUITE A GIRL...
LET'S GO.
THIS SHOULD LEAD US RIGHT TO 'EM.

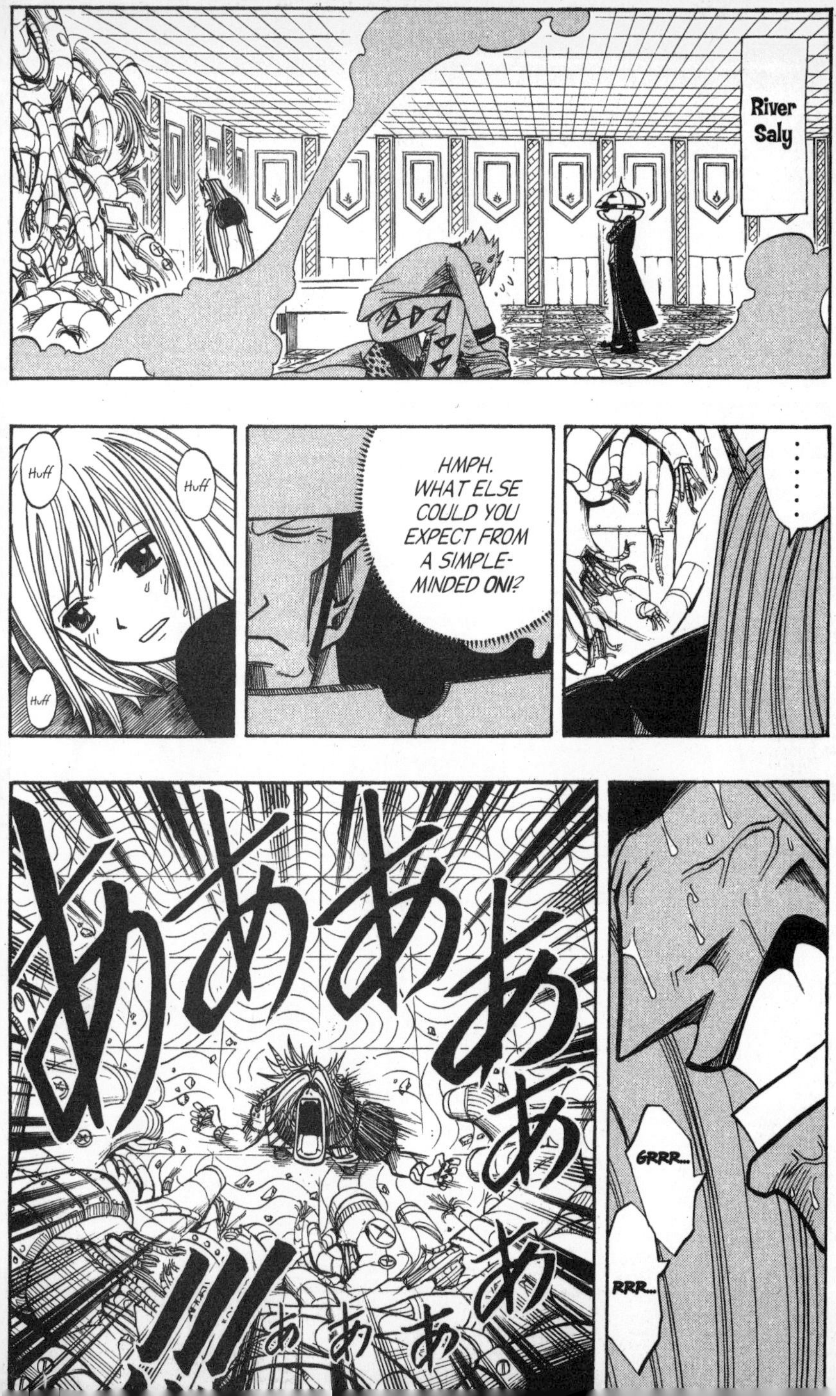
River Saly
......
HMPH. WHAT ELSE COULD YOU EXPECT FROM A SIMPLE-MINDED ONI?
Huff
Huff
Huff
GRRR...
RRR...
あああああああああ!!!

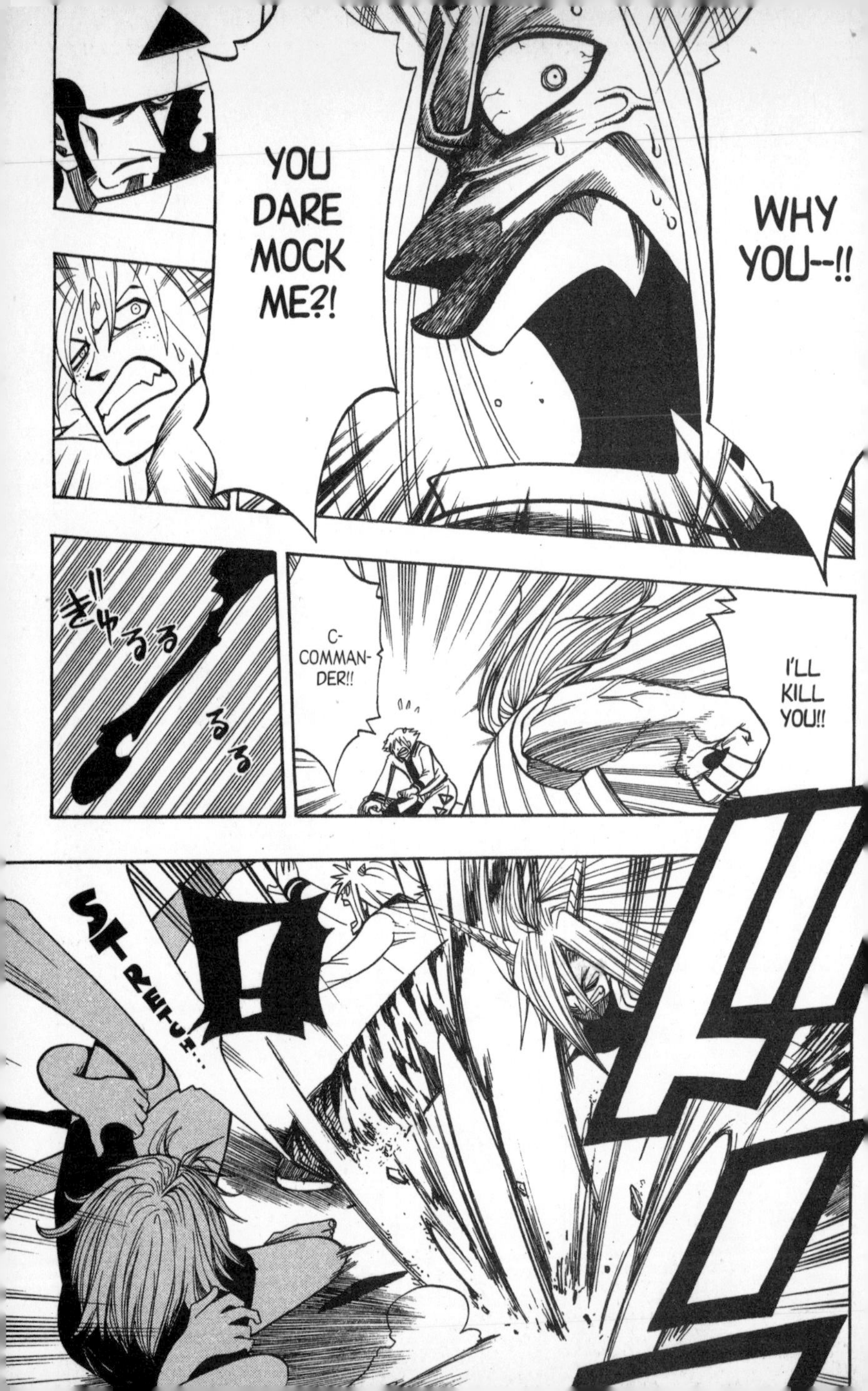
WHY YOU--!!
YOU DARE MOCK ME?!
I'LL KILL YOU!!
C-COMMANDER!!
ぎゅるるる
るる
!
STRETCH...

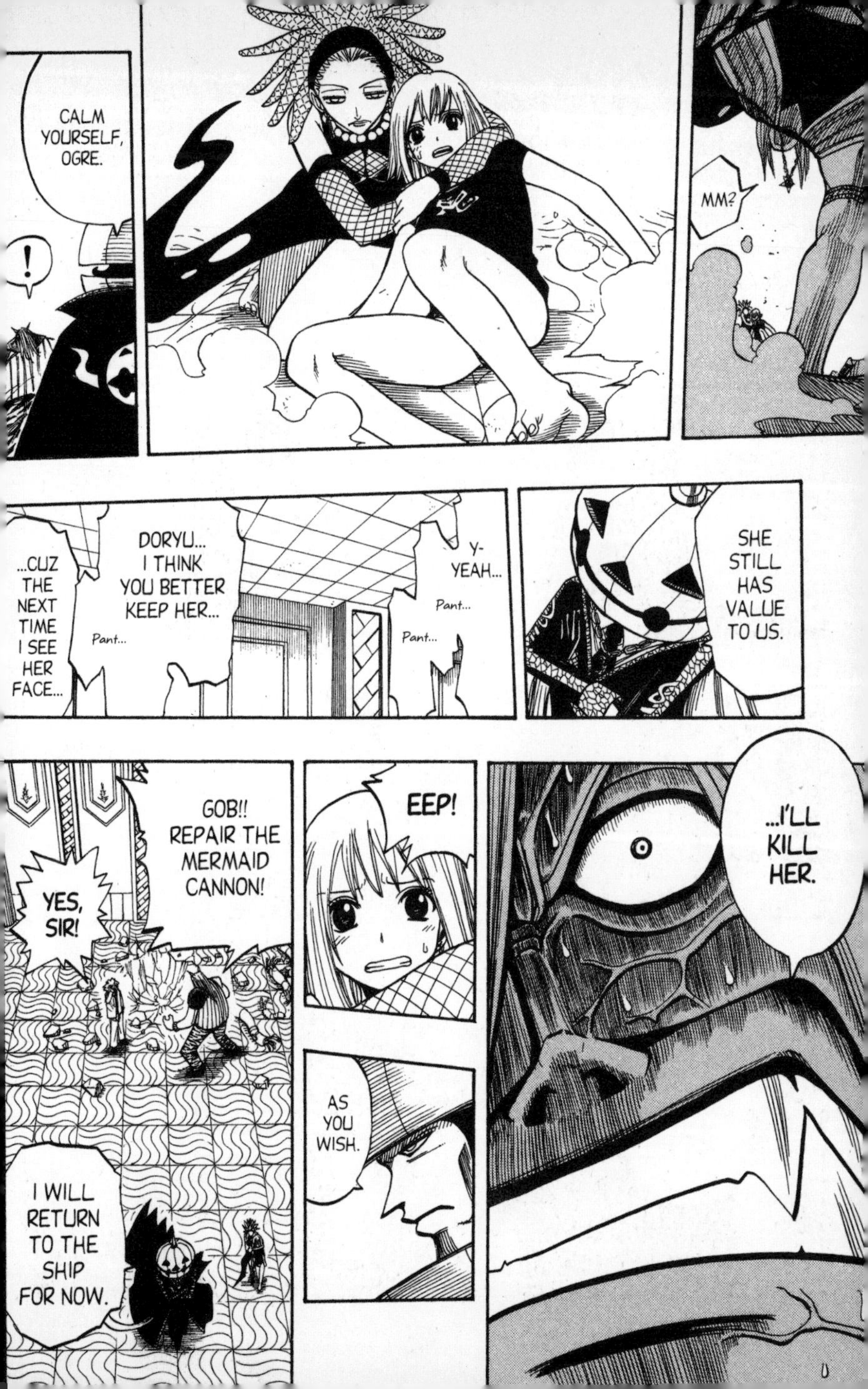
MM?
CALM YOURSELF, OGRE.
!
SHE STILL HAS VALUE TO US.
Y-YEAH...
Pant...
Pant...
DORYU... I THINK YOU BETTER KEEP HER...
Pant...
...CUZ THE NEXT TIME I SEE HER FACE...
...I'LL KILL HER.
EEP!
AS YOU WISH.
GOB!! REPAIR THE MERMAID CANNON!
YES, SIR!
I WILL RETURN TO THE SHIP FOR NOW.

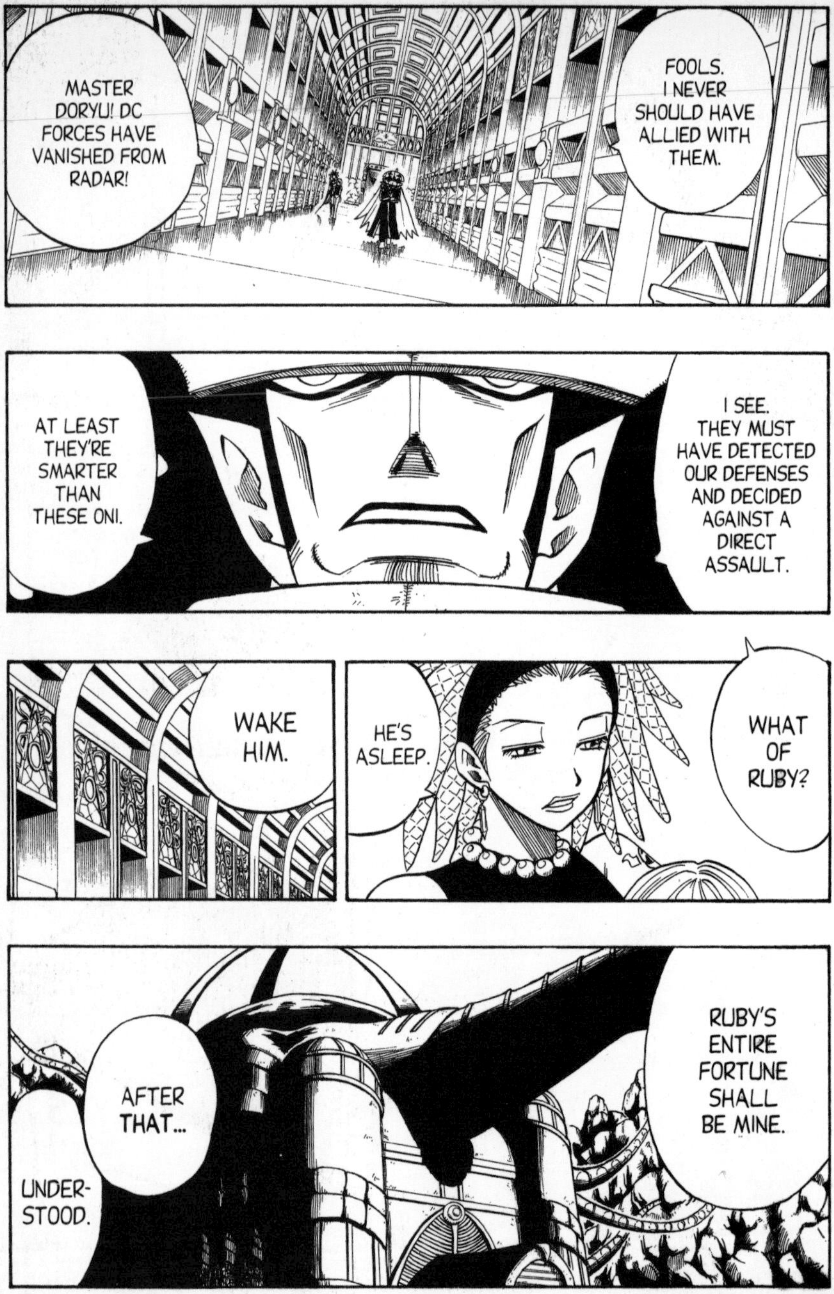
FOOLS. I NEVER SHOULD HAVE ALLIED WITH THEM.
MASTER DORYU! DC FORCES HAVE VANISHED FROM RADAR!
I SEE. THEY MUST HAVE DETECTED OUR DEFENSES AND DECIDED AGAINST A DIRECT ASSAULT.
AT LEAST THEY'RE SMARTER THAN THESE ONI.
WHAT OF RUBY?
HE'S ASLEEP.
WAKE HIM.
RUBY'S ENTIRE FORTUNE SHALL BE MINE.
AFTER THAT...
UNDER-STOOD.

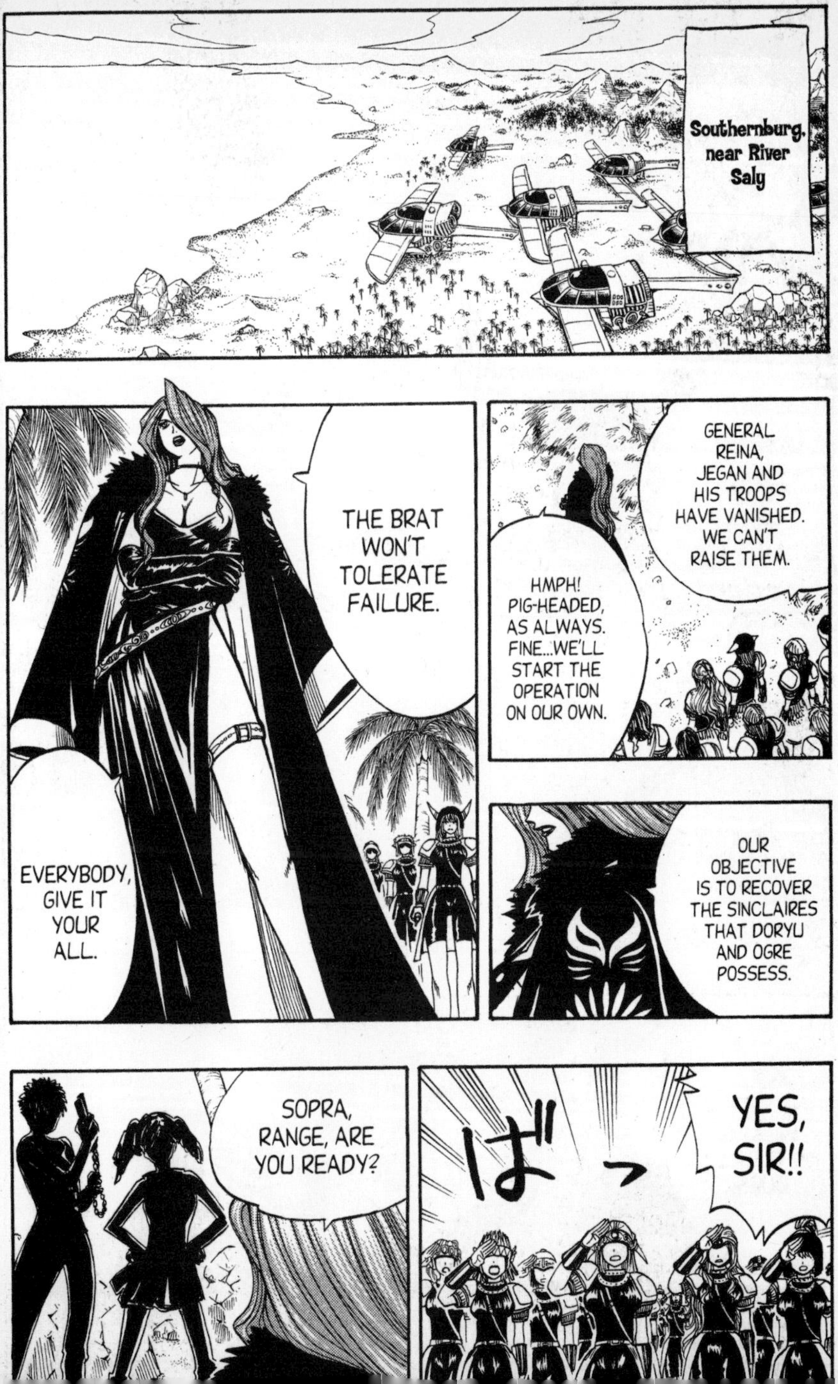
Southernburg, near River Saly
GENERAL REINA, JEGAN AND HIS TROOPS HAVE VANISHED. WE CAN'T RAISE THEM.
HMPH! PIG-HEADED, AS ALWAYS. FINE...WE'LL START THE OPERATION ON OUR OWN.
OUR OBJECTIVE IS TO RECOVER THE SINCLAIRES THAT DORYU AND OGRE POSSESS.
THE BRAT WON'T TOLERATE FAILURE.
EVERYBODY, GIVE IT YOUR ALL.
YES, SIR!!
ばっ
SOPRA, RANGE, ARE YOU READY?

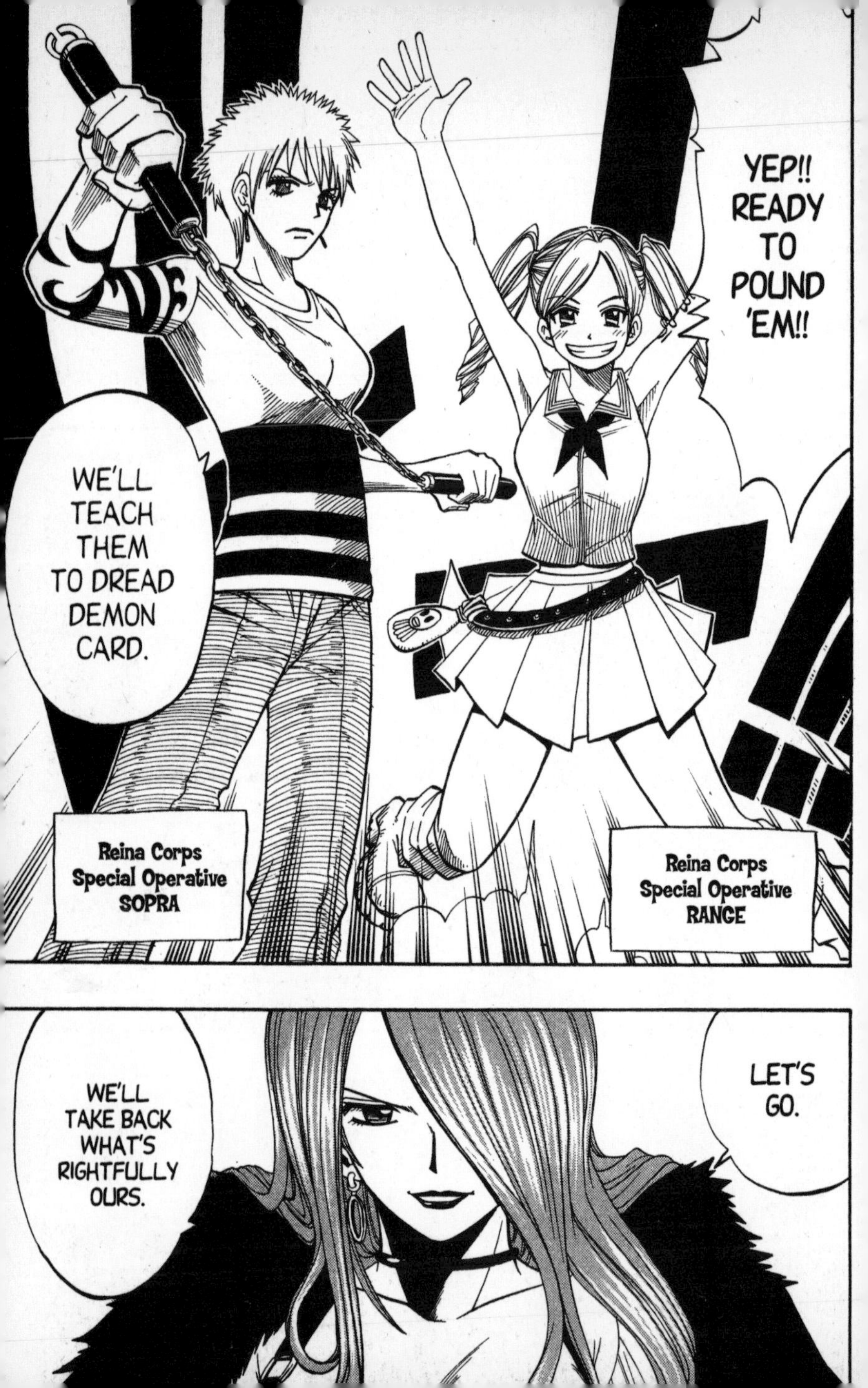
YEP!! READY TO POUND 'EM!!
WE'LL TEACH THEM TO DREAD DEMON CARD.
Reina Corps Special Operative RANGE
Reina Corps Special Operative SOPRA
LET'S GO.
WE'LL TAKE BACK WHAT'S RIGHTFULLY OURS.

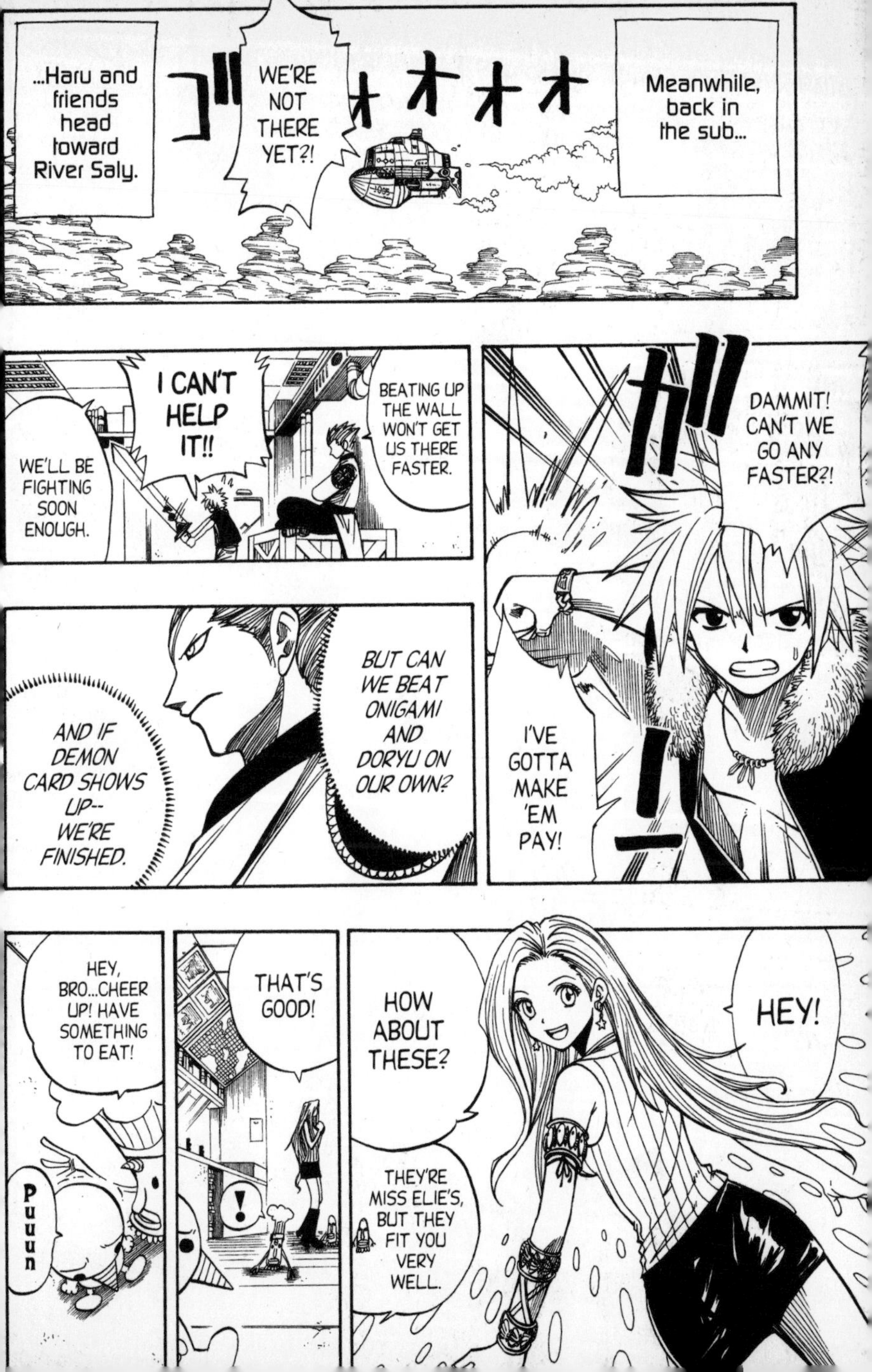

Meanwhile, back in the sub...
ゴオオオオ
WE'RE NOT THERE YET?!
...Haru and friends head toward River Saly.
ガ
DAMMIT! CAN'T WE GO ANY FASTER?!
I'VE GOTTA MAKE 'EM PAY!
BEATING UP THE WALL WON'T GET US THERE FASTER.
I CAN'T HELP IT!!
WE'LL BE FIGHTING SOON ENOUGH.
BUT CAN WE BEAT ONIGAMI AND DORYU ON OUR OWN?
AND IF DEMON CARD SHOWS UP-- WE'RE FINISHED.
HEY!
HOW ABOUT THESE?
THEY'RE MISS ELIE'S, BUT THEY FIT YOU VERY WELL.
THAT'S GOOD!
!
HEY, BRO...CHEER UP! HAVE SOMETHING TO EAT!
Puuun

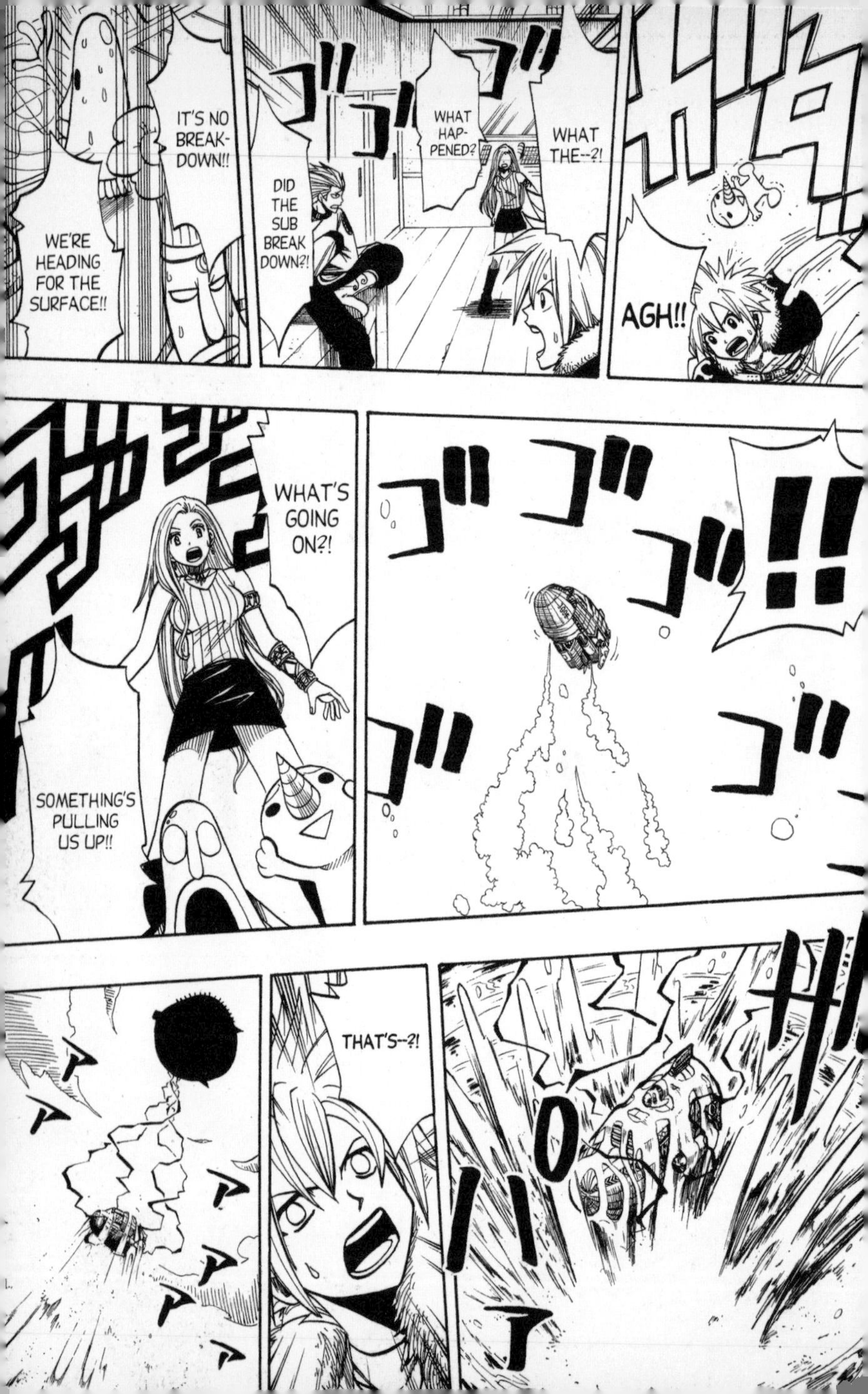
AGH!!
WHAT THE--?!
WHAT HAPPENED?
DID THE SUB BREAK DOWN?!
IT'S NO BREAKDOWN!!
WE'RE HEADING FOR THE SURFACE!!
WHAT'S GOING ON?!
SOMETHING'S PULLING US UP!!
THAT'S--?!

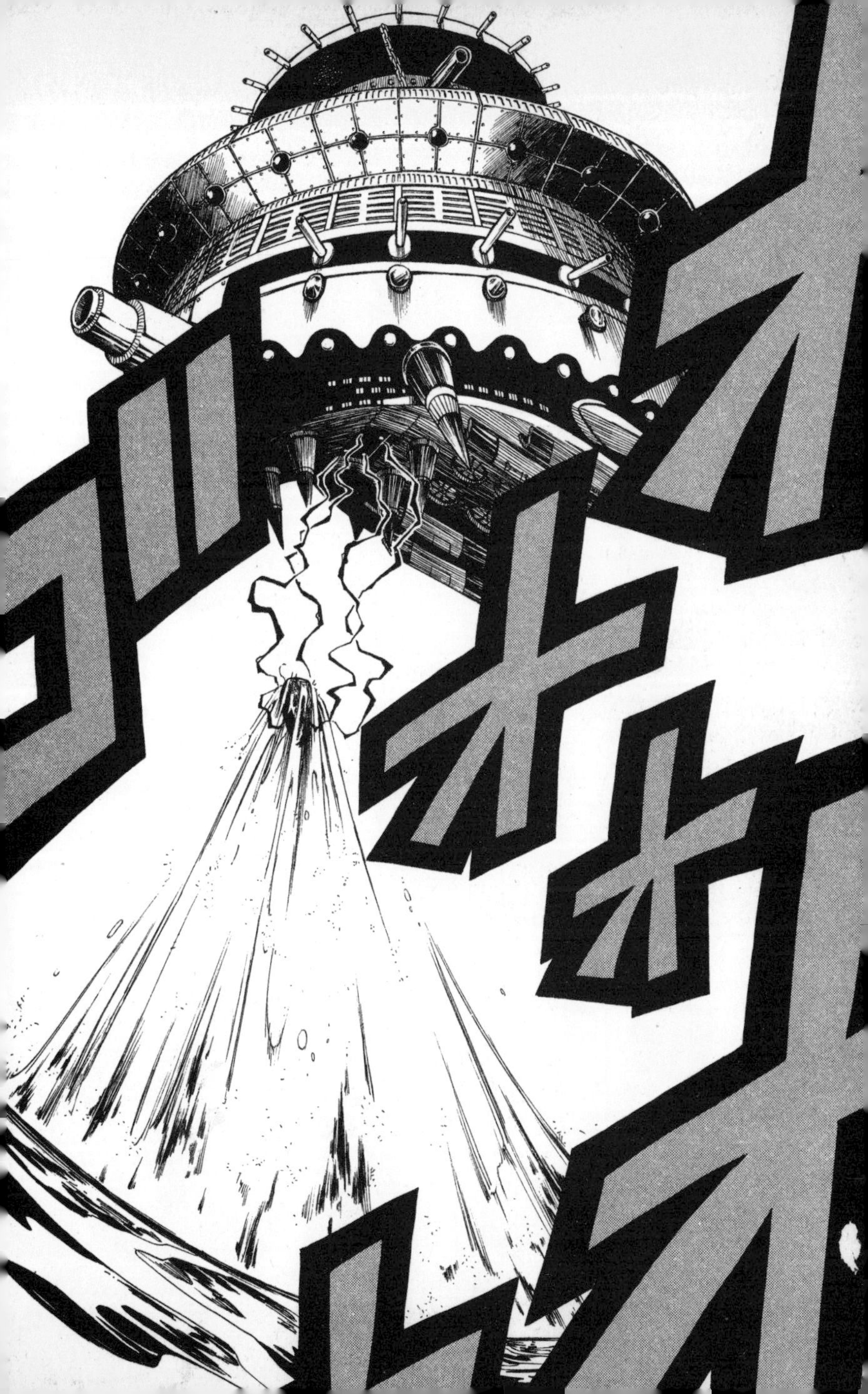

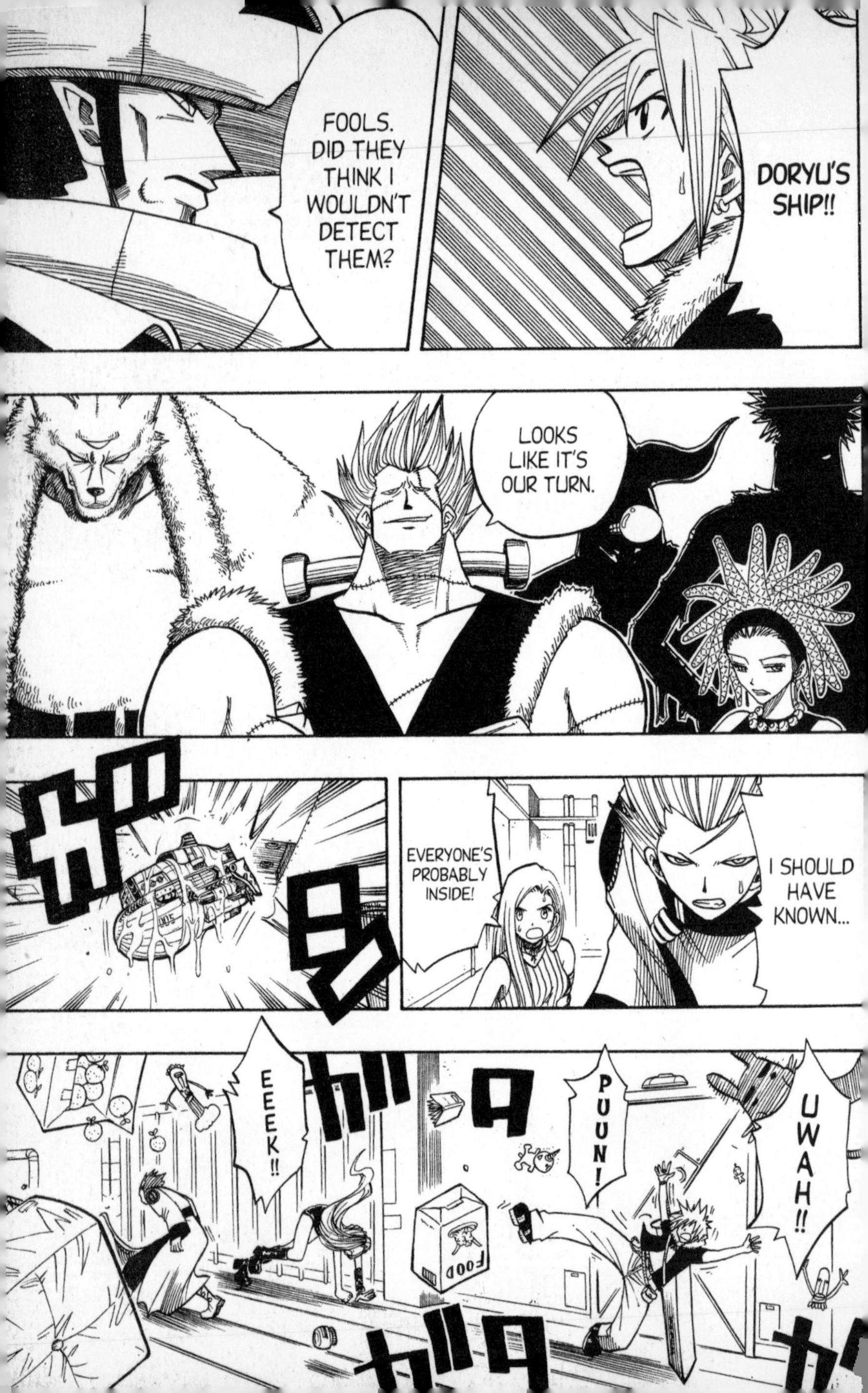
DORYU'S SHIP!!
FOOLS. DID THEY THINK I WOULDN'T DETECT THEM?
LOOKS LIKE IT'S OUR TURN.
I SHOULD HAVE KNOWN...
EVERYONE'S PROBABLY INSIDE!
UWAH!!
PUUN!
EEEK!!
FOOD

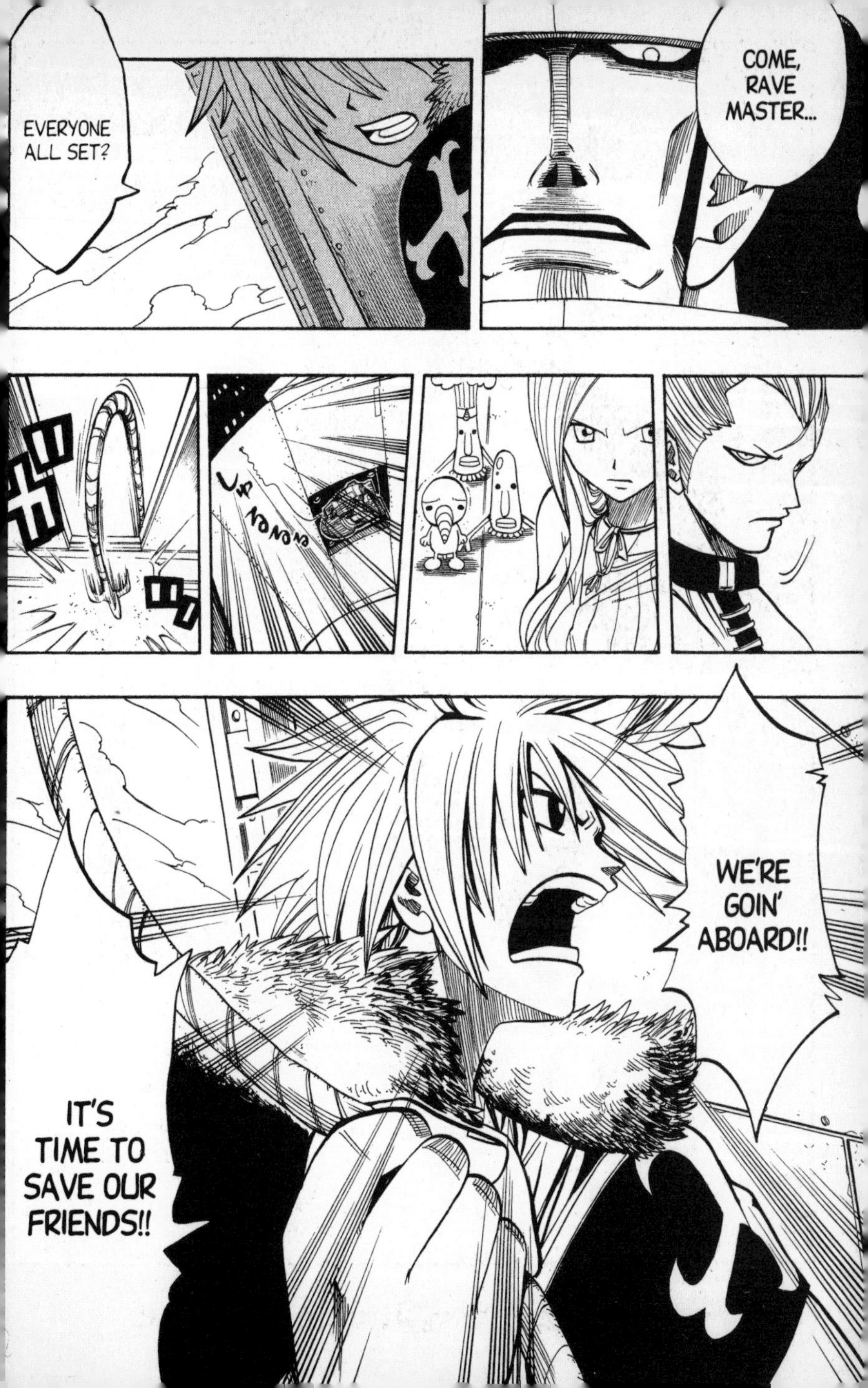
COME, RAVE MASTER...
EVERYONE ALL SET?
WE'RE GOIN' ABOARD!!
IT'S TIME TO SAVE OUR FRIENDS!!

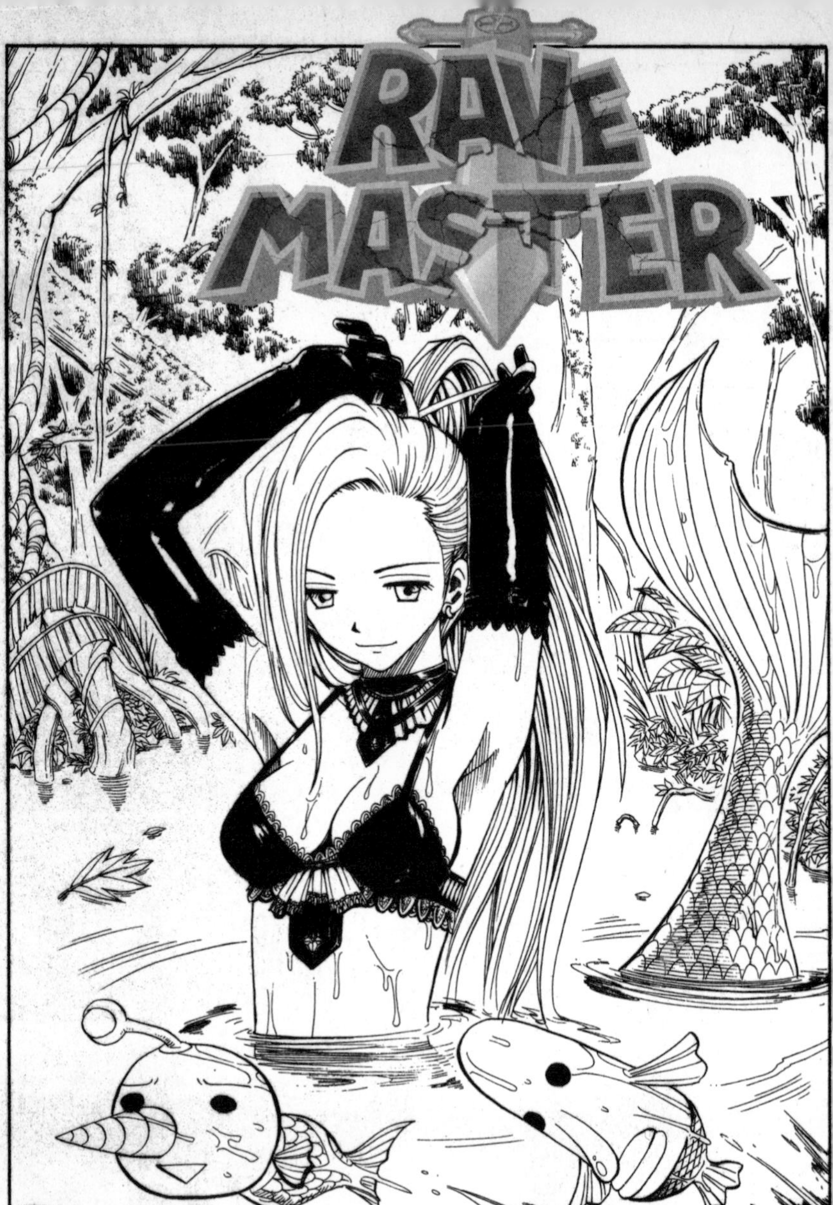
RAVE
MASTER

RAVE:114 ULTIMATE DARK

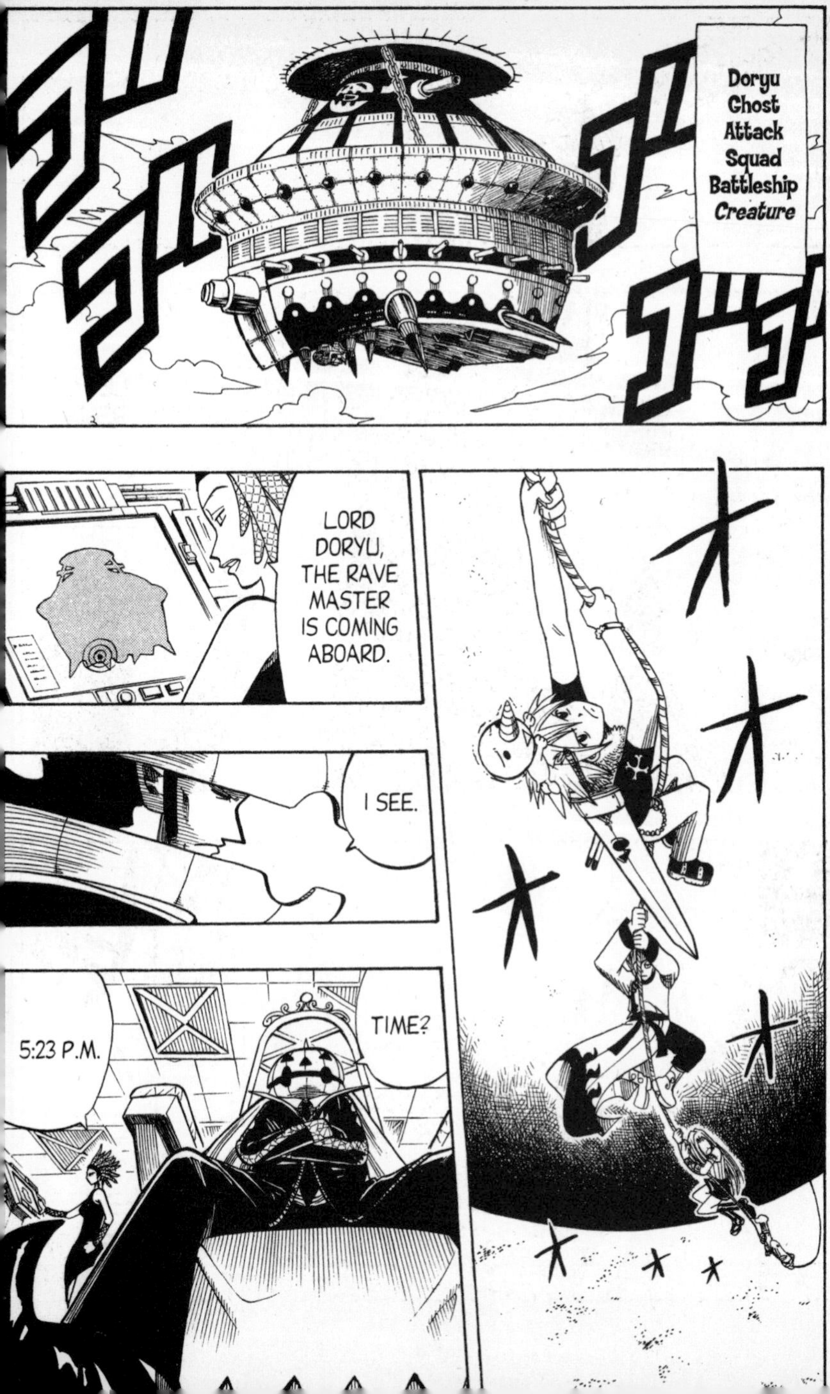
Doryu Ghost Attack Squad Battleship *Creature*
LORD DORYU, THE RAVE MASTER IS COMING ABOARD.
I SEE.
TIME?
5:23 P.M.

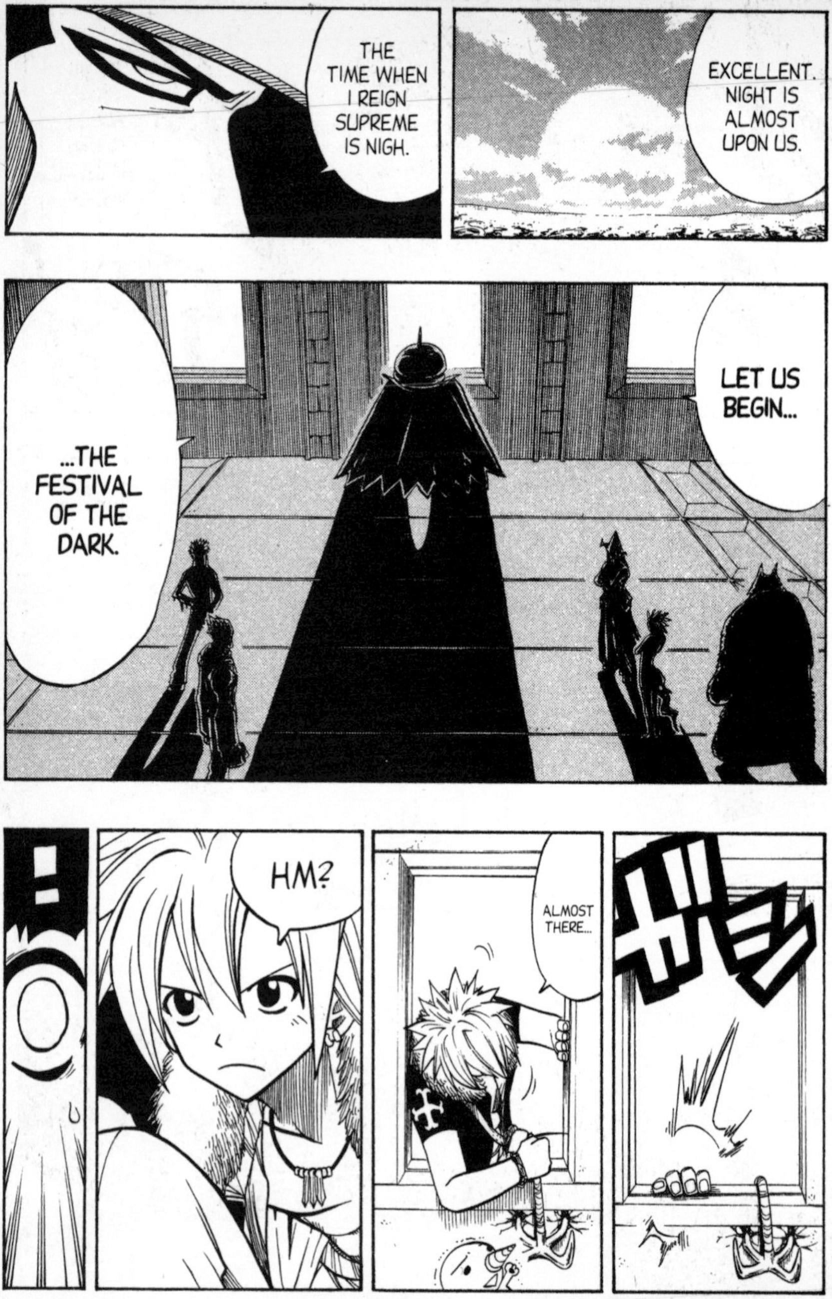
EXCELLENT. NIGHT IS ALMOST UPON US.
THE TIME WHEN I REIGN SUPREME IS NIGH.
LET US BEGIN...
...THE FESTIVAL OF THE DARK.
ALMOST THERE...
HM?
!

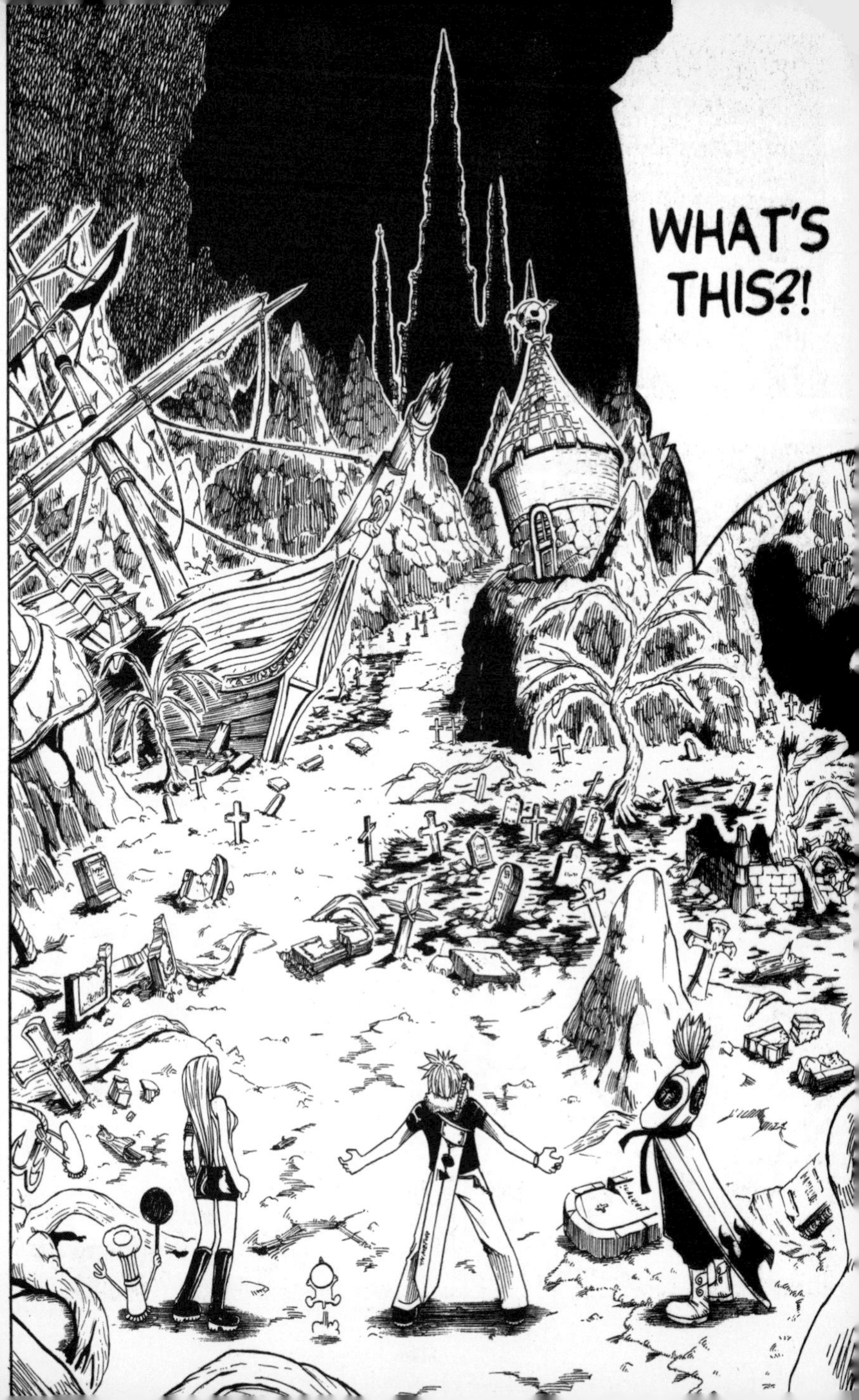
WHAT'S THIS?!

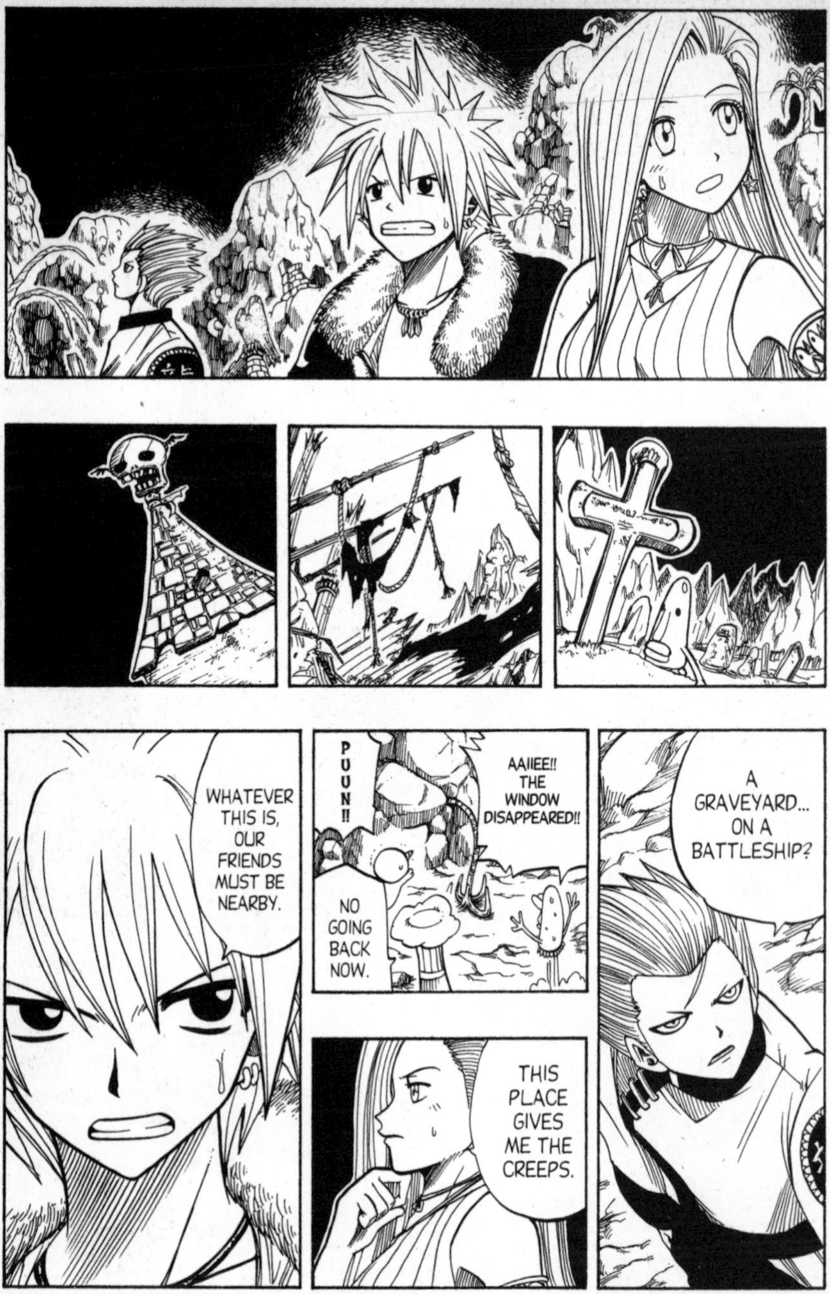
A GRAVEYARD... ON A BATTLESHIP?
AAIIEE!! THE WINDOW DISAPPEARED!!
PUUN!!
NO GOING BACK NOW.
THIS PLACE GIVES ME THE CREEPS.
WHATEVER THIS IS, OUR FRIENDS MUST BE NEARBY.

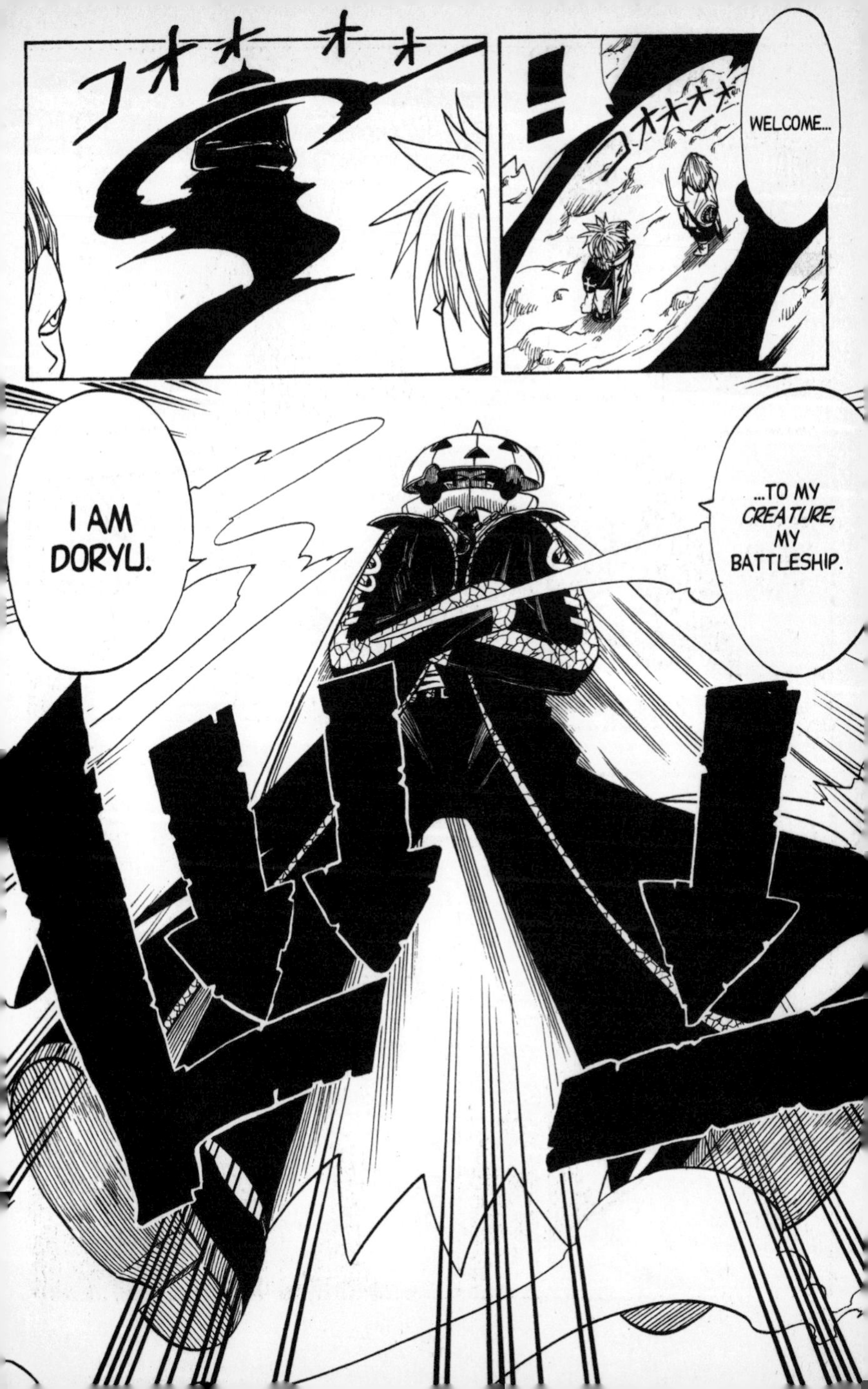
WELCOME...
フオオオオオ
フオオオ オオ
...TO MY *CREATURE*, MY BATTLESHIP.
I AM DORYU.

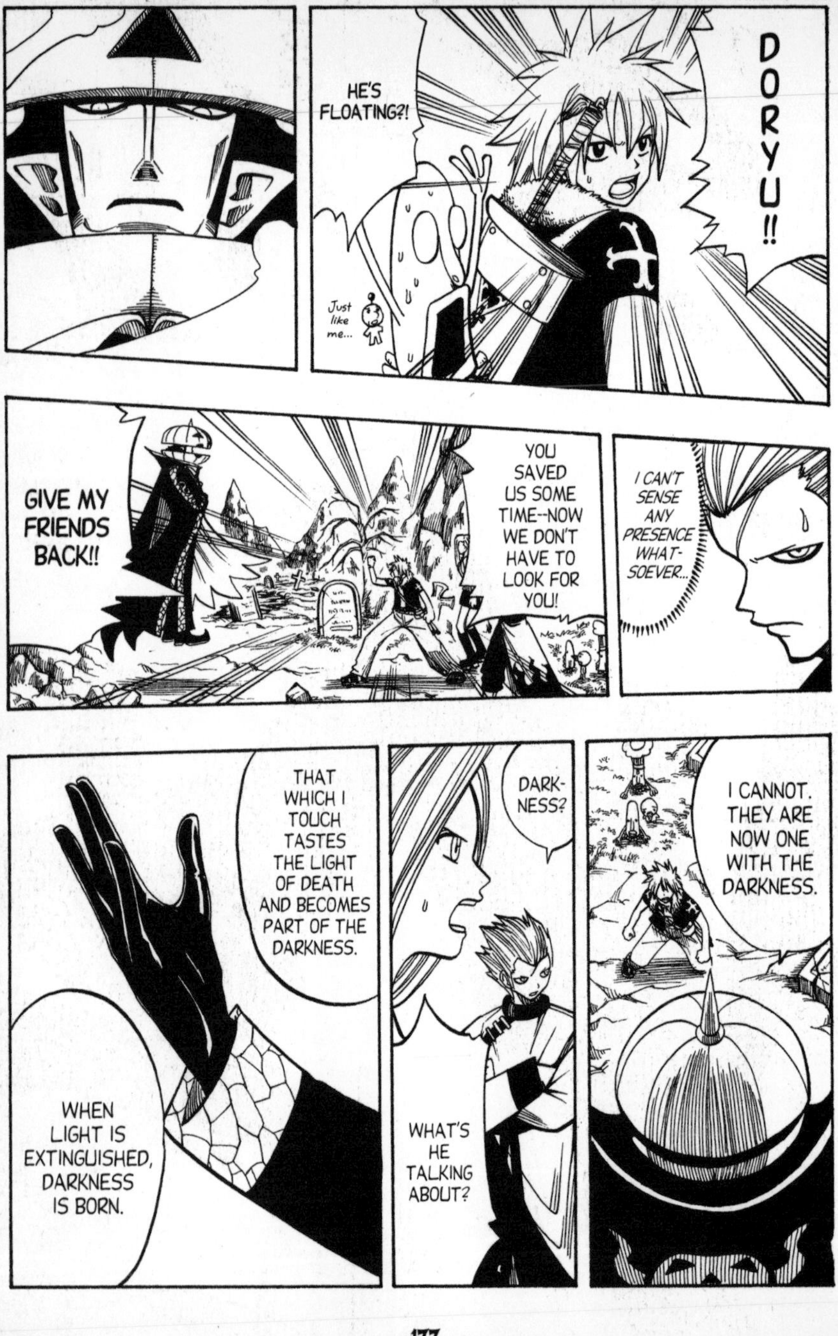
DORYU!!
HE'S FLOATING?!
Just like me...
I CAN'T SENSE ANY PRESENCE WHATSOEVER...
YOU SAVED US SOME TIME--NOW WE DON'T HAVE TO LOOK FOR YOU!
GIVE MY FRIENDS BACK!!
I CANNOT. THEY ARE NOW ONE WITH THE DARKNESS.
DARKNESS?
WHAT'S HE TALKING ABOUT?
THAT WHICH I TOUCH TASTES THE LIGHT OF DEATH AND BECOMES PART OF THE DARKNESS.
WHEN LIGHT IS EXTINGUISHED, DARKNESS IS BORN.

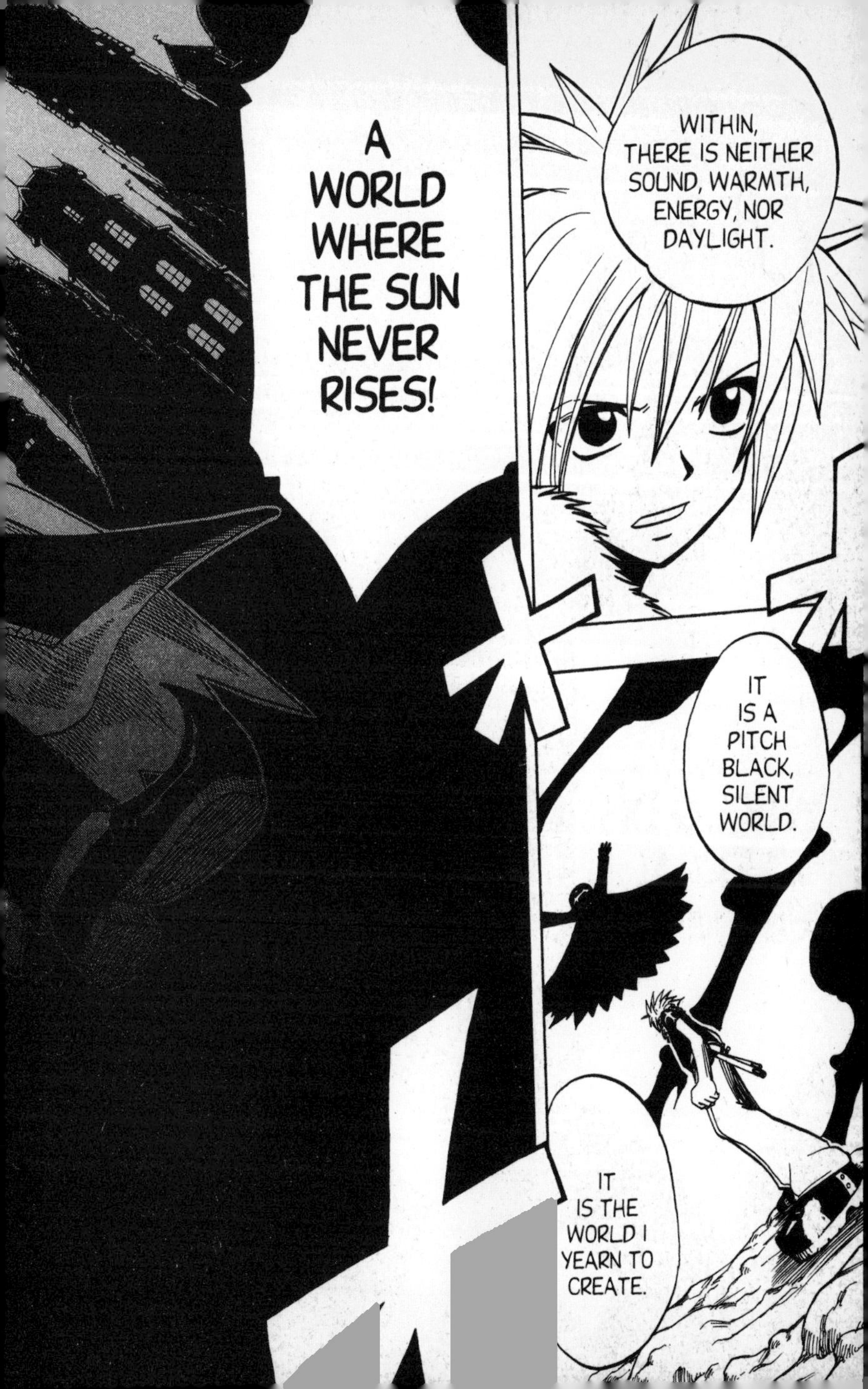
WITHIN, THERE IS NEITHER SOUND, WARMTH, ENERGY, NOR DAYLIGHT.
IT IS A PITCH BLACK, SILENT WORLD.
IT IS THE WORLD I YEARN TO CREATE.
A WORLD WHERE THE SUN NEVER RISES!

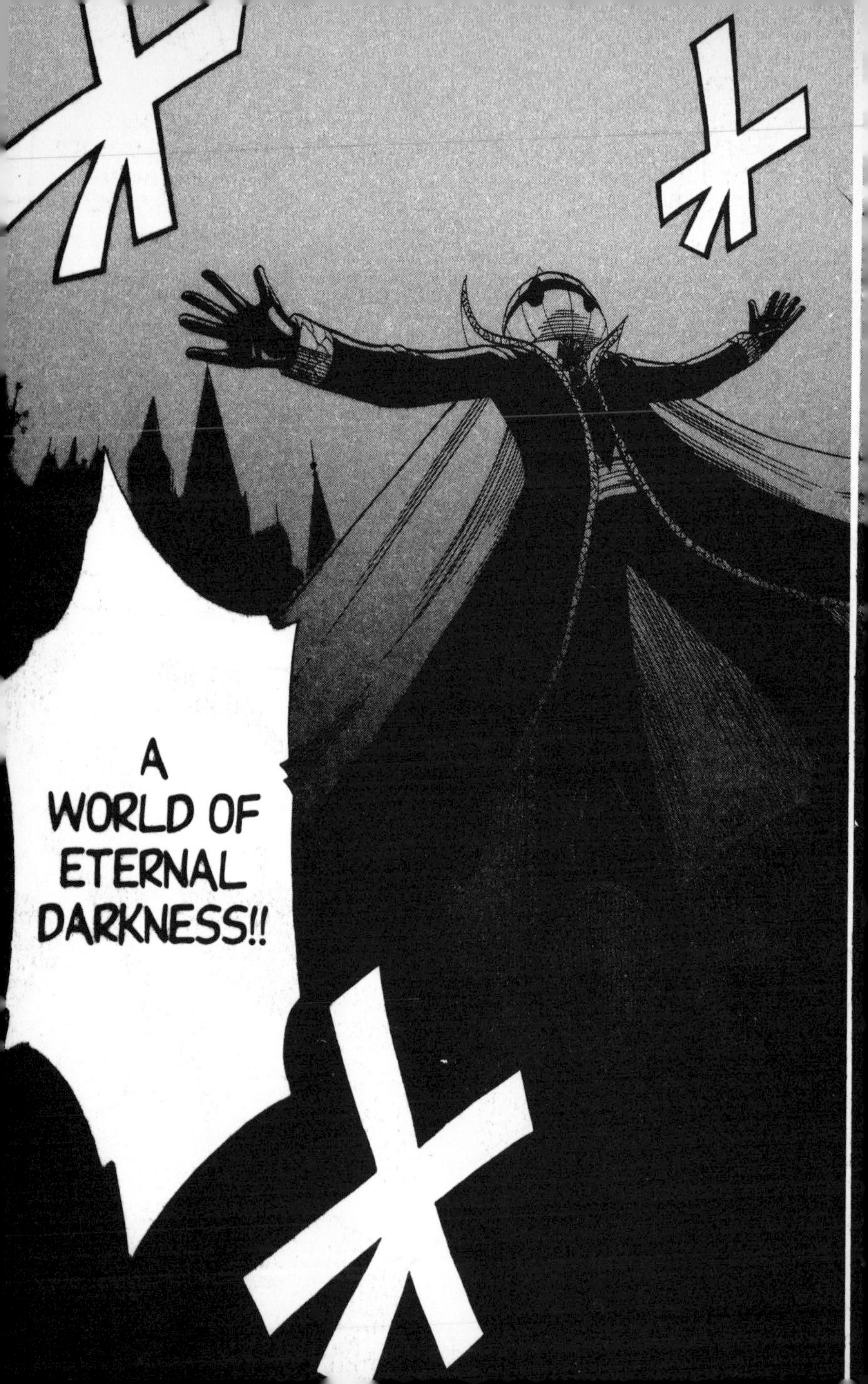
A WORLD OF ETERNAL DARKNESS!!

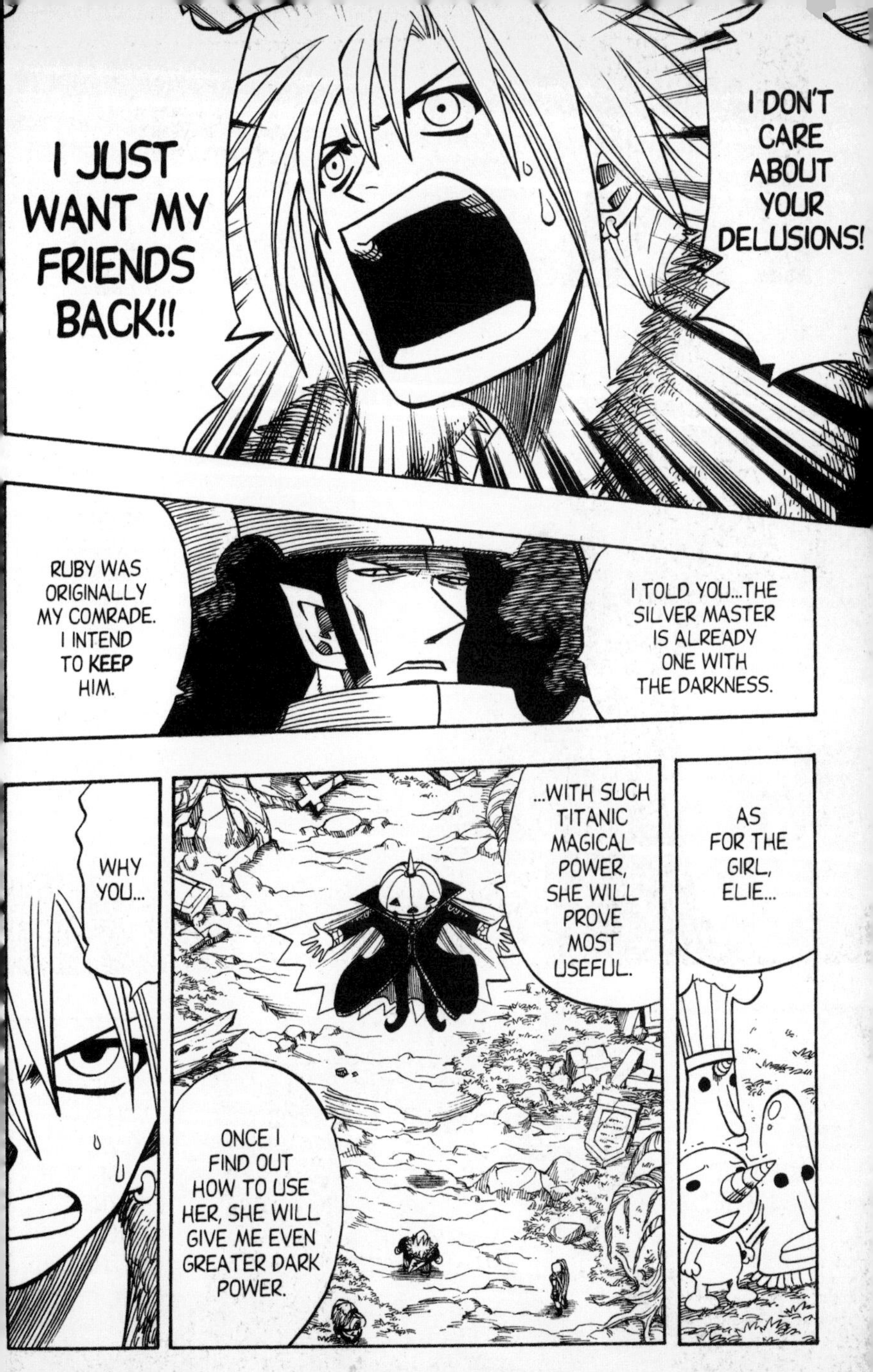
I DON'T CARE ABOUT YOUR DELUSIONS!
I JUST WANT MY FRIENDS BACK!!
I TOLD YOU...THE SILVER MASTER IS ALREADY ONE WITH THE DARKNESS.
RUBY WAS ORIGINALLY MY COMRADE. I INTEND TO KEEP HIM.
AS FOR THE GIRL, ELIE...
...WITH SUCH TITANIC MAGICAL POWER, SHE WILL PROVE MOST USEFUL.
ONCE I FIND OUT HOW TO USE HER, SHE WILL GIVE ME EVEN GREATER DARK POWER.
WHY YOU...

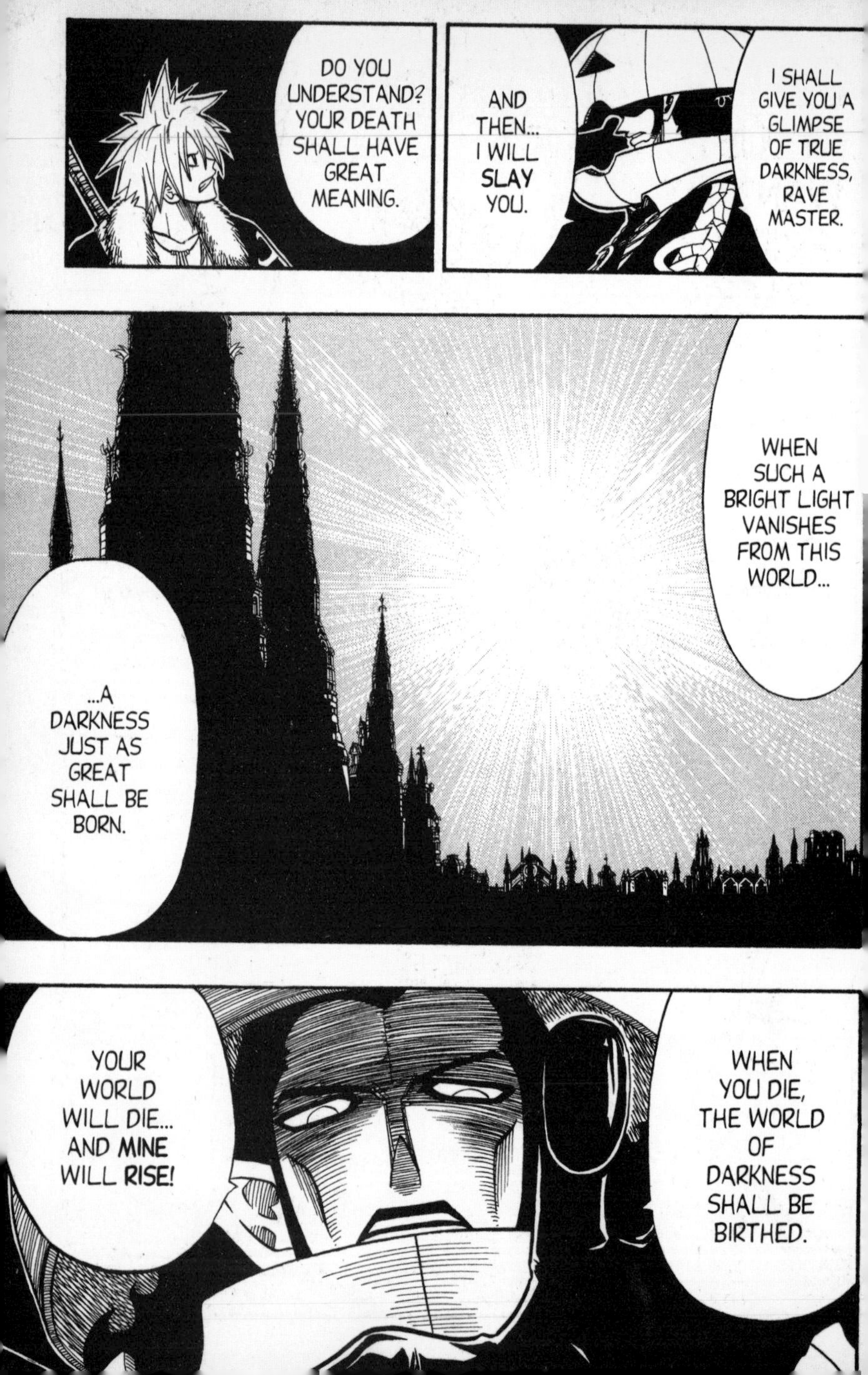
I SHALL GIVE YOU A GLIMPSE OF TRUE DARKNESS, RAVE MASTER.
AND THEN... I WILL SLAY YOU.
DO YOU UNDERSTAND? YOUR DEATH SHALL HAVE GREAT MEANING.
WHEN SUCH A BRIGHT LIGHT VANISHES FROM THIS WORLD...
...A DARKNESS JUST AS GREAT SHALL BE BORN.
WHEN YOU DIE, THE WORLD OF DARKNESS SHALL BE BIRTHED.
YOUR WORLD WILL DIE... AND MINE WILL RISE!

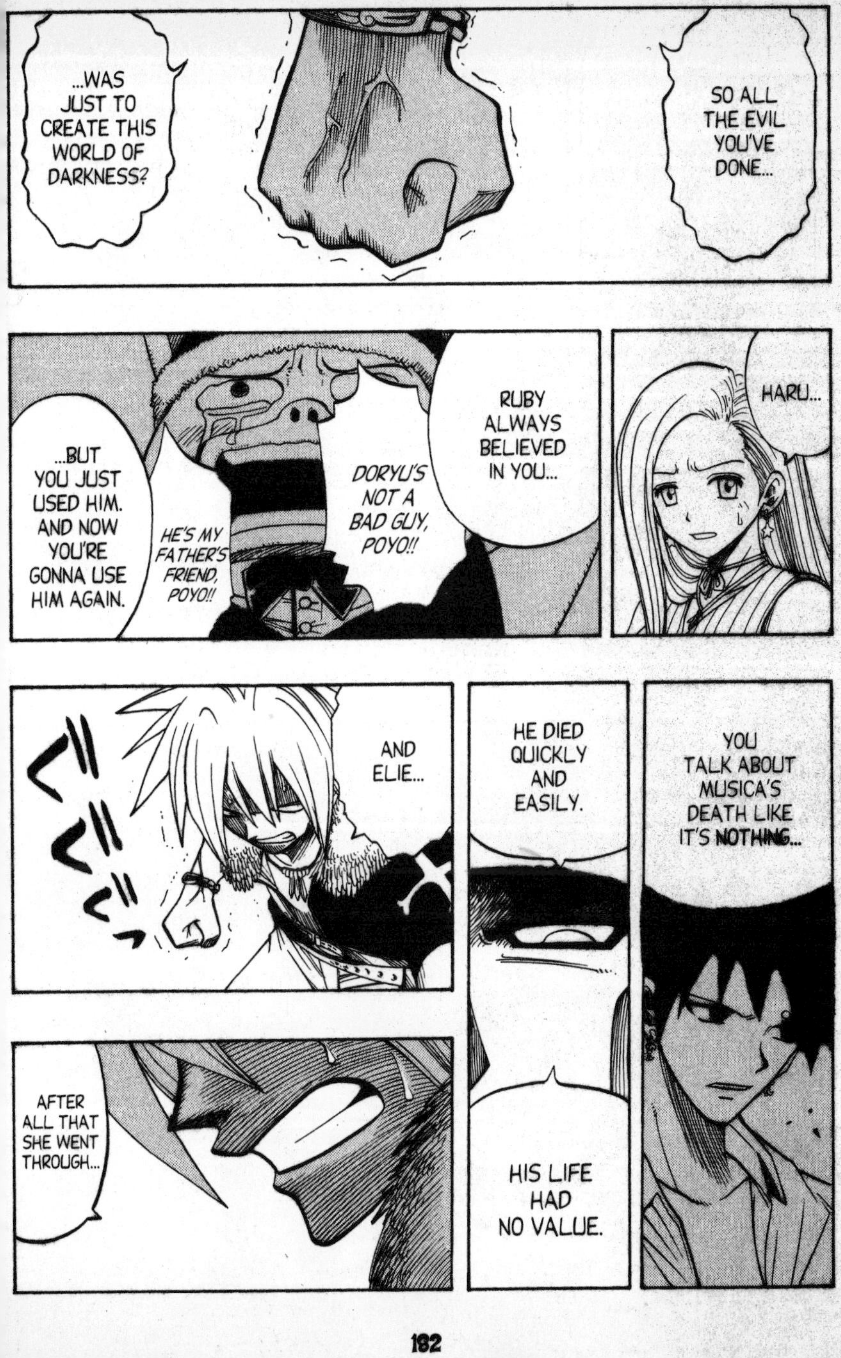
SO ALL THE EVIL YOU'VE DONE...
...WAS JUST TO CREATE THIS WORLD OF DARKNESS?
HARU...
RUBY ALWAYS BELIEVED IN YOU...
DORYU'S NOT A BAD GUY, POYO!!
HE'S MY FATHER'S FRIEND, POYO!!
...BUT YOU JUST USED HIM. AND NOW YOU'RE GONNA USE HIM AGAIN.
YOU TALK ABOUT MUSICA'S DEATH LIKE IT'S NOTHING...
HE DIED QUICKLY AND EASILY.
HIS LIFE HAD NO VALUE.
AND ELIE...
AFTER ALL THAT SHE WENT THROUGH...

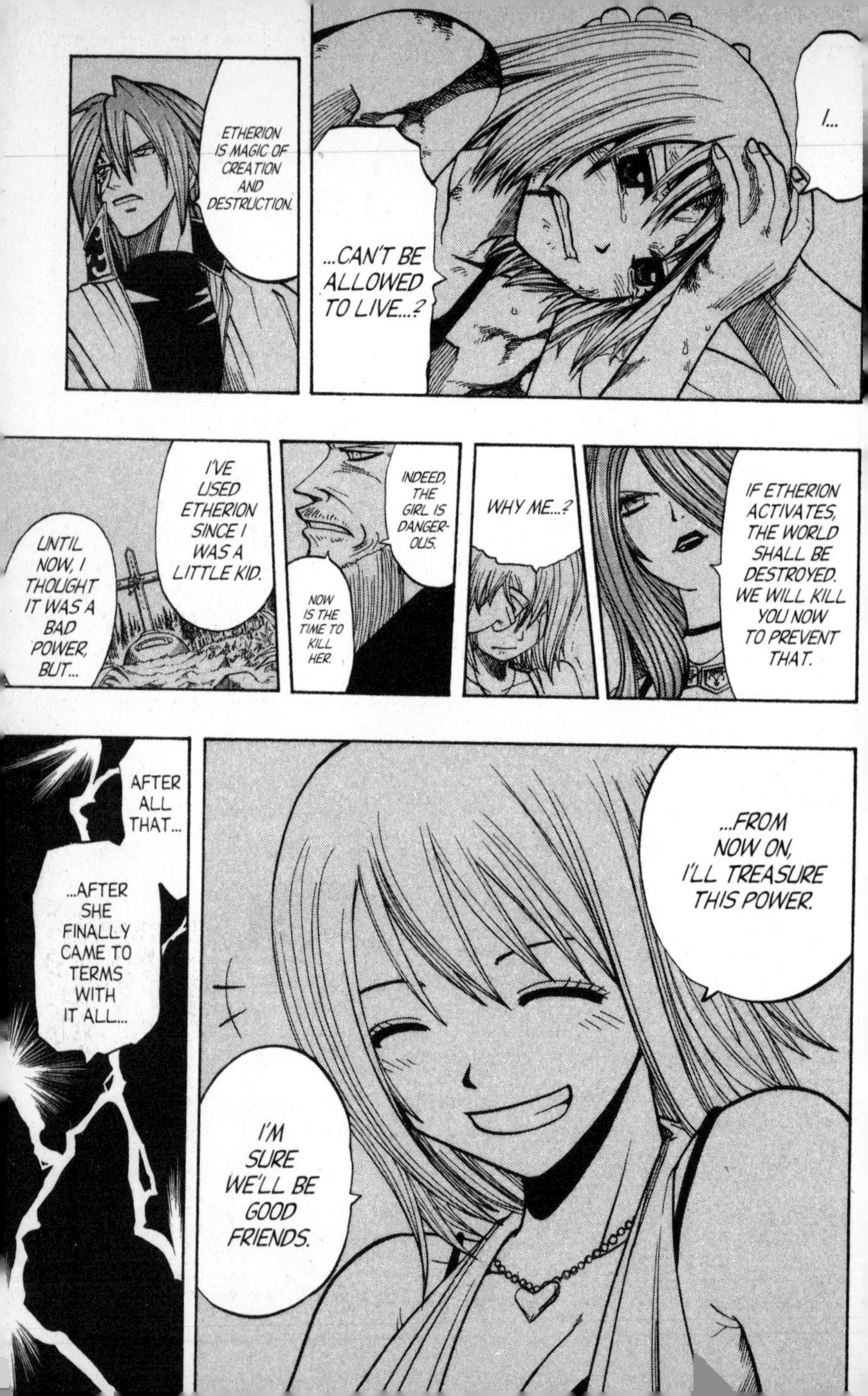
I...
...CAN'T BE ALLOWED TO LIVE...?
ETHERION IS MAGIC OF CREATION AND DESTRUCTION.
IF ETHERION ACTIVATES, THE WORLD SHALL BE DESTROYED. WE WILL KILL YOU NOW TO PREVENT THAT.
WHY ME...?
INDEED, THE GIRL IS DANGER-OUS.
NOW IS THE TIME TO KILL HER.
I'VE USED ETHERION SINCE I WAS A LITTLE KID.
UNTIL NOW, I THOUGHT IT WAS A BAD POWER, BUT...
...FROM NOW ON, I'LL TREASURE THIS POWER.
I'M SURE WE'LL BE GOOD FRIENDS.
AFTER ALL THAT...
...AFTER SHE FINALLY CAME TO TERMS WITH IT ALL...

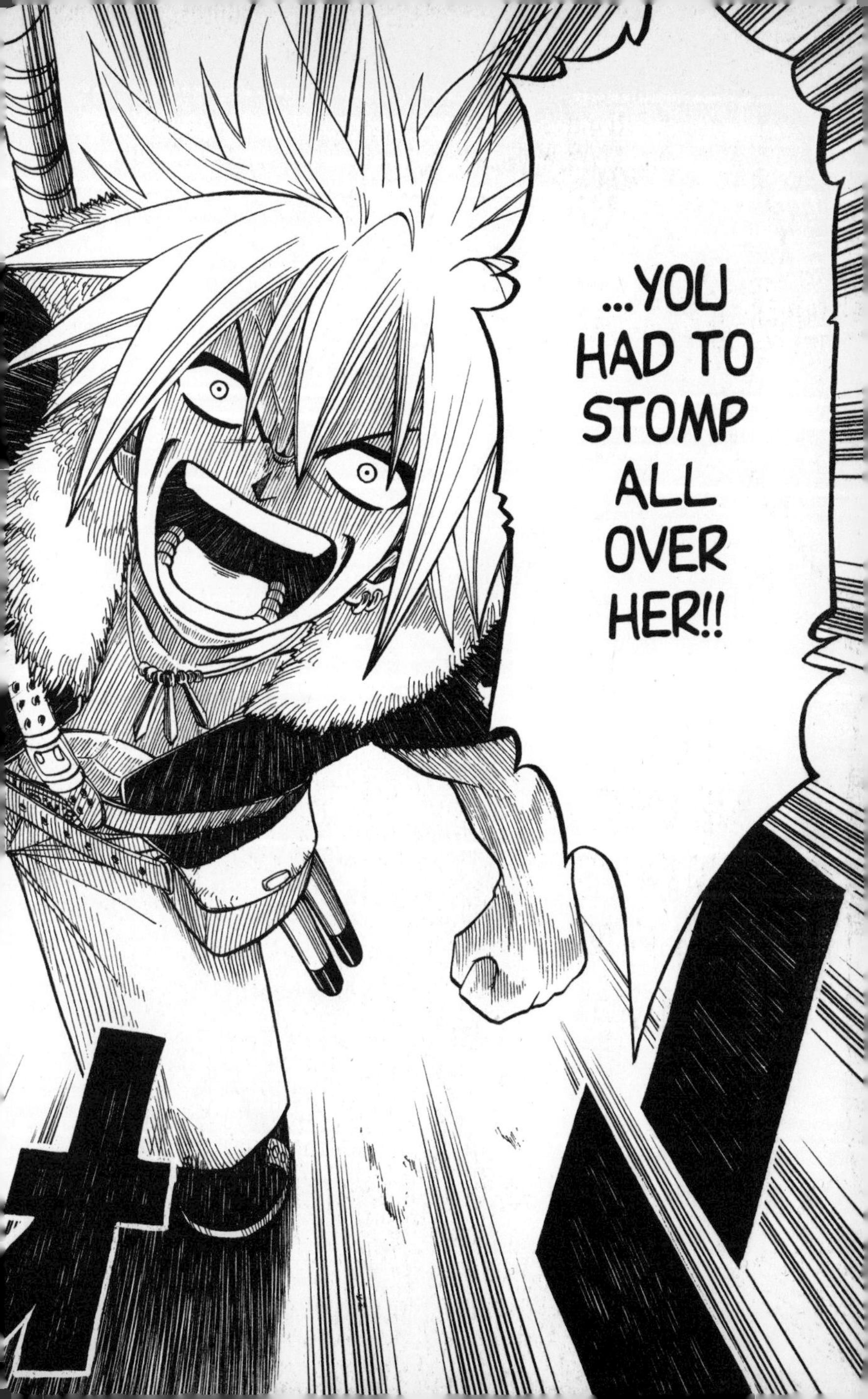
...YOU HAD TO STOMP ALL OVER HER!!

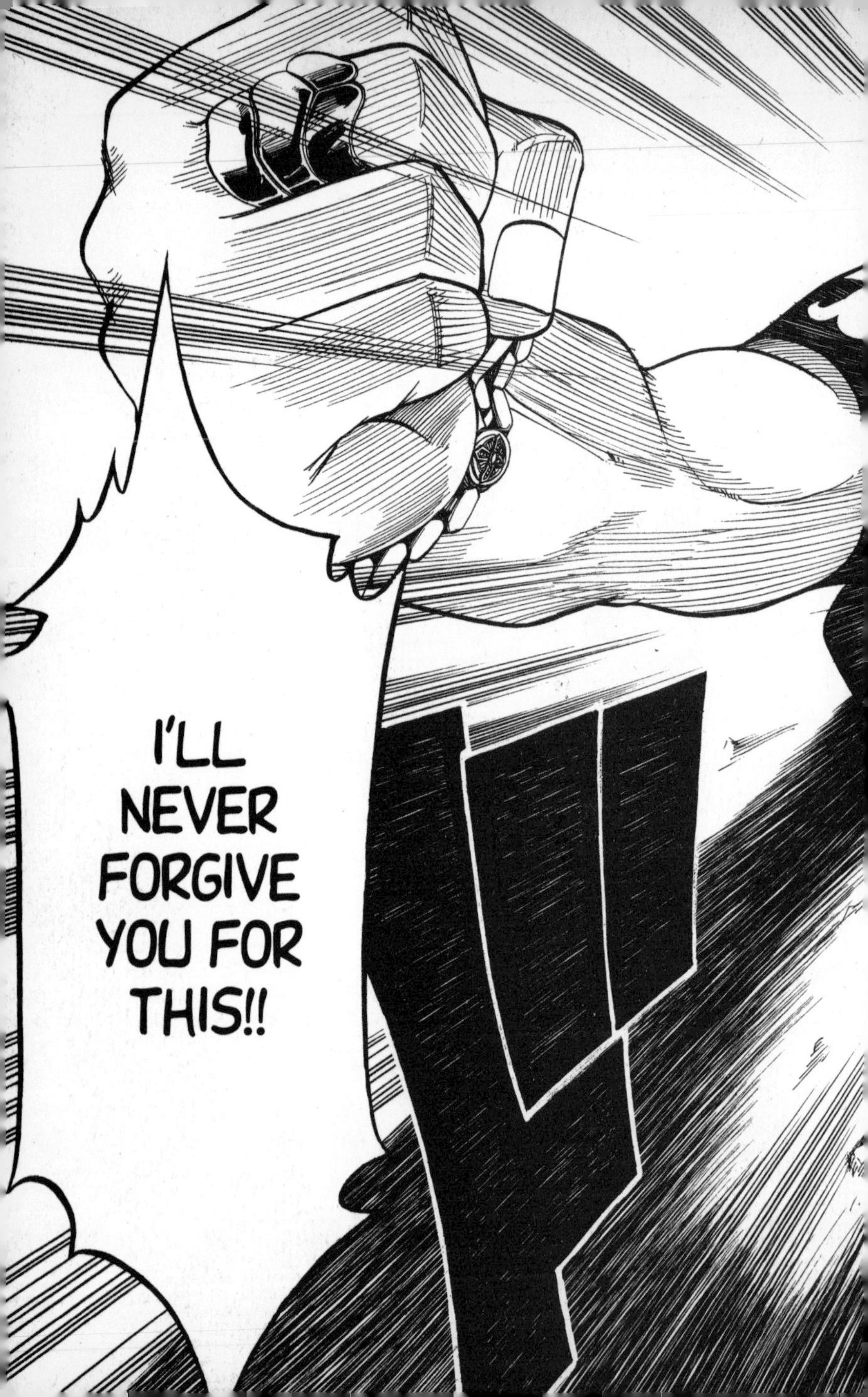
I'LL NEVER FORGIVE YOU FOR THIS!!

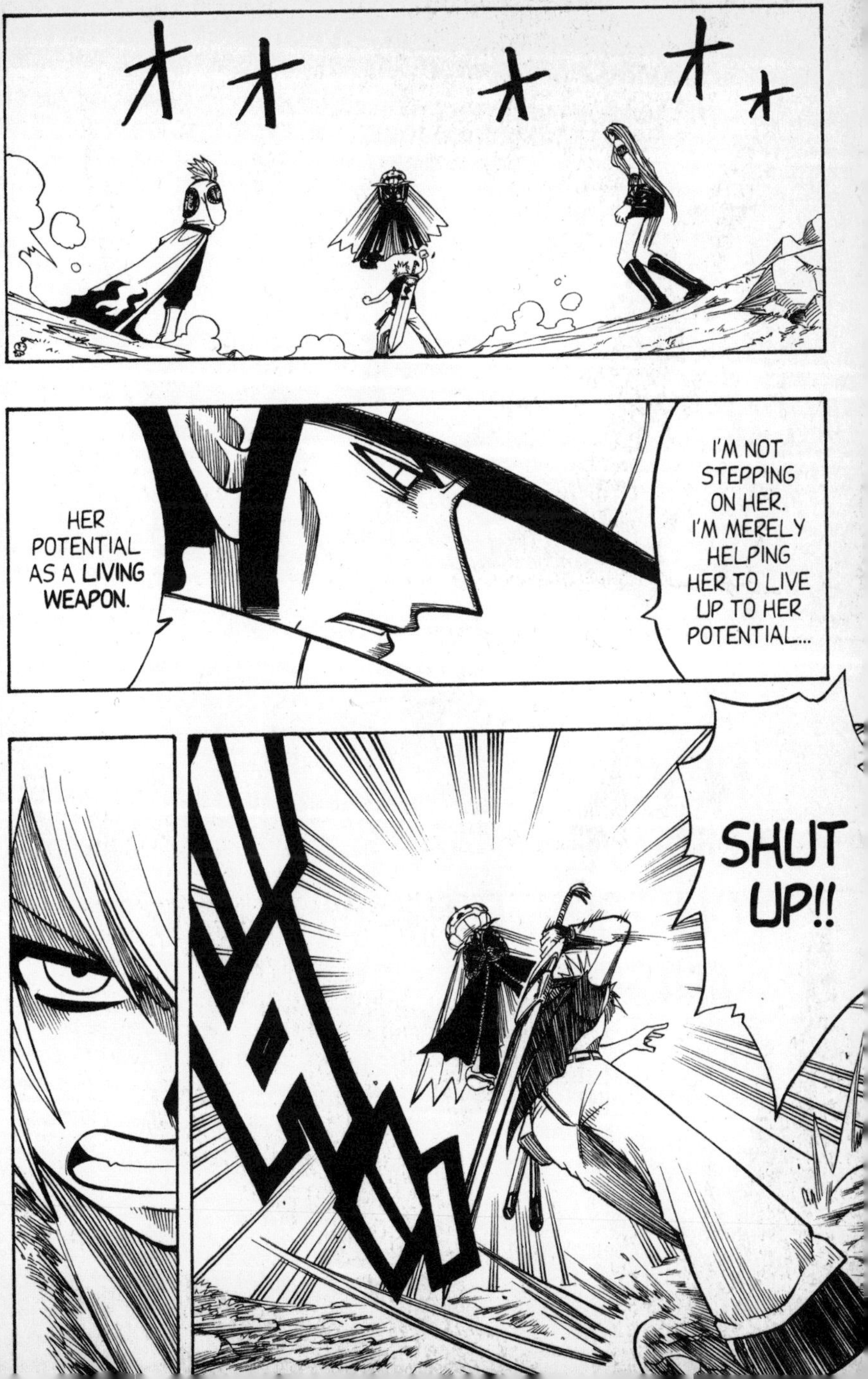
オオオオォ
I'M NOT STEPPING ON HER. I'M MERELY HELPING HER TO LIVE UP TO HER POTENTIAL...
HER POTENTIAL AS A LIVING WEAPON.
SHUT UP!!

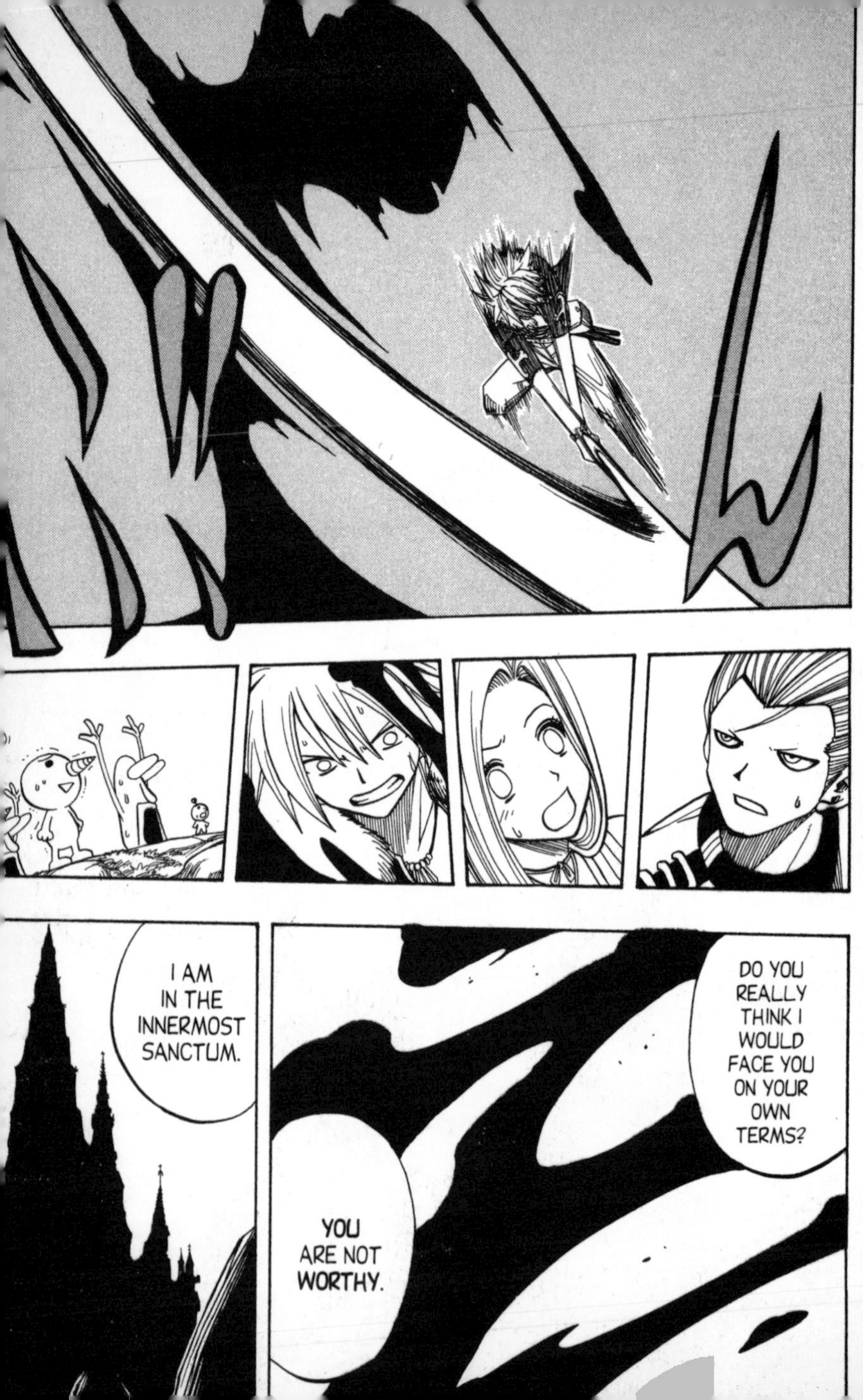
DO YOU REALLY THINK I WOULD FACE YOU ON YOUR OWN TERMS?
YOU ARE NOT WORTHY.
I AM IN THE INNERMOST SANCTUM.

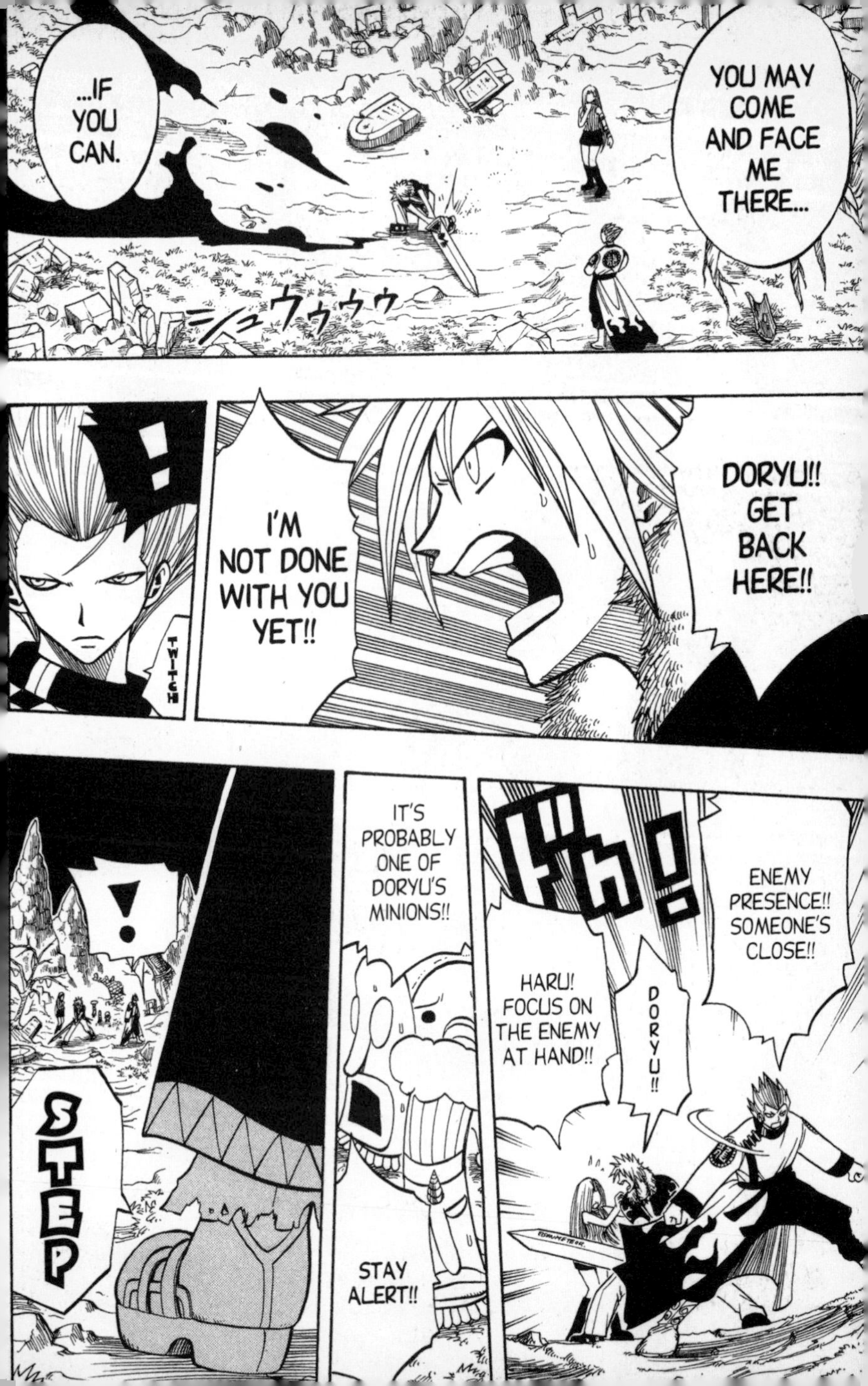
YOU MAY COME AND FACE ME THERE...
...IF YOU CAN.
DORYU!! GET BACK HERE!!
I'M NOT DONE WITH YOU YET!!
TWITCH
ENEMY PRESENCE!! SOMEONE'S CLOSE!!
DORYU!!
HARU! FOCUS ON THE ENEMY AT HAND!!
IT'S PROBABLY ONE OF DORYU'S MINIONS!!
STAY ALERT!!
STEP

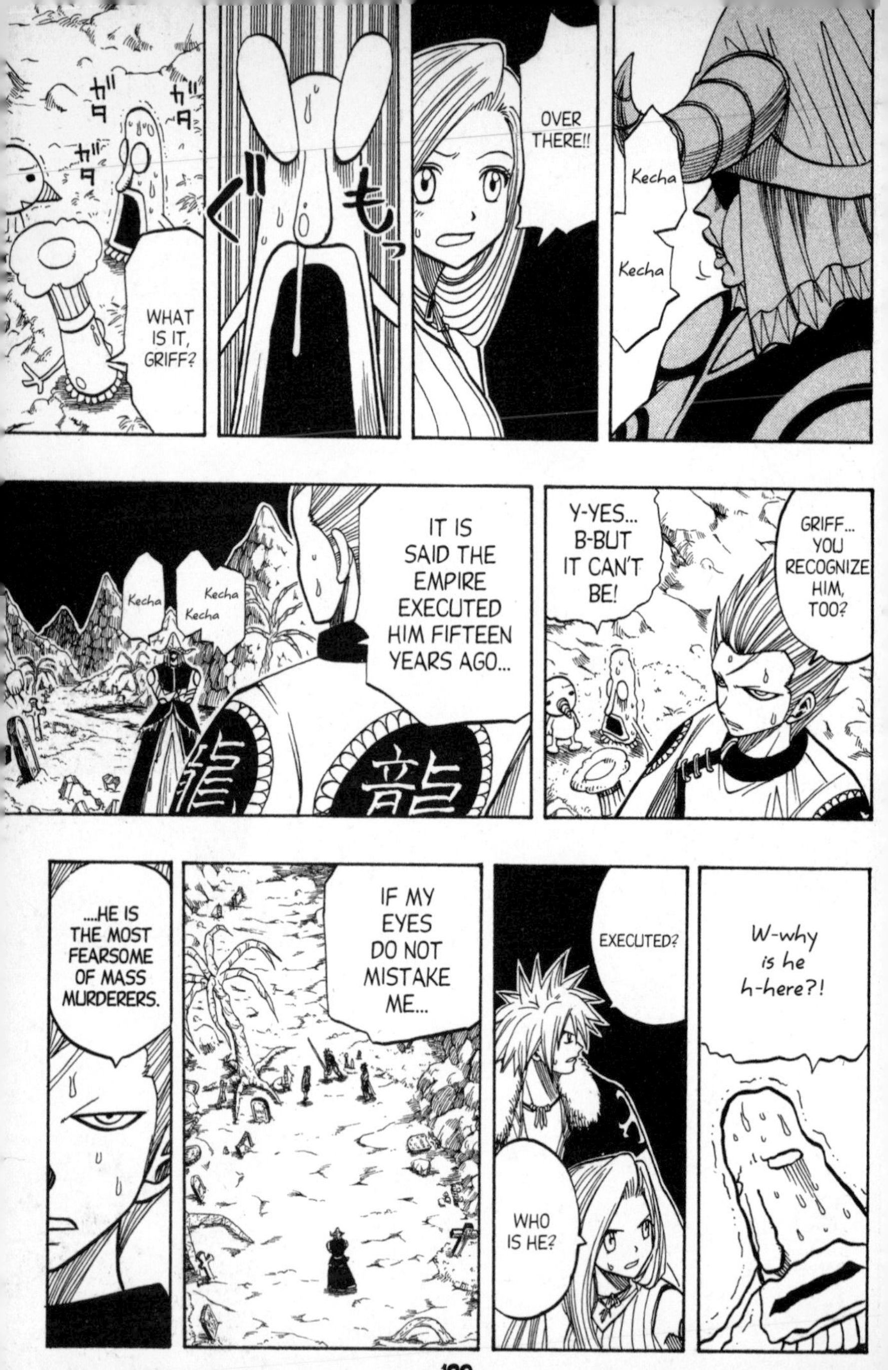
Kecha
Kecha
OVER THERE!!
ぐもっ
ガタ
ガタ
ガタ
WHAT IS IT, GRIFF?
GRIFF... YOU RECOGNIZE HIM, TOO?
Y-YES... B-BUT IT CAN'T BE!
IT IS SAID THE EMPIRE EXECUTED HIM FIFTEEN YEARS AGO...
Kecha
Kecha
Kecha
W-why is he h-here?!
EXECUTED?
WHO IS HE?
IF MY EYES DO NOT MISTAKE ME...
...HE IS THE MOST FEARSOME OF MASS MURDERERS.

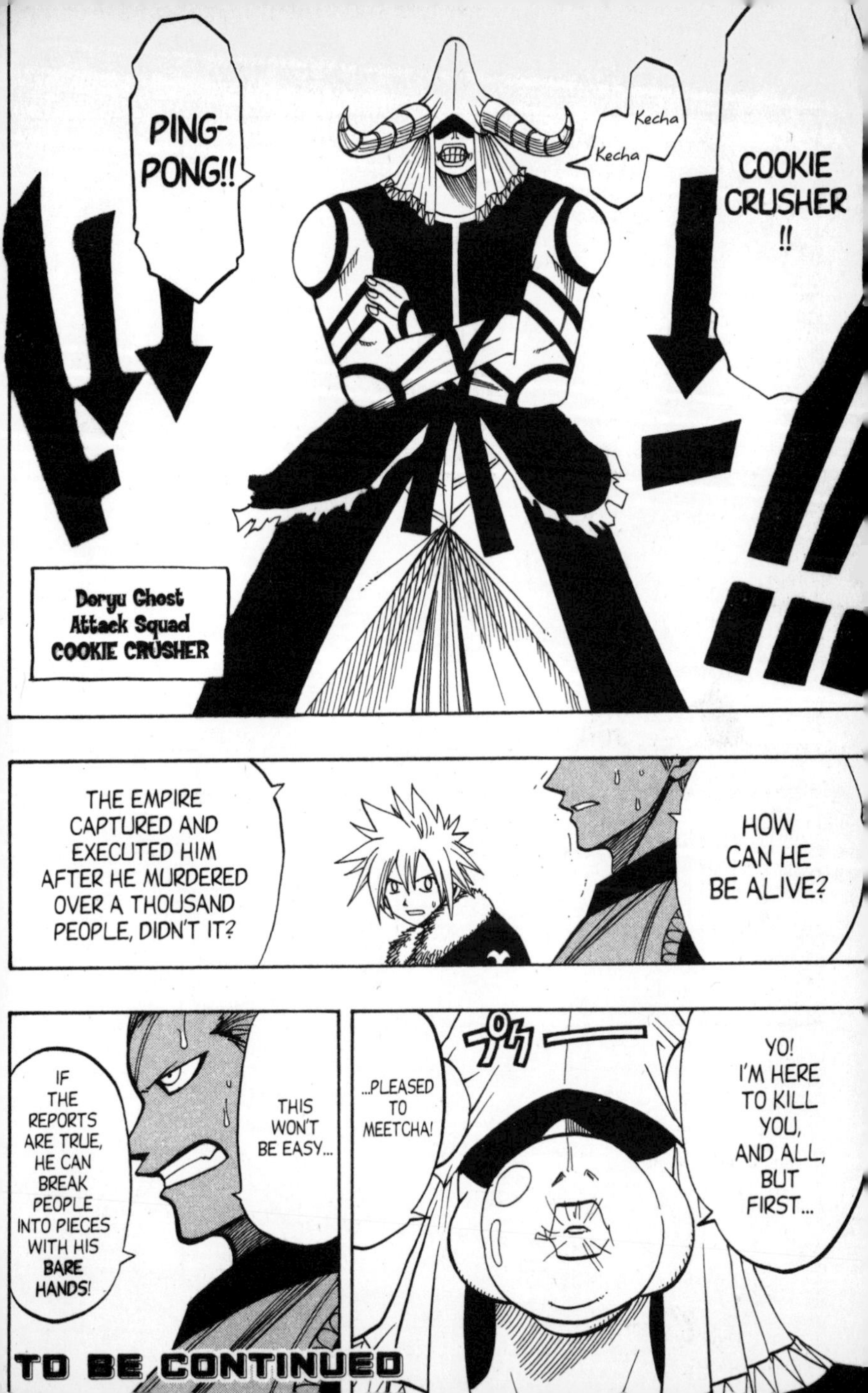
COOKIE CRUSHER !!
Kecha
Kecha
PING-PONG!!
Doryu Ghost Attack Squad COOKIE CRUSHER
HOW CAN HE BE ALIVE?
THE EMPIRE CAPTURED AND EXECUTED HIM AFTER HE MURDERED OVER A THOUSAND PEOPLE, DIDN'T IT?
YO! I'M HERE TO KILL YOU, AND ALL, BUT FIRST...
...PLEASED TO MEETCHA!
THIS WON'T BE EASY...
IF THE REPORTS ARE TRUE, HE CAN BREAK PEOPLE INTO PIECES WITH HIS BARE HANDS!
TO BE CONTINUED

RAVE0077

Levin Minds the House

#13 - CHARADES

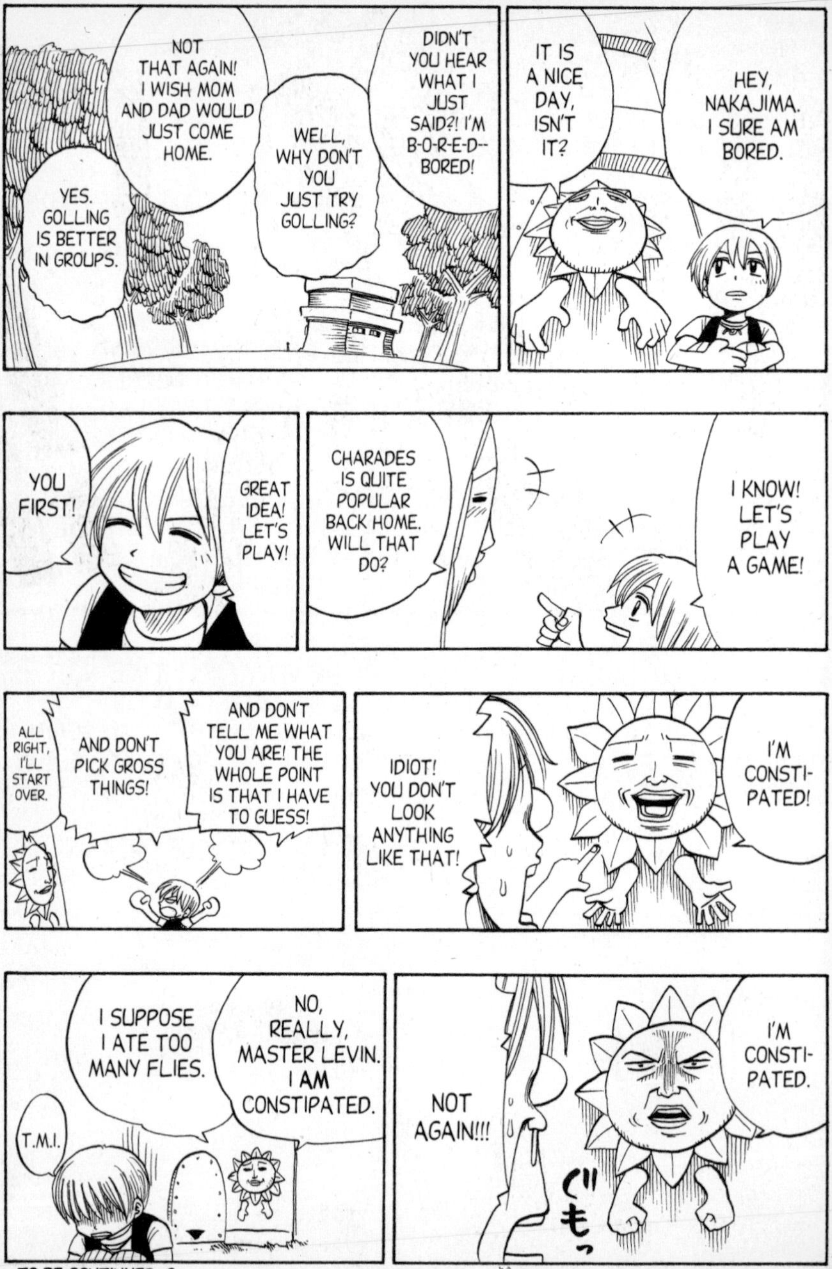
HEY, NAKAJIMA. I SURE AM BORED.
IT IS A NICE DAY, ISN'T IT?
DIDN'T YOU HEAR WHAT I JUST SAID?! I'M B-O-R-E-D-- BORED!
WELL, WHY DON'T YOU JUST TRY GOLLING?
NOT THAT AGAIN! I WISH MOM AND DAD WOULD JUST COME HOME.
YES. GOLLING IS BETTER IN GROUPS.
I KNOW! LET'S PLAY A GAME!
CHARADES IS QUITE POPULAR BACK HOME. WILL THAT DO?
GREAT IDEA! LET'S PLAY!
YOU FIRST!
I'M CONSTI-PATED!
IDIOT! YOU DON'T LOOK ANYTHING LIKE THAT!
AND DON'T TELL ME WHAT YOU ARE! THE WHOLE POINT IS THAT I HAVE TO GUESS!
AND DON'T PICK GROSS THINGS!
ALL RIGHT, I'LL START OVER.
I'M CONSTI-PATED.
NOT AGAIN!!!
ぐもっ
NO, REALLY, MASTER LEVIN. I AM CONSTIPATED.
I SUPPOSE I ATE TOO MANY FLIES.
T.M.I.

TO BE CONTINUED...?

"AFTERWORDS"

I'VE BEEN SO BUSY LATELY MY EYES ARE SPINNING. I TOOK ON SO MANY SIDE JOBS THAT I FORGOT ABOUT MY DEADLINE. (OUCH!)

IT'S FUN TO BE BUSY, THOUGH. IT FEELS GOOD TO BE LIVING LIFE TO ITS FULLEST.

WHEN I WAS IN SCHOOL I HAD WAY, WAY, **WAY** TOO MUCH TIME! IN HINDSIGHT, I THINK I WAS ALWAYS PREPARING MYSELF FOR MANGA, BUT AT THE TIME I WAS THINKING I'D END UP WITH A BAD CROWD. YOU KNOW, HANGING OUT WITH FRIENDS, DOING BAD THINGS TOGETHER... NOT EXACTLY HIGH AMBITIONS. BUT HERE I AM, A MANGA ARTIST!! AND A BAD ONE AT THAT. (HEH HEH...)

WHEN I WAS IN HIGH SCHOOL I DIDN'T REALLY HAVE ANY BIG, VAGUE DREAMS THAT I WANTED TO FOLLOW. I REGRET THAT NOW. I SHOULD'VE SPENT MY SPARE TIME STUDYING MORE MANGA!! WELL, IN MY LAST YEAR OF HIGH SCHOOL, STUFF HAPPENED AND I GOT SUSPENDED INDEFINITELY. IN THE END, MY TEACHERS AND FRIENDS BAILED ME OUT AND I GOT TO GRADUATE AFTER ALL. IT WAS THE BIGGEST INCIDENT IN MY LIFE TO DATE. I THOUGHT ABOUT MY FUTURE FOR THE VERY FIRST TIME. NOT "I WANNA BE A MANGA ARTIST," BUT, "I **WILL** BE A MANGA ARTIST!!" SO, I RELOCATED TO TOKYO AS SOON AS I GRADUATED AND DREW MANGA EVERY DAY AFTER I GOT OFF WORK AT MY PART-TIME JOB--AND I'VE BEEN BUSY EVER SINCE (^_^)!

HEY, YOU ALL HAD BETTER THINK SERIOUSLY ABOUT **YOUR DREAMS.** JUST REMEMBER YOUR FRIENDLY NEIGHBORHOOD MANGA ARTIST WHEN YOU DO...

- HIRO MASHIMA

This huffing, puffing, big, bad beastie eagerly awaits his showdown with the Rave Master! And wait till you get a load of his friends...

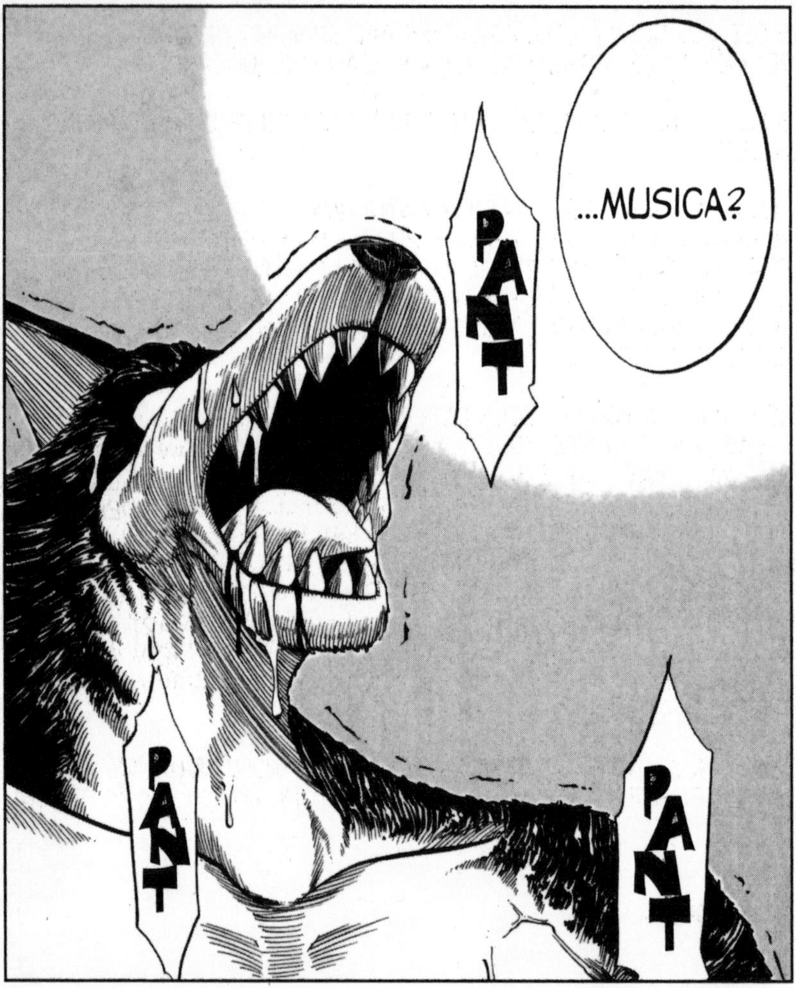

...MUSICA?
PANT
PANT
PANT

The creepy Cookie Crusher isn't the only villain to be vanquished as the Rave Master once again squares off against the Ghost Attack Squad. Plus, an old friend returns while another one falls!

TOKYOPOP SHOP

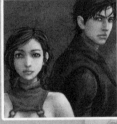
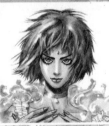

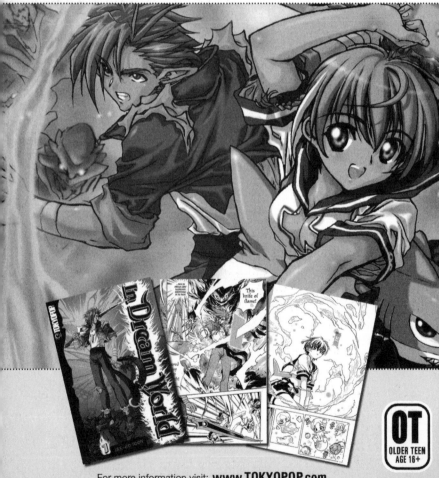

VAN VON HUNTER™

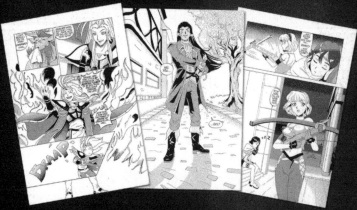

In the dark ages long ago, in a war-torn land where tranquility and harmony once blossomed, tyranny ruled with a flaming fist! At last, a hero arose to defeat the evildoers and returned hope to the people and peace to the countryside. Now...the sinister forces are back with a vengeance, and in their hour of direst-est need, the commoners once again seek a champion to right wrongs and triumph over villainy! Unfortunately, they could only get the mighty warrior Van Von Hunter, Hunter of Evil...Stuff!

Together with his loyal, memory-challenged sidekick, Van Von Hunter is on a never-ending quest to smite the bad guys—and believe us, they're real bad!

Preview the manga at:

www.TOKYOPOP.com/vanvonhunter
www.VanVonHunter.com

T
TEEN
AGE 13+

© Pseudome Studios LLC.

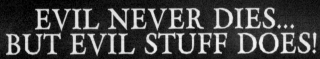

EVIL NEVER DIES...
BUT EVIL STUFF DOES!

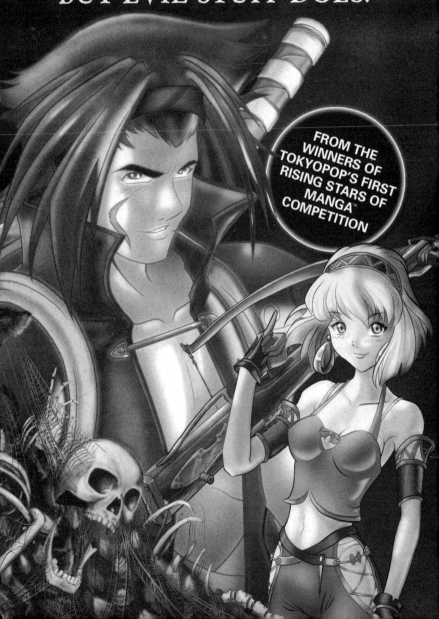

FROM THE WINNERS OF TOKYOPOP'S FIRST RISING STARS OF MANGA™ COMPETITION

EDITORS' PICKS

TOKYOPOP MANGA SUPPLEMENT

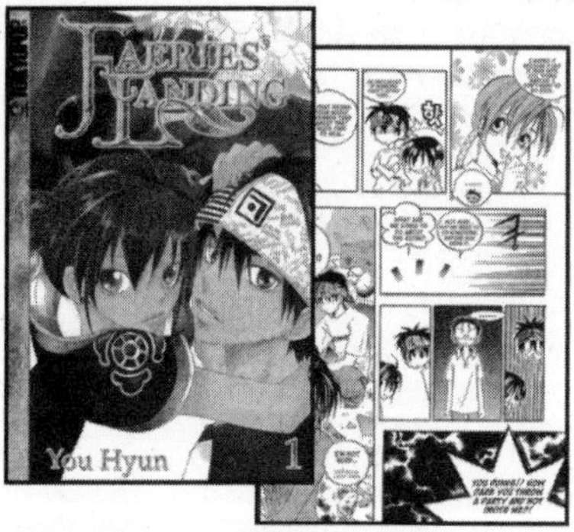

Faeries' Landing
You Hyun
1

BY YOU HYUN

FAERIES' LANDING

Following the misadventures of teenager Ryang Jegal and Fanta, a faerie who has fallen from the heavens straight into South Korea, *Faeries' Landing* is both a spoof of modern-day teen romance and a lighthearted fantasy epic. Imagine if Shakespeare's *A Midsummer Night's Dream* had come from the pen of Joss Whedon after about a dozen shots of espresso, and you have an idea of what to expect from You Hyun's funny little farce. Bursting with sharp wit, hip attitude and vibrant art, *Faeries' Landing* is guaranteed to get you giggling.

~Tim Beedle, Editor

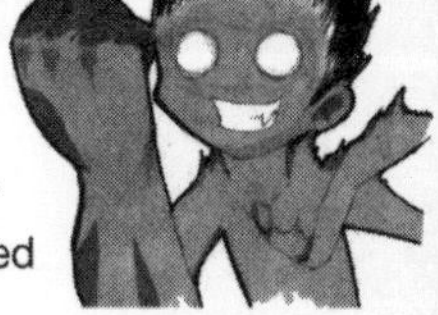

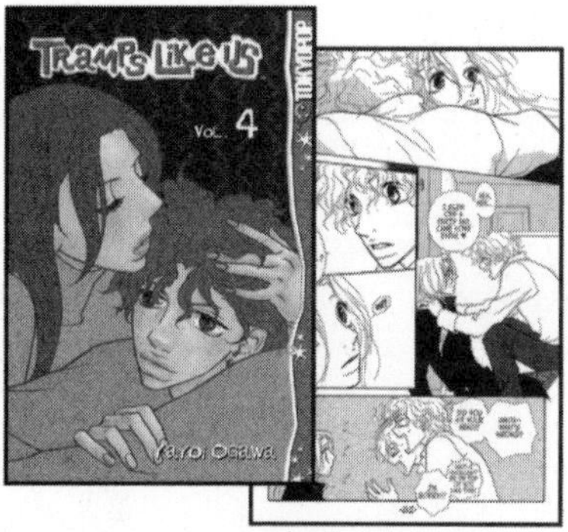

Tramps Like Us
Vol. 4
Yayoi Ogawa

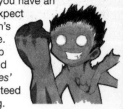

BY YAYOI OGAWA

TRAMPS LIKE US

Yayoi Ogawa's *Tramps Like Us*—known as *Kimi wa Pet* in Japan—is the touching and humorous story of Sumire, a woman whose striking looks and drive for success alienate her from her friends and co-workers...until she takes in Momo, a cute homeless boy, as her "pet." As sketchy as the situation sounds, it turns out to be the sanest thing in Sumire's hectic life. In his quiet way, Momo teaches Sumire how to care for another being while also caring for herself...in other words, how to love. And there ain't nothin' wrong with that.

~Carol Fox, Editor

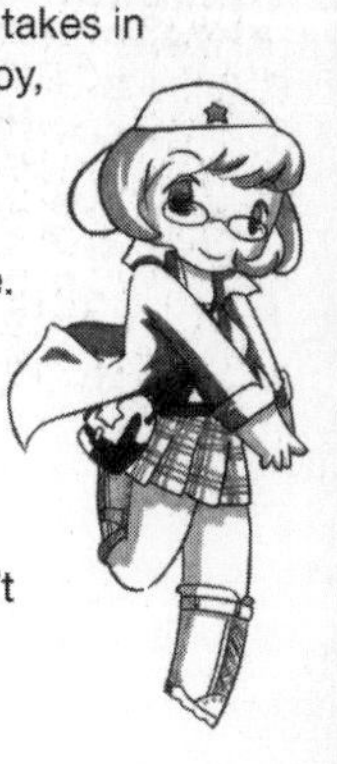

EDITORS' PICKS
TOKYOPOP MANGA SUPPLEMENT

SGT FROG

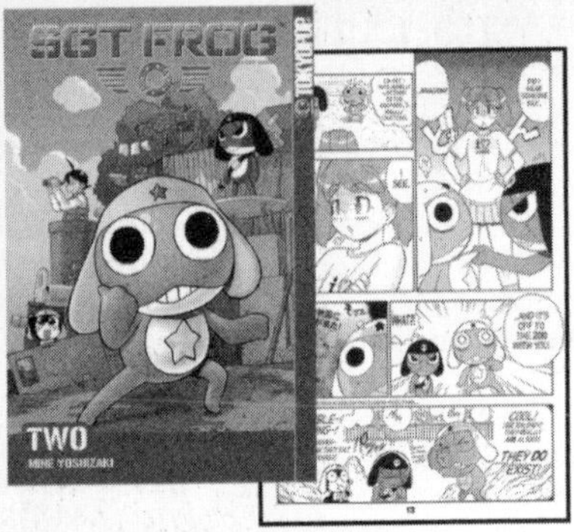
SGT FROG
TWO
MINE YOSHIZAKI
THEY DO EXIST!

BY MINE YOSHIZAKI

Sgt. Frog is so absurdly comical, it has me in stitches every time I edit it. Mine Yoshizaki's clever sci-fi spoof showcases the hijinks of Sergeant Keroro, a cuddly looking alien, diabolically determined to oppress our planet! While some E.T.s phone home, this otherworldly menace has your number! Abandoned on Earth, Keroro takes refuge in the Hinata home, whose residents quickly take advantage of his stellar cleaning skills. But between scrubbing, vacuuming and an unhealthy obsession with Gundam models, Keroro still finds time to plot the subjugation of humankind!

~ Paul Morrissey, Editor

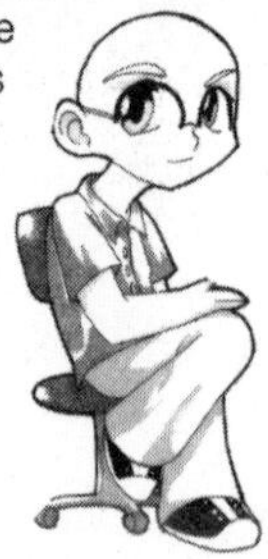

@LARGE

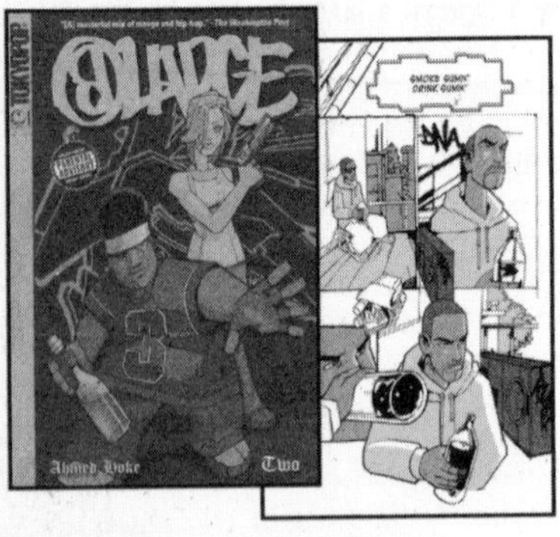
@LARGE
Ahmed Hoke
Two

BY AHMED HOKE

Ahmed Hoke's revolutionary hip-hop manga is a groundbreaking graphic novel. While at first glace this series may seem like a dramatic departure from traditional manga styles, on a deeper level one will find a rich, lyrical world full of wildly imaginative characters, intense action and heartfelt human emotions. This is a truly unique manga series that needs to be read by everyone—whether they are fans of hip-hop or not.

~Rob Valois, Editor

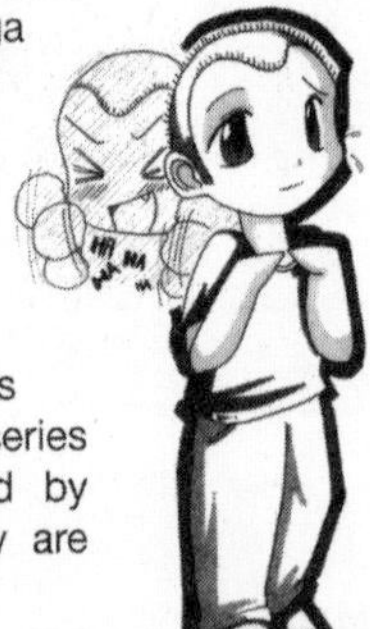

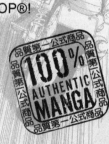

STOP!

This is the back of the book.
You wouldn't want to spoil a great ending!

This book is printed "manga-style," in the authentic Japanese right-to-left format. Since none of the artwork has been flipped or altered, readers get to experience the story just as the creator intended. You've been asking for it, so TOKYOPOP® delivered: authentic, hot-off-the-press, and far more fun!

DIRECTIONS

If this is your first time reading manga-style, here's a quick guide to help you understand how it works.

It's easy... just start in the top right panel and follow the numbers. Have fun, and look for more 100% authentic manga from TOKYOPOP®!

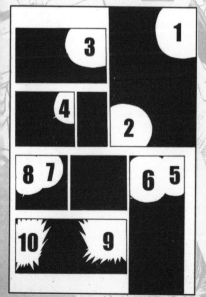